BUSINESS STRATEGY
AND
POLICY

BUSINESS STRATEGY
AND
POLICY

Third Edition

GARRY D. SMITH
Mississippi State University

DANNY R. ARNOLD
Mississippi State University

BOBBY G. BIZZELL
University of Houston—Downtown

HOUGHTON MIFFLIN COMPANY
· BOSTON
Dallas   Geneva, Illinois   Palo Alto
Princeton, New Jersey

To Our Families:
Charlotte, Brad, Ryan
Peggy, Wade, Daryl
Charlene, Laurie, Susan, Amy

Printed in the U.S.A.

Library of Congress Catalog Card Number: 90-83003

ISBN: 0-395-43367-3

ABCDEFGHIJ-AH-9876543210

BRIEF CONTENTS

CONTENTS

PREFACE

This text, accompanied by a companion volume, BUSINESS STRATEGY AND POLICY: CASES, is designed to meet the needs of students of business policy and strategic management. Our goals are to help students understand how to integrate knowledge of the various business disciplines and apply that knowledge to planning and managing strategic business activities. The text consists of strong coverage of policy and strategy concepts. The second volume is a collection of cases that helps students integrate and apply concepts and knowledge.

THE TEXT

The text material provides students with the most current information concerning the rapidly changing field of business policy and strategic management. We balance theory, research, and practice, integrating the coverage within a cohesive framework.

Ensuring readability is of primary importance. The wording and layout of the text enhance understanding, and the examples, some set aside as Perspectives on well-known organizations, illustrate applications of the concepts being presented. The Perspectives describe issues confronting firms such as Hasbro, Siemens, TWA, Quaker, Marriott, Blockbuster, K mart, GM, UPS, and Gillette.

STRUCTURE OF THE TEXT MATERIAL

The structure of the material is guided by a comprehensive model of the strategic management process. The model provides a display of the components of the strategic management process and its interrelationships.

The overall model and an overview of strategic management are presented in Chapter 1. Chapter 2 focuses on the need for maintaining a global perspective in the world of business. Chapter 3 provides a foundation in values, ethics, and social responsiveness. Chapter 4 entails a discussion of objective setting.

Chapters 5 through 7 deal in detail with the various environments faced by firms—the macroenvironment, task environment, and internal environment, respectively. Chapter 8 focuses on information management and environmental issue management, while Chapter 9 deals with environmental analysis, particularly competitive advantages and vulnerabilities.

Chapter 10 serves as a transition chapter to strategies by presenting portfolio analysis and other strategy analysis techniques. Specific corporate strategy alternatives are discussed in Chapter 11, while Chapter 12 covers business and functional strategies.

Strategy implementation and related issues are discussed in Chapter 13. The final chapter, Chapter 14, deals with evaluation and control issues.

ADDITIONS AND CHANGES

This third edition features some significant new material in the form of additions, updating, and organization. Specifically:

New chapters:
- Chapter 2—Global dimensions (All of the later chapters also have sections concerning global dimensions.)
- Chapter 3—Values, ethics, and social responsiveness
- Chapter 8—Environmental issue management

New or expanded sections:
- Responsibility for strategic management
- Strategic renewal
- Planning to plan
- Vision
- Industry structure, driving forces, and generic industry types
- Competitive forces
- Customer analysis
- Critical success factors, areas of excellence, and fundamental strategy
- Value chain activities
- Management and organizational considerations
- Competitive advantages and vulnerabilities (including critical underpinnings)
- Product/market (P/M) analysis
- An extended version of SWOT analysis
- Corporate development matrix
- Porter's competitive advantage approach
- PIMS

- Closure strategies
- Mergers and acquisitions
- Joint ventures
- Strategic alliances
- Generic strategies
- Market entry strategies
- Principles of competitive strategy
- Diversion and dissuasion strategies
- The impact of management characteristics on strategic decisions
- A more detailed discussion of the influence and analysis of organizational culture

THE CASES

Cases are the backbone of any text used for business policy and strategy courses, and this is no exception. The 29 cases are as up-to-date as possible—all include data from the late 1980s.

The volume of cases covers a variety of industries, such as computers (Apple Computer), communications (AT&T, Northern Telecom, Inc.), retail (Babbitt Brothers Trading Co.), steel (Chaparral Steel Co., Nucor), entertainment (General Cinema), food products (Kraft), transportation (Lewis Foods, Saunders Systems, Inc.), and manufacturing (Volvo Bus of North America, Springfield Remanufacturing). The cases involve businesses in many geographical areas. Although some involve large, recognizable firms such as AT&T and Polaroid, many involve small businesses. International firms and situations are covered in cases such as Survival Aids Ltd. (Great Britain) and Caterpillar (Latin America).

The highlighted issues are varied. Some of the cases stress complex strategic problems while others stress ethical/social responsibility or day-to-day planning issues.

HOW TO ANALYZE A CASE

How to Analyze a Case, designed to help students conduct effective case analysis, is included in both the main text and the cases text. This appendix bridges the gap between knowledge and application by demonstrating ways to apply the concepts presented in the text portion to actual case analysis. The framework of the appendix is the same as that underlying the entire text. It emphasizes quantitative analysis, particularly of financial data, and qualitative analysis, particularly of persons, events, and situations.

ACKNOWLEDGMENTS

As with all texts, many people were essential to our successful completion of this book. Our families deserve special thanks. To Charlotte, Peggy, Charlene, Laurie, Susan, Amy, Brad, Ryan, Wade, and Daryl, we give thanks for inspiration and apologize for the late nights, early mornings, and long days.

Others deserve thanks for a variety of manuscript production tasks: Glenda Johnson, Susan Cuculic, Charles Lopez, and Jane McLain. Their contributions were often made while facing severe time constraints. Our universities also contributed and we are grateful for their support.

This book would not have been possible without the efforts of another group—the case writers and the North American Case Research Association (especially those responsible for the case workshops).

Our reviewers also deserve many thanks. Their insights and suggestions were valuable. These special people are:

Daniel White, Drexel University; Jyoti Prasad, Western Illinois University; Frederick Clark, Clarion University of Pennsylvania; Mark Sharfman, Pennsylvania State University; Karl P. Ziethamel, Texas A & M University; Raymond L. Martin, University of Central Florida; Klaus D. Schmidt, San Francisco State University; John E. Prescott, University of Pittsburgh; Sexton Adams, North Texas State University; John N. Holscher, Ohio State University; Daniel A. Wren, University of Oklahoma; John C. Thompson, University of Connecticut; Scott H. Partridge, California State University at Hayward; Rosalie Tung, University of Pennsylvania; Peter J. Geib, Moorhead State University; Sheila A. Adams, Arizona State University; Michael A. McGinnis, Shippensburg State College; Joseph G. P. Paolillo, University of Wyoming; Charles D. McQuillen, University of Idaho; Stuart Wells, San Jose State University; William R. Soukup, San Diego State University; James D. Townsend, Kansas State University; B. C. Reimann, Cleveland State University; Peter R. Sugges, Jr., Arizona State University; and Belmont Haydel, Jr., Rider College.

We would like to thank our publisher, Houghton Mifflin Company, for the opportunity to revise these volumes. Many people there worked tirelessly to ensure that this final product is of superior quality.

We hope this text helps you better understand the many-faceted field of strategic management and helps ease your transition to the real world.

G.D.S.
D.R.A.
B.G.B.

PART ONE

Introduction

Part I, consisting of the first four chapters of the text, introduces the concepts of business policy and strategic management. Chapter 1 presents an overview of strategic management and planning. It focuses on these aspects: the strategic management model, process, and components; the levels of strategic management; who is responsible for strategic management; strategic renewal; planning to plan; and emerging trends in strategic management.

Chapter 2 considers the global, or international, perspective needed in today's business world, and Chapter 3 addresses the critically important question of values, ethics, and social responsiveness. The issues explored in these two chapters strongly influence decision making and the strategic management process; therefore, we raise them early in the text. Because they cannot be realistically separated from the other components of strategic management, both global and ethical issues are interwoven throughout the remaining chapters.

Chapter 4 concentrates on determining objectives, the first major component of the strategic management process. This chapter appears with the other introductory chapters because objectives form a major part of the foundation for strategic planning. Without sound objectives that specify what the organization wants to achieve, planning efforts would flounder. Objectives give these efforts direction.

CHAPTER 1

Introduction to Strategic Management

Most companies now face increasingly turbulent, complex, and threatening environments. In the past, many firms could apparently succeed by focusing management efforts on internal functions and on running their day-to-day affairs as efficiently as possible. Of course, efficient internal operations remain important. However, a company's adapting to changing environmental conditions has become an essential ingredient for success.[1]

The strategic management perspective highlights the value of analyzing environments and formulating strategies linked to environmental conditions. Strategic management does not reject proven management practices; it simply underscores a major responsibility of top management. The ultimate aim of strategic management is to help organizations increase performance through improved effectiveness, efficiency, and flexibility.[2]

Increased reliance on strategic management stems from three main factors: accelerating environmental change, growing competition for scarce resources, and mounting demands from a variety of special interest groups and individuals. Most firms, including giants such as General Electric, IBM, and Shell Oil, have been using some form of strategic management for several years now.[3] In the late 1970s, the publisher of *Business Week* observed that "strategic management has become the major thrust and emphasis in the management of U.S. corporations."[4] A decade later, one study found that 88.7 percent of the executives surveyed thought that reducing the emphasis on strategic planning would hurt their firms' long-term performance.[5]

As business turned its attention to strategic management, new scholarly journals were launched to deal with the topic—for instance, the *Strategic Management Journal* and the *Journal of Business Strategy*. Older scholarly journals, such as *Harvard Business Review* and the *Journal of Marketing*, began to include more articles on the subject. In addition, the words *strategic management* have appeared in many recent textbook titles.[6]

There is no single universally accepted way to introduce and practice strategic management. Since each organization is unique, the strategic management process must fit this uniqueness; consequently, no two strategic management systems will be exactly alike. Nonetheless, certain fundamental principles and practices form a common thread among successful strategic management systems.

WHAT IS STRATEGIC MANAGEMENT?

There are a number of workable definitions of **strategic management:**

> Strategic management is the process of managing the pursuit of organizational mission while managing the relationship of the organization to its environment.[7]

> Strategic management is that set of managerial decisions and actions that determine the long-run performance of a corporation.[8]

> Strategic management is defined as the set of decisions and actions resulting in the formulation and implementation of strategies designed to achieve the objectives of the organization.[9]

> Strategic management is the process whereby managers establish an organization's long-term direction, set specific performance objectives, develop strategies to achieve these objectives in the light of all the relevant internal and external circumstances, and undertake to execute the chosen action plans.[10]

The following definition serves as the foundation for this text:

> Strategic management is the process of examining both present and future environments, formulating the organization's objectives, and making, implementing, and controlling decisions focused on achieving these objectives in the present and future environments.

It is critical that management analyze both the external environments and the firm's internal capabilities and resources. The firm's internal strengths and weaknesses can then be deployed to take advantage of external opportunities and to minimize external problems. A major pioneer of strategic management, General Electric, defined strategy as "a statement of how what resources are going to be used to take advantage of which opportunities to minimize which threats to produce a desired result."[11] The specific components of this definition are described later in this introductory chapter and developed throughout the text.

3

Obviously, not all companies have a strategic management perspective. Those that lack it tend to have no focus, concentrate too heavily on internal efficiency or tactical details as the key to organizational effectiveness, or simply cope with crises as they arise. The absence of a strategic management perspective can limit a firm in other ways, such as the following:

1. Excessive concern with first analyzing the firm's resources (including skills) and then deciding how to process those resources efficiently into acceptable results. For example, if General Electric's management took this approach, its attitude would be that "we have the resources and skill to make electric gadgets, so let's make them." Conversely, strategic management focuses on first defining the desired results (objectives) and then assembling and processing the resources necessary to achieve those results. If producing electric gadgets enables GE to achieve the desired objectives, then GE's business will involve making electric gadgets; if the objectives cannot be met by making electric gadgets, GE would probably seek other ways to meet those objectives.
2. Planning based on the assumption that the environmental situation is stable. Although some firms do face relatively stable environments, many face dynamic environments in which turbulence and change are commonplace. Consider, for example, the oil industry, which during the past twenty years has experienced both sharply rising and sharply falling prices. Besides, many events, such as the rupturing of oil tankers, cannot be forecast and can cause many changes.
3. Inadequate use of long-range planning. Strategic management, on the other hand, highlights the need for long-range planning.

Why Use Strategic Management?

Although strategic management can benefit all types of organizations, it is still young enough to experience growing pains, and firms can still encounter problems in the planning process. Thus, before we move farther into the text, it is essential to explore both the advantages and the disadvantages of the strategic management process.

Advantages   First, the strategic management process provides organizations with clearer goals and direction. It forces management to consider and define where the organization should be heading and when it should reach a specific point.[12] Knowing the desired results, or outcomes, helps both management and employees understand what is required for success. Such understanding often encourages both groups to achieve short-term performances that are better focused on the firm's long-term welfare.

Second, rapid changes in the environmental conditions faced by organizations can create unexpected opportunities and threats. (See Perspective 1.1.) The strategic management approach helps management to focus on future opportunities and threats by encouraging the analysis and forecasting of both the near and the distant future environments. Better anticipation of future environments enhances management's ability to quickly take advantage of opportunities, fully exploit these opportunities, and reduce the risks associated with environmental threats.

Third, the strategic management process helps relate a firm's decision-making process to relevant environmental conditions. As environmental turbulence and complexity increase, it becomes more and more important for a firm to take either a proactive or an aggressive-reactive position. A **proactive decision** involves an attempt to forecast environmental conditions and then influence or change the forecast conditions so that the firm's objectives can be achieved. An **aggressive-reactive** decision involves forecasting future environments and taking action to optimize the firm's position in those environments; this action usually means avoiding expected problems and preparing the firm to pursue potential opportunities. Companies that do not use strategic management are much more

PERSPECTIVE 1.1

Hasbro Masters a Fickle Market

The story about the child who throws away the toy to play with the box may be amusing to most of us. To those charged with devising business strategies for toy companies, however, it is a tale of terror. In an industry that must somehow factor the whims of children into its plans of action, sudden changes in financial mood are not unusual. Consider the fate of Coleco: when sales of its Cabbage Patch dolls, which came from nowhere to gross $600 million in 1985, went into a tailspin, so did the company. In a few years it was bankrupt.

Is it possible for a toy company to grow at an impressive pace and yet avoid the boom-and-bust syndrome? Stephen Hassenfeld thought so. And the performance of Hasbro, the company whose chairman he became in 1980, suggests that he was right. Referred to by its competitors as a "Has been" when Hassenfeld took over, Hasbro is now the leading toy company in the United States. This development is all the more remarkable considering Hasbro's lack of success in developing blockbuster toys of its own.

The Hasbro approach has been to blanket the market—to produce a variety of toys and games for all ages—and thus avoid overdependence on any one product. To a large extent, Hasbro achieved diversity by acquisitions. Through the 1980s, Hasbro bought up makers of plush animals and board games, educational children's toys and outdoor furniture.

Hasbro also has demonstrated a talent for turning products into steady money makers. Hasbro's oldest toy—GI Joe turned 25 in 1989—is also its most profitable, and a number of its other steady sellers are over five years old. Such figures are impressive in a business where many products are stillborn and the usual growth period for successful items is four years. Hasbro keeps its toys young by marketing accessories to sell with them, and by changing these accessories every few years. Very often the basic toy is a relatively small-ticket item. The accessories, however, may be expensive. A ship to transport GI Joe, for example, may run $100.

In Europe, that same ship might cost considerably more. Hasbro successfully sells its products abroad at much higher prices.

References: Laura Jereski, "It's Kid Brother's Turn to Keep Hasbro Hot," *Business Week,* June 26, 1989, p. 152, 155; "How Hasbro Became King of the Toymakers," *Business Week,* September 22, 1986, pp. 90ff.; "Merry X-mas: It Has Already Come for Hasbro, Biggest U.S. Toymaker," *Barron's,* December 23, 1985, pp. 34–35.

likely to make **passive-reactive decisions**—that is, to take action only after the environment has changed. Although passive-reactive decisions can sometimes work, strategic management, with its focus on the environments, gives a firm stronger control of its destiny. Consider the different postures a firm could have assumed relative to the changing economic and political situation in Eastern Europe. A proactive firm would have involved itself directly in the negotiations that wrought these changes. An aggressive-reactive firm would have anticipated the changes and put itself in a position to take advantage of any resulting opportunities. A passive-reactive firm would have read about the changes in the newspaper and then considered its options for the future.

Fourth, firms using a well-designed strategic management process that facilitates both employee involvement and group analysis and decision making can expect several behavioral benefits:[13]

- Improved employee motivation due to greater understanding of the performance-reward relationship
- Consideration of the best available alternatives
- Reduction of gaps and overlaps in activities
- Reduction of resistance to change
- Enhanced problem-prevention capabilities

Fifth and perhaps most important, research shows that companies using strategic management significantly outperform their own past results and the results of the companies that do not use it.[14] Of course, a company using strategic management may still experience trouble or even go bankrupt. But using strategic management generally reduces the risk of catastrophic problems and increases the probability that a firm will take advantage of environmental opportunities as they arise.

Disadvantages   Planners must also take into account the disadvantages associated with strategic management. First, one of the principal drawbacks is the time and effort needed to institute the strategic management process. As an organization gains experience with this process, however, the time burden decreases. Eventually, strategic management saves time. Besides, the time required for planning becomes less important if it leads to greater compensating benefits.

Second, once committed to paper, strategic plans can come to be regarded as though written in stone. Such an approach is a gross misuse of strategic management. The strategic plan should be dynamic and evolving because (1) environmental conditions change and (2) the firm may decide to pursue new or modified objectives. To stick with initial plans regardless of new information can be self-defeating.

Third, the margin of error for long-range environmental forecasts is sometimes quite large. This difficulty does not lessen the need for predicting. Actually, long-range projections do not have to be accurate in the finest details. They are designed to ensure that the company will not have to make drastic changes but can adapt to the environment in a less disruptive manner. For example, computer manufacturers that did not anticipate market growth for smaller computers, especially personal computers, were ill prepared for that growth; typically, they had to undertake costly crash programs or enter the market late. (However, some latecomers, such as IBM, were quite successful.) Although firms that anticipated small to moderate market growth were also incorrect, they were generally able to avoid crash programs.

Fourth, some companies tend to remain almost perpetually in a planning stage, paying far too little need to implementation. This phenomenon has led some managers to question the usefulness of the strategic management process.[15] The problem, however, lies not with strategic management itself, but with its inappropriate use. Firms must obviously "plan for implementation" if any kind of planning activities are to be effective.

Although these disadvantages do keep some companies from adopting a strategic management process, potential problems can generally be overcome by using the process properly. The advantages of using a strategic process appear to far outweigh the disadvantages. Consequently, we recommend it for the majority of firms.

The Role of Strategic Management

Strategic planning and management do not directly provide decisions but rather a basis on which decisions can be made.[16] Strategic planning is a vehicle for announcing, selling, negotiation, rationalizing, and legitimizing strategic decisions. Its primary function is to help organizations develop strategies by creating a more rational approach to strategic choice. Strategic planning performs three other key functions.[17]

1. *Public relations:* influencing outsiders' opinions of the organization
2. *Information:* supplying information to individuals in the organization about vision, missions, and goals
3. *Group therapy:* encouraging individuals within the organization to participate in the strategic planning process and influence the organization's future

Despite its broad scope of applications, strategic management is not a panacea. There are several things that it does not attempt to do.[18] First, it does not try to blueprint the future. Plans cannot be cast in stone and followed into the far distant future when the environments assumed during the planning phase have changed. Rather, executives can try to foresee the desired future for the firm and achieve stated objectives by formulating appropriate strategies and detailed plans.

Second, strategic management involves more than simply forecasting sales and then determining what should be done to fulfill the forecasts. More basic questions must be addressed, such as: Are we in the right business? What are our basic objectives? Are our markets growing or eroding?

Third, strategic management is not a simple prescribed methodology, flow chart, or set of procedures. It embraces a wide range of specific types of planning systems and is inextricably interwoven into the entire management process.

Problems with Terminology

Different use of the same terms to define and describe real-world situations can cause confusion. For example, although it is easy to differentiate between *objectives* and *strategies*, in practice difficulties can arise. One firm may consider the statement of desired profit to be an objective, whereas another may consider it a strategy. Additional problems can develop with terms such as *tactics*, *policies*, and *procedures*. (Each of these terms is defined and described later in the discussion.)

To minimize such difficulties, we use our terms consistently throughout the text. Furthermore, our terminology by and large accords with current strategic management literature. Since the field has not perfected its terminology as yet, some discrepancies cannot be avoided. Thus you should carefully evaluate terms in their context to grasp their meaning fully.

THE STRATEGIC MANAGEMENT MODEL

Exhibit 1.1 presents a basic strategic management model, which organizes the major components of the strategic management process. Each of these major areas is discussed briefly in this section and in greater detail later in the text.

As you study the strategic management model, carefully consider the positioning of the environmental analysis component. Note that environmental analysis is actually a pervasive component because it occurs before, during, and after the execution of each of the other components. For example, some environmental analysis must be performed before determining the organization's vision, mission, and objectives.

Determining Vision, Mission, and Objectives

It is crucial that a firm know the direction it wants to take before it begins moving. Strategic planners can establish this direction by formulating objectives

---

EXHIBIT 1.1 · The Strategic Management Model

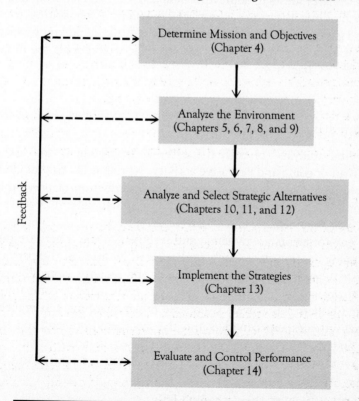

that enhance the firm's ability to fit successfully into current and forecast environments.

The concept of objectives is rather broad and can be separated into four components: vision, mission, long-term goals, and short-term goals. The first broad objective, **vision**, defines management's view of what it wants the organization's scope, scale, and size to be in the future. To define a vision clearly for a firm, management must first pose the question "What business are we in now?" In answering it, executives must consider the company's present scope, scale, and size and mix of activities, products, and markets. The result should be a meaningful picture of the firm's identity and character. If then a clear vision of each of these factors is defined from a futuristic perspective, managers can analyze the gap between what is and what will be. The nature of this gap should then determine the firm's direction and path.

The **mission** is a basic statement of the reason for a firm's existence and generally charts the firm's future direction and path. It defines how the firm intends to interact with its environments and how it intends to achieve the specified vision.

The **long-term goals** and **short-term goals** are the more specific targets or results that the firm wants to achieve. These goals are derived from and must be focused on fulfilling the firm's vision and mission. After stating the vision, mission, and goals of the company, everyone involved should know exactly what the organization wants to achieve. Vision, mission, and goals are discussed in greater detail in Chapter 4.

Analyzing the Environment

Environmental analysis (of both the external environment and the internal situation) is an ongoing and pervasive activity. Its role is (1) to provide much of the foundation for the mission statement (or confirmation of previously stated missions) and statements of objectives, and (2) to help determine what must be done to achieve the mission and objectives.

Some environments are dynamic and turbulent while others are rather stable. A dynamic environment, such as that faced by firms in the personal computer industry, makes planning more difficult and requires more adjustments in the original objectives. All the environments influencing a company must be analyzed and understood as well as possible before planning can proceed. Both the external environment (divided into the macroenvironment and task environment) and the internal situation are discussed in much greater detail in Chapters 5 through 7. Analysis of these environments is discussed in Chapters 8 and 9.

Analyzing and Selecting Strategic Alternatives

Strategic alternatives must be analyzed and an appropriate combination of corporate, business, and functional strategies must be selected. Accomplishing this task requires an understanding of appropriate analysis techniques, of the strategy alternatives, and of the strategy selection and evaluation process.

Analysis Techniques   Two phases of analysis form a critical part of strategy selection. First, the firm's competitive advantages and vulnerabilities must be analyzed. Environmental profiles, opportunity and threat matrices, and analysis of strengths, weaknesses, opportunities, and threats (SWOT) have proven to be useful tools for this task. They are discussed in Chapter 9.

The second phase involves applying various strategic analysis techniques, including portfolio analysis techniques. This phase of the analysis focuses on evaluating each business in which the company is involved. It can lead to a variety of strategies, ranging from a search for new opportunities to getting rid of present businesses. Approaches to strategy analysis and the overall strategy selection process are discussed in Chapter 10.

Strategy Alternatives   A number of corporate, business, and functional strategies are available for achieving the desired objectives. The broadest statement of how a firm will achieve the desired objectives is the strategy statement. Essentially, a **strategy** is an overall game plan or map to help guide the organization toward the desired objectives. This game plan forms the basis for policies (decision guidelines) and procedures (operating methods and techniques)—the more specific statements that outline what the firm will do in certain situations. (Note that other literature may use the term *tactics* to encompass both policies and procedures.)

Corporate strategies are often called **grand strategies** or **master strategies** and can be classified in a variety of ways. For the purposes of this text, we delineate six separate categories: concentrated growth strategies, integrative growth strategies, diversification growth strategies, stability strategies, decline strategies, and closure strategies. There are specific strategy alternatives for each of these categories, and companies may also pursue a combination of strategies. (See Perspective 1.2.)

1. **Concentrated growth strategies** center on improving current products and/or markets without changing any other factor.
   a. **Market penetration strategy** involves seeking growth for current products in current markets, normally through more aggressive marketing efforts.
   b. **Market development strategy** involves seeking growth by entering new markets with current products.

PERSPECTIVE 1.2

Honeywell Weighs Its Options

In 1986, with earnings that were good but below the industry average, Honeywell was ripe for a takeover. Stockholders seemed ready to make big profit by selling, at an inflated price, to a corporate raider. The raider would then presumably sell the divisions of Honeywell for more than it paid for the whole company. To remain intact and independent, it was argued, Honeywell would have to work up the price of its stock, by increasing either dividends or profitability. Higher stock prices would gratify current investors and reduce the potential profit of anyone looking to take over the firm.

Here are some survival steps analysts recommended for Honeywell at the time:

1. Sell assets to raise money to pay a sizable dividend. Honeywell could put its 50 percent share in Yamatake-Honeywell of Japan on the market. It could also sell its computer business, which many felt was its weakest point. As a computer maker the company was not big enough to compete with giant IBM, and it was involved in a mainframe computer market that was softening in the face of competition from increasingly powerful and versatile desktop systems.

2. Increase profits by expanding defense operations, making them more competitive. As it was, Honeywell was adversely affected by reduced Pentagon spending and intensified competition for the business that remained.

3. Reduce costs by cutting the workforce and combining operations. The computer and controls divisions—the latter devised systems for everything from factory automation to office-tower temperature regulation—might be efficiently meshed.

Honeywell in fact did adopt these cost-reduction measures. It did not, however, dispose of its computer operations. Instead, it took two aggressive steps it hoped would improve profits. One, it released a new minicomputer and announced that newer models were on the way. The new minicomputer was promoted for its high performance-to-price ratio. Two, Honeywell united with Groupe Bull, of France, and NEC Corp., of Japan, to form Honeywell Bull (later renamed Bull HN Information Systems). The combined assets of the three firms, it was hoped, would make the partnership competitive.

References: Gene G. Marcial, "Honeywell May Still Be Sweet," *Business Week,* July 31, 1989, p. 80; Charles Siler, "We Still Have More to Do," *Forbes,* December 11, 1989, p. 183; "Can Honeywell Turn Around in a Fishbowl?" *Business Week,* October 6, 1986, p. 73; "Honeywell Fights Back with New Mini (DPS 6Plus)," *Computer Decisions,* June 30, 1986, pp. 22ff.

c. **Product development strategy** involves seeking growth by developing new products for current markets.

2. **Integrative growth strategies** focus on moving to a different industry level. The company might deal with different products and technology, but the core or basic products, markets, industry, and technology would remain the same.

   a. **Backward vertical integration** involves seeking growth by acquiring ownership or increased control of supply sources.

   b. **Forward vertical integration** involves seeking growth by acquiring ownership or increased control of channel functions closer to the ultimate market, such as sales and distribution systems.

3. **Diversification growth strategies** attempt to change the characteristics of the business—the products, the markets, or the technology, or all three.

   a. **Concentric diversification** involves seeking growth by appealing to new markets with new products that have a meaningful technological or marketing fit, or synergy, with existing products.

   b. **Horizontal diversification** involves seeking growth by appealing to current markets with new products that are technologically unrelated to present products.

   c. **Conglomerate diversification** involves seeking growth by appealing to new markets with new products that have no technological relationship to current products.

4. **Stability strategy** (or *neutral strategy*) means continuing to maintain a competitive position by the same means as before. No major changes are made in products, markets, or production methods. Growth is possible, but will be slow and nonaggressive. Firms can consciously pursue a stability strategy when management is satisfied with the status quo.

5. **Decline strategies** involve regrouping to improve efficiency after a period of fast growth, or reductions of various types when long-run growth and profit opportunities are unavailable in an industry, during periods of economic uncertainty, or when other opportunities are simply more attractive than those presently being pursued.

   a. **Retrenchment** is a temporary, or short-run, strategy directed at alleviating organizational inefficiencies or temporary environmental problems—for instance, by reducing operating expenses or improving productivity.

   b. **Divestiture** means selling or closing a business to achieve a permanent change in the scope of operations.

   c. **Harvest** is the effort to maximize cash flow in the short run, regardless of the long-term effect. It is generally undertaken by businesses with a dim future and little likelihood of being sold for a profit, but still capable of yielding cash during the harvesting.

6. **Closure strategies** involve closing down the firm—an option management can resort to when all else fails.

   a. **Liquidation** means that the entire firm ceases to exist—for instance, in a situation such as when a firm cannot compete successfully in the current industry and does not have the resources necessary to pursue other promising strategies.

   b. **Bankruptcy** involves obtaining legal protection from creditors. It can be used as a permanent closure strategy or, in some cases, as a temporary defensive strategy. Chapter 11 bankruptcy allows a firm to protect itself from creditors and from enforcement of executory contracts. Essentially, Chapter 11 allows a firm the opportunity to rehabilitate itself and avoid insolvency.

Note that different firms may choose different objectives and strategies to achieve basically the same ends. As mentioned earlier, companies can also pursue **combination strategies,** that is, implement multiple corporate strategies simultaneously or sequentially over a period of time.

Growth through internal avenues involves using the existing corporate resources and competencies to develop the strategies. Growth through external avenues involves acquisitions of, mergers with, or joint ventures with other companies.

1. A **merger** takes place when two or more firms combine to form a single, new company.
2. **Acquisition** occurs when one company purchases another and absorbs or adds it to existing operations, often as an operating subsidiary or division.
3. **Joint ventures** come about when two or more firms join forces to accomplish something for which a single organization is not suited.

Corporate strategies are discussed in Chapter 11. Business- and functional-level strategic alternatives are discussed in Chapter 12.

Strategy Selection and Evaluation   To select the optimal combination of strategies, a number of issues must be considered, including financial resources, previous strategy, objectives, and others. Once chosen, strategies must undergo careful evaluation. Only then should the implementation process be launched. For example, planners should strive to avoid the following mistakes:[19]

1. Simple restructuring of old strategies
2. Diversifying rather than creating new products
3. Following other firms' ideas rather than creating new ideas
4. Participating in strategic alliances with other firms with similar characteristics
5. Blindly making acquisitions without a solid rationale

The strategy selection process and evaluation of the strategies are discussed in Chapter 11.

Implementing the Strategies

Implementing the selected strategies is a critical element of strategic management; yet too often it is overlooked or neglected by both practitioners and academicians. Strategy implementation is at least as significant as strategy formulation and can be more difficult to execute. What is particularly important for strategy implementation is getting the organization's members to accept the changes that strategies often dictate. (Note that this issue should also be considered when selecting objectives and strategies.) Other key issues include adjusting the organization structure to enhance the implementation of the strategic plan; developing appropriate budgets, reward systems, information systems, policies, and procedures; obtaining organizational and individual commitment to the strategies; and exerting leadership, which enhances the implementation process. Implementation and related issues are discussed in greater detail in Chapter 13.

Evaluating and Controlling Performance

After implementing its strategies, the firm must determine whether these strategies are working as intended. A given strategy may fail to attain the desired objectives for a variety of reasons—for instance, changes in the environment, the impossibility of implementing certain strategies, and inadequate commitment of resources. Feedback systems and control procedures must be designed and put into operation to monitor performance. Evaluation and control are discussed in greater detail in Chapter 14.

Words of Caution

Two caveats about the strategic planning process are in order. First, many firms still do not have a formal strategic planning and management process.[20] Although some of them manage to develop satisfactory plans, many would benefit from adding some formality to their planning.

Second, it is practically impossible to construct a strategic management model (such as that shown in Exhibit 1.1) that accurately portrays the dynamic, interactive nature of strategic management. Most models must be drawn in a sequential manner, which is only partially realistic. Not all environmental analyses, for example, are completed before any objectives are set and not all objectives are established before any strategies are selected.

The relationship between objectives and environmental analysis is particularly difficult to portray realistically. Some managers prefer to have most of the environmental analysis completed before selecting objectives; others might want to set all objectives and then perform the environmental analysis to find out how to achieve them. Still others might use their existing base of environmental knowledge to formulate a mission statement and perhaps long-term objectives and then conduct more specific environmental analyses to confirm the long-term objectives, form the basis for selecting short-term objectives, and provide input for selecting corporate, business, and functional strategies.

The last scenario highlights a critical issue: the component stages of the strategic management process are interactive and can occur *simultaneously*. In this sense, strategic management is a system. When managers are focusing on one specific component stage, such as setting objectives, all other components must be considered in the decision. For example, when setting objectives, managers must simultaneously consider the relevant environmental influences, potential strategy alternatives, implementation issues, and control issues. Failure to do so can easily lead to unrealistic objectives. Similar scenarios are also applicable for each of the other component stages.

LEVELS OF STRATEGIC MANAGEMENT

Strategic management can occur at different levels in an organization. Three basic levels of strategies can be identified.

1. **Corporate strategy** defines what business or businesses the firm is in or should be in (the scope and mix of corporate activities), how each business should be conducted (the degree of coordination and/or integration with other corporate divisions), how resources will be invested and allocated among activities, and how the organization and its businesses relate to society.
2. **Business strategy** defines how each strategic business unit (SBU) will attempt to achieve its mission and goals (and, therefore, contribute to achieving corporate strategy) within its chosen field of endeavor.
3. **Functional strategy** consists of the action plans for the major subordinate activities within a business unit and focuses on supporting the corporate and business strategies.

Exhibit 1.2 shows that the basic elements of the strategic management process are the same at each level. However, the focus of the relevant planning unit at each level is naturally different in scope. Corporate-level planners view each business as a planning unit, whereas business-level planners tend to view each product and/or market as the basic planning unit.

EXHIBIT 1.2 · **Levels of the Strategic Management Process**

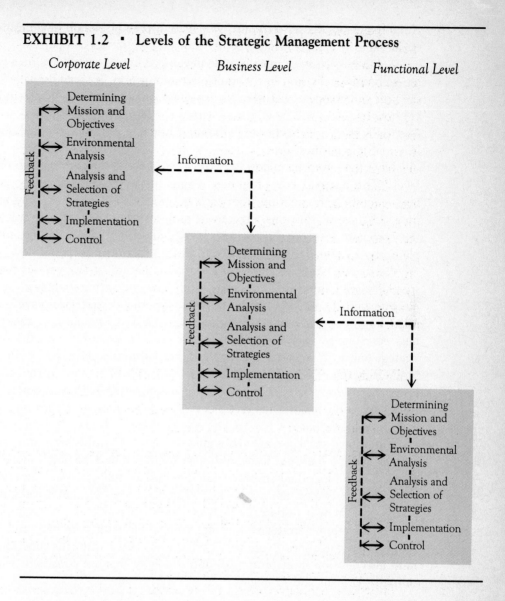

Corporate strategy must be developed for both single-business and multiple-business firms. Single-business firms have limited their operating domain to one major industry or trade. Multiple-business firms operate in more than one major domain; therefore, they face a more involved task of deciding whether to remain in present businesses, evaluating potential new businesses, and deciding how each of the chosen operating units should be conducted. For example, Eaton Corporation's corporate strategy would define which of its fifty-seven domestic and foreign subsidiaries to retain, which to dispose of, which new businesses to pursue, and which (or what type of) new major contracts to pursue.

A business strategy must also be developed for the single-business firm and for each unit or division in the multiple-business firm. It should specify (1) how the unit will compete, (2) what its expected competitive advantage will be, and (3) how resources will be allocated within the business unit. Business strategy is essentially the same for the single-business firm and for the individual businesses in a multiple-business firm.

Note the information flow in Exhibit 1.2 between the corporate and business levels. This complex flow often begins early in the process with corporate planners requesting information from each business unit to serve as input for planning. The vision, missions, objectives, and strategies are then transmitted from the corporate level to the business level and serve as input for business-level planning. Eventually, feedback is transmitted up to the corporate level.

Business strategy is supported by a combination of the various functional strategies (see Exhibit 1.3). For many companies, marketing strategy is the centerpiece of business strategy, with the other functional strategies playing integral roles. In other firms, production or research and development may dominate the business strategy. Each business strategy must be compatible with the corporate strategy and with the strategies of the other businesses operated by the firm. A business strategy of investing substantial amounts of money in semiconductor research, for example, would probably be incompatible with a corporate strategy that focuses on making major strides in high-technology electronics through external acquisitions.

Functional strategies are also similar for single-business firms and each business in multiple-business firms, although the latter may be much more complicated. These functional strategies are designed to support other strategies and, therefore, encompass areas such as production, research and development, finance, and human resources. Each of Eaton's subsidiaries, for example, must develop functional strategies that are compatible with corporate and business strategy and guidelines. Note that each department within the functional areas must also develop short-term goals and strategies that are consistent with functional-level goals and strategies.

WHO IS RESPONSIBLE FOR STRATEGIC MANAGEMENT?

Successful strategic management is the responsibility of every manager and employee of the organization. The planning aspects of strategic management, how-

EXHIBIT 1.3 · Levels of Strategic Planning Decisions

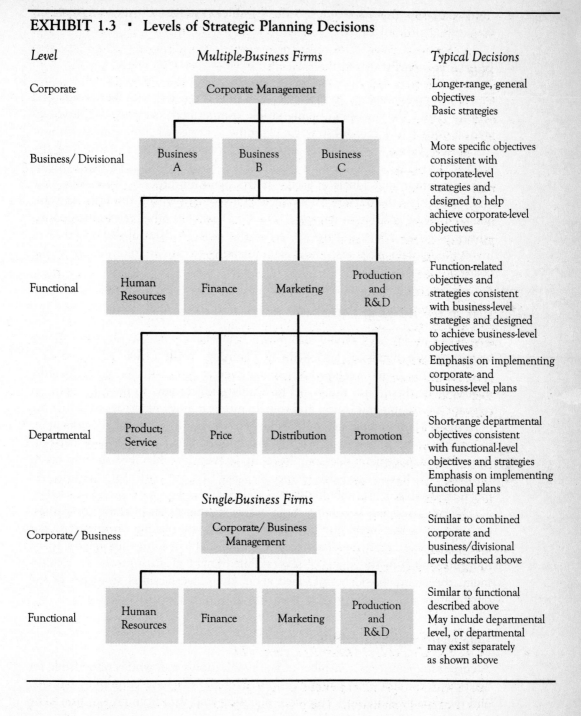

Level	Multiple-Business Firms	Typical Decisions
Corporate	Corporate Management	Longer-range, general objectives Basic strategies
Business/ Divisional	Business A Business B Business C	More specific objectives consistent with corporate-level strategies and designed to help achieve corporate-level objectives
Functional	Human Resources Finance Marketing Production and R&D	Function-related objectives and strategies consistent with business-level strategies and designed to achieve business-level objectives Emphasis on implementing corporate- and business-level plans
Departmental	Product; Service Price Distribution Promotion	Short-range departmental objectives consistent with functional-level objectives and strategies Emphasis on implementing functional plans

Single-Business Firms

Level		Typical Decisions
Corporate/ Business	Corporate/ Business Management	Similar to combined corporate and business/divisional level described above
Functional	Human Resources Finance Marketing Production and R&D	Similar to functional described above May include departmental level, or departmental may exist separately as shown above

ever, rest primarily with management; the **chief executive officer** (CEO) shoulders the major burden.

Role of the CEO

The CEO gives impetus to strategic planning through his or her words and actions. The CEO's real and highly visible commitment, support, and involvement is critical to successful strategic planning.[21] Professed commitment without the corresponding involvement and support typically leads to failure of the process. The CEO's involvement should take a hands-on form, including meetings with other individuals engaged in the planning process. Essentially, the CEO establishes the climate for strategic management within the firm, and this climate may be positive or negative. The CEO also has other relevant responsibilities, such as evaluating the design of the process, determining whether to involve corporate planners, and communicating pertinent information to the board of directors.

Role of the Board of Directors

The board of directors should also play a key role in strategic planning. Some boards provide hands-on leadership in planning, while others act more as a reviewer of the plans developed by others. Even in firms with less active boards, management should use the board to evaluate objectives, to provide input on relevant environmental issues, and to help monitor movement toward achieving objectives. Many companies could make better use of their boards. For example, in the area of environmental analysis, board members can often provide perspectives that management does not have. It is even possible that specific board members will have knowledge of special issues that are critical to the firm. As much as possible, a firm should select board members who have such knowledge.

Many boards are becoming more active in the affairs of their companies. One reason is the increasing liability that courts are placing on directors. For example, some board members have faced legal proceedings for failure to be diligent enough in the affairs of several failed financial institutions. At a minimum, the board should be informed about the objectives and strategies of the organization and should provide direction and oversight to its managers.

Role of the Corporate Planner

A **corporate planner** is a member of an organization's staff who is responsible for assisting in the strategic planning process. Not all firms have corporate planners, and the specific duties of a corporate planning staff vary from firm to firm. The primary role of a corporate planner is to coordinate, advise, and evaluate—rather than fully develop strategic plans. Typically, the planner helps devise the planning process and guides management through it, coordinates the conducting of environmental analyses, and generally serves as a catalyst for the entire strategic planning process.[22]

Role of the Line Manager

Implementing strategies and achieving the desired outcomes is the responsibility of **line managers.** Remember that line managers occupy positions throughout the organization. They include senior corporate-level executives, general managers of business units, managers of functional areas, managers of major operating departments, and managers of geographic field units. Since these managers run the parts of the firm in which the strategic outcomes must be achieved, they should also be given the responsibility and authority for strategy formulation and implementation.[23] The line managers' knowledge and capabilities in regard to strategic planning should dictate the kind of role that corporate planners should play.

STRATEGIC RENEWAL

Effective strategic management facilitates **strategic renewal,** or the adapting of strategies to take advantage of changing environmental conditions. Changing conditions call for *dynamic* strategies as opposed to *static* strategies. For example, Procter & Gamble transformed the diaper market with its introduction of Pampers in 1966. Procter & Gamble's strategy involved creating a competitive advantage by focusing on product features. New competitors entering the market, however, caused the disposable diaper to become rather standardized. Procter & Gamble subsequently dropped the product feature strategy and began to emphasize low prices, which enabled the company to capture about 60 percent of the market.[24] Note that the current concerns regarding the impact of disposable diapers on solid waste disposal may force Procter & Gamble to seek a new strategy or approach.

Robert Waterman proposes that operating values and attitudes form the underlying foundation for strategic renewal. He also isolates eight factors as critical to a company's strategic renewal efforts:[25]

1. Maintaining competitive advantages and flexibility by keeping abreast of the latest information through *informed opportunism*
2. Providing *direction and empowerment* by identifying required tasks and allowing subordinates the decision-making discretion to accomplish the tasks

3. Using *congenial controls,* primarily financial controls, as checks and balances while giving managers creative leeway

4. Using a *different mirror* to recognize that ideas can come from almost any source, including customers, competitors, and employees

5. Recognizing the interaction among and the necessity for *teamwork, trust, politics, and power*

6. Striving for *stability in motion* by responding consistently to changing conditions, while allowing rules to be broken occasionally

7. Recognizing that devoting *attention* to individuals is effective and that symbolic behavior enhances *attitudes*

8. Maintaining individuals' awareness that *causes and commitment* must be emphasized

PLANNING TO PLAN

The strategic planning process requires bringing together a great deal of complicated information and involves many individuals directly and indirectly, both inside and outside the firm. Consequently, it makes sense to devote adequate time to developing a plan for planning, or the process of planning. The overall process of strategic planning should be tailored to fit the needs and characteristics of a specific firm, including its culture, management and employees, and so on.

The plan to plan should be simple and systematic. However, it may not be simple to develop; a thorough understanding of the basic steps of the strategic planning process and the related analysis is only the starting point. Essentially, someone must carefully determine who does what, when do they begin, when is their deadline, how much analysis is required, what kind of input is needed, where can they get input and assistance, and so on. The more people and information involved and the tighter the planning time frame, the greater are the problems. Remember that every line manager and employee engaged in the planning process also has other important job duties.

Various approaches can be taken in any planning process. There are three basic ones:

1. **Top-down planning.** All critical planning is performed by top management; lower-level managers and subunits either prepare derivative plans or simply implement what is given to them.

2. **Bottom-up planning.** Lower-level employees, managers, and subunits prepare plans (either individually or collectively) and submit them to top management for review and approval, modification, or rejection.

3. **Top-down/bottom-up planning.** Plans can be initiated at either the top or the bottom of the organization, flow to the other direction (perhaps several

iterations), and ultimately be approved by top management. One variation of this approach involves the flow of objectives top-down and the subsequent return (bottom-up) of plans for strategies, implementation, and control. Still another variation involves the temporary integration of individuals from the top and bottom rungs of the organization into planning teams.

After settling on a planning process that should work for the specific organization, planners need to consider a number of dos and don'ts. The following factors should be incorporated into the process:

1. The planning process should have an "overseer" to help ensure that the planning gets done, and done in an acceptable manner.
2. Top managers must be involved in all stages of planning.
3. Line managers who have the responsibility for generating the desired outcomes must be involved in the planning. They should be encouraged to obtain quality input for the purpose of analysis, suggest new planning ideas, and communicate both vertically and horizontally.

Planners should strive to avoid the following traps:[26]

1. Blindly relying on mathematical or statistical calculations
2. Assuming that past trends can be extrapolated into the future
3. Drawing statistical inferences when sample size is insufficient
4. Assuming that a complex process is automatically sophisticated
5. Believing that the "ship" is unsinkable
6. Discounting or ignoring the environment and ignoring reports of unfavorable conditions

EMERGING TRENDS IN STRATEGIC MANAGEMENT

During its short life, the field of strategic management has grown rapidly. Many changes have occurred and are still occurring. These trends are currently observable:[27]

- Greater management involvement in the strategic planning process
- Shorter and simpler written strategic plans
- Expansion of the research base for strategists
- Relating management's rewards to the strategic plan

Trends that may grow into major issues in the future include the following:

- The planned development of managers as strategic planners and managers
- Greater emphasis on longer-term vision
- Greater emphasis on the development of corporate cultures

- Increased emphasis on developing an entrepreneurial (or intrapreneurial) climate within organizations, particularly at lower levels of the organization[28]
- Greater emphasis on research and other planning tools (for example, personal computers and decision support systems)[29]
- Increased emphasis on managerial control and on flexibility and innovation[30]
- Greater emphasis on global strategies[31]

ORGANIZATION OF THE TEXTBOOK

Although this textbook is organized around the strategic management model shown in Exhibit 1.1, two of the most pervasive influences on strategic management—global influences and also values, ethics, and social responsiveness—are discussed separately in Chapters 2 and 3, respectively. These two areas are part of the business environment, but they overlay business decision making to such an extent that planners should understand them thoroughly before addressing the specific components of strategic planning.

The remaining eleven chapters relate directly to the major steps in the strategic model. These chapters are designed to familiarize you with the strategic management process. The Appendix, which follows Chapter 14, is designed to acquaint you with the rudiments of case analysis.

Notes

1. George S. Yip, "Who Needs Strategic Planning?" *Journal of Business Strategy* (March 1985), 40–42.
2. M. D. Skipton, "Helping Managers to Develop Strategies," *Long Range Planning* (April 1985), 56–67.
3. Ronald N. Paul and James W. Taylor, "The State of Strategic Planning," *Business* (January-March 1986), 37.
4. "Publisher's Memo," *Business Week*, January 9, 1978.
5. V. Ramanujam, J. C. Camillus, and N. Venkatraman, "Trends in Strategic Planning," in *Strategic Planning and Management Handbook*, ed. W. R. King and D. I. Cleland (New York: Van Nostrand Reinhold, 1987), p. 619.
6. For example, see Arthur A. Thompson, Jr., and A. J. Strickland, *Strategic Management: Concepts and Cases*, 4th ed. (Plano, Tex.: Business Publications, 1987); George A. Steiner, John B. Miner, and Edmund R. Gray, *Management Policy and Strategy Text, Readings and Cases*, 3rd ed. (New York: Macmillan, 1986); John A. Pearce II and Richard B. Robinson, Jr., *Strategic Management*, 3rd ed. (Homewood, Ill.: Irwin, 1988); Thomas L. Wheelen and J. David Hunger, *Strategic Management and Business Policy*, 3rd ed. (Reading, Mass.: Addison-Wesley, 1989); Lawrence R. Jauch and William F. Glueck, *Business Policy and Strategic Management*, 5th ed. (New York: McGraw-

Hill, 1988); James M. Higgins, *Organizational Policy and Strategic Management: Text and Cases*, 2nd ed. (Chicago: The Dryden Press, 1983); Fred R. David, *Fundamentals of Strategic Management* (Columbus, Ohio: Merrill, 1986).

7. Higgins, p. 3.
8. Wheelen and Hunger, p. 7.
9. Pearce and Robinson, p. 6.
10. Thompson and Strickland, p. 4.
11. Ronald N. Paul and James W. Taylor, "The State of Strategic Planning," *Business*, (January-March 1986), 37–43.
12. Henry Mintzberg, "The Strategy Concept II: Another Look at Why Organizations Need Strategies," *California Management Review* (Fall 1987), 25–31.
13. J. A. Pearce II and W. A. Randolph, "Improving Strategy Formulation Pedagogies by Recognizing Behavioral Aspects," *Exchange* (December 1980), 7–10.
14. John A. Pearce II, Elizabeth B. Freeman, and Richard B. Robinson, Jr., "The Tenuous Link between Formal Strategic Planning and Financial Performance," *Academy of Management Review* (October 1987), 658–673; J. S. Bracker and J. N. Pearson, "Planning and Financial Performance of Small, Mature Firms," *Strategic Management Journal* (November-December 1986), 503–522; Lawrence C. Rhyme, "The Relationship of Strategic Planning to Financial Performance," *Strategic Management Journal* (September-October 1986), 423–436; Jonathan B. Welch, "Strategic Planning Could Improve Your Share Price," *Long Range Planning* (April 1984), 144–147; Richard B. Robinson, Jr., "The Importance of 'Outsiders' in Small Firm Strategic Planning," *Academy of Management Journal* (March 1982), 80–93; Richard W. Sapp and Robert E. Seiler, "The Relationship between Long-Range Planning and Financial Performance of U.S. Commercial Banks," *Managerial Planning* (September-October 1981), 32–36.

15. Walter Kiechel III, "Corporate Strategies Under Fire," *Fortune*, December 27, 1982, pp. 34–39.
16. Ann Langley, "The Role of Formal Strategic Planning," *Long Range Planning* (June 1988), 40–50.
17. Ibid.
18. Steiner, Miner, and Gray, pp. 173–174.
19. Michael Porter, "Corporate Strategy: The State of Strategic Thinking," *Economist* May 23, 1987, pp. 17–19+.
20. Paul and Taylor, p. 37.
21. George A. Steiner, *Strategic Planning: What Every Manager Must Know* (New York: The Free Press, 1979), pp. 93–94.
22. Ibid., p. 8.
23. Daniel H. Gray, "Uses and Misuses of Strategic Planning," *Harvard Business Review* (January-February 1986), 91.
24. Xavier Gilbert and Paul Strebal, "Strategies to Outpace the Competition," *Journal of Business Strategy* (Summer 1987).
25. Robert Waterman, *The Renewal Factor*, (New York: Bantam Books, 1987).
26. The first four traps are listed in M. R. Eigerman, "Who Should be Responsible for Business Strategy," *Journal of Business Strategy* (November-December 1988), 40–44, and the last two in Anthony V. Trowbridge, "Titanic Planning in an Uncertain Environment," *Long Range Planning* (April 1988), 86–90.
27. Ramanujam, Camillus, and Venkatraman, p. 621.
28. Robert H. Guest, "Management Imperatives for the Year 2000," *California Management Review* (Summer 1987), 30–36.
29. William J. Kent, "Administrative Management in 2000," *Administrative Management* (March-April 1988), 27–28.
30. Walter Kiechel III, "Corporate Strategy for the 1990's," *Fortune*, February 29, 1988, pp. 34–42.
31. Clemens Work, "The 21st Century Executive," *U.S. News and World Report*, March 7, 1988, pp. 48–51.

CHAPTER 2

A Global Perspective

At one time U.S. firms could ignore foreign companies and operate relatively safely. Since domestic markets were large enough and raw materials sufficiently plentiful, many companies could remain profitable without considering nondomestic markets or suppliers. Now, however, it is recognized widely that U.S. firms must adopt a global perspective and that this global perspective must be integrated throughout a firm's planning and decision-making processes.

An introductory overview of the global perspective, this chapter focuses on the importance of maintaining such a perspective. The key points include competing against foreign firms in domestic and international markets, international management, production, and marketing. Additional relevant global issues are treated in subsequent chapters and woven into the fabric of strategic planning and management.

THE IMPORTANCE OF GLOBAL PERSPECTIVE

Much has been written in recent years about the world becoming a smaller place. Nowhere is this phenomenon more important than in the formulation of business strategies and decisions. Few countries, including United States, have all the raw materials needed by manufacturers; some materials must be imported. Furthermore, many developed countries do not have adequate production capabilities to meet consumer demand for certain products; at the same time, they produce an overabundance of other products. This situation leads to both importing and exporting. Many firms throughout the world have also taken ownership positions in companies outside their domestic markets. Even very small firms cannot ignore the global environment. Foreign-made products offer new opportunities and threats. In essence, virtually no company is unaffected by this globalization trend.

As the global economy evolves, U.S. firms must be able to compete and operate effectively in the global marketplace. (See Perspective 2.1.) For instance, the European economic community could become even more united in 1992, making Europe one large market.[1] This market will be bigger than the U.S. market and contain many countries with high per capita incomes.[2]

The dramatic political and economic upheavals occurring in Eastern Europe since the late 1980s are also likely to have far-reaching ramifications.[3] The Eastern bloc countries—such as East Germany, Poland, and Romania—have relatively large populations and high pent-up demand. The upheavals within their borders could conceivably slow down the development of the 1992 European Common Market. However, further changes—such as the reunification of Germany—could also lead to a more attractive, as well as more formidable, European economic community. In addition, the 1990s may bring the opening of other markets formerly closed to United States—for example, Russia and China. Furthermore, these countries might compete with ours.

Another challenge may come from countries of the Asian Pacific Rim—for example, Japan, Korea, and Malaysia. One assessment terms the area "A worrisome threat. A fantastic opportunity. Bubbling with ambition. . . . In the 1990s this dynamic region will be a market as big as North America or Europe.[4]

These and other actual and potential changes throughout the world have led observers to conclude that all managers must learn to think globally. As Peter Drucker puts it, "If you don't think globally, you deserve to be unemployed, and you will be."[5]

What adds urgency to this warning is that the competition faced by U.S. managers—a European manager, for instance—is already likely to think in global terms. In many countries, the global/international perspective has long been part of business education and thinking, whereas in the United States it has remained a separate subject.

THE ADVANTAGES AND DISADVANTAGES OF GLOBAL INVOLVEMENT

A company may seek global involvement or try to enhance it for one of three basic reasons:

- To increase sales and profits by securing new markets and growth opportunities

PERSPECTIVE 2.1

McDonald's Goes to Moscow

The Soviet people eat meat and potatoes. McDonald's sells meat and potatoes. Therefore, McDonald's should open fast-food restaurants in the Soviet Union. This vision of international expansion—which sounds simple enough—cost George Cohon, president of McDonald's of Canada, some $50 million dollars and took him fourteen years to realize. It wasn't easy to introduce a highly standardized product and service into a society with very different social expectations and styles.

Take the problem of basic ingredients. While the Soviet Union raises its own cattle and grows its own potatoes, it does so in a highly regulated way. It has five-year plans, under which distribution is regulated. McDonald's was not part of anyone's five-year plan. And even if the fast-food giant had been part of such a plan, it would not have found the Soviet meat and potatoes quite right for its highly standardized Big Macs and fries. Accordingly, McDonald's, committed to dealing with local suppliers, imported potato seeds from its farm in the Netherlands and taught Soviet farmers how to produce beef to its exacting specifications.

Or take the problem of service. Eye contact and smiles, as obligatory as uniforms in the McDonald's system, are not automatic in the Soviet Union. Therefore, counter servers had to be instructed in professional cheeriness. Soviet managers—specially trained abroad—carried out this instruction.

Or take the problem of local eating habits. Unaccustomed to eating with their hands, Soviet people would tend to take their Big Macs apart and eat them with knives and forks. McDonald's mounted an ad campaign to show the right way to consume its burger sandwiches.

With the prospect of 290 million Soviet stomachs to fill, McDonald's of Canada is determined to build a local operation. The company is acting in partnership with the Moscow City Council Department of Foodservice. Its first restaurant sells its goods in Soviet rubles, rather than in the foreign currency demanded by most establishments offering exotic or expensive products. McDonald's first outlet, with 900 seats, 700 of them indoors, is regarded by the company as much as a training center for future McDonald's units as it is as a restaurant.

References: Ann Blackman, "Moscow's Big Mak Attack," Time, February 5, 1990, p. 51; Scott Hume, "How Big Mac Made It to Moscow," Advertising Age, January 22, 1990, p. 51ff. Rushworth M. Kidder, "What Moscow's Big Macs Mean," The Christian Science Monitor, February 12, 1990, p. 13. Reuters, "Soviet McDonald's Serves 30,000 Daily," The New York Times, March 1, 1990, section D, p. 5, col. 3, late edition.

- To improve the availability and/or cost of raw materials
- To gain a competitive advantage through lower-cost production facilities

However, it should recognize potential disadvantages as well:[6]

- A multiplicity of political, economic, legal, social, and cultural environments (each with a different level of environmental complexity and turbulence)
- Complex interactions with multiple national environments because of national sovereignties, widely disparate economic and social conditions, and so on
- Geographical distance, cultural and national differences, variations in business practices, and other differences that make communications difficult
- Disparities among countries in the availability, depth, and reliability of significant information required for planning
- Difficulties in analyzing present and future competition in some countries because of differences in industrial structure and business practices

TYPES OF GLOBAL INVOLVEMENT

Individual firms can vary widely in their global involvement, ranging from a retail store that carries a few foreign-made products to a company engaged in full production and marketing in an international setting. Several levels of global involvement are highlighted below.

Peripheral Involvement

Virtually all firms have at least a peripheral global involvement. There is hardly a retail store anywhere that does not carry at least a few products made outside the United States or made by U.S. plants owned by foreign companies. While these small retailing firms do not need as thorough a grasp of the global marketplace as do larger ones, they still must consider global possibilities and should not ignore them in formulating strategies and other decisions. For instance, a larger retailer may be able to deal directly with international suppliers to obtain lower prices and so move toward greater global involvement.

Competing with Foreign Firms

Many U.S. firms, even small producers, compete directly or indirectly with international firms. (See Perspective 2.2.) For example, small sewing plants that are scattered throughout the United States, particularly in the South, compete

PERSPECTIVE 2.2

Siemens: A New Major Player in Midrange Computers

Siemens, the giant German electronics firm, became a major player in midrange computers in January 1990, when it purchased Nixdorf Computer for an estimated $350 million. This acquisition is the latest phase of an aggressive expansion strategy—Siemens has acquired ownership of or made cooperative deals with Britain's Plessey, France's Franatome, Japan's Matsushita, and the United States' Rolm and Bendix. These moves have positioned Siemens as the seventh largest computer manufacturer in the world. The company should now be able to contend with Digital Equipment Corp. for the number-two slot in Europe, behind IBM. Nixdorf's customer base (50,000 installed minicomputer systems) also strengthens Siemens's previously weak position in mid-size computer systems.

Even though Nixdorf lost about $240 million in 1989, "everybody wanted to buy Nixdorf," according to the French industry minister. Other interested firms included France's Groupe Bull and Italy's Olivetti. Both the Nixdorf family (who controlled voting shares) and Deutsche Bank (Siemens's major lender) apparently wanted to keep Nixdorf out of non-German hands. Some observers believe that Siemens's acquisition sets the stage for a major competitive shakeout, one that a larger Siemens should be in a good position to survive.

Siemens's immediate plans include axing approximately a thousand Nixdorf employees, junking the Nixdorf 8870 series office computer, and introducing Siemens chips to Nixdorf products.

References: Igor Reichlin and Thane Peterson, "Why Siemens Wrote Such a Big Check," *Business Week*, January 22, 1990, p. 42; "Siemens' Bailout of Nixdorf: Financially Troubled Nixdorf Computer Found a Rescuer in Giant Siemens AG," *Mergers & Acquisitions*, March–April 1990, p. 64; Nell Margolis, "Fog Shrouds Future of Siemens Bid for Nixdorf," *Computerworld*, February 12, 1990, p. 96.

directly with clothing manufacturers from areas in the Caribbean Basin (for instance, from Barbados, Haiti, and Jamaica) and the Pacific Rim (for example, Hong Kong, Korea, and Thailand). The low cost of labor in these areas makes it difficult for U.S. firms to compete in some markets.

Larger companies, such as those in the automobile and electronics industries, also face formidable competition in both domestic and international markets. Note that these firms often compete on the basis of technology rather than low labor rates.

Firms competing domestically against foreign competitors must analyze the global situation carefully and formulate appropriate strategies. Key points to consider include competitors' collective strength in the market, potential barriers to market entry, and the likely intensity of a competitor's reaction to specific strategies.[7]

Operating Plants Outside the United States

Many U.S. firms have established production facilities outside the U.S. boundaries, chiefly because of lower labor costs in certain countries, particularly in the developing Third World. Firms at this level of global involvement must move to a different plane of thought concerning globalization. The company must familiarize itself with the governance of the country in which it operates. It must also study the culture of the host country to ensure a meshing with dominant cultural elements, particularly regarding labor and labor-management relationships. Some U.S. firms have encountered difficulties with their foreign operations because they did not understand the culture—such as the mandatory nature of religious holidays in some countries—and dealt with foreign nationals as they would with labor in the United States. It is crucial for managers to recognize that differences in cultures and in the way people think require the use of a different management approach.

Selling in International Markets

U.S. firms have a long history of selling in markets outside the United States. However, the relative sales as measured by the balance of trade have fallen in recent years. Nevertheless, several major U.S. companies earn more abroad than in the United States. Gillette and Colgate-Palmolive, for example, each grossed almost two-thirds of their 1988 net income abroad, while General Motors and Goodyear generated well over one-half of their earnings in non-U.S. markets.[8]

It is critically important for companies selling in international markets to understand what the customers are looking for and avoid violating these customers' cultural norms or taboos. The upheavals in Eastern Europe are likely to open new markets in which U.S. companies have little experience. Situations such as this one require that firms study them carefully and try to develop an understanding of the new customers' needs and wants. It will also be interesting to observe how these countries, which have relatively little hard currency and little significant experience in international trade, will deal with global competition.

Foreign Plants Operating in the United States

Foreign firms and investors are buying or building more and more plants in the United States. In the late 1980s much was written about the increasing amount of foreign investment—for instance, the Japanese purchase of Rockefeller Center and of large tracts of U.S. agricultural land. Despite much concern in the United States, foreigners apparently will continue to make inroads into our economy.

Indeed, as U.S. firms keep moving production facilities out of the country and nondomestic firms keep locating here, foreign companies could easily become the major employers in some industries. For example, while U.S. firms such as General Motors are shifting production facilities to Korea and other countries, Japanese firms are setting up their plants in the United States to take advantage of trade barriers or to lessen their impact. If the present trend continues, then by the year 2000 the only cars produced in the United States may well be Japanese cars. It is quite possible that many of today's college students will work for a firm that is owned wholly or partially by foreign investors. In such a situation, understanding and appreciating other cultures become critical assets.

Combination Approaches

The five types of global involvement we have discussed so far may also appear in various combinations. For instance, today's typical firm may have some production facilities abroad, may compete directly and indirectly with foreign-owned businesses, and may also have major groups of foreign investors. To function effectively, managers and employees of such firms must have a grasp of foreign cultures and must be able to think in a global context. Emphasizing global context is perhaps the greatest change we need in the way we approach business strategy and decisions. Merely stressing international trade—trade laws, trade regulations, and so on—as U.S. business schools have done in the past, is no longer enough.

THE CONSTANTS OF GLOBAL MANAGEMENT

Along with the differences, many elements of global management remain the same across cultural boundaries. First, business firms in virtually all cultures have *financial targets* such as quotas, expenses, and profits. Even in cultures that de-emphasize profits, profits or "excess revenues" have some importance. In these countries, profits may go to the government rather than to private investors, but excess revenues are desirable and expected in most organizations.

Second, a *nationalistic focus* exists in most countries. Owners, managers, and employees are likely to focus heavily on issues related to their native land. Few individuals possess a truly global perspective, and even fewer focus primarily on another country. Consequently, major events occurring in the United States may matter little to people elsewhere.

Third, virtually all developed countries use the *corporate form of ownership* or its equivalent. That is, the money needed to operate a business is placed in the hands of professional managers, who attempt to increase that pool of money. The extent to which government invests funds in business varies from country to country. In some countries, for example, the government may be the major stockholder in many firms. Such situations can influence the competitive situation. For instance, a government that owns a major portion of some of the businesses may give those businesses special privileges and protection.

Fourth, every company in every country has some type of formal or informal *organizational structure*. Although there are many structure possibilities, even within the United States, all the structures have essentially the same focus: someone at the top has the power, and the authority vested in that individual is delegated to subordinates. Just as in the United States, so elsewhere, too, serious differences between the informal and the formal structure can cause management problems.

Fifth, the *basic functions and principles of management* have existed for many years and are constant across many different cultures. In fact, Henri Fayol, who is credited with first writing down the functions and the principles of management, was a French industrialist. Thus U.S. managers can utilize in international dealings what they learned in U.S. schools. They can manage in other cultures by adjusting their ideas about the functions and principles of management rather than trying to adopt totally new ideas. It is crucial, however, for U.S.-trained managers to recognize the need for making adjustments because there are sometimes major differences in the application of functions and principles.

MAJOR DIFFERENCES IN GLOBAL MANAGEMENT

The differences in global management practices stem from differences in culture, degrees of government involvement, and relative size. Failure to take these differences into account can lead to general failure on global issues.[9]

Culture

Culture is a very broad concept, encompassing many issues related to different countries and groups within countries. As discussed later in the text, individual firms also have their own cultures. An operational definition of culture is "the way that a group of people tend to act or react in given situations." The major components of culture are religion, norms of society, and several other less obvious factors.

Religion   The basic religious beliefs of a country form a critical cornerstone of culture. To make good decisions in the global marketplace, managers must try to gain a basic understanding of the world's major religions. This is especially necessary when a company moves from domestic markets into markets where a radically different religion exists. For instance, U.S. firms moving into countries dominated by Moslem or Hindu religions must examine those religions carefully to assess their effect on decision making.

Perhaps the worst mistake that a manager can make is to assume that religious beliefs of other cultures resemble those found in the United States. Violating major components of another land's religion is a particularly grave error. Thus foreign managers in Middle Eastern countries must not underestimate the importance of Mecca to those of the Moslem faith. For example, a U.S. bus manufacturer obtained a contract to build buses for the Saudi government to take Moslem worshippers to Mecca. Since each Moslem is required to go to Mecca at least once, people save for a lifetime to make the trip. Therefore, anything that interferes with the comfort or enjoyment of that journey can cause resentment and ill will. But these buses did not please the government or the travelers; they were deemed substandard. Had the company's managers realized how important a visit to Mecca is for a Moslem, they might have reached a different decision about the quality of materials for their buses.

Nothing we have said so far is meant to suggest that U.S. managers should adopt religions from other parts of the world. But they do need to acknowledge the presence of different religions and the right of those who believe in them to practice their faith. Thus a company may have to adjust work hours, work rules, or other elements to conform to the religious requirements of the host country.

Norms   Norms are the prevailing informal rules under which a given society operates; they vary from one society to another. For instance, some Eastern cultures respect age much more than we do in the United States. A company operating in such a culture may find it advantageous to place in supervisory positions people who are older than the population in general.

Other Aspects of Culture   Besides religion and norms, managers should keep in mind some other aspects of local culture when operating internationally. For instance, working on a daily basis is not the prevailing custom in some countries, especially the less developed ones; thus employees may not comprehend the need for coming to work every day. In such situations, U.S. managers should be prepared to make special provisions to get the job done. They should also be aware of major local holidays and adjust schedules and production accordingly.

Government Involvement in Business

Historically, the U.S. government has had relatively minor involvement with the ownership and management of businesses. The reverse holds true in many other countries. In several European countries, for instance, the government partially owns major industries. In developing countries, this difference is even greater, for the government controls most industries, as well as the information related to those industries.[10] To succeed, a U.S. firm operating in such areas must adapt to more government control and answer to the government as a major owner of the business.[11]

Much has been written about *Japan, Inc.*—a term that has come to indicate the Japanese government's heavy involvement with domestic Japanese companies. For instance, the Japanese government may have an institute that supports research for a given industry and may provide other special supports for the industry, such as tariffs or other trade barriers to outsiders. Foreign firms must learn to live within this system. U.S. companies must be willing to deal with the situation as it exists since they are not likely to be able to change it. The Japanese market, however, appears to be more open to U.S. firms than it had been in the past.[12]

The apparent shift of many Eastern European governments away from communism will create interesting situations for many U.S. companies. Eastern European firms are likely to be doing much more business globally than in the past, yet their ownership structure is almost exclusively state ownership. How this competitive situation will work out is certainly unclear as we move into the decade of the 1990s. Perhaps the governments will maintain ownership and operate the firms in a way to best help the country, or perhaps these companies will be reorganized into more independent corporate forms. This will certainly be one of the major challenges facing managers as we approach the twenty-first century.

Size Relative to the United States

Some major countries are extremely small geographically when compared with the United States. For instance, many European countries are smaller than a number of our states in both land mass and population. Consequently, American and European managers may have trouble understanding how business must be conducted in each other's country. Some European managers may not realize initially that it can take many hours or even several days to go from one corner of the United States to the other. They may assume that a plant in Florida and a plant in Washington are very close whereas, in fact, the distance between the two plants would be approximately twice that between Paris and Moscow. Conversely, a U.S. manager operating in a European country could underestimate the response time of competitors from other European countries.

If a U.S. firm intends to do business with several different European companies, the problem of size can be further complicated by the problem of language, since in Europe several very distinct languages can exist within a relatively short distance, even in the same country. Just look at a map and see how close Great Britain, France, and Spain are to each other. Yet these three countries represent three major languages of the world.

MANAGING IN THE GLOBAL MARKETPLACE

To survive in the global marketplace, a firm's leadership has to perceive the world as a global village, see the firm as a multinational firm, and take actions that show a multinational attitude.[13] If U.S. managers recognize that they must manage differently as they move into worldwide competition, they can succeed. If they are unwilling to take cultural differences into account, they may flounder.[14] A firm may wish to consider setting up a team to bring in cultural diversity when individuals do not have a sufficiently broad global perspective and appreciation of cultural differences.[15]

U.S. managers must recognize that, although U.S. businesses are strong competitors in the global marketplace, there are also other strong competitors. Failure to recognize this will likely result in major difficulties of survival as the twenty-first century approaches.[16]

Before a U.S. firm begins to internationalize, its management needs to take these steps:[17]

1. *Scan the international situation.* Read journals and patent reports, check other printed sources, meet people at scientific/technical conferences and in-house seminars.
2. *Make connections with academic and research organizations.*
3. *Increase the firm's global visibility.* Participate in technology trade fairs, circulate brochures illustrating the firm's products and inventions.
4. *Undertake cooperative research projects.*

U.S. firms can do business in newly opened markets. Doing business in the Soviet Union, for example, appears to be based on the following caveats:[18]

1. *Show an unshakable corporate commitment from the top of the organization.* The Soviets place a premium on protocol and prefer to deal top executive to top executive.
2. *Do not expect quick business decisions.* Layers of Soviet bureaucracy slow decision making.
3. *Be conscious of the Soviets' wariness of the quarter-to-quarter management orientation of many U.S. firms.* They want to be convinced of the U.S. firm's long-term commitment.
4. *Know that there is no formal research regarding the size of the Soviet market for a product, price elasticity, consumer demographics, and other information.* A Soviet adviser with appropriate experience may be indispensable.
5. *Be familiar with relevant terms of trade.* The Soviet ruble is not convertible to hard currency, but efforts are under way to remedy this.

U.S. businesspeople are very fortunate that much global business is transacted in English. In fact, English has become the most significant "language of business," giving Americans an advantage. The drawback of this situation is that Americans feel little need to learn other languages, whereas in many countries foreign languages are part of the educational requirement.

As future managers, you should be very concerned with how you will cope with the international, or global, situation. You may not need to understand numerous foreign languages, but you will need to appreciate other cultures. Although it may be too late in your college career to take additional courses in geography or foreign languages, you should make every effort to improve your understanding of the global marketplace. Because they have lacked such understanding, some U.S. companies are now at risk of fading out of existence.

Notes

1. For a more complete discussion of the 1992 situation, see John A. Quelch, Robert D. Buzzell, and Eric R. Salama, *The Marketing Challenge of 1992,* (Boston: Addison-Wesley, 1990). See also Sandra Vandermerwe and Marc-André L'Huillier, "Euro-Consumers in 1992," *Business Horizons* (January-February 1989), 23–27.
2. David Mitchell, "1992: The Implications for Management," *Long Range Planning* (February 1989), 32–40.
3. Peter Nulty, "How the World Will Change," *Fortune,* January 15, 1990, pp. 44–54.
4. See "The Challenge of Asia in the 1990s," *Fortune,* Special Issue (Fall 1989), 10–11 and the remainder of the same issue for an excellent discussion on doing business in Pacific Rim countries.
5. Peter F. Drucker, "New World According to Drucker" *Business Month,* 133 (May 1989), 50.
6. Adapted from W. A. Dymsza, *Multinational Business Strategy* (New York: McGraw-Hill, 1972), pp. 50–51.

7. W. Chan Kim and R. A. Mauborgne, "Becoming an Effective Global Competitor," *Journal of Business Strategy* (January-February 1988), 33–37.

8. W. J. Holstein, "The Action is Abroad," *Business Week*, May 1, 1989, p. 28.

9. Rose Knotts, "Cross-Cultural Management: Transformation and Adaptations," *Business Horizons* (January-February 1989), 29–33.

10. W. R. Haines, "Making Corporate Planning Work in Developing Countries," *Long Range Planning* (April 1988), 91–95.

11. Mark Alpert, "Wary Hope on Eastern Europe," *Fortune*, January 29, 1990, pp. 125–126.

12. Carla Rapoport, "You Can Make Money in Japan," *Fortune*, February 12, 1990, pp. 85–92.

13. James Bolt, "Global competitors: Some Criteria for Success," *Business Horizons* (January 1988), 32–37. See also Mark M. Colodny, "How to Manage in the New Era," *Fortune*, January 15, 1990, pp. 58–72.

14. "International Business Blunders: An Update," *Business and Economic Review* (January-March 1988), 11–14.

15. Thomas Gross, Ernie Turner, and Lars Cederman, "Building Teams for Global Operations," *Management Review* (June 1987), 32–36.

16. John J. Dyment, "Strategies and Management Controls for Global Corporations," *Journal Business Strategy* (Spring 1987), 20–24.

17. R. Ronstadt and R. Kramer, "Getting the Most Out of Innovation Abroad," *Harvard Business Review* (March-April 1982), 94–99.

18. Kari Seppala and Mark A. Meyer, "Time Ripe for U.S. Firms to Enter Soviet Market," *Marketing News*, February 5, 1990, pp. 6, 9.

CHAPTER 3

Values, Ethics, and Social Responsiveness

It has become increasingly important for businesses to make decisions that are correct in the eyes of society. People are demanding that all types of business organizations exhibit corporate consciousness. One of the reasons for this trend is the heightened visibility of corporate decisions. News organizations are reporting business affairs more diligently, informing the public about corporate decisions and their consequences. The negative publicity stemming from decisions that go against the society's wishes can injure or destroy even the largest corporations. Hence, firms have begun to look more closely at their obligations to society. The level of corporate citizenship depends on three critical elements: values, ethics and social responsiveness.

VALUES

Values are *those ideas and things that a group of individuals considers important or desirable.* Values are acquired from influential people (such as parents, teachers) early in life. Every manager brings his or her own set of values to the firm. These personal values have been classified in various ways. William D. Guth and Renato Taguiri proposed six value categories:[1]

- *Theoretical:* primarily interested in the discovery of truth and knowledge
- *Economic:* primarily interested in what is useful and economically practical
- *Aesthetic:* primarily interested in the artistic aspects of life
- *Social:* primarily interested in the love of other people
- *Political:* primarily interested in acquiring power
- *Religious:* primarily interested in relating to the universe

George England offered a three-category value scheme:[2]

- *Pragmatic:* views ideas and concepts in terms of whether or not they work or are successful
- *Ethical-moral:* views ideas in terms of being right or wrong
- *Feeling:* views ideas in terms of whether or not they are pleasant

Values may be positive or negative from a social perspective. For instance, one company's value system may prompt it to act in ways that will be beneficial to society. But another firm's value system may put the owners' best interest first, regardless of the impact on society. Values are crucial to any discussion of strategic thinking, planning, and management because they are part of a firm's culture and control the consistency of its decisions.

Corporate Culture

Corporate culture represents the *sum of the values of all the people within an organization.* It is the normal way of doing things within an organization. Like the broader concept of a society's culture, corporate (or organizational) culture includes norms, mores, and other related factors. Just as in society, culture in a company is strongly influenced by people with power: managers, owners, and so on. Indeed, these individuals set the tone for firm's culture. Management needs to recognize this fact and strive to foster a culture that supports achievement of the organization's objectives.

It is no accident that when scrutinizing firms that have experienced strong, sustained growth, such as Wal-Mart and Federal Express, one finds strong, positive cultures. By contrast, many less successful firms appear to have weak or poorly defined cultures. In researching the subject, Thomas J. Peters and Robert H. Waterman have concluded that the cultures of successful firms incorporate the following basic beliefs:[3]

1. Belief in being the best
2. Belief in the importance of the details of execution, the nuts and bolts of doing the job well
3. Belief in the importance of people as individuals
4. Belief in superior quality and service
5. Belief that most members of the organization should be innovators, and its corollary, the willingness to support failure
6. Belief in the importance of informality to enhance communication
7. Belief in a recognition of the importance of economic growth and profits

Note that the issue for a company is not whether to have a culture; that is unavoidable. The question is whether a given culture is the most desirable one for a particular organization.

The Need for Pervasive Corporate Values

Corporate decisions should be relatively consistent. Strong values that permeate the entire firm enhance this consistency because managers at all levels are likely to make decisions that are consistent with decisions made at other organization levels. Such consonance in decision making is especially important for issues that influence society in general. For instance, if top management decides that the firm will respect the environment and takes steps to reduce any harm to it, managers at all levels should conform to this posture. If a manager of a small facility in the organization violates this environmental posture, the company is likely to receive bad publicity and be accused of hypocrisy.

Generating companywide knowledge and appreciation of corporate values generally requires that higher-level management publish and discuss a *code of conduct* or *code of ethics* clearly stating the firm's core values. For instance, management may formulate a set of statements declaring the firm's fundamental beliefs. This document should be furnished to all managers and all employees, and they should be expected to abide by its tenets. The document can also prove a valuable public relations tool and thus may be published on posters, in financial statements, and so on.

ETHICS

Ethics may be defined as "a theory or morality which attempts to systematize moral judgments, and establish and defend basic moral principles."[4] The ethical quality of an act or decision is usually assessed through either the teleological or the deontological approach.[5]

The **teleological approach** is based on the consequences of a decision: if they are beneficial, the decision is deemed ethical. Utilitarianism is a teleological philosophy, advocated in the nineteenth century by John Stuart Mill and Jeremy Bentham. According to the utilitarian criterion, a decision is ethical when it benefits the largest number of people.

There are three basic forms of utilitarianism:[6]

1. *Hedonistic utilitarianism* judges the basic morality of an action by estimating the degree of pleasure or pain that it offers to society as a whole.

2. *Eudaimonistic utilitarianism* measures the degree of happiness an act engenders for society.
3. *Ideal utilitarianism* encompasses a larger view of valuable consequences and considers "all intrinsically valuable human goods, which also include friendship, knowledge, and a host of other goods valuable in themselves."

The **deontological approach** is based on the idea that decisions are ethical if they have characteristics that we associate with "good." Thus ethical conduct is self-evident and is not judged by its consequences. The theories related to this approach often have a religious or moral framework.

It is important that you begin to develop your own way of evaluating ethical behavior. Books such as *Ethical Managing* by F. Neil Brady can aid you in this process.[7]

Defining Ethical Behavior

Top management sets and transmits the ethical tone of an organization through both words and actions. If a firm does not have a written code of ethics, the top management should, at the very least, make it clear to all members of the organization that unethical behavior or misconduct will not be tolerated and rationalizations for it will not be accepted.

It particularly needs to stress these four rationalizations as unacceptable.[8]

- *The activity was within reasonable ethical and legal limits—that is, it was not "really" illegal or immoral.* "Everybody does it" is not an acceptable rationalization.
- *The activity was in the individual's or the organization's best interests—the individual was expected to undertake the activity.* "I did it for the company" is not an acceptable rationalization.
- *The activity was "safe" because it will never be found out or publicized—the classic crime-and-punishment issue of risk of discovery.* "No one will ever find out" is not an acceptable rationalization.
- *Because the activity helps the company, the company will condone it and even protect the person who engaged in it.* "My boss will protect me because I made money for the company" is not an acceptable rationalization.

Table 3.1 lists fourteen ethical propositions. If understood and heeded, they can improve the ethical climate of an organization.

Every organization must define how it will judge whether a decision is ethical or unethical. It may do so through a code of ethics or simply through statements

TABLE 3.1 · Ethical Propositions

- Ethical conflicts and choices are inherent in business decision making.

- Proper ethical behavior exists on a plane above the law. The law merely specifies the lowest common denominator of acceptable behavior.

- There is no single satisfactory standard of ethical action agreeable to everyone that a manager can use to make specific operational decisions.

- Managers should be familiar with a wide variety of ethical standards.

- The discussion of business cases or of situations having ethical implications can make managers more ethically sensitive.

- There are diverse and sometimes conflicting determinants of ethical action. These stem primarily from the individual, from the organization, from professional norms, and from the values of society.

- Individual values are the final standard, although not necessarily the determining reason, for ethical behavior.

- Consensus regarding what constitutes proper ethical behavior in a decision-making situation diminishes as the level of analysis proceeds from abstract to specific.

- The moral tone of an organization is set by top management.

- The lower the organizational level of a manager, the greater the perceived pressure to act unethically.

- Individual managers perceive themselves as more ethical than their colleagues.

- Effective codes of ethics should contain meaningful and clearly stated provisions, along with enforced sanctions for noncompliance.

- Employees must have a nonpunitive, fail-safe mechanism for reporting ethical abuses in the organization.

- Every organization should appoint a top-level manager or director to be responsible for acting as an ethical advocate in the organization.

Source: From Gene Laczniak, "Business Ethics: A Manager's Primer," *Business,* March 1983, pp. 23–29. Copyright 1983 by the College of Business Administration, Georgia State University, Atlanta. Reprinted by permission of the publisher.

of what the firm believes and how it will ensure that its decisions conform to those beliefs.

That a firm take ethics into account is more important than the particular ethical behaviors that it favors. Individuals may disagree on the specifics of ethical behavior. What is vital is that the company consider decisions from an ethical angle before acting on them. This approach will stand it in good stead when it confronts ethical dilemmas.

Ethical Dilemmas

Ethical dilemmas stem from issues on which there is little agreement regarding what is right and what would benefit society the most. Consider, for instance, the issue of testing drugs with animals. Some people believe that drug companies should never use animals in such tests, but others are convinced that some type of testing is necessary before new drugs are used on humans. The dilemma involves determining how much drug testing should be done on the animals. If a firm tests too much, it may be viewed by society as being "anti-animals"; if it tests too little, it may produce drugs injurious to humans.

Another highly charged issue today is the drug testing of employees. This dilemma pits a worker's right to privacy against a firm's right to ensure that its employees' performance is unimpaired by drugs. Apparently, society has determined that in some cases it is more important to prevent impairment by drugs, while in others it is more important to preserve the right to privacy. There seems to be general agreement that it is appropriate to test those who hold jobs where error can pose grave risks—for instance, aircraft pilots. There is much less agreement, however, about testing baggage handlers employed by the same airline.

The Importance of Acting Ethically

Since ethical behavior is expected from today's business organizations, companies that adhere to high ethical standards may not reap any particular rewards. (See Perspective 3.1.) Unethical behavior, on the other hand, gets widely publicized by the news media and draws public censure. A firm branded as unethical in its actions can lose both reputation and revenue. Thus even self-interest should dictate an ethical approach as the best policy for running a business.[9]

SOCIAL RESPONSIVENESS

Social responsiveness and ethics are related issues with some subtle differences. **Social responsiveness** involves responding to the needs and wants of society. It has fewer moralistic overtones than ethics, but shares many of the problems. For instance, ethical dilemmas are related to the social responsiveness issue of satisfying different stakeholders—important groups that have some claim on the organization.

Note that many authors use the term **social responsibility** rather than **social responsiveness.** We prefer the latter term because all firms have a social responsibility to various stakeholders, but not all are responsive to social needs. Further-

PERSPECTIVE 3.1

Firms' Responsiveness to Working Women

Although much progress is still needed, many businesses have begun to respond to the different needs of working women and dual-career couples. Examples of changes that have been made include the following:

RELOCATION

When an employee with a working spouse is transferred, more and more companies are providing child-care assistance, as well as job-search services for the "trailing" spouse.

CHILD CARE

About 2,500 firms provided some form of child-care aid in 1985, up from 600 in 1982. For example:

- Campbell Soup Company has a child-care center—offering breakfast—at its headquarters.
- Merck & Co. has a child-care center near its headquarters.

Some firms are beginning to institute a two-track career plan that includes the so-called Mommy Track, which allows part-time work. Career advancement is allowed, but at a slower pace.

In addition, some firms are trying to stimulate the supply of day care in the general community:

- BankAmerica put up $100,000 to start a pilot program that eventually generated $700,000 and created 1,000 new day-care slots.
- AT&T is beginning several experiments, creating on-site centers and giving employees a building to start their own facility.
- IBM spent $1 million in 1984 to set up a nationwide corporate service for referring employees to community child care. Now with a $2 million budget, the service has referred 16,000 children.
- Dayton-Hudson Corporation and First Bank System Inc. contribute to Chicken Soup, a firm that cares for ill children so their parents can work rather than stay at home.

FLEXIBLE WORKING HOURS

Merck & Co. began letting its employees start work at any point from 7 A.M. to 9:30 A.M.

PARENTAL LEAVES

About 35 percent of the major companies have increased the length of paid maternity leave in the past five years. In addition:

- Merck allows some parents of infants to work part-time or at home.
- Hewlett-Packard allows employees to combine sick leave and annual leave and add them to maternity leave.

- Lotus Development Corp. offers up to four weeks of paid time off to adoptive parents (men or women).
- BankAmerica reimburses some adoption expenses up to $2,000.

FRINGE BENEFITS

Instead of offering the same benefits to everyone, some 500 firms offer flexible packages that let employees choose what they need, for example, child care versus higher take-home pay.

PROMOTION SYSTEMS

BankAmerica now bases seniority (for promotion) on cumulative service rather than consecutive employment. This policy helps mothers who take maternity leave.

References: Stephen L. Guinn, "The Changing Workforce," *Training & Development Journal*, December 1989, pp. 38–39; "Business Starts Tailoring Itself to Suit Working Women," *Business Week*, October 6, 1986, pp. 50–54; "Working Women and Employee Benefits," *Personnel Journal*, September 1985, pp. 73–74ff.

more, social responsibility implies a state of being, whereas social responsiveness implies action.

Responding to Different Stakeholders

An organization's stakeholders can be found at each environmental level (discussed in Chapters 5 through 7). A **stakeholder** is *any group that has an actual or potential interest or impact on an organization's ability to achieve its objectives.*[10] The terms *constituency, coalition, public,* and *claimants* are often used interchangeably with *stakeholder.*[11]

Stakeholder groups, which can help or hinder an organization in accomplishing its objectives, fall into three main segments. *Reciprocal stakeholders* are those in whom the firm is interested and who are interested in the firm, such as stockholders. *Sought stakeholders* are those in whom the firm is interested but who do not take a strong interest in the firm, such as the press, from which the firm wants good news coverage. *Unwelcome stakeholders* are those whom the firm shuns but who insist on taking an interest in the firm, such as citizen-action groups.[12]

The Importance of Socially Responsive Action

Regardless of the problems associated with determining how to respond to social needs, a firm must still respond to these needs. At a minimum, society expects companies to avoid injuring the various elements of society. Even though a firm may not be able to satisfy stakeholder wants exactly, it should strive to avoid damaging any relevant stakeholder. Firms should also attempt to improve their stakeholders' situation or positions. As indicated previously, damaging stakeholders or failing to improve their position can lead to extremely negative publicity and hurt not only the firm's reputation, but also its chances for survival.

DEALING WITH SOCIAL AND ETHICAL DILEMMAS

The difficulty of dealing with social and ethical dilemmas is no excuse for avoiding these issues. To find ways of tackling them, we might look back to the philosophical bases of ethical conduct discussed earlier: doing the greatest good and doing the right thing.

The Greatest Good

Many people take the position that business firms should base their decisions on the concept of doing the greatest good for the largest portion of the population. If the outcome of a decision does indeed help the greatest number of people, it validates the decision as *good*. Thus, in coping with dilemmas, management should certainly evaluate where the greatest good lies.

If a decision favoring one group over another must be made, the rationale for such a decision comes from our democratic system, which is based on responding to the needs of the majority. But blindly following the principle of the greatest good may result in decisions that harm smaller, or minority, groups. Since such groups can become the proverbial "squeaky wheel," it is important that management also consider what is "right."

The "Right" Decision

A classic philosophical dilemma deals with a society whose members can have all the things they desire, but only if they are willing to keep a small child in a state of extreme pain. In the strictest sense, the "greatest good" approach would appear to support keeping the child in pain. Most people, however, would agree that this is not the right thing to do. Business firms are sometimes faced with similar decisions. For instance, should a firm produce chemicals that are extremely valuable to society and relatively safe in use, but extremely dangerous to the workers who produce them? Are the benefits to society worth damaging the health of a few employees or possibly killing them? Asbestos provides another good example. Its insulating qualities can reduce energy consumption, but people exposed to it face a high health risk.

Every manager should realize that it is impossible to satisfy all of society's wants; it is also impossible to always know what the "greatest good" is or "what is right." Yet even in nebulous situations, management must strive to be a good citizen through ethical and responsive behavior.

BECOMING AN ETHICAL, RESPONSIVE ORGANIZATION

When businesspeople view social responsibility as simple compliance with laws and regulations, businesses may react quite slowly to social pressures. Such laggardness has provoked increasingly restrictive government regulations. Had some U.S. businesses acted in a more desirable manner, they might have averted government action. For instance, had the automobile industry devoted more effort to obtaining better gasoline mileage, fleet mileage regulations might have been avoided.

More firms are starting to realize that social responsiveness may be the best way to protect long-run profitability. Firms such as Sears, Roebuck & Co. and General Electric Co. have developed programs to assess the evolving social and political environment.[13] Other firms have taken specific steps before government agencies forced action. Procter & Gamble Co., for instance, incurred an enormous cost in removing Rely tampons from the market after the Centers for Disease Control uncovered a possible link between the use of Rely and toxic shock syndrome. Similarly, McNeilabs, the manufacturer of Tylenol, took immediate action to remove its product from the market after seven people died in the Chicago area from poisoned Tylenol capsules. Although the company had not poisoned the capsules, it bore the full expense—estimated at $100 million— of replacing them with tablets for the customers who wanted this exchange.[14] Thus McNeilabs may have bolstered its long-term profitability by incurring a rather steep short-term loss.

If companies act in a socially responsive manner, fewer new and stringent regulations are likely to ensue. But if they fail to pay enough attention to social responsiveness, they can expect tighter controls.

Firms must realize that business decisions have a social impact and that managing social impact is a necessity. George Sawyer proposes the following nine principles of social impact management:[15]

1. *Responsibility:* A firm bears responsibility for the consequences of its actions in proportion to its discretion or freedom to take those actions.
2. *Social costs:* A firm must either avoid or balance social costs, or face the resulting social stress.

3. *Law:* A firm depends on respect for the law from itself and others because the law is the major bulwark upon which the existence, success, and security of the firm depends.
4. *Resources:* A firm must use natural resources wisely or risk challenge of its right to use them at all.
5. *Continuity:* A firm must balance any costs it causes when it breaks an ongoing relationship that others assume is ongoing.
6. *Opportunity costs:* A firm must consider the opportunity costs it has created for the other parties when breaking ongoing relationships.
7. *Community:* A firm should ensure that the total of the contributions it has made to the community represents a fair share of the total requirement.
8. *Ethics:* A firm's actions and words help shape the ethics and culture of the community, and the firm will be judged according to those ethics.
9. *Public:* The social impact of a firm's actions puts it in an important public role, and self-interest requires that the firm carefully manage that role.

Most firms should be addressing the question "How can we become a better citizen?" or "How can we improve our ethical behavior and social responsiveness?" Tackling these questions begins with listing the values important to the organization. Management should examine these values to ensure their ethical soundness. It needs to ask whether the values result in good for a large number of people and whether they are good in and of themselves. It also needs to ascertain if each value is reasonably acceptable to society. The list of values should be distributed to all personnel and strongly emphasized to every manager within the organization. All decisions should be made in the light of these values.

Sawyer provides twenty-six guidelines that can serve as comprehensive, flexible norms:[16]

1. *Quality:* Ensure that goods and services will fulfill customer expectations.
2. *Service:* Meet reasonable requirements for after-sale and continued support of routine use patterns.
3. *Safety:* Keep goods and services free of danger and unexpected side effects in normal use, attempt to ensure safety in the light of predictable product misuse, and attempt to prevent products and packaging from causing unacceptable environmental aftereffects.
4. *Conservation:* Manage operations with a sensitivity that minimizes the risk of losing our right to use resources, particularly scarce resources.
5. *Value:* Provide all personnel with fair compensation and safe working conditions.
6. *Opportunity:* Provide personnel with meaningful tasks, challenging career paths, and equal opportunity.

7. *Pollution:* Do not allow wastes discharged from company operations to cause any measurable damage to the environment.

8. *Waste:* Minimize energy and resource content of waste streams by recovery or recycling.

9. *Dependence:* Recognize the degree to which the firm depends on and is served by the health of the local community and encourage this health whenever possible.

10. *Contributor:* Support a fair share of the costs of community services, including those used by the firm and needed by both the employees and by those in the community who cannot support themselves.

11. *Neighborhood:* Recognize the firm's effect on the nature and character of the surrounding neighborhood and minimize adverse effects.

12. *Self-Interest:* Recognize and pursue the firm's self-interest in public processes and cultivate an understanding of this self-interest as it relates to the social and political processes so that neither the anger of society nor its political power will be aroused.

13. *Standards:* Create appropriate standards when encountering areas where social standards are needed but do not yet exist.

14. *Allegiance:* Give primary allegiance to the society that makes the rules controlling the firm's existence and blend in as a sound corporate citizen to ensure long-term acceptance and survival.

15. *Federal management:* Encourage each subsidiary (particularly those in different rule-making social units and countries) to become part of the local society, recognize the divergent allegiances of subsidiaries, and develop economic and managerial unity in a framework consistent with local ties.

16. *Power:* Use economic power and political influence carefully to avoid presenting a threat to the society or alarming the political power of that society.

17. *Loyalty:* Expect and require allegiance from organization members within the legal scope of the business and within the personal scope of the employee's normal growth and progressions as individuals, and recognize the likelihood of unrest or defection if the firm tries to require legal or unethical actions or actions detrimental to an employee's self-interest.

18. *Wealth production:* Attempt to make productive processes as efficient in the use of materials, energy, and labor as competitive circumstances will permit.

19. *Social control:* Strive to build public information about the basic issues underlying the firm's choice of the most efficient pattern for regulating itself and its industry.

20. *Regulation:* Learn the network of rules and regulations applicable to the firm's operations, determine which are relevant, viable, and under enforcement, and work quietly and constructively with the various regulatory authorities, confronting them only as business self-interest truly requires.

21. *Technology:* Develop an understanding of the firm's level of dependence on technology and seek opportunities to encourage the replenishment of this technology.

22. *New products:* Make an effort to minimize the social stress caused by introducing goods that change lifestyles and cultural patterns, hasten adoption, and avoid challenge of the right to introduce such goods or services.

23. *Capital:* Conserve and expand the firm's resource base to maintain and increase the level of opportunity for the firm, its employees, and its community.

24. *Profits:* Handle profits in such a way as to minimize the economic, social, and political impact of their use.

25. *Severance:* Make a serious effort to find alternative profitable uses for previously employed resources when evolution of the business creates a surplus of plants or people.

26. *Social change:* Use the power to mold and reshape society wisely by selecting areas where social forces supporting such change have already been set in motion and by not encouraging attempts at change that will be rejected by society's governance processes.

Besides establishing the firm's values, management should constantly monitor society regarding societal wants and the firm's *ethical/social fit.* Societal values and wants can change over time, and may change quite rapidly. For example, although by and large U.S. society has viewed drugs negatively for quite some time, the strength of those views seems to have increased dramatically in recent years. Firms may need to respond to this sentiment by increasing antidrug efforts, providing assistance to employees who have drug-related problems, and helping communities cope with drug-related problems.

Management must also carefully consider which ethical and social issues it will respond to. Obviously, a firm cannot possibly fill every need and attack every problem. However, it is almost mandatory that it respond to such issues as pollution control, equal opportunity, public health and welfare, drug abuse, and safety. On some other issues, a company may have more discretion. For instance, it may elect to satisfy the desires of a specific stakeholder group in one situation, while responding to a different stakeholder group in another situation. What is vital is that management make such decisions consciously and not just allow them to happen.

GLOBAL ETHICAL DIMENSIONS

Multinational corporations (MNCs) face an interesting ethical situation. Formulating a code of ethics for global use is difficult because of variances in countries' customs, morals, and values. These varying standards imply that the firm should adapt its behavior to that of the host country. But would the MNC be hypocritical if its code of ethics varied from country to country? For example, what if bribery is against an MNC's code of ethics, but an acceptable business practice in a specific country? What if bribery is the only way to clear goods through customs? Should bribery be accepted as a cost of doing business? A firm may even need to withdraw from some countries because of their laws, rules, or accepted behavior. For instance, many firms have cut their ties with South Africa because of the country's practice of apartheid.

Succeeding in a country requires the understanding and accommodation of differing values and customs and resulting ethics. The quandary is in not compromising so much that the ethics of the MNC lead to a double standard and, hence, hypocritical ethical norms.[17]

Notes

1. William D. Guth and Renato Taguiri, "Personal Values and Corporate Strategy," *Harvard Business Review* (September-October 1965), 124–25.

2. George England, "Personal Value Systems of Managers and Administrators," *Academy of Management Proceedings* (August 1973), 81–94.

3. Thomas J. Peters and Robert H. Waterman, Jr., *In Search of Excellence*, (New York: Harper & Row, 1982), p. 285.

4. R. T. DeGeorge, *Business Ethics*, (New York: Macmillan, 1982), p. 37.

5. Ibid. For a discussion of utilitarianism and its three basic forms, see p. 41.

6. DeGeorge, p. 41.

7. F. Neil Brady, *Ethical Managing: Rules and Results*, (New York: Macmillian, 1990).

8. Saul W. Gellerman, "Why 'Good' Managers Make Bad Ethical Choices," *Harvard Business Review* (July-August 1986), 85–90.

9. Kenneth Blanchard and Norman Vincent Peale, *The Power of Ethical Management*, (New York: Morrow, 1988).

10. Philip Kotler, *Marketing Management*, 5th ed. (Englewood Cliffs, N.J.: Prentice-Hall, 1984), p. 84.

11. These four terms are used by the following authors, respectively: George A. Steiner, John B. Miner, and Edmund R. Gray, *Management Policy and Strategy*, (New York: Macmillan, 1982), p. 176; William F. Glueck, *Business Policy and Strategic Management*, (New York: McGraw-Hill, 1980), p. 39; Kotler, p. 84; John A. Pearce II and Richard B. Robinson, Jr., *Strategic Management*, 3rd ed. (Homewood, Ill.: Irwin, 1988), p. 87.

12. Kotler, p. 84.

13. See Robert E. Barmeier, "Public Issues Analysis in Corporate Planning," and Ian H. Wilson, "Environmental Scanning and Strategic Planning," both in *Business Environment/Public Policy*, ed. Lee E. Preston, 1980 Conference Papers. St. Louis, Mo.: American Assembly of Collegiate Schools of Business, 1980, pp. 158 and 160–161, respectively.

14. Thomas Moore, "The Fight to Save Tylenol," *Fortune*, November 29, 1982, p. 49.

15. Excerpts from *Business Policy and Strategic Management* by George Sawyer, copyright © 1990 by Harcourt Brace Jovanovich, Inc., reprinted by permission of the publisher.

16. Ibid.

17. Fred Luthans, Richard M. Hodgetts, and Kenneth R. Thompson, *Social Issues in Business*, 5th edition (New York: Macmillan, 1987), p. 100.

CHAPTER 4

Determining Objectives: Vision, Mission, and Goals

Objectives are not set in one session. Some are set before an environmental analysis is conducted, some during environmental analysis and strategy formulation, and others after the environmental analysis. Thus, objectives both serve as the basis for environmental analysis and are themselves based on this analysis. The desired outcomes specified by objectives become the targets at which the firm aims its strategies and decisions. This chapter starts by describing different types of objectives and then considers the hierarchy of objectives, growth objectives, criteria for good objectives, who sets the objectives, objectives for different stakeholders, how objectives are set, problems associated with overemphasizing objectives, changing objectives, and international dimensions.

WHAT ARE OBJECTIVES?

The term **objectives** refers to all the target results, or outcomes, desired by a firm. These desired results, or outcomes, can be separated into four categories: company vision, missions, long-term goals, and short-term goals.

Vision

The first broad objective, **vision,** defines management's view of what the organization's scope, scale, size, and general characteristics should be in the future. (See Perspective 4.1.) The vision embraced by the chief executive officer (CEO) is critically important to a firm's future. A successful vision embodies a desirable future and can be communicated throughout the organization and readily understood. It should also attract broad internal support. In short, it should motivate individuals and serve as a structure for allocating resources.

Defining a clear vision for a firm involves first asking the question "What business are we in now?" To answer this question, executives must consider the firm's present scope, scale, and size and mix of activities, products, and markets. The answer should provide a meaningful picture of the firm's identity and character.

Subsequently defining a clear vision based on each of these factors permits analysis of the gap between "what is" and "what will be." The nature of this gap should then determine the firm's direction and path.[1]

Although analysis and strategic thinking can serve as the base and help spur the development of a vision statement, a successful vision often arises from creativity and intuition. Many of today's major industries—including the radio, personal computer, telecommunication, and television industries—were the result of someone's creative vision. Such a vision also generally provides the driving force for successful firms, such as McDonald's, IBM, Disneyland, and General Electric.

A clear vision can help managers with what Daniel J. Isenberg refers to as *strategic opportunism.*[2] Ideally, managers should stay on a general strategic path while maintaining enough flexibility to deal with current opportunities. Current opportunities can make objectives outmoded; managers need to be ready and willing to ignore outmoded objectives and pursue superior current opportunities. However, strategic opportunism should not be confused with myopic management. Far too many firms "steal from the future" by investing heavily in projects with quick payoffs.[3] Pursuit of current opportunities must be anchored to the long-term vision of the firm.

Mission

A firm's mission consists of the purpose that distinguishes it from other similar firms. The **mission statement** is an "enduring statement of purpose that distinguishes one business from other similar firms."[4] The terms *mission* and *mission statement* are used interchangeably. Such declarations may also be called statements of a firm's creed, philosophy, purpose, business principles, or corporate beliefs. They all define the firm's business domain(s), usually in terms of basic product or service class, primary customer groups, market need, technological field, or some combination of these. The mission statement may also contain more general statements of desired accomplishments outside the firm, such as the

---

PERSPECTIVE 4.1

Daimler-Benz Develops

In 1980 Daimler-Benz was basically a one-product company. It made Mercedes Benz luxury cars and trucks. In 1990 there was still a Daimler-Benz, which still made the Mercedes Benz, still prized as a symbol of luxury. In the intervening decade, however, Daimler, cash-rich from its success with prestige automobiles, had gone shopping.

What it bought changed the company dramatically. In early 1985 Daimler completed purchase of MTU, a maker of aircraft engines and diesel motors for tanks and ships. A little later that same year it picked up Dornier, a manufacturer of commuter planes, rocket and satellite parts, and medical equipment. The next year Daimler took control of AEG, a conglomerate that manufactured computers, household appliances, automation equipment, public transportation systems, and broadcasting equipment. In 1989 Daimler added Messerschmitt-Bolkow-Blohm, a prominent aerospace firm.

Daimler's vision in all this? According to Werner Breitschwerdt, the Daimler chief executive responsible for the MTU, Dornier, and AEG purchases, his acquisitions would provide the kind of high technology that would give Daimler a competitive advantage in the production of increasingly sophisticated luxury cars. Materials developed by Dornier might find their way into a rustproof Mercedes body. Daimler could also draw on AEG's work in mobile telephones, automotive electrical equipment, and radar, which could aid future Mercedes owners when driving in inclement weather. To Breitschwerdt, an engineer by training and a long-time Daimler employee, Daimler-Benz would remain primarily an auto maker.

Edzard Reuter, finance officer at the time of the earlier acquisitions and—as Breitschwerdt's successor in 1987—the architect of the Messerschmitt deal, speaks of a different objective: diversification. Assembled into a separate subsidiary, the aerospace components of the various acquisitions constitute much more than a laboratory for devising the technology of the luxury car of the future. They make up one of the largest aerospace firms in the world. That such a business has little to do with luxury cars may be considered more of an advantage than a disadvantage. The idea of diversification is to lessen overall financial risk. If a corporation owns a number of different businesses and one of them slumps, the argument goes, the other businesses may hold the corporation up.

References: "On the Runway," *The Economist*, April 8, 1989, p. 72ff; "Diverse Daimler Versus Brilliant BMW," *The Economist*, June 3, 1989, pp. 65–66; "Daimler-Benz Conglomerates," *Fortune*, October 27, 1986, p. 84ff.; "How Takeover of AEG Will Change Daimler's Outlook," *International Management*, December 1985, p. 11ff.

firm's desired public image and the general manner in which the company will conduct itself.

A mission statement should: (1) define what the organization is and what it aspires to be, (2) distinguish an organization from all others, and (3) serve as a framework for evaluating both current and prospective activities.[5] According to W. R. King and D. I. Cleland, the mission should also accomplish the following:[6]

1. Ensure unanimity of purpose within the firm
2. Provide a basis for motivating the firm's resources
3. Provide a standard for allocating the firm's resources
4. Establish the desired businesslike tone or climate
5. Serve as a focal point for those who can identify with the firm's purpose and direction
6. Facilitate translating the organizational purposes into appropriate objectives
7. Facilitate the translation of objectives into strategies and other specific activities

Mission statements are designed to provide guidance and declare attitudes rather than express concrete ends. They should be limited enough to exclude some ventures and broad enough to allow for creative growth; they should also be stated in terms sufficiently clear to be widely understood throughout the organization.[7] There are several good reasons for the lack of specificity. Detail attracts opposition (particularly from stakeholders with diverse interests), tends to stifle management's creativity, promotes organizational rigidity and resistance to change, and reduces flexibility in adapting to environmental changes.[8]

The mission should be stated in the light of at least five key factors: (1) the firm's history, (2) current preferences of management and owners, (3) environmental considerations, (4) available resources, and (5) distinctive competencies.[9]

Mission statements sometimes appear in corporate annual reports, such as those in Tables 4.1 and 4.2. Note, however, that all components of the mission are not necessarily included in the publicized mission statement. Closely held corporations, for example, may have an unwritten mission to provide employment for shareholders.

A wide variety of criteria can be applied to evaluate mission statements. The major criterion involves priorities: "Does the mission statement indicate which components are more important than others?" The following questions indicate some additional common criteria:[10]

1. Is the mission consistent with the present and expected environment?
2. Does the mission statement clarify how organizational activities will lead to the desired outcomes?

TABLE 4.1 · Statements of Corporate Objectives for K mart Corp.

MISSION

To provide superior value and quality products with low prices to both the company's customers and shareholders as the world's largest discount retailer and major operator of superdrugstores, warehouse home improvement centers, and bookstores.

LONG-RUN GOALS

1. Implement a sound, long-term marketing and merchandising strategy for the 1990s.
2. Bring high-quality, well-made merchandise to all American customers at low everyday prices within a friendly, courteous, and pleasant shopping experience.
3. Capitalize on customer franchise in retailing.
4. Create dominant lifestyle departments that customers will shop first for that type of merchandise and, at the same time, lower everyday prices throughout the store.

SHORT-RUN GOALS

1. Install point-of-sale systems in all K mart stores by the end of 1990.
2. Facilitate a more centralized approach to merchandising our stores.
3. Place curtains and drapes, bed and bath products and floor coverings of home fashions division under the K mart apparel umbrella within the next twelve to eighteen months.
4. Plans call for other lifestyle departments, such as jewelry, sporting goods, automotive accessories and home care, to be centrally merchandised in the near future.
5. Differentiate our stores from those of our competitors by the strongest advertising program.
6. Improve our in-stock position on high-margin merchandise.
7. Continue the everyday low-pricing program and extend it to more and more items.
8. Open a second American Fare Store in the Charlotte, North Carolina, market.

Source: Adapted with permission from K mart Corp. 1988 Annual Report.

---

3. Is the mission statement congruent with existing policies, procedures, and plans?
4. Does the mission integrate major components of the organization, such as scope of operations, resource allocation, competitive advantages and disadvantages?
5. Is the mission attainable, realistic, and challenging?

TABLE 4.2 · **Statements of Corporate Objectives for Xerox Corp.**

MISSION

- **For Xerox Business Products and Systems:** To provide business products and systems activities that encompass developing, manufacturing, marketing and servicing document-processing products and systems for making offices more productive
- **For Xerox Financial Services:** To offer a wide range of quality financial products and services on a wholesale basis, primarily for the domestic market
- **Overall:** To provide uncommon and unparalleled customer satisfaction, as well as to maximize growth and the return to Xerox shareholders

LONG-RUN GOALS

1. To be more competitive, to enhance technological leadership and to build solid customer relationships in response to changes in markets at present and in the future by
   a. strengthening market position
   b. enhancing service to customers
   c. improving financial returns
   d. increasing shareholder value
2. To grow value for shareholders by continuing to expand existing businesses by using the combined capabilities of operating units to develop new products and markets and by adding niche businesses that build on current strengths
3. To understand the needs of customers and help them provide solutions to their real problems; to work with customers to provide value-added solutions
4. To form partnerships between Xerox and Xerox customers in order to give value to the customer, business to Xerox, and value to shareholders

SHORT-RUN GOALS

1. To improve profit performance by $50–60 million in 1989 and by $100–$120 million in 1990 and subsequent years
2. To reach the goal of 15 percent return on assets in 1990, to make substantial progress in 1989, and to provide solid shareholder value
3. To further focus our strategic direction and concentrate resources on the core business—document processing
4. To disengage from Xerox Medical Systems
5. To scale back electronic typing business to bring these resources in line with declining worldwide demand
6. To focus worldwide document systems marketing into one organization
7. To reduce overhead costs without sacrificing quality and customer satisfaction

Source: Adapted with permission from Xerox Corporation. 1988 Annual Report.

The mission statement also helps executives to determine more specific objectives. They need this guidance particularly in the early stages of planning and it also aids them when they consider changes in strategy or operation.

Goals

Goals refer to the specific targets or results that the business will try to achieve. Although the goals should flow directly from the mission statement, they should be more specific and concrete. For example, the mission may include a general statement focusing on the firm's efforts to help handicapped workers. The corresponding goal might be the hiring of a specific number of handicapped workers. Other common areas for goal statements include profitability, sales growth, market share, risk diversification, and innovation.

We will consider two types of goals here: long-term goals and short-term goals. Before discussing each type in detail, we need to clarify their time frames. Short-term and long-term goals are normally distinguished by specifying a number of years. *Short-term goals* are often defined as the goals that should be accomplished within one year, whereas *long-term goals* are those that should be accomplished in more than one year. Sometimes a third category, *intermediate-term goals*, is also defined. *Intermediate-term goals* may range from one to five years. This simplistic approach, however, does not fully clarify the distinction between short- and long-term goals.

Long-term and short-term goals must be defined relative to the length of the specific firm's normal decision cycle. A *decision cycle* refers to the time it takes for a decision to reach full implementation. Automobile manufacturers, for example, face a decision cycle of about five years for introducing new models because some resources must be committed about five years prior to introducing a new model. Consequently, any goal related to new models that should be accomplished in five years or less can be viewed as a short-term goal. The key issue is that the short-term and long-term designations depend on the industry and on specific businesses rather than on some arbitrary number of years. Tables 4.1 and 4.2 illustrate this issue as well.

Long-term Goals   As noted earlier, long-term goals indicate desired outcomes for a fairly long time period; although the specific number of years varies, it is generally longer than one decision cycle. Long-term goals are more specific than the mission statement but somewhat less specific than the short-term goals. Tables 4.1 and 4.2 illustrate this difference. Long-term goals are often established for eight performance areas.[11]

1. Market standing
2. Innovation

3. Productivity
4. Physical and financial resources
5. Profitability
6. Manager performance and development
7. Worker performance and attitude
8. Public responsibility

Customer-related and product-related objectives should also be viewed as critically important.

To understand the relationship between missions and long-term goals, consider a firm with a stated mission of becoming a nationwide distributor of men's outerwear. A corresponding long-term goal statement might include the goal of increasing geographical distribution by selling in all states east of the Mississippi River within ten years. This long-term goal gives much more direction than the mission statement but is not so specific as to prescribe what decisions should be made immediately.

Short-term Goals   Short-term goals should be very specific and state detailed target results that the business intends to generate during the next decision cycle. (For illustration, see Tables 4.1 and 4.2.) A short-term goal for the distributor we discussed in the preceding paragraph could involve obtaining distribution in the states of Kentucky and Tennessee and preparing for the introduction of the product in Georgia during the next year.

HIERARCHY OF OBJECTIVES

Besides missions, long-term goals, and short-term goals, all firms have a hierarchy of objectives. This hierarchy can be seen more easily in larger firms, which have several layers of management. Objectives set at the higher levels of management are usually broader and planned for the longer run, whereas those at the lower levels are narrower and planned for the shorter run. Exhibit 4.1 provides an example of the hierarchy situation. As the table shows, higher-level goals serve as benchmarks for subsequent goals. This hierarchy extends from the mission statement to the lowest levels of the firm. The hierarchical concept is also relevant for strategies, and we will discuss it later in that context. The concept should aid in understanding who sets objectives and how objectives are set, topics that we will take up later in this chapter.

EXHIBIT 4.1 · Hierarchy of Short-Run Goals

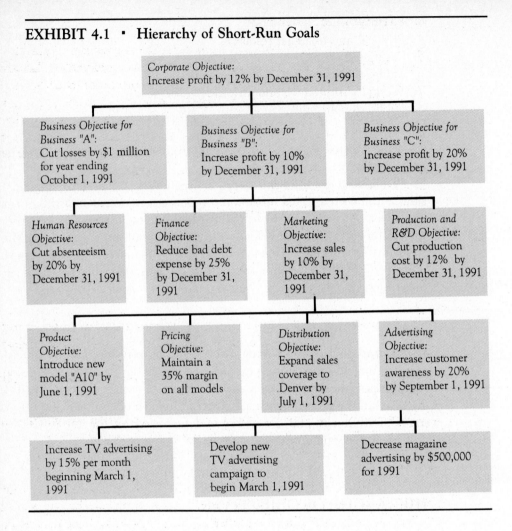

GROWTH OBJECTIVES

Top management should formulate growth objectives for the company. These growth objectives serve as important guidelines for selecting corporate strategies and can be stated in a variety of ways. For our purposes, a firm's growth objective should be stated in terms of percentage change in sales and profits relative to the industry percentage change in sales and profits. This perception of growth can be organized to yield three basic growth objectives: fast growth, stable growth, and decline.

Fast-Growth Objective

A firm may select a fast-growth objective and try to grow faster than the rest of the industry. Many feel that fast growth or expansion is extremely desirable and, depending on the environmental threats and opportunities faced by the firm, a fast-growth objective is hard to criticize. Fast growth, however, is not without problems. For instance, the Atari division of Warner Communications has experienced some rather serious difficulties, partially because the company grew so fast that it became somewhat unwieldy. One observer lists seven basic requirements for successfully pursuing a fast-growth objective:[12]

1. Intelligent risk taking
2. Utilization of experienced management
3. Understanding of markets
4. Selecting a target market and focusing resources on it
5. Formulating a clear corporate strategy
6. Successful management of assets
7. Timing and luck

After selecting a fast-growth objective, management must refine it to specify exactly how much faster—for example, 10 percent faster—than the industry the firm should grow.

A firm may adopt a fast-growth objective for one or more of the following reasons:[13]

1. Management may believe that environmental conditions are volatile and that the only means of survival is to pursue a fast-growth objective.
2. Management equates fast growth or expansion with effectiveness.
3. Management believes that society benefits from fast growth.
4. Management associates incremental personal rewards with fast growth.
5. Management believes in the experience curve, or that as the firm grows in size and experience it gets better at what it is doing—reducing costs and improving productivity.
6. Management believes that fast growth will yield monopoly power.
7. Management is experiencing external pressure to expand—for instance, pressure from stockholders.

Stable-Growth Objective

The second type of growth objective is stable growth, or growth at about the same speed as the industry. A firm could experience fairly substantial percentage increases in sales volume and profits and still be in a stable-growth pattern. For instance, if industry sales were growing 20 percent and the firm intended to grow at about 20 percent, the firm would have a stable-growth objective. A stable-growth objective does not necessarily imply a "do-nothing" approach. It can, for example, involve activities to increase profit, such as improving efficiency.

A firm may choose a stable-growth objective for a variety of defendable reasons:[14]

1. Management perceives that the firm is doing well and wants to "continue doing things the way we always have."
2. Management views the environment as stable.
3. A stability strategy is less risky.
4. Too much expansion can lead to inefficiencies.
5. Environmental conditions prevent a fast-growth objective.

A stable-growth objective may also be pursued for some less defendable reasons, such as (1) management never gets around to considering any other objectives because it prefers action to thought, and (2) it is easier and less disruptive to pursue a stable-growth objective.

Decline Objective

The last growth objective is a decline (sometimes called retrenchment), which is a growth intentionally slower than that of the industry or even at a rate that causes the firm to decrease in size. A decline objective can mean reducing the number of product or service lines, markets, or functions. From the corporate perspective, units with negative or low cash flow or profitability may be eliminated.

A decline objective is typically difficult to pursue. It goes against the grain of most executives, largely because it implies failure. Although a decline objective can be beneficial in a variety of circumstances, it tends to be reserved for addressing crises.

There are many situations in which a decline objective can be appropriate. For instance, any time a firm is performing poorly, a decline objective should be at least considered. More specifically, a firm may have become too large too quickly and need to reduce its growth rate substantially while improving efficiency in various areas. Environmental factors may threaten to overwhelm the firm on certain fronts. Lastly, one of the most positive reasons for pursuing a decline objective involves the discovery of attractive opportunities, which cannot be pursued without a temporary decline in order to allow efficient reallocation of resources.

Temporal Considerations for Growth Objectives

Selecting the appropriate growth objective involves considering a variety of factors, such as relevant environmental opportunities and threats, management's

---

EXHIBIT 4.2 · Examples of Growth Objectives

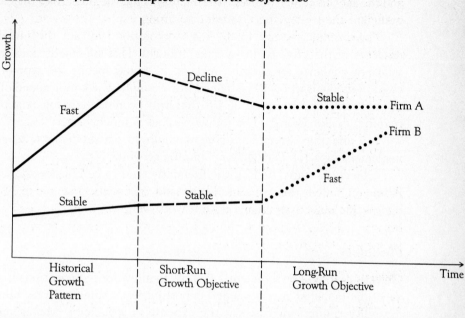

attitude toward risk, and stockholder objectives. Growth objectives can be divided into long-term and short-term growth goals, which are not necessarily identical. For example, consider a long-term goal of stable growth and a recent history of fast growth. The short-term growth goal most appropriate for enhancing the attainment of the long-term goal could be decline, because fast growth may no longer be possible and stable growth might not be possible until undesirable businesses or products are discarded. This pattern is illustrated in Exhibit 4.2.

CRITERIA FOR GOOD OBJECTIVES

All good objectives should normally meet six criteria: specificity, flexibility, measurability, attainability, congruency, and acceptability. Although these criteria are directed more toward the long- and short-term goals, the mission statement should also generally meet the criteria.

Specificity

Good objectives should be specific so that they are easily understood by those responsible for achieving them. A statement of objectives should indicate to what each objective is related, the time frame for accomplishing the objective, and the specific results desired. The more specific the objective, the easier it is to formulate the strategy necessary for attaining it.

For example, to say that "Ace Corporation will aid the underprivileged residents of the city" is not specific enough. This statement does not provide sufficient guidance for decision makers. It should specify the type of disadvantaged individuals who will be helped (for example, the handicapped or hard-core unemployed) and the type of aid that will be rendered (for example, hiring, training, or donations). The following goal is much better: "Ace Corporation will hire and train twenty hard-core unemployed city residents by developing and implementing a Job Partnership Training program."

Objectives stated high in the hierarchy tend to be broader and less specific. However, unless the firm intends to add specificity and greater detail later, nonspecific objectives usually do not work well.

Flexibility

Objectives should be sufficiently flexible to allow for modifications to accommodate unanticipated environmental opportunities or threats. Note, however, that flexibility is often increased at the expense of specificity. Management should exercise caution when modifying an objective and make corresponding changes in related strategies and action plans.

Measurability

Measurability is related to specificity. To satisfy the measurability criterion, an objective must be stated in terms that can be evaluated or quantified. This is important because objectives often evolve into control standards for appraising performance. (These standards are discussed more fully in Chapter 14.)

Consider the first goal statement about aiding disadvantaged individuals. To meet the measurability criterion, the statement must mention the number of people who will be aided and the level of aid to be delivered. The second statement has these elements. A statement of goal with this amount of detail is a useful guide in managerial decision making; those responsible for implementation will know exactly what and how much is expected of them.

Attainability

Objectives should simultaneously motivate and challenge both management and personnel, but they must also be realistic and attainable. To determine whether a goal is attainable, a certain amount of environmental analysis and forecasting may be necessary.

Setting unattainable goals is at best a waste of time and can even be counter-productive. For instance, consider the sales manager who believes that salespeople can achieve a 12 percent sales increase if they work diligently. However, after skimming a text on motivation, the manager decides to place the goal at a higher level, perhaps 15 percent. If the salespeople increase sales by 14 percent, the sales manager is likely to credit the strategy of placing the sales goal abnormally high. The salespeople, however, might conclude that their best efforts were not good enough. If the sales manager continues with this strategy for several years, the salespeople are likely to lose their motivation to achieve the firm's goals and may seek alternate goals, perhaps outside the organization. Once such a situation arises, objectives have little use from a motivational standpoint, or any other standpoint.

Congruency

Objectives should be congruent with each other; that is, they must fit together, and attaining one objective should not preclude attaining another. For instance, if the marketing objective is to increase sales by 10 percent and the credit department's objective is to cut bad debt losses by 25 percent, it is likely that attaining either of these goals will eliminate the possibility of attaining the other. Similarly, striving to achieve aggressive market share and profit goals can compromise other financial goals such as liquidity and debt-to-equity goals.[15]

Incongruent objectives often lead to great conflict within an organization. Note, however, that congruent objectives may not be perfectly compatible. Friction is to be expected, especially in large, complex organizations. If this friction and conflict become intense enough to indicate real incongruencies, tradeoffs in the accomplishment of objectives will become necessary.

Reducing potential inconsistencies requires priority ranking, tradeoffs, and compromise. Robert Weinberg has identified eight potential strategic tradeoffs:[16]

1. Short-term profits versus long-term growth
2. Profit margin versus competitive position
3. Direct sales effort versus market development effort
4. Penetration of existing markets versus development of new markets
5. Related versus nonrelated new opportunities as a source of long-term growth
6. Profit versus nonprofit goals (for example, social responsibilities)
7. Growth versus stability
8. Risk-free environment versus high-risk environment

Acceptability

Good objectives must be acceptable to those responsible for achieving them and to the firm's major stakeholders. Acceptability implies and leads to management and employee commitment. Such commitment is crucial to success in achieving objectives. For example, the acceptability criterion may increase in importance as employees become less likely to subordinate their own objectives to those dictated by management. In order to formulate acceptable goals, management must therefore have a good understanding of its employees' needs and desires.

It should also be noted that management cannot influence the acceptability criterion as it does the other criteria, even though it can try to persuade stakeholders to accept an objective. If management believes that key stakeholder groups will not readily accept a given objective, it should plan to sway these groups before finalizing the objective. (A relevant discussion on change theory appears in Chapter 13.)

Problems with the Criteria

Although theoretically all objectives should meet the six criteria we have been discussing, there are "real-world" problems with the criteria. This is especially true of publicly reported objectives. For instance, Tables 4.1, 4.2 and 4.3 include some objectives of real firms as reported in annual statements. The specificity and measurability criteria are obviously violated. This is not a serious problem if the firms have more specific and measurable objectives in internal documents.

Other problems are more difficult to explain. For instance, all firms have multiple goals, and as the number of goals increases, so does the probability of violating the congruency and attainability criteria. These and other problems with the criteria do not negate their importance. Those who set objectives must strive to meet the criteria or take action to lessen the negative effects of not meeting them. One such action is to prioritize goals so that, if incongruency becomes a problem, decision makers will have help in choosing which goals to pursue. However, if possible, the criteria should be considered and followed.

WHO SETS THE OBJECTIVES?

The question of who sets objectives is not easily answered. Different organizations use different objective-setting procedures, which may range from highly centralized to decentralized.

Centralized Objective Setting

In some firms, the board of directors or corporate-level executives set the objectives for the entire business. This centralized objective setting typically results in more congruent goals than does decentralized objective setting (in which lower-level employees set goals for the firm). Further, centralized objective setting also focuses more directly on achieving corporate goals.

Along with these important advantages, centralized objective setting has some potentially significant drawbacks. One of them is that the setters of objectives may know little about the specific opportunities and threats faced by lower-level managers. If all goal-setting and decision-making discretion is withheld from these managers, inflexibility and lower profits can sometimes result. Besides, lower-level managers may resist directives coming from the top, especially if they do not understand the reasons behind the objectives. In order to overcome such problems, many firms have adopted some form of decentralized objective setting.

Decentralized Objective Setting

As the term implies, firms using decentralized objective setting allow managers at each level to have the dominant influence on their unit's objective. There are two basic approaches, with many intermediate variations. The first is a *top-to-bottom* procedure, in which the board, the corporate-level managers, or both groups together, set the corporate objectives and the head of each division or business unit sets the divisional or business-level objectives. This same pattern applies to the rest of the organizational levels. Usually, higher-level managers, especially those at the next higher level, must approve the goals of lower-level managers.

The second, or *bottom-up*, approach allows lower levels to set their goals and then requires higher-level managers to set their goals in line with the lower-level goals. Based on Theory Y thinking about human nature, this approach is sometimes less likely to yield a coordinated effort and congruent goals. It might be wise to reserve it for special situations, such as firms in high-technology industries.

However, since management normally has power over rewards and punishment, higher-level managers strongly influence objectives even when objective setting is decentralized. The decision to use centralized or decentralized objective setting also affects strategy selection, organizational structure, and the management of the firm in general.

HOW ARE OBJECTIVES SET?

Although top management is responsible for formulating a firm's objectives, the objective-setting process normally takes into account a variety of factors. The interaction of four key categories of factors is important.[17] First, *forces in the external environment* often exert a large influence on objectives. External stakeholders (such as owners, suppliers, competitors) influence the firm through social norms, specific constraints, pressure campaigns, direct controls, and memberships on boards of directors. Setting objectives is therefore part of the process of establishing a favorable balance of power between the firm and external environmental factors.[18]

Second, the *firm's resources* influence the character and level of objectives. Companies with large resource bases are in a better position to respond to environmental forces. The larger resource base permits consideration of a greater range of objectives. IBM, for example, has many more competitive options available in the personal computer industry than does one of the much smaller firms.

Third, the firm's *internal political and power relationships* also affect the setting of objectives. Firms that have the overall support of employees and of key employee groups can generally set higher-level and perhaps more ambitious objectives. Furthermore, the power relationships among those who set objectives can strongly influence the final choice of objectives. These individuals often bargain with each other over objectives by using the influence of money, position, status, and power. A manager's ability to sway others is predicated on his or her **power base,** which comprises such factors as prior performance, professional reputation, relationships with other managers, ownership position, and ability to recognize and utilize available resources.[19]

Fourth, the *value system of top executives* affects formulation of objectives. These values develop from education, general experience, and information received on the job. Values can exert a strong influence on an individual's decision making and general attitudes.

To sum up, each manager brings his or her own value system to the objective-setting process. The nature of these values and the strength with which they are held helps to filter and shade the interaction among setters of objectives (managers). The relative power of each executive also affects this direct interaction. The executive group responsible for formulating objectives must also consider the direct and indirect influence of other internal stakeholders and the firm's overall resource base. External factors that must be considered include stakeholders' desired objectives and general external forces (for example, economic factors).

Management does not normally set completely new objectives each year. Rather, the previous year's objectives are used as a starting point are updated and revised. Major changes in the objectives would result from (1) increased demands from external or internal stakeholders, (2) a change in managers' aspiration levels, or (3) major crises, such as the disappearance of the firm's market or of its reason for being.[20]

Intraorganizational Conflict

Intraorganizational conflict almost always flares up in the setting of objectives because of the interactive way in which objectives are set. For example, as Table 4.4 indicates, since marketing is to help attain a short-run goal of increasing profit by 10 percent, the marketing manager has determined that the marketing objective should be to increase sales by 10 percent. At the same time, the production manager has decided that the production objective should be to cut costs by 12 percent. Although these two goals may not appear to conflict at first glance, they may cause trouble. For example, if the production manager intends to cut costs by minimizing the number of different models produced, the sales manager may find it hard to increase the number of units sold.

The finance and marketing managers might have an even greater conflict. A credit objective of reducing bad debt expense by 25 percent will mean more stringent criteria for granting credit. But if credit is less available, it may be virtually impossible to increase sales.

The positive side of intraorganizational conflict is discussed in Chapter 13.

OBJECTIVES FOR DIFFERENT STAKEHOLDERS

Objectives are not formulated in a vacuum. A number of variables affect the process. An organization's stakeholders are among the key variables, and careful study of these stakeholders (internal and external) can lead to a greater understanding of both business and social responsibilities. In this section, we look at four of the major stakeholders: owners, employees, customers, and society. Other influences on the objective-setting process are discussed later in the chapter.

Owners

Historically, management has been responsible only to the firm's owners or stockholders. Although the situation has changed somewhat as other stakeholders have gained importance, owners can still be considered the most significant stakeholders.

Owners who invest in a firm—especially absentee owners, such as stockholders—are interested in the value and general growth of their investment through dividends or increases in stock price. Businesses serve this interest by generating profits. Managers often have more relevant training and experience in setting profit-related objectives than in setting other types of objectives.

Management must exercise caution, however, in setting the profit objectives specifically desired by owners. The primary caution is not to overemphasize short-term profitability at the expense of long-term profitability. Short-run profits must sometimes be suboptimized in order to optimize long-run profitability. Unfortunately, many managers hesitate to make this kind of decision because they are often evaluated only on short-run performance.

Employees

Employees, too, are stakeholders and are demanding more attention from management. (See Perspective 4.2.) Normally, employees have been concerned with objectives that influence their direct wages, benefits, safety, job security, and the like. Present-day managers can generally deal satisfactorily with these types of demands. Employees' demands, however, have evolved in recent years to include matters such as obtaining more input regarding job-related activities and the fulfillment of higher-order needs. The average manager may find these objectives much more difficult to deal with. Although employees should not dictate an organization's objectives, many firms are heeding these demands by formulating objectives that are generally compatible with employee desires.

Customers

Customers are also demanding increased consideration from management, particularly lower prices, higher-quality and safer products, an assured supply of them, and better services. The well-managed firm knows that customers determine the success of the business; if customers are not considered in setting objectives, the business is much less likely to succeed.

As customers have become more knowledgeable and vocal, companies have had to give priority to customer demands. Consumerism, which grew to rather large proportions during the 1960s and 1970s has made most managers aware that the customer has clout and can make or break a company. Indeed, it is almost impossible to achieve profit objectives unless appropriate customer-related objectives are formulated and achieved.

Society

Those who are not owners, employees, or customers can be broadly classified as society. In recent years, society has begun to insist more and more that businesses act in a responsible manner toward all stakeholders and societal issues. For example, pollution control and proper utilization of resources are two types of objectives that society has increasingly forced businesses to adopt. Firms that fail to set and achieve society-related objectives have little chance to succeed in the long run.

PERSPECTIVE 4.2

TWA and Its Unions

In 1986, using money he raised by offering a high rate of interest, Carl Icahn took control of TWA through a corporate buyout. Key to Icahn's acquisition were concessions he won from TWA's unions, concessions that would amount to about a billion dollars over the next five years. TWA had made money only once in that decade. Icahn would turn the airline around.

If only on paper, he did, at least at first. In 1987 and 1988 TWA showed a profit. Much of this was achieved through cost cutting: besides gaining concessions from the unions, Icahn reduced his white-collar payroll, from executives on down, and minimized capital investment in such items as new airplanes. Then there were Icahn's stock market investments, which added to the plus side of the TWA balance sheet. Not even Icahn's acquisition of Ozark Airlines dug into short-term profits. By selling Ozark's planes and leasing them back, Icahn was able to reduce the cost of the purchase to a mere $20 million.

Nevertheless, by 1990 TWA was tumbling into debt. Repayments of money Icahn borrowed to buy the airline were a drain on its resources, and Icahn's stock dealings were not looking as good as they once had. Compounding TWA's problems was its aging fleet of planes. Older planes have higher maintenance costs and are difficult to sell or lease should you need to raise money.

Icahn's solution to his financial problems was to sell TWA's domestic routes to America West, a Phoenix-based carrier with coast-to-coast ambitions. To make the deal attractive to America West, Icahn offered to buy and include in the transaction twenty new planes. Icahn hoped to finance this purchase through further union concessions.

This time, the union response was negative. Union officials seemed displeased by what they saw as Icahn's use of union concessions to pay back takeover debts rather than to build up the airline. Adding to union displeasure was America West's nonunion status. America West was as famous for its good treatment of its employees, highly paid by industry standards, as it was for its resistance to unionization.

References: Todd Vogel, James E. Ellis, and Eric Schine, "Will American West Hand Carl Icahn a Parachute?" Business Week, May 14, 1990, pp. 110–111; P. Fling, "Elbowed Aside," Air Transportation World, December 1989, p. 46–48ff.; D. K. Henderson, "Rolling the Dice in the Desert," Air Transportation World, December 1989, pp. 22–24ff.

Specific groups of society, such as suppliers, competitors, government, and special interest groups, could also be discussed in detail. Because of space limitations, we cannot discuss them here, but we remind you that these groups are pressing their demands upon the business community.

INCONGRUENCIES OF OBJECTIVES DESIRED BY THE STAKEHOLDERS

The difficulty of setting objectives that satisfy specific stakeholder groups is compounded by the problem of setting objectives that meet the desires of all the relevant publics and individual stakeholders. Different stakeholders have incongruent desires, and hence, objectives may conflict. Table 4.3 summarizes some of the desires or claims that the firm's stakeholders may have.

Intragroup Incongruencies

Before tackling the incongruencies among the different stakeholders, we need to examine some incongruencies within specific stakeholder groups. Consider, for example, the stockholders of a corporation. Corporate executives often encounter stockholders with a variety of demands, even in such matters as the desired form of financial return. (See Perspective 4.3.) One group (for example, retirees) is likely to want high dividends to serve as regular income. Other, perhaps younger, stockholders may not care much about dividends because of their tax

---

TABLE 4.3 · Stakeholders' Desires

Stakeholders or Public	Desires
Owners	High profits, security, high dividends, stock value growth
Employees	High wages, job security, high fringe benefits, safe working conditions, advancement opportunities, job satisfaction, decision input, long vacations, short hours, convenient hours
Customers	Low prices, high-quality products, assured supply, easy credit, safe products, good warranties, quick service, friendliness, long hours (open), convenient locations
Society	Low pollution, environmental concern, community development, proper utilization of scarce resources, support of good government, support of community activities, aid to underprivileged and needy, generally "responsible" decisions

---

PERSPECTIVE 4.3

USX and Its Largest Shareholder

David M. Roderick and Charles A. Corry were the top executives who, from 1979, saved USX, then an ailing steel corporation. Their strategy involved cutting costs, shedding unprofitable businesses, and, last but not least, diversifying, mostly into energy companies. This last element was intended to protect USX from recessions. The theory was that, when the steel business, always cyclical, was down, oil might be up. Up until 1990, the time of this writing, the strategy more or less worked. USX kept making money, and kept paying dividends. Long-term stockholders looking for a fairly steady source of income, were happy.

Not happy was a stockholder named Carl Icahn who, through TWA, the airline he controlled, had purchased 13 percent of USX, and announced plans to take the company over through a leveraged buyout. Unlike long-term stockholders, Icahn wanted fast results. And USX's return on equity, though slightly higher than other steel companies, was lower than most energy companies. Spin off the various components, argued Icahn, let them earn their proper return—and let the stockholders earn their proper profit. Otherwise, Icahn indicated that he would buy the company himself and oversee its dissolution in the interest of the stockholders.

Had Carl Icahn made his move three or four years earlier, he might have struck more fear in the hearts of USX management. As it was, they were reported to have taken his bid to up his stake in USX rather lightly. For one thing, "junk bonds," the high-interest device for financing takeovers, stood in much lower repute with investors than they once had. For another thing, Icahn's TWA was having serious financial and labor problems, so that it would be difficult to buy more USX stock with TWA money. Even the USX stock he held would be something of a problem to sell off in a hurry. The demand for USX was not great enough for the market to absorb TWA's $800 million holdings without a significant drop in the stock's price. Icahn had made a handsome profit on his investment, as long as he didn't try to cash it in. To quote one analyst: "USX has become a long-term investment, whether Carl likes it or not."

References: Gregory L. Miles, "Why USX Isn't Afraid of the Bogeyman," Business Week, May 14, 1990, p. 112; "USX Resists Icahn's Bid for Restructuring the Corporation," Iron Age, January 1990, p. 11–12; Todd Vogel, James E. Ellis, and Eric Schine, "Will American West Hand Carl Icahn a Parachute?" Business Week, May 14, 1990, p. 110–111.

situation but want long-term growth in the value of their holdings. Consequently, management might be torn between two incongruent goals: paying the highest possible dividends or reinvesting funds to maximize the stock value. Because of this conflict, corporations often focus on satisfying one type of stockholder and develop a reputation either for paying regular dividends, as do AT&T and Exxon, or for being a high-growth company, as many in the computer industry have been.

Different groups of employees and individual employees can also have inconsistent desires. One group may want higher wages, whereas another group may want greater job security. An individual may want higher wages but not want to relocate. As we have seen during recessions, employees may be willing to solve their own incongruencies by making or accepting tradeoffs—for instance, accepting lower wages so that the employer stays afloat and they can retain their job security. Thus Chrysler employees accepted lower wages to help protect their jobs. Normally, however, management must be prepared to make judicious tradeoffs.

Customer groups also provide some rather large incongruencies. For example, one group may want low prices and another group high quality or more services. Firms often encounter difficulties when trying to satisfy both groups.

Intergroup Incongruencies

Incongruencies among the desires of different stakeholder groups do not always matter. On occasion, however, they can pose an acute problem for management. For example, maximizing short-run profit, which the owners may desire, would require paying the lowest possible wages, charging the highest possible prices, and not worrying much about damaging the environment. Obviously, such profit-maximization objectives would perturb most of the firm's other stakeholders. To balance the demands of the various groups, the company must formulate satisfactory, rather than optimum, objectives for each group. For example, stockholders may have to accept returns no higher than the industry average so that the firm can pay employees acceptable, but not excessive, wages. Both stockholders and employees may have to accept less return so that the firm can install pollution-control equipment.

Sometimes the various stakeholders may desire certain things so strongly that they demand government regulations or laws to force the firm to act in certain ways. Table 4.4 indicates several areas in which the government has placed regulations on business to force compliance with the desires of the public. For example, society's desire for a cleaner environment is enforced primarily by the Environmental Protection Agency (EPA), and employees' desires for safety are enforced primarily through the Occupational Safety and Health Agency

(OSHA). The high cost of complying with these and other regulations forces companies to suboptimize other objectives, such as lower prices for customers and higher returns for owners.

PROBLEMS CAUSED BY OVEREMPHASIZING OBJECTIVES

Management must be very careful in defining the degree of emphasis for objectives and their achievement. Overemphasizing objectives can spell trouble—chiefly, near misses or neglect of other major objectives.

Near Misses

If challenging objectives are set, some of them will not be achieved. The environmental situation could change or perhaps the firm does not have the ability or resources to achieve the goal. Near misses can cause morale problems among employees, who tried diligently but failed to achieve the objectives continually stressed by management. To illustrate this problem, consider an analogy from the world of sports. If an athlete trains hard toward achieving an Olympic gold medal and even beats the existing world record while coming in second for a silver medal, that athlete may still feel like a failure. Yet even though a gold medal was the objective, the silver medal represents a high accomplishment. Similar situations can develop in business. Therefore, management must be careful to properly emphasize achieving objectives without letting overemphasis create unnecessary stress and other problems.

Overlooking Other Objectives

Most business firms have many different objectives. Some, however, are more important than others. Problems can arise when one or a few of the more important objectives are emphasized heavily but little attention is paid to the others. For example, a firm might have an objective to increase profit by 10 percent and another objective to reduce pollution by 10 percent. If top management regularly and heavily stresses the profit objective to the plant manager, the plant manager may focus on profits and neglect pollution control. This situation can even lead to illegal and unethical acts to increase profitability, such as excessive dumping of pollutants into the air. To avoid these potential problems, management should prioritize goals while making it clear to all concerned that all goals are important. It is also the responsibility of top management to ensure that the employees know their limits or constraints while striving to achieve even high-priority objectives.

SETTING OBJECTIVES AT AN ELECTRIC UTILITY

To illustrate more fully the difficulties and importance of setting objectives, let us consider a hypothetical electric utility company. We are choosing a utility company because utilities are somewhat controversial and require extremely long-range objectives. One major long-term objective involves the types of generating stations that should be built. Certain types of generating stations take twenty years to construct. Consequently, twenty years must be viewed as the decision cycle in setting long-term objectives for these generating stations.

The Stakeholders

Like other firms, electric utilities must try to balance conflicting desires of their diverse stakeholders, chiefly customers, employees, and society.

Customers   The major customer demands are for low-cost electricity and continuous, uninterrupted service. Just these two items underscore how difficult it is to set objectives for the utility. The total generating capacity of the utility is a crucial issue. Customers want a consistent flow of electricity upon demand, which means that the utility must be able to generate sufficient electricity for peak demand periods. However, if the utility builds enough generating capacity for peak demand, there will be excess capacity during periods of normal demand. The public's desire for electricity on a continuous basis, therefore, means that the utility must spend much more money than would be necessary to handle normal demand.

The utility must also maintain reasonable prices while providing continuous electric service. Many utilities have begun trying to persuade customers to use electricity during off-peak periods and so decrease peak demand. For example, they have aimed promotional campaigns at customers, urging them to run some appliances, such as dishwashers, late at night or at certain other times. Some utilities are also trying to convince customers to attach nonessential electric appliances to devices the utility itself can shut off during peak times. From this perspective, the utility has tried to reduce the demand for electricity during peak periods so that it can fulfill the public's other desire, low prices.

Employees   Employees of the utility have various demands—for instance, continuous employment. They do not want the utility to keep hiring and laying off workers depending on the amount of service required at a particular time. Although this demand is fully justifiable, it conflicts with the utilities' need to offer customers the lowest possible prices.

If the utility hires and maintains enough employees for peak demand periods for both electricity and repair services, it will obviously have to charge customers higher prices. On the other hand, if the utility minimizes the number of employees, irregular service and slower repair will result. To lessen this problem, utilities generally assist each other during periods of high repair work. For instance, when a hurricane inflicts damage in one area, utilities elsewhere may send employees to aid the affected utilities.

Since few customers are aware of the tradeoffs that a utility must make, they continue to clamor for complete and quick service and low prices. The utility must try to appease these demands along with those of other stakeholders.

Society   The utility must also consider society in general, particularly with regard to pollution. The utility could provide cheaper energy if it could ignore pollution control. The public, however, wants a clean environment, as well as low costs. Again, the two demands conflict and no utility company can satisfy them totally. Management must, therefore, choose a satisfactory tradeoff by determining how much pollution control the public is willing to pay for. Although representatives of few utility companies speak favorably of government regulations, the regulations that specify how much pollution is allowable may actually simplify the setting of objectives.

Our discussion of some of the problems in setting objectives does not mean, of course, that the utility management cannot or should not set objectives. On the contrary, it must strive to satisfy its stakeholders' desires as much as possible. But it will not be able to meet any of these demands fully, regardless of the types of generating facilities it constructs.

Electric Generating Facilities

A major objective of any utility involves constructing the most appropriate types of generating stations. Although some scientists expect new methods of generating electricity to be developed during the next fifty years, at present utilities must choose among natural gas, coal, and nuclear generators. Table 4.4 contains selected information crucial to this objective. The key information concerns construction time, cost, resources utilized, and pollution characteristics for each type of facility.

Construction of a nuclear reactor takes a long time and is very costly, but such reactors are thought to be inexpensive to operate. Conversely, the plant fixed by natural gas has low construction costs but is expensive to operate and may become more expensive in the future. The coal-fired plant costs more to build than a natural-gas plant but is less expensive than a nuclear plant. The coal plant also costs more to operate than a nuclear plant but less than a gas plant.

TABLE 4.4 · **Information Needed to Select Optimal Generating Facilities for an Electric Utility**[a]

Facility	Cost		Supply of Fuel (years)		Pollution	
	Construction	Operations	Known	Probable	Known	Potential
Natural gas	Low	High	10	100+	Low	Low
Coal	Moderate	Moderate	200+	200+	High	High
Nuclear	Very high	Low?	∞	∞	Low	Extremely high?

[a]The evaluations in the table are intended as discussion motivators rather than definitive evaluations of types of generating stations.

In the area of resource utilization, the key issue involves the years of supply available of the resource needed to fire the plant. The natural-gas plant presents an interesting problem. Only a few years ago experts were predicting a ten-year supply of natural gas for the United States. More recently, however, new deep gas wells have increased the estimates to as much as a hundred-year supply. Whether the supply will last ten or one hundred years has a tremendous bearing on the type of plant utilities should construct. Since there appears to be a several hundred years' supply of coal on hand and virtually an unlimited supply of nuclear fuel, either of these resources could carry a utility for years.

Pollution is also a major factor. At present, coal-fired plants create the most pollution. However, the intensity of the problem could decrease if ongoing research can deliver more cost-efficient means of pollution control. The natural-gas plant has a relatively low pollution level. The nuclear plant creates the greatest societal concern. Some believe that nuclear power is the least polluting, while others see potential radiation leakage and waste disposal as the greatest pollution hazards of all.

The difficulties suggested even by this limited data indicate some of the vexing issues facing a utility as it considers what type of generating facility to construct. Individuals might decide that they are not able to choose among the generating facilities, but every utility's management must make that choice. The executives must balance present stakeholder desires while deciding on a generating facility that will be operating in the year 2000 and beyond. This decision would be easier to make if management could answer some of the questions noted earlier.

Missing Information

Several pieces of vital information would help the utility select the type of generating facility it should build. For instance, if indeed the natural gas supply would be exhausted in ten years, building gas-fired generating stations would be ridiculous. On the other hand, a hundred-year supply might be enough to sustain the utility until new generating resources and technology are discovered.

The nuclear plant also raises several questions. Are nuclear reactors actually safe? Can nuclear waste be stored safely? Even if both answers are, in fact, yes, would society accept the answers? If all three answers were yes, the construction of nuclear-fired plants would be much more appealing.

An additional piece of information that would carry weight with those setting objectives pertains to the potential demand for electricity. The demand for electricity in the United States grew at a very rapid pace until the late 1970s. Then the growth rate began slowing as society became more energy conscious and people started building energy-efficient homes and factories. If this trend should continue, fewer generating stations of any type would be needed and the supply of natural gas would last much longer.

These and other questions highlight the need for continuous development of information sources. As the quality of information improves, the difficulties associated with setting objectives will diminish.

CHANGING OBJECTIVES

Although objectives, particularly mission statements, should be stable, they should not be irrevocable. A variety of factors, such as new technology, new government regulations, and different stakeholder demands, can render good objectives obsolete. Management must be on the alert for such changes and update objectives as needed.

Some firms, such as Xerox Corp. and American Hospital Supply Corporation, use **rolling planning**. Long-range objectives and strategies are developed, often covering five years (some firms use three years). The annual plan is a detailed version of the first year of the long-range plan. Each year the five-year plan is reviewed and updated to reflect any environmental changes and new assumptions. Thus a five-year plan always exists, but it is "rolled over" each year.

Long-term goals require a great deal of attention because of their future impact on the company. As noted earlier, long-term goals serve primarily to point the firm in the right direction rather than to give it exact results for achievement at some future date.

For example, the utility discussed in the previous section may have to change objectives, or at least rethink them, as additional information begins to unfold. Assume that the utility decided to invest heavily in nuclear energy because it had concluded that the gas supply would run out before long and because it was also concerned about the high levels of pollution from coal. If management later discovers or becomes convinced that there is plenty of gas to fire plants for one hundred to two hundred years, the company may want to reevaluate its objectives. Similarly, if growth in demand were to decrease substantially, the firm may simply decide not to build as many plants as originally planned.

Objectives, then, should not only be based on careful evaluation, but should also be continuously evaluated. This process can lead to modifications of the original objectives. If the strategic management process operates correctly and efficiently, these modifications will normally be slight rather than dramatic.

INTERNATIONAL DIMENSIONS

The goal-setting process for the multinational firm is not unlike that of a strictly domestic firm. However, there may be more goals, and the specific nature of the goals may differ. For example, culture disparities may affect the acceptability of a particular goal in a particular foreign country. Essentially, goals for multinational firms should be formulated as described in this text and then adjusted for cultural or political differences. An international expert can assist this process. This specialist can help ensure that goals are stated in culturally and politically expedient terms.

Notes

1. Elinor Morris, "Vision and Strategy: A Focus for the Future," *Journal of Business Strategy* (November 1987), 51–58.

2. Daniel J. Isenberg, "The Tactics of Strategic Opportunism," *Harvard Business Review* (March-April 1987), 92–97.

3. John J. Curran, "Companies That Rob the Future," *Fortune,* July 4, 1988, pp. 84–88.

4. John A. Pearce II, "The Company Mission as a Strategic Tool," *Sloan Management Review* (Spring 1982), 15.

5. Vern McGinnis, "The Mission Statement: A Key Step in Strategic Planning," *Business* (January 1981) p. 41.

6. W. R. King and D. I. Cleland, *Strategic Planning and Policy* (New York: Van Nostrand Reinhold, 1979), p. 124.

7. Ibid.

8. George Steiner, *Strategic Planning: What Every Manager Must Know* (New York: The Free Press, 1979), p. 160.

9. Philip Kotler, *Marketing Management,* 5th ed. (Englewood Cliffs, N.J.: Prentice-Hall, 1984), p. 45.

10. J. P. Campbell, "On the Nature of Orga-

nizational Effectiveness," in *New Perspectives on Organizational Effectiveness*, ed. P. S. Goodman and J. M. Pennings, (San Francisco: Jossey-Bass, 1977), pp. 15–55.

11. Peter Drucker, *Management Tasks, Responsibilities, Practices*, (New York: Harper and Row, 1974), p. 100.

12. David A. Norman, "Success Strategy for Growth," *Industrial Management* (September-October 1985), 1–4.

13. Lawrence R. Jauch and William F. Glueck, *Business Policy and Strategic Management*, 5th ed. (New York: McGraw-Hill, 1988), pp. 204–206.

14. Ibid., pp. 207–208.

15. Gordon Donaldson, "Financial Goals and Strategic Consequences," *Harvard Business Review* (May-June 1985), 57–66.

16. Robert Weinberg, "Developing Management Strategies for Short-Term Profits and Long-Term Growth" (seminar presentation sponsored by Advanced Management Research, Inc., Regency Hotel, New York City, September 29, 1969).

17. James Thompson and William McEwen, "Organizational Goals and Environment," *American Sociological Review*, 23 (1958), 23–30.

18. Richard Cyert and James March, *A Behavioral View of the Firm* (Englewood Cliffs, N.J.: Prentice-Hall, 1963), and Henry Mintzberg, "Organizational Power and Goals: A Skeletal Theory," in *Strategic Management: A New View of Business Policy and Planning* ed. Charles Hofer and Dan Schendel, (Boston: Little, Brown, 1979), pp. 64–80.

19. Virginia E. Schein, "Strategic Management and the Politics of Power," *Personnel Administrator* (October 1983), 56.

20. William F. Glueck and Lawrence R. Jauch, *Business Policy and Strategic Management*, 4th ed. (New York: McGraw-Hill, 1984), pp. 58–61.

PART TWO

Environmental Analysis

Environmental analysis is one of the most critical elements of strategic planning and management. Firms that properly analyze the environment are much more likely to succeed than those that do not. Conversely, a major mistake, such as assuming that environmental conditions will not change, is very likely to seriously harm the firm.

The outcome of proper environmental analysis should be an understanding of the situation confronting the company. Whereas setting objectives addresses where the firm wants to go, environmental analysis addresses what the firm is facing and allows managers to select strategies that will lead to the reaching of objectives.

All five chapters of this part focus on environmental analysis. They are designed to help you determine both the present and the likely future internal and external situations the firm faces. Chapters 5 through 7 describe environments: Chapter 5, the macroenvironment; Chapter 6, the task environment; and Chapter 7, the internal environment. These three chapters should give you an overall grasp of the nature of the factors affecting a firm's operations. Chapter 8 examines the processes and procedures needed to perform an environmental analysis, and Chapter 9 shows how to conduct this analysis. Chapter 9 begins the shift from analysis to decision making, for several of the analytical techniques presented also suggest strategy alternatives.

As you read these five chapters, remember that a chief aim of strategic management is to select and implement strategies that are likely to succeed. If you know what environments a company faces, you stand a much better chance of selecting workable strategies.

CHAPTER 5

The Macroenvironment

Good strategic management depends on a thorough knowledge of the environments faced by an organization. Government regulations and the needs, demands, and actions of suppliers, competitors, and customers all help constitute these environments. Since environmental components affect all other steps of the strategic management process, strategies must be designed in the light of expected environmental conditions.

The total environment faced by an organization can be divided into three levels: the macroenvironment, the task environment, and the internal situation. The **macroenvironment** is most remote from the firm and consists of components such as regulations, economic conditions, sociocultural factors, and technological factors. It influences all businesses, but not necessarily in the same way. The **task environment** is defined for a specific industry, and that industry's task environment affects all its firms. The macroenvironment and task environment are sometimes combined and called the *external*, or *uncontrollable*, *environment*.

The **internal situation** consists of the factors inside a specific firm; in effect, a firm is the sum of its internal situation factors. The internal situation is sometimes referred to as the *internal*, or *controllable*, *environment*. Exhibit 5.1 defines these three environmental levels and shows their interrelation.

When analyzing environmental influences, organizations must take two other factors into account: environmental complexity and environmental turbulence. **Environmental complexity** refers to the number of components influencing an organization's efforts.[1] The more complex the environment, the more difficult it is to make effective decisions. **Environmental turbulence** means the dynamism, or rate of change, in the relevant environments. A stable environment tends to change quite slowly and predictably, but in a turbulent environment change is rapid and hard to predict. Environmental complexity and turbulence are especially critical when the firm analyzes its macro- and task environments, since both of these are external to the firm.

Of the many different macroenvironment areas, we will address the five listed in Figure 5.1: economic, governmental and political, societal, natural, and technological. Table 5.1 gives specific examples of the factors we selected. Each of these macroenvironmental factors can influence an organization singly or in combination with other factors.

As you read the rest of this chapter, keep in mind two important points, which will help prepare you for the discussion of environmental analysis in Chapters 8 and 9. First, one of the most significant aspects of environmental analysis is detecting emerging trends, or impending changes that will influence a

---

EXHIBIT 5.1 · Environmental Definitions and Relationships

Macroenvironment consists of those factors external to the organization that shape and influence the task and internal environments and pose opportunities and threats to the organization. **Task environment** consists of those factors external to the organization that serve to drive industry competition. **Internal situation** consists of forces and resources from the organization.

Macroenvironment
1. Economic factors
2. Governmental and political factors
3. Sociocultural factors
4. Natural factors
5. Technological factors

Task Environment
1. Competitors
2. Customers
3. Suppliers
4. Potential entrants
5. Substitutes

Internal Situation
1. Human resources
2. Research and development
3. Production
4. Financial and accounting
5. Marketing
6. Organizational culture

TABLE 5.1 · Examples of Macroenvironmental Factors

Economic	Governmental and Political
Stage of economic cycle	Consumer lending regulations
Money supply	Antitrust regulations
GNP trends	Environmental protection laws
Inflation rates	Tax laws
Interest rates	Special incentives
Monetary policies	International trade regulations
Unemployment levels	Regulations on hiring and promotions
Fiscal policies	Stability of government
Wage/price controls	
Balance of payments	

Societal	Natural	Technological
Attitudes toward quality of life	Pollution	Federal R&D spending
Lifestyles	Energy shortages	Industry R&D spending
Women in work force	Wasting of natural resources	Focus of technological efforts
Career expectations		Patent protection
Consumer activism		New products
Growth rate of population		New technology transfer
Shifts in population		Automation
Birthrates		Robotics

---

firm or its opportunities as society adapts to new technology, new products and services, or different rules and requirements. Seeking out patterns of change also helps. For example, in 1984 John Naisbitt identified ten trends pointing to these major shifts:[2]

1. From an industrial society to an information society
2. From forced technology to high tech/high touch (instead of mass production of standard products, use of high technology to improve the quality of life)
3. From a national economy to a world economy
4. From short-term to long-term decisions in businesses
5. From centralization to decentralization of our society
6. From institutional help to self-help and self-reliance
7. From representative democracy to participatory democracy
8. From management hierarchies to management networking

9. From the North to the South in the United States
10. From "either/or" choices to multiple options (a broader horizon for our lives)

Some of these shifts have already occurred.

Second, major macroenvironmental issues present potential *opportunities or threats* to a company and must be examined from that point of view. The chief purpose of defining and understanding the relevant environments is to pinpoint the factors most likely to have an impact on the organization's decisions.[3] A list of key influences serves this purpose. The influences listed indicate which environmental factors are actually monitored by the firm. A survey of 180 manufacturing firms reported five key areas:[4]

- Organizational characteristics
- Industry structure
- Market and consumer behavior
- Supplier behavior
- Social, economic, and political factors

These and other potentially critical areas are discussed in this chapter and in Chapters 6 and 7.

ECONOMIC FACTORS

Economic factors have a tremendous impact on business firms. Fortunately, firms know more about analyzing economic factors than any other set of factors. Furthermore, various governmental bodies keep statistics on components of the economy. Thus a company can quite easily obtain data on interest rates, unemployment, price levels, and so forth. Some experts even predict future levels of various economic factors. Although a firm may make incorrect projections relative to the economy, there is no excuse for not having economic data. It is available to all firms at little cost.

Key economic influences include interest rates, stage of the economic cycle, trends in gross national product (GNP), unemployment level, balance of payments, fiscal policies, monetary policies, and other factors (see Table 5.1). Since these factors are rather broad, individual firms should try to refine them in order to identify the specific forces that will most directly affect the firm.

Each of these economic factors can serve either as an opportunity or as a threat. For example, various economic factors—such as inflation and high interest rates—sometimes combine to drive down the sales of automobiles. At the same time, however, manufacturers of auto parts may experience increases in sales.

GOVERNMENTAL AND POLITICAL FACTORS

Governmental and political factors are exerting an ever stronger influence on how businesses operate. Firms must cope with government policy regarding economic policies, regulatory policies, and firm- or industry-specific intervention. They must comply with regulations dealing with antitrust activities, hiring practices, taxes (see Perspective 5.1), consumer lending, safety, pricing, advertising, plant location, and pollution. Since public opinion, special interest groups, elected politicians, and bureaucrats influence trends in government policy and regulation, companies need to monitor such groups.

Governmental activity also provides both opportunities and threats. For example, some government programs, such as tariffs on competing foreign goods and tax reductions, provide growth or survival opportunities. Conversely, increased taxes in certain industries (for example, video arcades) can threaten profitability.

In general, businesses operate as they do at present because society allows them to. If and when society no longer approves of certain practices or situations, it can withdraw that permission by demanding government intervention through regulation or the judicial system. Society's concern about pollution and energy conservation, for example, has been reflected in governmental action. Society has also demanded more stringent safety regulations for consumer products. Thus businesses need to recognize that strict compliance with existing rules may not be enough. They must also consider their own influence on potential regulations: that is, how their own activities could provoke restrictions. Self-regulation may be more appealing than government regulation.

SOCIOCULTURAL FACTORS

All companies should analyze a broad range of sociocultural factors to determine potential threats and opportunities. These factors range from demographic trends, recreational patterns, and behavioral patterns to attitudes toward quality of life, the business community, or women working.

Since these sociocultural factors often evolve slowly, they may be hard to perceive. For instance, the large-scale entry of women into the work force was preceded by changes in both women's and men's attitudes. Very few companies however, discussed these changes, forecast their impact, and formulated appropriate strategy.

External interruptions in sociocultural behavior patterns can cause rapid change. For example, the energy shortages and tremendous price increases in the

---

PERSPECTIVE 5.1

Taxing Times for Marriott Corporation

Hard work and determination are still keys to success in American business—and so is a knowledge of the tax laws. Such is the lesson of the Marriott Corporation. What began in 1927 as a small root-beer stand was built by three generations over sixty years into an $8 billion hotel and restaurant empire. Son followed father from kitchen to board room, learning the basics of the trade. The key lesson was not acquiring a knack for peeling potatoes. Rather, at least until 1986, it was mastering the art of the tax shelter.

Until 1986, Marriott did not own the hotels that bore its name. It built them and then sold most of the equity in them as tax shelters. Under existing tax laws the buyers received a tax break. Marriott made money from the sale of the ownership, from management contracts, and from the minority stake it retained in the operation.

When, in 1986, the tax law changed, Marriott had to seek a new formula for success. Without the prospect of tax relief, investors had less reason to buy into Marriott properties. Marriott responded with a new incentive: the company would guarantee a 10 percent return.

Initially, the strategy worked. Soon, however, problems arose—not through any intrinsic fault, but because the business environment had changed. The success of Marriott and others in the hotel business had encouraged a rash of new construction, creating an oversupply of rooms. This intensified competition. (Rival Hyatt, for one, began a strong promotional campaign designed to lure away Marriott's top customers.) It also lowered room occupancy rates. Where 68 percent occupancy is needed to break even, the industry-wide rate stood, in 1990, at 64 percent. Marriott's occupancy rate was nearly 75 percent, but the company's roster of unsold properties was growing.

To shore itself up financially, Marriott sold off its less profitable fast-food operations (it owned Roy Rogers) and its airline in-flight food-service business. Among Marriott's other moves: it built hotels abroad, and it decided to enter the life-care business, through apartment-like facilities offering meals and health care to better-off senior citizens.

References: Dean Foust and Mark Maremont, "The Baggage Weighing Marriott Down," *Business Week*, January 29, 1990, pp. 64, 66; Robin Amster, "Hyatt Ad Hurls Challenge at Marriott," *Travel Weekly*, March 1, 1990, p. 1; "The Big Bite at Marriott: Marriott Corp. Is Hitching Its Future to Being a Leader in Lodging and High-Traffic Restaurants," *Mergers & Acquisitions*, March-April 1990, p. 16.

mid-1970s spurred interest in energy conservation. As a result, sales of home insulation went up.

Sociocultural factors also affect a firm's *cost and availability of supplies, operations, and markets.* Demographic trends, for instance, determine the availability and quality of the labor force, and shifts in sociocultural opinions, attitudes, and beliefs (OABs) influence the firm's ability to motivate its workers. Changing demographics and OABs can also create new market opportunities and literally destroy other markets. Society's interest in health and fitness, for example, has created a market opportunity for sports-related shoes and contributed to the decline of the tobacco industry.

NATURAL FACTORS

Business firms have long acknowledged the impact of the natural environment on business decisions. Until recently, though, factors related to maintaining the natural environment have been almost totally ignored. Now public concern for the quality of the natural environment has prompted business decision makers to pay heed to it as well. In fact, many trend spotters see the 1990s as the *Earth Decade*, both in the United States and worldwide, and predict that environmentalism will be the most important issue in business.[5] Examples of the actions that concerned firms are already taking include the following:

- DuPont is pulling out of a $750 million-a-year business because it may harm the environment.
- McDonald's, already a leading crusader for recycling, is planning to become a leading educator on environmental issues.
- 3M is investing much more in pollution controls for its plants than the law requires.
- Procter & Gamble is emphasizing environmental concerns in relation to its products (for instance, it is emphasizing recycled packaging material).
- Pacific Gas & Electric is teaming up with environmental groups to do joint projects, such as a $10 million study of energy efficiency.

Public interest groups have brought various environmental problems to public and government attention. Pollution, energy shortages, and the wasting of natural resources, coupled with increasing demands on our limited resources, have motivated the public, as well as businesses, to make some radical changes in this way of doing things. Yet even such environmentally conscious companies as those just listed are by no means perfect in handling environmental issues. For example, DuPont makes numerous chemicals that some experts deem harmful. McDonald's uses styrofoam for many of its products, and some of it ends up along roadsides and in landfills. Procter & Gamble produces disposable diapers in large quantities, even though many people believe that solid wastes, such as disposable diapers, are our most pressing environmental problem.

TECHNOLOGICAL FACTORS

Few industries and firms in this country do not depend on an increasingly sophisticated technological base. The high probability for continued technological advances provides both opportunities and threats for entire industries and for specific companies. Leaders in technology development and technology transfer generally assume an offensive posture by seeking new technical solutions to existing problems and by identifying existing technologies that can be exploited in existing markets.

Firms must also be on the alert for new technologies that can directly or indirectly make their products obsolete. Many of these innovations come from outside existing industries. As N. H. Snyder points out, "History teaches that most new developments which threaten existing business practices and technologies do not come from traditional industries."[6] NCR, for example, was not well prepared for a major assault on its market for electromechanical cash registers and adding machines by firms offering electronic units.

Typically, established firms experience great difficulty in mounting an effective response to major technological innovations in their industry, especially those introduced during the maturity stage of the product life cycle.[7] In addition, large and complex firms tend to introduce fewer technological innovations than firms in their early stages of growth.[8]

Major upheavals do not always result from technological breakthroughs. In recent decades, **technology transfer**—the process of taking new technology from the laboratory to the marketplace—has attracted increasing attention. (There is even an annual World's Fair for Technology Exchange.) Integrated circuit technology, for example, was transferred to the watchmaking industry by firms such as Texas Instruments. Timex, Seiko, and Swiss firms found that their market had changed almost overnight and were forced to invest heavily in the new technology. Developing technologies that may soon be transferred to other industries include biological engineering, robotics, and telecommunications.

How vulnerable firms can be to technological advances is illustrated by the **technology life cycle** concept. In Exhibit 5.2, each S-shaped curve relates research and development (R&D) efforts to improvements in a specific technology. The typical pattern is that increased effort does not yield constant technological improvements. Early R&D effort in Technology A, for example, may yield only small increments in performance. Later efforts may cause a sharp rise

EXHIBIT 5.2 · The Technology Life Cycle

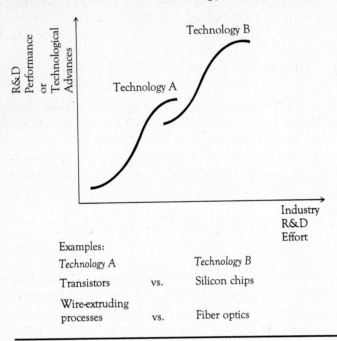

Examples:

Technology A		*Technology B*
Transistors	vs.	Silicon chips
Wire-extruding processes	vs.	Fiber optics

in R&D performance. Eventually, however, increased R&D efforts are likely to yield only marginal improvements in performance. Technology A is, therefore, "played out."

To get further improvement in performance, a new technology (Technology B) must replace the old, thereby launching another technology curve. The firm must therefore predict movements along the current technology curve and "jump" from one curve to the other. To be caught investing heavily in a technology that is soon to be obsolete can cause severe problems. For instance, a firm that is building a plant geared to use the latest vacuum tube technology just as transistors are developed, or geared to use the latest transistor technology just as silicon chips are developed, is creating handicaps for itself. If a firm predicts that a given technology is nearing its maximum potential, it might hold off making long-term investments until the new technology can be anticipated with some accuracy.

Whereas new technology life cycles are considered to be macroenvironmental influences, advances along an existing curve are most likely to originate within the industry. Thus movements along a technology life cycle curve could be considered as task environment influences (discussed in Chapter 6). Technological factors influence several components of the task environment (for example, suppliers and substitute products) and the internal situation (for instance, R&D and marketing). Although technological factors are not discussed in those sections, you should be aware of their influence.

Technology has two basic components. The tangible component consist of machines, tools, and materials. The much more important intangible component consist of knowledge and expertise.[9] Planners should analyze the technology being used by their firm and scan the environment to discover what technology is being used by competitors. They also need to discern new technologies that may be on the horizon for a given industry and its key stakeholder industries (including those which might accomplish similar functions for the firm).

INTERACTION OF MACROENVIRONMENTAL FACTORS

Macroenvironmental forces also interact with each other to influence businesses. Exhibit 5.3 illustrates how selected factors and their interrelationships are linked to the increased demand for better-quality smaller cars.

Exhibit 5.3 also helps to highlight the hazards of misinterpreting a changing macroenvironment. As indicated, a variety of macroenvironmental factors combined to increase the demand for smaller cars. When this demand became more apparent to the U.S. automobile companies, most of them assumed that the underlying causal factors were all related to the economy and that some customers would put up with a smaller car only if it cost much less than a larger car and obtained much greater gas mileage.

Although this interpretation may have been accurate at one point, hindsight reveals that other macroenvironmental forces were also at work. For instance, auto manufacturers apparently ignored one key factor: the changing attitudes of women. Dual-income families with fewer children often need two or more cars, but do not necessarily want a large, comfortable family car and a small, spartan second car. They may prefer two small, comfortable cars. Correct interpretation of these factors might have speeded up the U.S. firms' entry into this market. Instead, they lagged behind foreign companies.

GLOBAL DIMENSIONS

Firms that deal directly in foreign markets, use foreign suppliers, or have foreign production facilities obviously must consider international environmental influ-

EXHIBIT 5.3 · Synopsis of Macroenvironmental Impact on the Demand for Smaller Automobiles

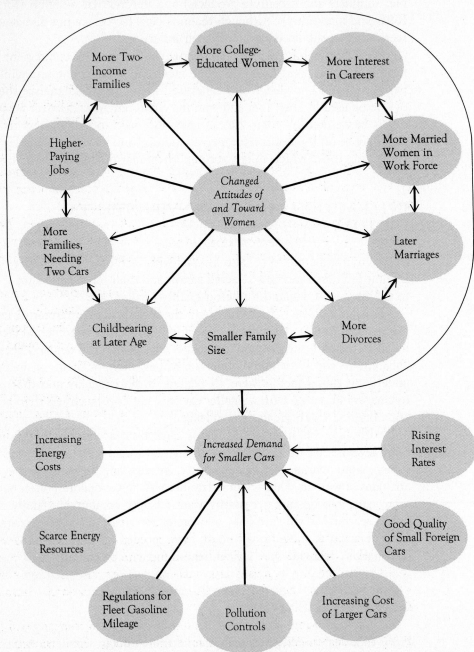

ences. However, companies without such involvement must do so as well. We will discuss each group separately.

Firms with Only Domestic Operations

Most of the macroenvironmental categories discussed earlier in this chapter can contain international components. For example, global economic factors influenced the U.S. economy, affecting the balance of payments and the relative strength of the dollar.

Governmental and political influences have a bearing on international trade relations. Many U.S. farmers, for instance, have suffered because strained political relations, along with other factors, have caused certain countries to buy less grain from the United States, thereby driving down prices.

techno Advances in technology by foreign firms must also be watched. New technology for production purposes (such as an improved process for making steel) or as part of the final product (such as more efficient automobile engines) can have an impact on a domestic firms' operations.

Even if a firm does not have foreign operations or markets, sociocultural factors in foreign countries can influence its strategy. For example, a firm might sell production equipment to companies that make and distribute their products primarily overseas. If societal factors in foreign countries lessen demand for those products, then the equipment manufacturer will also suffer.

The natural environment in certain foreign countries can also exert an influence. For example, although U.S. firms may purchase energy from other U.S. firms, much of the raw petroleum for this energy comes from foreign countries. Thus continual depletion of oil deposits is a natural environmental factor with a potentially large impact.

Firms with Global Operations

Firms with global operations face an even more complex environmental situation. (See Perspective 5.2.) Whether dealing with foreign markets, production facilities, or suppliers, domestic firms must analyze the macroenvironment of the particular country. Table 5.2 offers examples of key international macroenvironmental factors.

When marketing its products in a foreign country, a company will be influenced by macroenvironmental factors of that country. First, economic factors will influence, for example, the consumers' ability to pay for the products.

PERSPECTIVE 5.2

Gatorade Goes Global

As of the late 1980s, Gatorade was riding high. The sports beverage controlled well over 90 percent of its U.S. market—a market projected to expand at more than 14 percent a year. Still, Quaker Oats, the maker of Gatorade, was concerned. Given the market growth rate and the recent introduction of sports beverages by such heavy hitters as Coca-Cola, PepsiCo, and H. J. Heinz, Quaker would be challenged to maintain Gatorade's annual growth rate of 30 percent. Some experts maintained that, even if Quaker did everything right, it was bound to lose at least some market share to such tough competition.

The solution? Develop new markets. To keep profits soaring, Quaker decided to take Gatorade abroad. By 1990 overseas sales of Gatorade were still minute compared to domestic sales. Yet Quaker intended, through the aggressive marketing that has made its drink so successful at home, to make a big splash worldwide.

In Italy, the campaign seems to be working. Ads are showing prominent athletes keeping up their strength with the help of Gatorade. In the name of Gatorade, Quaker has sponsored Italian Olympic athletes. And Quaker has captured 93 percent of the sports beverage market.

In Brazil, however, held back by a troubled economy and a price freeze, Gatorade has not achieved its modest ambition of 0.1 percent of the soft-drink market.

Essentially, Quaker has promoted Gatorade abroad the same way it promoted the drink in the United States. The company has, however, paid attention to the particularities of individual markets. In Italy, Quaker has concentrated on its lemon and orange flavors, packaged in half-liter bottles and four-packs. In Brazil, Gatorade is available in lemon and tangerine, both sold in natural colors.

Quaker hopes that a successful Gatorade will set the stage for the promotion of other Quaker products in foreign markets. The company's pet foods in particular could use a boost from overseas sales!

References: Julie Liesse Erickson, "Gatorade Gusher Set," *Advertising Age*, April 17, 1989, p. 10; Lois Therrien, "How Swallowing Gatorade Gave Quaker Oats a Boost," *Business Week*, January 15, 1990, p. 56; Julie Liesse and Patricia Winters, "Gatorade Set to Bench New Rivals," *Advertising Age*, March 19, 1990, p. 4.

TABLE 5.2 · Examples of Key International Environmental Factors

Legal Environment	Cultural Environment
Legal tradition	Customs, norms, values, beliefs
Effectiveness of legal system	Language
Treaties with foreign nations	Attitudes
Patent trademark laws	Motivations
Laws affecting business firms	Social institutions
	Status symbols
	Religious beliefs

Economic Environment	Political System
Level of economic development	Form of government
Population	Political ideology
Gross national product	Stability of government
Per capita income	Strength of opposition parties and groups
Literacy level	Social unrest
Social infrastructure	Political strife and insurgency
Natural resources	Governmental attitude toward foreign firms
Climate	Foreign policy
Membership in regional economic blocks (EEC; LAFTA; etc.)	
Monetary and fiscal policies	
Nature of competition	
Currency convertibility	
Inflation	
Taxation system	
Interest rates	
Wage and salary levels	

Source: From Arvind V. Phatak, *International Dimensions of Management* (Boston: Kent Publishing Company, 1983), p. 6. © 1983 by Wadsworth, Inc. Reprinted by permission of PWS-KENT Publishing Company.

Second, government and legal regulations may mandate partnerships with local businesses. Third, societal and cultural factors (including language or even the colors of packages) can create barriers to certain products. The color blue, for instance, is taboo in certain countries because it has special religious significance. Fourth, the technological environment may be such that certain products will not have a market. The market for personal computers in most developing countries is not very large. Fifth, natural factors can preclude the need for certain products in a given foreign country. The market for heavy coats in tropical climates is obviously quite small.

When a domestic firm's only international involvement is with foreign suppliers, the firm must address the macroenvironment of the suppliers' home country. Depending on the situation, companies purchasing foreign goods usually need a continuous, dependable supply of goods at a reasonable price. Each macroenvironmental factor in a given country must be viewed in the light of this objective. Economic factors, such as inflation and monetary instability, can potentially damage sources of supply. Governmental factors, such as export restrictions and political instability, can also cause barriers to imports from a country. Sociocultural factors, such as attitudes toward quality of life, might narrow the export possibilities for certain goods. In addition, technological limitations might restrict a country's ability to support the production of certain types of goods, and a lack of certain natural resources might cramp potential suppliers in producing and exporting goods.

Firms seeking to establish production facilities abroad must also analyze the macroenvironment in the target country. Both economic factors, such as average wage rates, and governmental factors, such as tax laws, special incentives, and regulations on local hiring, would affect the country's attractiveness as a production site. Social factors, such as general attitudes toward work and quality of life, would determine the size and ability of the local work force. Technological factors could influence the quality of the product, and natural factors, such as climate and terrain, could affect both production and transportation.

Notes

1. F. John Pessolano, "Futurism: Design for Survival," *Enterprise* (February 1979), 6–11.

2. John Naisbitt, *Megatrends* (New York: Warner Books, 1984).

3. L. J. Bourgeois III, "Strategy and Environment: A Conceptual Integration," *Academy of Management Review*, 5, No. 1 (1980), 25–39.

4. James F. Brown, Jr., "How U.S. Firms Conduct Strategic Planning," *Management Accounting* (February 1986), 38+.

5. David Kirkpatrick, "Environmentalism: The New Crusade," *Fortune*, February 12, 1990, pp. 44–55.

6. N. H. Snyder, "Environmental Volatility, Scanning Intensity and Organization Performance," *Journal of Contemporary Business* (September 1981), 16.

7. A. C. Cooper et al., "Strategic Responses

to Technological Threats," *Proceedings,* Academy of Management, 1974.

8. J. M. Utterback and M. J. Abernathy, "The Test of a Conceptual Model Linking States in Firms' Process and Product Innovation" (Working Paper No. 74–23, Harvard School of Business, 1974).

9. Alan J. Rowe, Richard O. Mason, Dickel, and Neil H. Snyder, *Strategic agement: A Methodological Approach,* edition, (Reading, Mass.: Addison-Wesl 1989), p. 117.

6

The Task Environment

The task environment consists of the industry and those industry factors external to the firm that determine the nature and strength of industry competition. Sometimes analysis of the task environment is called *industry analysis*. This chapter focuses on describing the components of the task environment. The five key ones are competitors, buyers, suppliers, potential entrants, and substitutes, and Exhibit 6.1 shows their interrelation. The key for developing a successful strategy is to analyze each major factor. Knowledge of these sources of competitive pressure helps to highlight the firm's strengths and weaknesses relative to the threats and opportunities facing the industry.[1]

THE INDUSTRY SITUATION

Before considering the components of the task environment, the strategist must gain a firm grasp of the industry situation regarding its overall attractiveness and long-run profit potential. Five categories of factors are relevant: industry structure, driving forces, generic industry type, economic and business characteristics, and industrywide strategic issues.

Industry Structure

An industry can be viewed as a group of firms that attempt to serve essentially similar customer needs in the same markets with similar products and services. The input needed to gain an overall understanding of industry structure consists of factors such as market size and growth rate, production capacity, capital requirements, the number of buyers and sellers, and so on.

Note that different competitors can fit this description while using very different market approaches. These competitive subgroups, or clusters, are referred to as *strategic groups*.[2] Defining the strategic groups requires more than gathering descriptive information. Essentially, the strategist must assume the perspective of the customer to determine which competitive factors are important to various groups of customers. For example, are there sufficient numbers of customers interested in products with high, medium, and low price and quality dimensions to attract three distinct clusters of competitors? Furthermore, does each one of these clusters offer product lines of the same or different breadth and depth? Answers to these questions help pinpoint the factors that differentiate individual competitors.

Driving Forces

Driving forces are factors exerting the dominant influence on what kind of changes take place in an industry.[3] The following often serve as driving forces because they can cause strategy-related changes in an industry:

- *Changes in the long-term industry growth rate* can influence the investment decisions of existing competitors and cause more firms to enter or exit the industry.
- *Changes in the customer base* can mandate changes in the marketing approach, including products and product lines, service requirements, pricing, channels of distribution, and promotional programs.
- *Product innovation* can influence a variety of strategic factors, including marketing costs and programs, manufacturing methods, demand, and so on.
- *Process innovation* can alter factors such as capital requirements, unit costs, and the cost structure of rival firms.
- *Marketing innovation* can influence the nature of demand, product differentiation opportunities, and unit costs.
- *Entry of a major firm* with new ideas about applying skills and resources can change the rules for competing.
- *Exit of a major firm* reduces the number of players and can cause a stampede to capture former customers.
- *Diffusion of proprietary knowledge* erodes the advantages held by firms that possess it, thereby potentially attracting new firms.
- *Improved cost and efficiency* through learning curve effects or economies of scale can cause many firms to adopt market-share-building approaches.
- *Rising costs* can cause competitors to intensely seek reliable supplies at affordable prices or search out lower-cost substitutes.

EXHIBIT 6.1 · General Diagram of Industry Task Environment

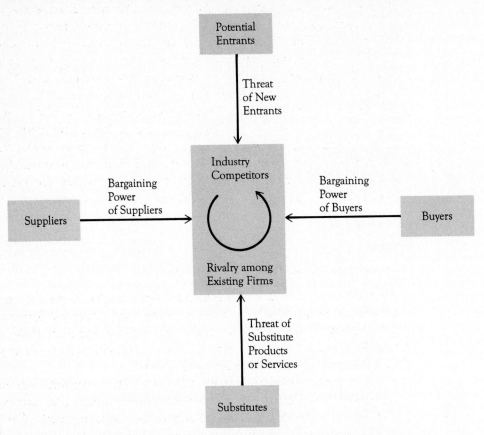

Source: Reprinted with permission of the Free Press, a Division of Macmillan, Inc., from *Competitive Strategy: Techniques for Analyzing Industries and Competitors* by Michael E. Porter. Copyright © 1980 by The Free Press.

- *Shifts in demand away from differentiated products to commodity products* can mandate a price-oriented focus, thereby reducing competitors' strategic freedom.
- *Shifts in demand away from commodities to differentiated products* can cause rivals to stress product differentiation.
- *Regulatory influences and government policy changes* can place heavy burdens on an industry (for instance, the utility industries) or create attractive opportunities (for example, deregulation in the trucking and banking industries).

Generic Industry Type

Planners should also determine the generic industry type. An **emerging industry** involves the formation of a group of competitors around a new product or service, which arose through a technological innovation, cost shift, or other environmental event. A **maturing industry** has grown rapidly at some point but now faces slower growth and the corresponding greater domestic and international competition, overexpansion of capacity, more brand-oriented buyers, and greater emphasis on cost and service. A **declining industry** suffers from declining sales over a long period of time for reasons such as technological substitution, demographic shifts, and changing buyer preferences. A **fragmented industry** contains no dominant competitors and has numerous small and medium-sized firms. A **global industry** develops when competition in a specific geographical area is influenced by competitors who compete globally or across national boundaries.

Business and Economic Characteristics[4]

An industry's business and economic characteristics define the constraints or parameters within which firms must operate to be successful. Business characteristics consist of the "what and how" needed to compete successfully in an industry. Key business characteristics include factors such as the role of advertising, location, production efficiencies, and so on.

The dominant business characteristics lead to the critical economic characteristics of the industry. The links among price, revenue, cost, and profit vary in each industry and are driven by factors such as economies of scale, capital requirements, elasticity of demand, and so on.

Understanding an industry's business and economic characteristics serves as the foundation for discovering the industry's **key success factors.** An industry's key success factors are the three or four major determinants of success in that industry. These factors should serve as the cornerstone for a firm's competitive strategy.

Industry-Wide Strategic Issues

An industry-wide strategic issue can be viewed as one that presents an opportunity or threat to the industry as a whole. These issues typically arise from some change in one of the external environmental components. Understanding these issues can provide insight regarding the overall attractiveness of the industry and competitors' resource allocations and strategic focus.

COMPETITORS AND COMPETITIVE FORCES

Competition is the most dangerous environmental factor because competitors are intelligent adversaries whose activities in pursuit of their objectives can impede another firm's pursuit of its objectives. In addition, competitors are dangerous because competitors are not static but can consciously take action in response to another firm's action. This reaction often occurs in three distinct stages.[5] The first stage, *blindness*, involves hoping that nothing will change and that everything will continue to go on as before. The second stage is an *attempt to destroy* the competitor or its strategy. This attempt can mean cutting off sources of supply or trying to secure legislation that would prevent a certain mode of operation. The third stage is *direct confrontation*, perhaps with overcompensation. For example, price cuts are met with greater price cuts, and increased promotional activities are met with even greater promotional efforts.

Competitive Forces

Competitive forces influence each firm differently, even if they are in the same industry. An industry's competitive environment can be viewed as consisting of the ten major forces discussed below.[6]

Potential Rate of Growth in the Industry   Industries with low growth rates, such as typewriters, hold few opportunities and, consequently, attract relatively few new competitors. High-growth industries, such as microcomputers, present substantial opportunity, thereby attracting the attention of many more firms. Low- and high-growth industries therefore require different types of strategies.

Threat of Entry by New Competitors   The threat of entry into an industry by new competitors decreases when the barriers to entry are high and a strong reaction from existing competitors is likely. High entry barriers can result from high startup capital requirements, the ability of established companies to practice economies of scale, established firms' exclusive access to patents, information, or raw materials, preferred locations, superior facilities, and strong product differentiation. The threat of a new automobile manufacturer arising in the United States, for example, is fairly low because of the high level of startup capital required.

The threat of entry is high when effective barriers are lacking. It is relatively easy, for example, to launch a new computer software firm because of low entry barriers. Conversely, the more difficult it is for new firms to enter the industry, the stronger the competitive position of existing firms.

Intensity of Rivalry Among Existing Competitors   A highly intense rivalry among existing competitors makes it difficult for them to survive and for new firms to enter the industry. Few firms desire to enter an industry in which every action generates fierce countermeasures from competitors. Highly intense rivalry occurs when (1) competitors are numerous, (2) competitors are similar in size, skills, and market power, (3) competitors face exit barriers (find it difficult to leave the industry) and choose to stay and "fight it out," (4) the industry is stagnant or declining, thereby increasing the pressure on competitors to fight for market share, and (5) one or more competitors are extremely aggressive or simply extremely committed to succeeding in the industry.

Pressure from Substitute Products   Substitute products often arise from new technology and often from outside the industry, as discussed in Chapter 5. A typical pattern involves the competitors in an industry focusing their attention almost exclusively on present competitors and getting blind-sided. The plastics industry, for example, has made serious inroads in markets dominated previously by the metals industry.

Dependence on Complementary Products and Services   Two different products are complementary when their demand is somehow related, such as computers, printers, and continuous-feed paper. A high degree of dependence on complementary products is a danger signal, particularly if the complementary product represents another industry. As long as the other industry is healthy, both can be healthy. However, a stagnant or unstable complementary industry can damage both industries.

Bargaining Power of Buyers   The bargaining power of buyers tends to be high in industries that have many sellers and few buyers. The greater the bargaining power of buyers, the lesser are the advantages available to sellers. The low-price and high-service levels in such industries make profits hard to find.

Bargaining Power of Suppliers   Suppliers tend to have more power if there are just a few of them, if there are few alternative sources of supply, if their product is important for the buyer's business, and if they do not depend on the buyer's purchases to have a successful business. For example, firms that make cooling towers must purchase large amounts of copper tubing from copper suppliers; copper suppliers are relatively large and powerful, which allows them to exert great influence. The greater the bargaining power of suppliers, the less advantage the buyer has.

Sophistication of Technologies Applied in the Industry   Competitive forces in both high- and low-tech industries can be powerful. Firms in high-tech industries typically must invest heavily in research and development and strive to protect their position through secrecy, patents, and copyrights. Low-tech firms face potentially intense competition because of low barriers to entry.

Rate of Innovation   If the rate of innovation in an industry is high, competitors must be flexible and committed to keeping up through R&D spending and strategic planning. The personal computer industry, for example, has been characterized by rapid innovation; firms that lagged behind the industry's innovation rate are no longer in the industry. Low rates of innovation call for emphasis on marketing, sales, and cost reduction. The primary stimuli for innovation are technological progress and strategic thinking (or new ways of thinking about products and services).

Capability of Management   Competition tends to be more intense in industries containing many firms with highly capable managers. A competitor with good managers in an industry generally lacking good managers has a strong potential competitive advantage. Note that the definition of a good manager is not the same in all industries. In the grocery business, for example, the better managers focus on cost control and operational efficiency. However, the best managers in the computer software industry are likely to be innovative thinkers.

Components of Competitor Analysis

Knowledge about specific competitors is important to a firm for a variety of reasons. First, competitors determine the nature and level of industry rivalry or jockeying for position. The intensity of this rivalry depends on the interaction of several factors, including the number of firms, industry growth rate, fixed cost structure, and degree of product differentiation.[7] The presence of these factors tends to increase a firm's need and/or desire to gain and defend market share, thereby intensifying the competitive rivalry. (See Perspective 6.1.) Firms must also recognize that competitive rivalry is not stable. Maturing industries, for example, normally encounter intensified rivalry as growth rates and profits decline. (Integrated circuit, hand calculator, and snowmobile industries illustrate this situation.) Furthermore, new competitors and technological innovations often change the level and nature of competitive rivalry.

Firms must analyze each competitor to gain a sense of its probable actions and responses. Exhibit 6.2 shows the key components of a competitor analysis, and we discuss them in the rest of this section.

PERSPECTIVE 6.1

K mart Fights Back

The glory days of youthful expansion had passed for K mart with the 1970s. By the late 1980s the discount retailer had settled into middle age. Its stores were lackluster, the profits were off, and it trailed behind industry leader Wal-Mart Stores. New chairman Joseph E. Antonini had a plan, however. Cut prices, play catch-up, and expand into specialty retailing.

The first part didn't work. K mart slashed prices on some 8,000 items—and lost money. One reason was because it was so successful; the heavily discounted items disappeared from the shelves faster than K mart's distribution could replace them. And, of course, unreliable supply generates customer dissatisfaction, which leads to the second part of K mart's plan.

For K mart, playing catch-up meant catching up to Wal-Mart. One of Wal-Mart's strong points is its highly efficient computerized distribution system. K mart's plan called for spending a billion dollars on a better computerized distribution system (due to be on-line by the end of 1990). It also called for spending $1.3 billion enlarging and modernizing K mart

stores—for example, by widening aisles, improving lighting, and installing wider shelves. And the plan provided for enlivening the store's image. To that end, Antonini hired Jacklyn Smith to promote K mart clothing and author-caterer Martha Stewart to promote K mart housewares.

Part of Antonini's strategy also included specialty retailing ventures, such as Pace Membership Warehouse, Inc., huge outlets offering wholesale prices; American Fare, an enormous "hypermarket" in Atlanta, formed in partnership with Bruno's of Birmingham, Alabama; and Builders Square, a chain of home-improvement stores.

References: David Woodruff, "Will K mart Ever Be a Silk Purse?" *Business Week,* January 22, 1990, p. 46; Francine Schwadel, "K mart to Speed Store Openings, Renovations," *Wall Street Journal,* February 27, 1990, p. A3; Faye Rice, "Why K mart Has Stalled," *Fortune, October* 9, 1989, p. 79; Stephen Dowdell, "American Fare: Big on Quality," *Supermarket News,* February 20, 1989, p. 1.

Future Goals   Knowledge of competitors' goals allows a firm to predict (1) how satisfied each competitor is with its present position and financial results, (2) how likely that competitor is to change its strategy, (3) the vigor with which it will react to outside events (such as other firm's strategic changes), and (4) the seriousness of initiatives the competitor takes.

EXHIBIT 6.2 · The Components of Competitor Analysis

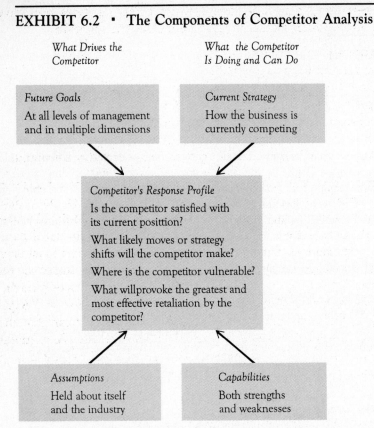

Source: Reprinted with permission of The Free Press, a Division of Macmillan, Inc., from *Competitive Strategy: Techniques for Analyzing Industries and Competitors* by Michael E. Porter, Copyright © 1980 by The Free Press

There are many factors to examine relative to a competitor's **business unit goals.**[8] For example, a firm that requires its investments to yield a high rate of return or to have a short payback period is not likely to make moves that provide low short-run returns, even if the investment would yield a large return in the long run. Consequently, knowing a competitor's *financial goals* can help a firm predict what that competitor will do. *Attitudes toward risk* can also be revealing—competitors aversive to risk usually move cautiously and may be "beaten to the punch" by quicker action. Other, less obvious, factors can also be important in predicting a competitor's moves. For example, the *organizational structure* and the *composition of the board of directors* may provide insight into likely competitive strategy. If the board has several entrepreneurial members, the firm may be more likely to pursue relatively risky strategies, and pursue them earlier. Similarly, if the organization structure is dominated by marketing, more risky investments may be made. Other factors to examine include the following:

- Organizational values or beliefs
- Control and incentive systems
- Accounting systems and conventions
- Types of managers, particularly the CEO
- Managerial consensus about future directions
- Contractual commitments that may limit alternatives
- Regulatory, antitrust, or other governmental or social constraints

When a competitor is part of a larger parent organization, the parent might impose certain constraints or requirements on the business unit. Since these conditions may affect the competitor's behavior, several additional issues must be addressed.[9] One of these issues involves *top management's emotional attachment* to the unit. For example, Sara Lee is likely to give heavy support to its Bryan Foods division because the CEO of Sara Lee is George Bryan, the son of the founder of Bryan Foods. The *parent firm's performance* in terms of sales growth, rate of return, and the related factors may also help predict what will happen to a business unit or division. Poor overall performance may mean that the parent will spin off a strategic business unit (SBU) to generate cash. Furthermore, SBUs that are performing below the parent's average are likely to be sold or changed. Other issues to examine include the following:

- Parent firm's overall goals
- Importance of the business unit to parent
- Parent firm's reasons for entering the particular business, such as excess capacity, need for vertical integration, wish to exploit distribution channels, and so on
- Economic relationship between parent firm's units, such as vertical integration and shared R&D
- Values or beliefs of top management
- Common generic strategies used by parent company
- Sales targets, hurdles for returns on investment, and constraints on capital due to the performance and needs of parent firm's other units
- Diversification plans
- Parent firm's organizational structure, including the relative status, position, and goals of the particular unit
- Control and compensation schemes for divisional management
- Type of executives commonly rewarded (which reinforces certain types of strategic behavior)
- Recruiting strategy
- Sensitivity to antitrust, regulatory, or social issues

Planners can also gain insight by analyzing the parent firm's portfolio strategy and noting how the competing unit fits. These key questions form the backbone of such an analysis:[10]

- What criteria are used to classify businesses?
- Which businesses are classified as cash generators?
- Which businesses are likely to be harvested or divested?
- Which businesses provide stability to offset fluctuations elsewhere in the portfolio?
- Which businesses are positioned to protect other major businesses?
- In which businesses is the parent likely to invest resources and attempt to build market share?
- Which businesses tend to have the largest impact on the parent's overall portfolio relative to stability, earnings, cash flow, sales growth, and so on?

Information gleaned from answers to these questions can help a firm locate positions in the market where it can meet its objectives without threatening competitors and perhaps touching off bitter warfare. If such a position is not available, the firm has at least become better prepared to develop strategies that it can defend against existing and potential competitors.

Assumptions   Gaining an understanding of a competitor's assumptions about both *itself* and *other firms* in the industry can also benefit a company. When these assumptions are inaccurate, they can create "blind spots," which make the competitor vulnerable. If a competitor believes, for example, that it has unusually strong customer loyalty, it may be vulnerable to competitive moves such as price cuts and new product introductions. Similarly, a firm can hold inaccurate assumptions about the industry or its environment. U.S. automobile manufacturers, for example, had long regarded the demand for small cars as based strictly on economics; this error made them vulnerable to foreign competitors whose cars offered more luxury components and were perceived to be of higher quality.

The following questions can help identify competitors' assumptions, including potentially erroneous assumptions:[11]

1. What are the competitor's beliefs about its strengths, weaknesses, and overall position in the industry relative to costs, product quality, technological sophistication, and so on? Are the beliefs accurate?
2. How strongly from a historical or emotional perspective does the competitor identify with particular products and policies, such as selling approach, desire for product quality, and approach to product design?
3. What is the impact of cultural, regional, or national differences on the competitor's attitudes and perception of events?

4. Are there strongly institutionalized values or canons, such as those ~ by the competing firm's founder, that influence attitudes?
5. What does the competitor believe about future demand for its products and other industry trends?
6. What does the competitor believe about its competitors' goals and capabilities? Are these beliefs accurate?
7. Does the competitor believe in conventional wisdom or rules of thumb, such as "We must have a full line" and "Centralization is the key to success"? Do these beliefs make it vulnerable?

Note that a thorough analysis of a competitor's history and the backgrounds of its managers and advisers can yield insight into its goals, in addition to its assumptions.

Current Strategy The current strategy of each competitor, whether explicit or implicit, must be understood. Essentially, a firm must determine how the competitor is currently competing. The focus, therefore, is on the competitor's key operating policies in each functional area and how it seeks to interrelate the functions.

Capabilities The goals, assumptions, and current strategy of a competitor influence the likelihood, timing, nature, and intensity of its reactions. The competitor's ability to initiate or react to strategic moves and deal with environmental events is based on its strengths and weaknesses. Firms should examine the competitor's *core capabilities*—its strengths and weaknesses in each of the following functional areas:[12]

- Products
- Dealer/distribution system
- Marketing and selling
- Operations/manufacturing
- Research and engineering
- Overall costs
- Financial strength
- Organization
- General managerial ability
- Corporate portfolio
- Human resources
- Relationship with key publics (for example, government)

The consistency of the competitor's goals and strategy should also be examined. Does it have *internal consistency*, which exists when goals are mutually achievable, when key operating policies address the goals, and when goals and policies reinforce each other? *Environmental fit* is also significant; it exists when the goals and policies exploit industry opportunities, deal with threats, and respond to broader societal concerns. *Resource fit* occurs when the goals and policies match the resources available to the firm. Successful *communication and implementation* depend on these factors: the key implementers understanding the goals; sufficient congruence between goals and policies and the key implementers' values to ensure commitment; and sufficient managerial capability to allow for effective implementation. A firm must also determine whether the competitor's strengths, weaknesses, and consistency will change over time and in what direction.

Still another factor requiring examination is the competitor's *ability to grow*. A company needs to evaluate (1) whether the competitor's capabilities would increase or diminish if it did grow; (2) the competitor's potential for growth in terms of people, skills, and plant capacity; and (3) the degree of growth the competitor could sustain from a financial perspective.

The competitor's *quick-response capability*—its ability to mount an immediate counteroffensive—is, of course, important. Specific factors to analyze include uncommitted cash reserves, reserve borrowing power, excess plant capacity, and unintroduced new products that could quickly be placed on the shelf.

Knowing the competitor's *ability to adapt to change* is critical. Firms should examine the competitor's ability to respond to external events such as technological advances, inflation, and greater governmental intervention. The ability to adapt to changes relative to each functional area must also be scrutinized. For example, can the competitor adapt to an escalation in marketing activity or manage a more complex product line? The competitor's ability to adapt to change will be influenced by (1) fixed versus variable costs, (2) cost of unused capacity, (3) existence of exit barriers, and (4) shared manufacturing or other facilities or personnel, such as a sales force, with other units of its corporate parent.

The competitor's *staying power* involves its ability to sustain a protracted battle. Staying power will be a function of cash reserves, unanimity within management, long time horizon in its financial goals, and lack of stock market pressure.

A full understanding of key competitors is so valuable that it justifies developing competitor analysis procedures and maintaining competitor files, which should contain all relevant and legally obtainable information on each major competitor. Table 6.1 presents a list of the necessary information. The files should be continually updated and periodically evaluated.

TABLE 6.1 · Information Needed for Competitor Analysis

Conceptive Design	Physical Resources	Marketing	Finance	Management
Technical resources	Capacity	Sales force	Long-term	Key people
Concepts	Plant	Skills	Debt/equity ratio	Objectives and
Patents and	Size	Size	Cost of debt	priorities
copyrights	Location	Type	Short-term	Values
Technological	Age	Location	Line of credit	Reward systems
sophistication	Equipment	Distribution network	Type of debt	Decision making
Technical	Automation	Research	Cost of debt	Location
integration	Maintenance	Skills	Liquidity	Type
Human resources	Flexibility	Type	Cash flow	Speed
Key people and	Processes	Service and sales	Days of	Planning
skills	Uniqueness	policies	receivables	Type
Use of external	Flexibility	Advertising	Inventory	Emphasis
technical	Degree of integration	Skills	turnover	Time span
groups	Human resources	Type	Accounting	Staffing
Funding	Key people and	Human resources	practices	Longevity and
Total	skills	Key people and	Human resources	turnover
Percentage of	Work force	skills	Key people and	Experience
sales	Skills mix	Turnover	skills	Replacement
Consistency over	Unions	Funding	Turnover	policies
time	Turnover	Total	Systems	Organization
Internally	Position on	Consistency over	Budgeting	Centralization
generated	experience	time	Forecasting	Functions
Government	curve	Percentage of	Controlling	Use of staff
supplied	Raw material costs	sales		Climate
	Production cost	Reward systems		Corporate strategy
		Market share		
		Product line		
		Quality		
		Breadth		
		Depth		
		Standing in each		
		market		
		Price		
		Competitiveness		
		General image		

Source: Reprinted, by permission of the publisher, from *Management Review*, July 1979. © 1979 by American Management Association, New York. All rights reserved.

CUSTOMERS

Customers are an integral part of a firm's task environment. A base of loyal customers can be a firm's most precious asset. This loyalty is created by satisfying customers' needs and desires better than the competitors do. Customers must be understood from several perspectives: as individuals, as consumers, as groups of buyers, and as markets. Each of these perspectives has different implications for the strategist.

Customers as Individuals (Micro Perspective)

From a micro perspective, the strategist must understand how individuals make decisions to purchase a specific brand of a product. Major areas to address include the customers' decision-making processes, psychological inputs (personality, attitudes, learning, perceptions, motivation), and social inputs (culture, subcultures, social classes, reference groups). When the customer is a buyer for an organization, the strategist must understand issues such as committee buying, joint decision making, organizational constraints, and so on.

Customers as Consumers (Macro Perspective)

From a macro perspective, major trends inconsumers' behavior in the marketplace must be evaluated. One observer, for example, identifies four themes underlying current changes in consumers' behavior: (1) the tempering of traditional American optimism and confidence, (2) cost-effectiveness emphasis by the consumer, (3) focus on strategic thinking, action, and winning, and (4) a rise in local identification. Based on these themes, she predicts:[13]

- Less impulse buying
- Less response to novelty change and variety
- More emphasis on quality, durability, and appropriateness
- Increased tradeoffs of time versus convenience in purchasing
- Reduced store loyalty
- Loyalty to brands with selective behavior among products
- More time and thus more money spent in in-home shopping
- A willingness to forgo present comforts for future benefits
- More personal responsibility for making the right product choice
- An emphasis on local products, brands, and those who influence their purchase

Customers as Groups of Buyers

A key issue in viewing customers as groups of buyers is their overall bargaining power. Powerful buyers can reduce industry profitability by forcing prices down or by demanding higher quality or more services. Buyers have a relatively large amount of power when factors such as the following are present:[14]

1. A buyer's purchases represent a large proportion of seller sales volume, as when General Motors buys from a small component-parts manufacturer.
2. The cost of switching to another seller is small.
3. Buyers represent a believable threat of backward integration, as do the major automobile manufacturers.

4. The seller's product has little impact on the quality of the buyer's product.

If these conditions interact to prevent a firm from achieving its objectives, the firm should try to change its bargaining position by altering one (or more) of the conditions or finding less powerful customers.

Customers as Markets

A group of customers with similar needs for similar products can be viewed as a market. As such, the customer market can be segmented, or divided, in a variety of ways—for instance on the basis of demographics, geography, psychographics, lifestyle, benefit desired, and behavioral characteristics. Note that markets can also be defined on the basis of products, such as the "market for convertible automobiles."

The Customer Profile

Firms should develop a **customer file** of present and prospective customers. The understanding gained from this profile and its development is an important fundamental guide for strategic planning, particularly in regard to marketing. Table 6.2 shows the key variables to consider.

SUPPLIERS

Business firms must also deal with the suppliers of various resources, such as materials and equipment, labor, and financing.

Vendors of Materials and Equipment

Powerful material and equipment suppliers can squeeze profits by raising prices, reducing the quality of products, or reducing the level of services. The conditions that make a supplier group powerful are similar to those that make buyers powerful: few suppliers, no substitutes, and suppliers who offer differentiated products.[15] For example, Nutra-Sweet, a division of Monsanto Company, now holds the patent for aspartame and is in a very strong position until its patent expires in 1991. If the presence of these conditions fosters powerful suppliers, the buying firm can seek to improve its position by influencing one or more of the conditions. It might threaten to integrate vertically by buying its own supplier, or perhaps obtain an exclusive license.

TABLE 6.2 · Customer Profile Considerations

Variable	Typical Breakdowns
GEOGRAPHIC	
Region	Pacific, Mountain, West North Central, West South Central, East North Central, East South Central, South Atlantic, Middle Atlantic, New England
County size	A, B, C, D
City or SMSA size	Under 5,000; 5,000–20,000; 20,000–50,000; 50,000–100,000; 100,000–250,000; 250,000–500,000; 500,000–1,000,000; 1,000,000–4,000,000; 4,000,000 or over
Density	Urban, suburban, rural
Climate	Northern, southern
DEMOGRAPHIC	
Age	Under 6, 6–11, 12–19, 20–34, 35–49, 50–64, 65+
Sex	Male, female
Family size	1–2, 3–4, 5+
Family life cycle	Young, single; young, married, no children; young, married, youngest child under 6; young, married, youngest child 6 or over; older, married, with children; older, married, no children under 18; older, single; other
Income	Under $2,500; $2,500–$5,000; $5,000–$7,500; $7,500–$10,000; $10,000–$15,000; $15,000–$20,000; $20,000–$30,000; $30,000–$50,000; $50,000 and over
Occupation	Professional and technical; managers, officials, and proprietors; clerical, sales; craftsmen, foremen; operatives; farmers; retired; students; housewives; unemployed
Education	Grade school or less; some high school; high school graduate; some college; college graduate
Religion	Catholic, Protestant, Jewish, other
Race	White, black, Oriental
Nationality	American, British, French, German, Scandinavian, Italian, Latin American, Middle Eastern, Japanese
PSYCHOGRAPHIC	
Social class	Lower lowers, upper lowers, lower middles, upper middles, lower uppers, upper uppers
Lifestyle	Straights, swingers, longhairs
Personality	Compulsive, gregarious, authoritarian, ambitious
BEHAVIORAL	
Use occasion	Regular occasion, special occasion
Benefits sought	Quality, service, economy
User status	Nonuser, ex-user, potential user, first-time user, regular user
Usage rate	Light user, medium user, heavy user
Loyalty status	None, medium, strong, absolute
Readiness stage	Unaware, aware, informed, interested, desirous, intending to buy
Attitude toward product	Enthusiastic, positive, indifferent, negative, hostile

Source: From Philip Kotler, *Marketing Management: Analysis, Planning and Control,* 5th ed. © 1984, p. 256. Reprinted by permission of Prentice-Hall, Inc., Englewood Cliffs, N.J.

Selection of suppliers should be based on vendor analysis. Each potential supplier should be analyzed on the factors considered important to the individual firm. Records of vendors' past performance are also valuable.

These performance descriptions should at least summarize ordering/receiving discrepancies regarding content and dates, terms of sale, and any extenuating circumstance that has affected the supplier.

Financial Community

Most firms, including profitable ones, must at some point acquire temporary cash resources from the financial community. These cash resources can be acquired through short-term or long-term borrowing or issuance of stock. A firm should focus its analysis of the financial community primarily on determining its standing with the various members of that community. Basic questions such as the following must be addressed:[16]

1. Is the firm's stock fairly valued?
2. Do potential creditors perceive the firm to have an acceptable record of paying debts? A strong working capital position?
3. Are creditors' current loan terms compatible with the firm's profitability objectives?
4. Are creditors able to extend the necessary line of credit?

Labor Supply

The supply of labor, too, is a key part of a firm's task environment. The ability to attract and hold capable employees is a prerequisite for a successful firm. Key factors to assess include the total labor pool (including its skill level and trainability), the firm's relative attractiveness as an employer, and the prevailing wage rates.

Organized labor unions also play a significant role in a firm's task environment. The specific nature of the relationship between the firm and relevant unions as suppliers of labor can have a large impact on the firm's ability to achieve its objectives. An adversarial relationship would likely have a negative influence.

POTENTIAL ENTRANTS

New entrants into an industry can reduce profitability by bringing in new capacity, the desire to gain market share, and substantial resources. Note that acquisition in an industry with the intention of building market share essentially represents a new entrant.

Although firms do not regularly deal with potential entrants, the threat of entry into an industry both influences and is influenced by a firm's strategy. Among other things, defending a competitive position involves maintaining legitimate barriers to entry. These barriers include large economies of scale, product differentiation, large financial requirements, high product switching costs, limited access to viable channels of distribution, and cost advantages not replicable by potential entrants (for example, proprietary technology and favorable access to raw materials). Another entry barrier arises when potential entrants expect stiff retaliation from entrenched firms. Xerox and General Electric found that the barriers to entry in the mainframe computer industry have been scale economies in production, research, marketing, and service.[17]

SUBSTITUTES

Pressure from substitute products limits an industry's profit potential by placing a ceiling on prices. Firms that ignore potential substitutes can find themselves left with very small markets, as has happened to manufacturers of pinball machines, who ignored the boom in video arcade games. Thus companies should continually search for and examine potential substitutes.

Most new substitute products are the result of the continuing technological explosion. Firms that intend to be successful must devote attention and resources to developing new technology and integrating it into their strategies.

GLOBAL DIMENSIONS

The discussion of the task environment as it relates to the international dimension is structured around domestic and global operations.

Firms with Only Domestic Operations

Each of the components of the task environment can be influenced by international environmental factors. Many U.S. markets now include foreign competitors, some of them quite strong. The automobile market, for example, contains Nissan Toyota, Hyundai, and others.

A firm with only domestic markets obviously does not have to be directly concerned with foreign customers. However, many such firms must consider *potential* foreign customers, particularly when growth opportunities in the United States are limited.

For firms lacking direct involvement with foreign suppliers, such suppliers, again, are not a major consideration. But foreign suppliers must be taken into account as *potential* suppliers, particularly when cost advantages are possible. The same factor applies to the possibility of establishing foreign production facilities in the future.

Potential substitute products can come from any type of company, including a foreign company. Consequently, innovative foreign companies in similar fields should be monitored for product developments and strategy possibilities.

Potential entrants can also come from foreign countries. Many makers of small computers, for example, have been somewhat anxiously awaiting the entry of Japanese manufacturers into the personal computer market.

Firms with Global Operations

International involvement of any kind also calls for consideration of the task environment of that country. Table 6.3 indicates the differences between the United States and international macro- and task environments.

Firms seeking foreign markets must consider the following factors:

- *Competition:* U.S. firms doing business abroad encounter competition from other global firms, large national firms of the target country, and a host of small competitors.
- *Customers:* Customers from different cultures often pose cross-cultural problems. If foreign intermediaries must be used, they, too, can present a unique set of problems, such as ties with complex, multilayered channels of distribution.
- *Suppliers:* Although the U.S. firm may export its goods, local supplies of various types must often be purchased. In addition, distribution channels in foreign countries may be quite complex.
- *Substitute products:* Local alternatives to U.S. products often present formidable competition. McDonald's, for example, competes against a host of street vendors in many countries.
- *Potential entrants:* Even firms successfully established in foreign countries face potential competition from other global firms, which are attracted by the opportunities for profit.

Firms seeking foreign suppliers must also analyze the task environment, but from a different perspective than those seeking markets. Since the purchasing firm is interested in continuous supply, the relevant task environment factors are those that influence the supplying firm's ability to survive and compete successfully in the long run.

TABLE 6.3 · Differences Between U.S. and Multinational Operations That Affect Strategic Management

Factor	U.S. Operations	International Operations
Language	English used almost universally	Local language must be used in many situations
Culture	Relatively homogeneous	Quite diverse, both between countries and within a country
Politics	Stable and relatively unimportant	Often volatile and of decisive importance
Economy	Relatively uniform	Wide variations among countries and between regions within countries
Government interference	Minimal and reasonably predictable	Extensive and subject to rapid change
Labor	Skilled labor available	Skilled labor often scarce, requiring training or redesign of production methods
Financing	Well-developed financial markets	Poorly developed financial markets; capital flows subject to government control
Market research	Data easy to collect	Data difficult and expensive to collect
Advertising	Many media available; few restrictions	Media limited; many restrictions; low literacy rates rule out print media in some countries
Money	U.S. dollar used universally	Must change from one currency to another; changing exchange rates and government restrictions are problems
Transportation/communication	Among the best in the world	Often inadequate
Control	Always a problem. Centralized control will work	A worse problem; centralized control won't work; must walk a tightrope between overcentralizing and losing control through too much decentralizing
Contracts	Once signed, are binding on both parties, even if one party makes a bad deal	Can be voided and renegotiated if one party becomes dissatisfied
Labor relations	Collective bargaining; can lay off workers easily	Often cannot lay off workers; may have mandatory worker participation in management; workers may seek change through political process rather than collective bargaining
Trade barriers	Nonexistent	Extensive and very important

Source: From R. G. Murdick, R. C. Moor, R. H. Eckhouse, and T. W. Zimmerer, *Business Policy: A Framework for Analysis*, 4th ed., p. 275. Copyright © 1984 by Grid Publishing Company. Reprinted by permission of Grid Publishing Company, 5701 N. High St., Worthington, Ohio 43085.

Firms seeking to establish production facilities abroad should also examine selected task environment factors. The most critical of these factors will generally be the availability of sufficient supplies of raw materials and necessary equipment.

The changes in Eastern Europe and the Soviet Union have dramatically altered the task environment for many firms. Many Eastern European customers, for example, have not had the ability or opportunity to buy Western products, which may unleash a wave of pent-up demand. Besides, many Eastern European firms may soon enter markets in other areas of the world. These changes put U.S. companies in a predicament: so little is known about these potential customers or firms that it is difficult to take action. U.S. strategists need to start studying the new prospects immediately.

Notes

1. Adapted/reprinted with permission of The Free Press, a division of Macmillan, Inc. from *Competitive Strategy: Techniques for Analyzing Industries and Competitors* by Michael E. Porter. Copyright © 1980 by The Free Press.
2. Ibid., ch. 7.
3. Ibid., pp. 164–183.
4. This section is drawn from Porter, chs. 9–13.
5. William A. Cohen, *The Practice of Marketing Management* (New York: Macmillan Publishing Company, 1988), pp. 137–138.
6. Porter, pp. 3–33.
7. Ibid., pp. 18–19.
8. Ibid., pp. 51–53.
9. Ibid., pp. 53–56.
10. Ibid., pp. 56–57.
11. Ibid., pp. 59–60.
12. Ibid., pp. 64–65.
13. "Social Changes Provide Valuable Clues to Consumer Behavior in the Marketplace," *Marketing News*, March 2, 1984, p. 21.
14. Porter, p. 25.
15. Ibid., p. 27.
16. John A. Pearce II and Richard B. Robinson, Jr., *Strategic Management* (Homewood, Ill.: Irwin, 1982), p. 112.
17. Porter, pp. 7–11.

CHAPTER 7

Internal Environment

A firm's internal environment consists of all elements and systems that exist within the firm. Firms should attempt to determine their capabilities, strengths and weaknesses, and advantages and vulnerabilities by carefully analyzing these internal factors. Steps can then be taken to reduce any weaknesses and deploy available strengths to the best possible advantage. Internal factors can be viewed in several ways. We first discuss briefly, from a functional perspective, the functional areas of human resources, research and development, production, finance and accounting, and marketing. Then we consider internal factors from a value chain perspective. We also examine critical managerial and organizational factors.

One view of the internal situation assumes that the survival of a firm ultimately depends upon its ability to obtain resources from the external environment. The major resources that the firm requires for survival include cash, people, and material. Each of the firm's functional areas is responsible for either obtaining or conserving one or more of these resources for the firm. Since the desired resources are possessed by various external groups, each functional area normally specializes in dealing with one or more of these external groups by serving as "linking pins" between them and the firm. Marketing, for example, is responsible for fostering positive relationships with consumers, thereby helping the firm acquire cash resources. The financial function is also responsible for acquiring cash, but from stockholder and lender groups.[1]

CRITICAL SUCCESS FACTORS

The driving forces and key success factors for an industry were discussed in Chapter 6. The concepts of **driving forces** and **critical success factors** (CSF) are also relevant for individual firms. Michel Robert contends that a driving force is what gives an organization its momentum in a certain direction. This momentum should be focused on CSFs, which are the limited number of areas where satisfactory results are needed to ensure performance. Opportunities tend to be evaluated in relation to how well they fit in with the firm's driving forces and CSFs.

Robert suggests that every firm contains the same basic important strategic areas and that one or a few of these areas should serve as the firm's primary driving force. Furthermore, the firm should develop a corresponding *area of excellence* for its primary driving force. This effort forms the basis for the firm's fundamental strategy.[2] Eight of these driving forces are

1. A *product/service-driven firm* uses a "product concept" as the basis for future product-related decisions. Such firms maintain their competitive advantage by cultivating excellence in product quality, product development, and/or customer service. Federal Express is an example of such a firm.

2. A *market/customer class-driven firm* anchors to a market type or category or to a class of customers. Required areas of excellence include obtaining and interpreting market or user research and building customer loyalty. (See Perspective 7.1.) Wal-Mart exemplifies this type of firm.

3. A *production capacity/capability-driven firm* has a substantial investment in its production facility and emphasizes "keeping it running." Key areas of excellence include manufacturing or plant efficiency and substitute marketing (that is, substituting the firm's product, such as paper, for plastic).

4. A *technology-driven firm* focuses on the ability to develop or obtain technology that can be translated into commercial applications. Technology research and applications marketing are important areas of excellence for these firms, for example, Minolta.

5. A *sales/marketing method-driven firm* emphasizes the technique or approach used to sell or market the product (for instance, Mary Kay Cosmetics, Avon). The areas of excellence required to win are recruiting and training.

6. A *distribution method-driven firm* focuses on a unique way of getting the product or service to the customer. The primary areas of excellence involve having the most effective channel of distribution and channel efficiency. L. L. Bean is such a firm.

7. A *natural resource-driven firm* depends on access to or pursuit of natural resources. Success with this strategy involves excellence at exploration, such as for mining companies and oil firms like Exxon.

8. A *size/growth-driven firm* or a *profit/return-driven firm* focuses on increasing the size or profits, respectively. Both of these strategies require excellence in portfolio management and information systems. Sara Lee is such a firm.

PERSPECTIVE 7.1

BMW's Hands-On Approach

BMW's 1989 worldwide auto sales topped $16 billion. Sales in the United States, however, decreased to 65,000 units, which was 33 percent lower than its peak in 1986. This slide can be attributed to changes in tax laws that restricted auto loan deductions, as well as higher prices resulting from the strong West German mark. In addition, new Japanese car models are competing at the lower end of the luxury market, and cars selling under $30,000 account for one-third of BMW's sales in the United States.

While BMW North America hopes that two new models priced around $20,000 will attract younger customers, the company is pushing a new strategy for its 400 dealers. BMW has discovered that local advertising and promotion can be more effective than a national strategy because local dealers can pinpoint their individual market's needs. Thus the new strategy focuses on a more active approach that will get dealers out of their showrooms.

The strategy was presented first at sales conferences held in late 1989. Dealers were advised to try some of the following:

- To make "cold" calls to potential buyers
- To search out more well-to-do customers, including less obvious choices, such as local building contractors
- To take cars to customers' homes and offices for test drives, thus saving potential buyers' time
- To plan local promotional events
- To organize direct-mail advertising and promotional campaigns

Follow-up manuals on how to find new customers have been sent to dealers. BMW has also targeted conventions and other gatherings as good places to scout out buyers. For example, the company sent salespeople and sample cars to a convention for private airplane owners. One dealer has sent promotional videotapes to potential buyers and then dropped off cars for them to try for a short time; he even has been known to negotiate deals with a fax.

References: Bruce Hager and John Templeman, "Now, They're Selling BMWs Door-to-Door—Almost," *Business Week,* May 14, 1990, p. 65; J. Henry, "BMW Disbands Dealer Advertising Groups," *Automotive News,* January 8, 1990, p. 3; William Baldwin and Peter Fuhrman, "The Company Behind the Image," *Forbes,* November 27, 1989, p. 89.

These driving forces help to articulate the overall business concept of the organization and to limit the scope of products and markets served.

Driving forces vary from industry to industry. Furthermore, firms within the same industry can choose to compete in different ways, thereby utilizing a different combination of driving forces and CSFs. Internal CSFs must be compatible with the industry driving forces and provide the firm with a reasonable chance for success.

Pinpointing the internal CSFs is based on a thorough analysis of the internal environment, with specific attention focused on the firm's *strategic skills pool*— the skills possessed by a firm that can be used to create a meaningful strategic advantage or to "beat the competition." A broad three-step process can facilitate this analysis. First, identifying strategic skills pools involves separating the skills that can yield a competitive advantage from those that represent the minimum requirements to compete. Second, strategic skills pools should be developed at all levels of the company, with specific attention to emerging skills and competitive skills. Third, strategic skills pools should be monitored regarding the financial support devoted to acquiring, developing, and maintaining the pool.

INTERNAL FUNCTIONS

Planners can develop a better understanding of the firm's internal situation by analyzing key internal functions to determine strengths and weaknesses. Table 7.1 lists these functions and provides examples of the major factors within them.

Human Resource Factors

Human resources are especially critical to a firm's success. People provide the input for setting objectives, analyzing the environmental situation, and selecting, implementing, and controlling the firm's strategies. Regardless of the conceptual soundness of the overall planning system, it will not be effective without effective personnel.

Unfortunately, human resource factors are not always given adequate consideration in strategy selection. Many firms—for instance W. T. Grant—have pursued rapid growth strategies without ensuring that adequate human resources were "in the pipeline." Similarly to other resources, human resources must be acquired and allocated in such a way that the firm's objectives can be achieved.[3]

Research and Development Factors

The quality of a firm's research and development (R&D) efforts can keep it at the forefront of its industry (for example, Mercedes-Benz), or cause it to lag far behind industry leaders in areas such as new product development, product quality, cost control, and production technology. Good R&D is based on more than pure scientific skill or expertise. The R&D function must also constantly monitor the external environments for information on technological innovations in production processes, products, and materials. Efficient communication chan-

TABLE 7.1 · Key Internal Factors: Potential Strengths and Weaknesses

MARKETING

Firm's products/services; breadth of product line
Concentration of sales in a few products or to a few customers
Ability to gather needed information about markets
Market share or submarket shares
Product/service mix and expansion potential: life cycle of key products; profit/sales
    balance in product/service
Channels of distribution: number, coverage, and control
Effective sales organization; knowledge of customer needs
Product/service image, reputation, and quality
Imaginative, efficient, and effective sales promotion and advertising
Pricing strategy and pricing flexibility
Procedures for digesting market feedback and developing new product, services, or
    markets
After sale service and follow-up
Goodwill/brand loyalty

FINANCE AND ACCOUNTING

Ability to raise short-term capital
Ability to raise long-term capital: debt/equity
Corporate-level resources (multibusiness firm)
Cost of capital relative to industry and competitors
Tax considerations
Relations with owners, investors, and stockholders
Leverage position: capacity to utilize alternative financial strategies such as lease or
    sale and lease back
Cost of entry and barriers to entry
Price-earnings ratio
Working capital; flexibility of capital structure
Effective cost control; ability to reduce cost
Financial size
Efficient and effective accounting system for cost, budget, and profit planning

PRODUCTION/OPERATIONS/TECHNICAL

Raw materials cost and availability; supplier relationships
Inventory control systems; inventory turnover
Location of facilities; layout and utilization of facilities
Economies of scale
Technical efficiency of facilities and utilization of capacity
Effective use of subcontracting
Degree of vertical integration; value added and profit margin
Efficiency and cost/benefit of equipment
Effective operation control procedures; design, scheduling, purchasing, quality control,
    and efficiency

TABLE 7.1   (*continued*)

Costs and technological competencies relative to industry and competitors
Research and development/technology/innovation
Patents, trademarks, and similar legal protection

PERSONNEL

Management personnel
Employees' skill and morale
Labor relations costs compared to industry and competition
Efficient and effective personnel policies
Effective use of incentives to motivate performance
Ability to level peaks and valleys of employment
Employee turnover and absenteeism
Specialized skills
Experience

ORGANIZATION AND GENERAL MANAGEMENT

Organizational structure
Firm's image and prestige
Firm's record for achieving objectives
Organization of communication system
Overall organizational control system (effectiveness and utilization)
Organizational climate; culture
Use of systematic procedures and techniques in decision making
Top management skill, capabilities, and interest
Strategic planning system
Intraorganizational synergy (multibusiness firms)

Source: From John A. Pearce II and Richard D. Robinson, Jr., *Strategic Management*, 2nd ed., pp. 186–187. © Richard D. Irwin, Inc. Reprinted by permission of the publisher.

---

nels between R&D and other functional areas, particularly marketing, are critical to the firm's success.

Production Factors

Production is the segment of a company concerned with the creation of products and services. As one of the major functional areas of a business, it has a strong influence both on a firm's overall ability to succeed and on each of the other functional areas.

Consider the positive influences of a production department that delivers relatively high-quality products and services at relatively low cost. The marketing function benefits because good-quality products and services that can be priced relatively low are easier to market. The burden on the financial function is eased when efficient production capabilities help conserve financial resources. Production can also have a major influence on the human resources function by enhancing morale. Conversely, a weak production function may deliver products that will not sell; it may also become an insurmountable financial drain, and alienate employees as well.

Finance and Accounting Factors

The financial function involves the analysis, planning, and control of the financial performance and position of the firm. Smaller firms may employ one person to handle all financial matters and refer to this person as the accountant, bookkeeper, business manager, or finance manager. Larger firms may have a variety of departments, such as accounting, finance, office of the comptroller (or controller), treasury, audit staff, and planning.

The financial function's influence is pervasive in a firm. Financial considerations and the firm's overall objectives and strategy are intertwined because all plans and decisions involving the firm's financial resources must be analyzed from a financial perspective. All functional areas share in this responsibility, which generally leads to direct interaction between the financial function and other functional areas. Furthermore, the financial function provides all areas with a wide variety of information through the normal accounting or bookkeeping system.

As with the other areas, the financial function has major responsibilities in regard to resources. First, resource acquisition responsibilities normally involve the acquisition of cash. Second, control and disbursal of financial resources are typically financial responsibilities. Examples of specific financial and accounting factors that can yield strengths or weaknesses appear in Table 7.1. Financial information and analysis are discussed in the Appendix.

Marketing Factors

The marketing function involves the analysis, planning, implementation, and control of programs focused on creating and maintaining mutually beneficial exchanges and relationships with target customers. Thus the task of marketing management is generally viewed as regulating the level, timing, and character of demand in a way that will help the organization achieve its objectives.

Marketing management analyzes the needs, wants, perceptions, and preferences of target markets and formulates effective product, pricing, communication, and distribution strategies for these markets.

VALUE CHAIN ACTIVITIES

Another way to view a firm's internal situation is to examine the firm's activities that give value to its products and services. Value refers to how the ultimate consumer or user perceives the product or service relative to competitive offerings. **Value chain activities** refer to those activities required to design, produce, market, deliver, and support a product or service. Each firm exists in a large value chain composed of itself and other organizations, including suppliers, facilitating organizations, and members of the firm's channel of distribution. Each firm creates value through an interlocking chain of activities. These value-creating activities and their linkages often serve as the basis for the firm's competitive advantage.

Components of Value Chains

A firm's value chain consists of two major parts: primary activities and support functions.[4] Primary activities comprise five groups:

- *Inbound logistics* consists of those activities concerned with the receipt, storage, and distribution of the inputs or raw materials needed to produce the product/service. Examples include inbound transportation, materials han-
- *Operations* (or production/manufacturing) consists of those activities necessary to transform the input/raw materials into the final product or service, such as refining, distilling, machining, packaging, assembling, and testing.
- *Outbound logistics* consists of those activities concerned with the accumulation, storage, and distribution of the product to the customer, such as warehousing, materials handling, and transportation.
- *Marketing and sales* consist of those activities concerned with communicating with the customer, making the product/service attractive to the customer, and transferring title to the customer. Examples include advertising, selling, and pricing.
- *Service* consists of those activities concerned with maintaining or enhancing the value of a product/service and the firm's relationship with the customer, such as installation, training, and repair.

Essentially, the firm creates value by obtaining input, processing this input into a form attractive to customers, making it available to customers, and helping customers use the item.

Support functions can be viewed as the activities, systems, and resources needed to drive the functions. The major *support activities* are procurement, technology development, and human resource management; note that *each of the support activities is carried out for each of the primary activities* (see Table 7.2). Each support activity has a focal point, which varies for each relevant primary activity. Procurement activities, for example, can focus on arranging transportation for inbound logistics, acquiring machinery for operations, securing warehousing for outbound logistics, obtaining patent protection for marketing and sales, and obtaining additional franchisees for service.

Support systems can also be associated with each of the three support activities for any of the primary activities. As shown in Table 7.2, procurement-related systems, for example, can involve materials handling, quality control, delivery scheduling, order processing, and work/service order systems. Note also that other management or organization systems can focus on other activities and on resources.

Table 7.2 shows fifteen (three for each of the five primary activities) cells, or combinations of primary value chain activities and support functions. In addition

TABLE 7.2 · Examples of Value Chain Activities

Support Functions	Primary Activities				
	Inbound Logistics	Operations	Outbound Logistics	Marketing and Sales	Service
PROCUREMENT					
Activity	Transport	Machinery	Warehousing	Patents	Franchises
System	Materials handling	Quality control	Delivery scheduling	Order processing	Work/service orders
TECHNOLOGY DEVELOPMENT					
Activity	Materials handling technology	Process technology	Materials handling technology	Marketing information systems	Repair technology
System	The systems for technology development activities consist largely of processes focused on obtaining new ideas for how to do the primary activities.				
HUMAN RESOURCE MANAGEMENT					
Activity	Supplier relations	Morale	Subcontractor relations	Sales force productivity	Installation crew morale
System	Incentives for buyers	Maternity leaves	On-time incentives	Commission system	Vacation options

Source: Adapted from Michael E. Porter, *Competitive Advantage* (New York: The Free Press, 1985) ch. 2.

to analyzing the activities and systems in each cell, the strategist must also analyze the firm's resources allocated to each cell. The resources should be analyzed relative to their quantity, quality, and systems associated with them. Resources can be categorized as financial, human, and physical.

- Analysis of *financial resources* should focus on cash and working capital balances, cash and working capital management, capital structure, ability to obtain capital, relationships with suppliers of capital, and so on. The essential question for value chain analysis is, "Do those individuals responsible for the primary/support activity combinations have sufficient financial resources at their disposal to accomplish their tasks?"
- Analysis of *human resources* should focus on the numbers and types of skills available, the adaptability of skills, and so on. The essential question for value chain analysis is, "Do those individuals responsible for the primary/ support activity combinations have sufficient human resources at their disposal to accomplish their tasks?"
- Analysis of *physical resources* such as land, buildings, and equipment should focus on the availability, age, condition, capability, location, and so on. The essential question for value chain analysis is, "Do those individuals responsible for the primary/support activity combinations have sufficient physical resources at their disposal to accomplish their tasks?"

Besides analyzing tangible resources for each of the activity combinations, the strategist must also evaluate relevant external relationships to pinpoint "intangible resources." Examples include the firm's relationship with customers, suppliers, distributors, and other external groups. Note that certain more tangible items, such as contracts, patents, and copyrights, can also serve as valuable resources.

Resource Utilization

Part of resource analysis involves evaluating how resources are being utilized, particularly in regard to enhancing the value chain activities and the linkages between them. The use of resources in a particular manner in one primary activity can influence a different primary activity. Increased promotional activity, for example, could result in greater revenues. If not coordinated with all other primary components, however, it could skew the scheduling of inbound logistics, production, outbound logistics, and service (that is, installation scheduling) and increase the cost of operations.

Resource Efficiency   A key part of resource analysis involves evaluating resource efficiency, or how well resources are utilized. This evaluation focuses on "doing things right" as compared with "doing the right thing," which has to do with resource effectiveness. Common measures of resource efficiency include the following:[5]

- *Capacity utilization:* a measure of the degree of capacity being used (particularly important when fixed overhead is high)
- *Labor productivity:* a measure of how well human resources are being used
- *Profitability:* an overall measure of how well the firm is doing, and using its capital
- *Working capital:* a measure of how well the firm's financial resources are being used
- *Yield:* a measure of how well raw materials and/or energy are being converted into the finished product (particularly important when it represents a major part of cost)

Resource Effectiveness   As mentioned earlier, resource effectiveness involves the idea of "doing the right thing." The analyst wants to know if the right people are deployed to the right jobs, if working capital is allocated to the right activities, if marketing efforts are being focused in the right directions, and so on.

So far, few techniques have been developed to measure effectiveness. Often a relatively efficient firm discovers its lack of effectiveness only when it begins to fail. For example, the firm may be very efficient at producing products and services that are not wanted by customers, which indicates a lack of effectiveness. Obviously, this kind of company is very likely to fail. Unfortunately, such firms often work harder and harder at being more efficient rather than examining effectiveness.

MANAGEMENT CONSIDERATIONS

Management is one of the dominant influences in the internal environment and must be considered in strategic planning. Individual managers can be analyzed from a variety of perspectives, including personality, degree of concern for subordinates,[6] methods of exerting influence within their organization,[7] management preferences, and others. Managements' beliefs and management styles in the light of the strategic situation are of particular interest.

Management's Beliefs

In general, a belief can range from a casual endorsement of an idea to a deep, emotional conviction (or value). Through a learning process based on their experience, managers develop beliefs about a variety of subjects, including themselves, their colleagues, competitors, and strategic issues. These beliefs serve as filters to incoming information and also provide a context in which managers make strategic decisions. Since managers tend to prefer doing what they believe they do best, a strong chief executive officer may guide a firm toward his or her strength. In fact, some researchers feel that the plethora of mergers and acquisitions is directly related to CEO backgrounds in law and finance; the CEOs are doing what they do best, perhaps at the expense of fundamental development of their firms.[8]

Beliefs also influence managers' preferences for particular strategies.[9] Examples of beliefs regarding strategic objectives include these three:

- "We must grow in volume and ROI."
- "We must be measured against the best."
- "We want a dividend payout of x percent because we can make better use of the money than shareholders."

The following statements illustrate beliefs regarding product market strategy:

- "Don't diversify except where our technology can be applied."
- "We must not be dependent on one single product line."
- "We can manage in a range of industries."

Examples of beliefs regarding competitive strategy include these views:

- "Market share comes through technically superior products."
- "We much compete on innovation in processes and basic products, not price."
- "We must be a leader in manufacturing methods to keep costs down and quality up."

Management Style

Management style is relevant to both the strategic planning process and the strategic situation. In relation to strategic planning, Thomas P. Mullen and Stephen A. Stumpf offer the ISSUES model, which depicts six management styles representing unique approaches to organizing and interpreting information: (ISSUES is an acronym for the six styles.)[10]

- *Identifiers* tend to set agendas and list issues in an unbiased way, often solicit data from others, cluster specific strategic issues into broad groups, and scan all that may affect their business. They avoid risks. Essentially, they address the question "What are the key issues affecting our business?"
- *Sorters* tend to arrange issues by priority, concentrate on issues oriented toward action, focus on well-defined problems that can be forecast confidently. They are willing to take calculated risks and essentially address the question "What are the issues on which we can act?"

- *Selectors* tend to concentrate on issues affecting their specific business area, make decisions based on preferences, and prefer to make strategic plans on an individual basis. They address the question "Will this issue affect my area of the business?"
- *Unilateral discriminators* tend to identify issues relating to current or anticipated problems. They tend to be self-confident, impulsive, and "dominated" by their problems. The question that concerns them is "What issues solve my area's problem?"
- *Evolvers* Try to develop an overall understanding of all issues relating to the business and then develop an agenda. They appear passive and unorganized to coworkers, follow their intuition, and are insightful, original, and idealistic. They focus on the question "How does this issue fit with or relate to other issues?"
- *Searchers* tend to focus on gathering as much information as possible before establishing strategic planning goals. They are likely to be good investigators, good at interacting with others, and methodical and cooperative. They address the question "Can we get additional data on that before we proceed?"

The strategic situation faced by a company can influence the way decisions are made at the top of the organization. Competition is one of the key components of the strategic situation. Researchers have found that intense competition encourages more delegation and sharing of decisions, but that this participation tends to involve selected issues, depending on the specific situation. Furthermore, the participation comes with more controls, to ensure that the delegated decisions are made and carried out appropriately.[11]

Another potentially important issue to address involves the overall strategic stance, or posture, being taken by the firm. A small but increasing amount of evidence indicates that certain types of managers appear to be better suited for certain strategic stances.[12]

ORGANIZATIONAL CONSIDERATIONS

Evaluating the internal environment would not be complete without addressing the organization itself. Of the many possible factors, two categories are of interest—organizational style and organizational culture.

Organizational Style

The strategic planning process and outcomes can be influenced by organizational style. Although not all firms have an identifiable or consistent style, those which do merit evaluation by planners.

George Stiner, John B. Miner, and Edmund R. Gray discuss four organizational style alternatives, which revolve around the dominant orientation.[13]

1. *Power orientation* means a focus on dominating and controlling the environment and avoiding control by external stakeholders; insiders strive to use their power within the organization.
2. *Role orientation* means a focus on rationality, orderliness, legality, legitimacy, and responsibility.
3. *Task orientation* means a focus on achieving a superordinate goal and evaluating all functions and activities in terms of contribution to stated goals.
4. *Person orientation* means a focus on serving needs of the organization's members.

Understanding an organization's style as it relates to strategy issues is also potentially important because the style helps determine likely responses to environmental changes. Raymond E. Miles and Charles C. Snow describe four organizational styles and their related characteristics (see Table 7.3).[14]

Furthermore, an organization's style helps determine its reputation as a winner. *Fortune* publishes the results of an annual survey, which employs eight key attributes of reputation. These are the attributes and the 1990 "winners":[15]

- *Ability to attract, develop, and keep talented people:* Merck
- *Innovativeness:* Merck
- *Financial soundness:* Merck
- *Community and environmental responsibility:* Johnson & Johnson
- *Use of corporate assets:* Berkshire Hathaway
- *Value as a long-term investment:* Philip Morris
- *Quality of management:* Philip Morris
- *Quality of products or services:* Merck

Merck was the overall "winner."

Organizational Culture

A firm is a living organization; it is people who make the firm work and who form the culture that gives meaning and purpose to its activities. An organization's culture is the totality of its experience, personality, values, and atmosphere, which, combined, form "the way we get things done around here." Essentially, a firm's culture is its mechanism for interacting with environments.[16]

Every firm has an organizational culture, and this culture guides most of what goes on in the company.[17] It influences the way managers make decisions and how they view the firm's environments and strategies.[18]

TABLE 7.3 · A Set of Strategy-Related Organizational Styles

DEFENDERS

1. Narrow and stable product market domain
2. Tendency to ignore developments outside the domain
3. Growth dependent on ability to maintain prominence and achieve deeper penetration into market
4. Tendency to have a single core technology
5. Tendency to integrate vertically
6. Power held by financial and production experts
7. Tendency to have functional structure, extensive division of labor, a high degree of formalization, and centralized control

PROSPECTORS

1. Broad and continually developing domain
2. Major change agent in industry
3. Achieve by finding new markets and developing new products
4. Tendency to use multiple technologies
5. Tendency of marketing and research to form the dominant coalition
6. Tendency to have a product structure, low division of labor, low degree of formalization, and results-oriented controls

ANALYZERS

1. Domain mixed, with stability in some parts and change in others
2. Tendency to follow change
3. Use of extensive market surveillance mechanisms
4. Growth obtained through market penetration and product/market development
5. Concentration on a stable technological core, combined with emphasis on flexibility through intense applied research
6. Dominant coalition includes marketing, applied research, and production
7. Often have a matrix structure and both simple and complex control mechanisms

REACTORS

1. No viable organizational strategy, or
2. Established strategy not linked appropriately to technology, structure, and processes, or
3. Outmoded strategy/structure

Source: Adapted from Raymond E. Miles and Charles C. Snow, *Organizational Strategy, Structure, and Process.* Copyright © 1978 by McGraw-Hill, Inc. Reprinted by permission of the publisher, McGraw-Hill, Inc.

The culture can be a strength or a weakness. It can serve as a strength when it eases and economizes communications, facilitates organizational decision making and control, enhances strategic planning and implementation, and generates higher levels of cooperation and commitment in the company. It is a weakness when important shared beliefs and values interfere with the needs of the business, its strategy, and the people working on the company's behalf.[19] One K mart manager, for example, made the following statement about K mart's CEO: "There is no one to tell him things are going wrong. The culture here is to tell the chairman what he wants to hear."[20] Firms with strong, positive cultures have a much better chance of succeeding than those with weak or negative cultures.

Achieving a strong culture, which encourages employees to internalize positive attitudes and behavioral patterns, is critical for an organization. If the culture allows flexibility and encourages an external focus, the company can adapt more easily to environmental changes. One of the major responsibilities of managers is to shape an organization's values by directing employees' attention to those things that are important.[21]

A strong culture makes employees feel better about what they do, leading them to work harder to achieve organizational goals. A strong culture can also provide behavioral parameters, or a system of informal rules, that tell employees how to behave most of the time. Conversely, in a weak culture, employees waste time just trying to figure out what they should do and how to do it. According to T. Peters and R. Waterman, cultures in well-run companies show these traits:[22]

1. *A bias for action:* little formality, much flexibility
2. *Closeness to the customer:* adoption of the marketing concept and an obsession with quality, reliability, and/or service
3. *Autonomy and entrepreneurship:* encouragement of creativity and risk taking
4. *Productivity through people:* maintaining a trusting, positive atmosphere and free-flowing, two-way communications
5. *Hands-on, value-driven operations:* shaping values and the corporate culture
6. *Careful diversification:* staying away from unrelated businesses
7. *Simple form and lean staff:* stable organization structure and small staff
8. *Simultaneous loose-tight properties:* tight control of core values, but autonomy, entrepreneurship, and innovation pushed to lower levels

Components of Culture   There are several schemes for classifying the various components of an organization's culture. Terrence E. Deal and Allan A. Kennedy note four basic elements, management consultants McKinsey and Co. identify seven variables, and Stephen P. Robbins points out seven characteristics.

In the Deal and Kennedy scheme, the critical elements of organizational culture are values, heroes, rituals and ceremonies, and a cultural network.[23] Values are the fundamental concepts and beliefs that establish standards of achievement and success within the firm in concrete terms, such as "If you do this, you will be a success." *Core values*—the concepts and beliefs generally held by all members of the organization—form the heart of a firm's culture. *Secondary values* compromise the concepts and beliefs held by members of significant sub-cultures, such as the marketing department or the home appliance division. In a strong culture, secondary values are not in conflict with the firm's core values and can provide necessary support.

Individuals who personify the culture's values constitute its *heroes.* They serve as tangible role models for employees. Lee Iacocca of Chrysler, for instance, sets an example that pervades the organization. Employees also learn what kind of behavior is expected of them through *rituals and ceremonies*—the systematic and programmed routines of day-to-day life in the firm. Rituals are relatively routine manifestations that show employees the kind of behavior that is expected of them, such as special privileges. Ceremonies are extravaganzas providing visible and potent examples of what the firm stands for.

What transmits the firm's values and heroic mythology is the *cultural network*—the primary (but informal) means of communicating within a firm. This network is often the only effective way to get things done or to understand what is really going on.

McKinsey & Co. uses a different perspective of culture, comprising seven variables:[24]

1. *Staff:* what kind of people a firm has
2. *Style:* how managers and employees conduct themselves
3. *Skills:* what a firm knows how to do
4. *Systems:* what patterns of communication are used both inside the firm and outside
5. *Structure:* the firm's organizational design
6. *Shared values:* superordinate goals of the corporate culture
7. *Strategy:* plans

The key idea is that when there is a "goodness of fit" among these seven variables, corporate strategies are more easily implemented and corporate objectives are therefore more readily accomplished. (See Perspective 7.2.)

Robbins suggests seven different characteristics, which captures the essence of a culture:[25]

1. *Individual autonomy* given to employees
2. *Structure* relative to number of rules and regulations

Reebok: Set to Spring Back to the Top

Almost everyone has heard of Reeboks. In fact, market research done in the late 1980s indicated that Reebok was among the best-known brand names in the world. For a company that got its start about a decade ago, that kind of brand identity is proof of phenomenal success. Indeed, as of 1989, Reebok was the fastest-growing U.S. firm of all time.

It got that way because it found a niche no one else had: athletic shoes that were stylish as well as functional. The company's first big hit—and perennial big-seller—was the Free-style aerobic shoe. The shoe had a sturdy rubber sole that could stand up to heavy exercise, yet it also had a stylish, comfortable upper that appealed to the fashion-conscious. Early on, Reebok figured out what the company now calls the "80-20 rule": 80 percent of athletic shoes are not worn for athletic pursuits. People tend to buy them for comfort shoes.

As Reebok grew, so did the athletic shoe market. Between 1986 and 1989, it increased 45 percent, with sales around $10 billion retail. More than one-third of all shoes sold in the United States are athletic shoes, which translates, by one count, to 377 million pairs. The profit margins are enormous: even the biggest-ticket shoes may have manufacturing costs less than $30 per pair. Clearly, the stakes are high for maintaining market share.

In the last few years, Reebok has faced an increasing challenge from Nike. In 1989, Ree-bok's profits increased by 28 percent—certainly a sizable growth—but Nike's increased 40 percent, carrying it to the number-one spot in the athletic shoe industry.

What happened? Analysts point to several things. Reebok has the reputation of being more of a fashion shoe company than Nike, which has always stressed performance. And the fashion world is fickle. For that matter, so is the athletic shoe industry. (Remember Adidas?) Right now there seems to be more of an interest in performance than in fashion, regardless of the 80-20 rule. Also, some believe that the athletic shoe market has reached saturation.

Reebok has also had some problems with its advertising campaigns. Its expensive "UBU" campaign, for example, seemed to confuse more than inspire, and it ran head to head with Nike's successful "Doing It" campaign, which stressed performance.

At the same time, Reebok had undergone some management changes. Founder Paul B. Fireman had always emphasized a "gung-ho culture," encouraging managers to make regular visits to retailers to consult on styles. But after Fireman handed over the reins to a new president, retailers began to complain that it was hard to get in touch with the company.

Fireman admits that the company was "getting stale." So, in late 1989 he took back day-to-day control of the company, ousting the president. He also reorganized Reebok's shoe lines—Reebok, Rockport, and Avia—into separate divisions that report directly to him. In a related move, in March 1990 he promoted John Duerden to president of the reorganized Reebok division. Duerden is re-emphasizing the need for managers to stay in touch with retailers, encouraging them to spend three days a week in stores. Already the company has displayed greater flexibility in such things as changing order, runs of certain sizes, and delivery. In addition, Reebok has switched ad agencies, in the hopes of developing a successful campaign that will put the spring back in the "gung-ho" company's step.

References: Laura Jereski, "Can Paul Fireman Put the Bounce Back in Reebok?" *Business Week,* June 18, 1990, pp. 181–182; P. Sloan, "Reebok Chief Looks Beyond Nike," *Advertising Age,* January 29, 1990, p. 16ff; Bernice Kanner, "Reebok on the Rebound," *New York,* October 16, 1989, pp. 26, 28; John Sedgwick, "Treading on Air: Dumb Luck and Marketing Dazzle Made Reebok the Hot Company of the '80s," *Business Month,* January 1989, p. 28ff.

3. *Support* given by managers to subordinates
4. *Identification* with organization rather than with individual work groups
5. *Performance-reward* relationship
6. *Conflict tolerance,* or willingness to be open about differences
7. *Risk tolerance,* or degree to which employees are encouraged to be aggressive and innovative

Although each of these perspectives seems different, close examination should also reveal great similarities. One thread that runs through each is the trust between management and employees. Heroes, for example, are trusted to do the right thing and firms that give autonomy trust employees. Another thread which is that of the individual striving to make the organization better by supporting organizational goals, even when other goals might fit the person better.

Strength of Culture   The strength of an organization's culture influences its members' degree of compliance. This strength is a composite of three factors: thickness, extent of sharing, and clarity of ordering.[26]

The number of important shared assumptions determines the *thickness* of a culture. *Thick* cultures have many shared assumptions, whereas *thin* cultures have few. Thick cultures tend to have a greater influence on organizational life.

The *extent of sharing* refers to the degree to which important assumptions are shared. Cultures with widely shared assumptions, beliefs, and values tend to have a greater impact on the organization.

Clarity of ordering refers to the level of ambiguity associated with the priority of key beliefs and values. Cultures with a high degree of clarity of ordering tend to have a greater impact than those with low levels of clarity of ordering.

In summary, the intensity of a culture's influence on organizational behavior depends largely on the culture's strength. Stronger cultures are thicker, more widely shared, and more clearly ordered. As a result, they have a stronger influence on organizational behavior. This influence can be a strength or a weakness, depending on the culture's compatibility with the stated strategies.

Influence of Culture   Culture can influence the basic processes that constitute a company's foundation.[27] First, it influences the degree of true *cooperation* in the firm. Cooperation cannot be mandated; it must arise from mutual trust and good will.

Second, *decision-making* is influenced because the culture provides a consistent set of basic assumptions and preferences. Fewer disagreements arise over which assumptions and premises should prevail in the decision-making process.

Third, *control* is affected by the **clan mechanism**—that is, a strong reference group for members—which provides a "compass" that members rely on to choose appropriate courses of action. Most firms also have formal procedures to guide action, including rules, guidelines, budgets, and directives. The clan mechanism tends to be highly efficient, but can lose its effectiveness when the "clan" does not support adjustments necessary to meet new environmental conditions.

Fourth, culture can enhance *communications* by reducing miscommunications in two ways. Matters for which shared assumptions already exist do not need to be communicated, and such assumptions provide guidelines to help interpret messages.

Fifth, a strong culture fosters identification and feelings, which serve as the basis for *commitment*. Committed employees typically need less direction and are likely to do whatever it takes to get the job done for the organization.

Culture has several other major implications for strategy.[28] First, harmony between corporate culture and corporate strategy is critical. Second, multibusiness firms should attempt to capitalize on their strong subcultures by acquiring compatible businesses and divesting those that are not compatible. Third, autonomous divisions can be established to capitalize on strong existing subcultures or to encourage the development of unique subcultures. Fourth, the concept of mobility or flexibility should be nourished as a desirable core value. Fifth, a well-defined set of core values should be established. Sixth, culture plays a major role in all aspects of strategic management, particularly those aspects that involve changes (for example, implementation).

Ralph H. Kilmann, Marry J. Saxton, and Roy Serpa suggest that these five basic questions can help in evaluating a firm's culture:[29]

1. *What is the impact of culture on the organization's ability to carry out its activities and plans?* Both direction (positive or negative) and strength are relevant.

2. *How deep-seated is the culture?* Deep-seated cultures are difficult to change and can foster resistance to change.

3. *How many cultures does the organization have?* Different cultures or subcultures can exist in different divisions, functional departments, new acquisitions, and so on. Although a culture can have a number of different "flavors," diverse cultures without an overriding common theme tend to be negative.

4. *How changeable is the culture?* This answer depends largely on the answers to the first three questions. In addition, the degree and type of reinforcement offered by top management is also relevant

5. *Can culture alone be changed?* Generally, no. Organizational structure, reward systems, work procedures, knowledge, skills, attitudes and so on may also have to be changed to give new strategies a chance.

In conclusion, the culture of an organization is an important internal consideration. Although the concept is difficult to understand perfectly, it is an important part of the internal situation of all organizations and can affect an organization either positively or negatively.

GLOBAL DIMENSIONS

A firm seeking foreign markets must consider certain internal environmental factors, for instance, whether its management and marketing skills are transferable, what business skills local management candidates are likely to have, and whether the firm can finance expansion. In seeking foreign supply, a company must consider its purchasing ability. A company seeking to establish foreign production facilities must evaluate its management skills and ability to deal with unusual production situations.

Notes

1. Paul F. Anderson, "Marketing, Strategic Planning and the Theory of the Firm," *Journal of Marketing* (Spring 1982), 15–26.

2. Michel Robert, *The Strategist CEO* (New York: Quorum Books, 1988), chs. 6 and 7.

3. Stella M. Nkomo, "Strategic Planning for Human Resources—Let's Get Started," *Long Range Planning* (February 1988), 66–72.

4. Michael E. Porter, *Competitive Advantage*, (New York: The Free Press, 1985), ch. 2.

5. Gerry Johnson, Kevan Scholes, and Robert W. Sexty, *Exploring Strategic Management* (Scarborough, Ont.: Prentice-Hall Canada, 1989), pp. 108–109.

6. R. H. George Field, "A Test of the Vroom-Yetton Normative Model of Leadership," *Journal of Applied Psychology* (October 1982).

7. David Kipnis and Stuart M. Schmidt,

"An Influence Perspective on Bargaining Within Organizations," in *Negotiating in Organizations*, ed. Max H. Bazerman and Roy J. Lewicki (Beverly Hills, Calif.: Sage, 1983), p. 307.

8. Robert H. Hayes and William J. Abernathy, "Managing Our Way to Economic Decline," *Harvard Business Review* (July-August 1980), 67–77.

9. Gordon Donaldson and Jay W. Lorsch, *Decision Making at the Top* (New York: Basic Books, 1983), p. 7.

10. Thomas P. Mullen and Stephen A. Stumpf, "The Effect of Management Styles on Strategic Planning," Journal of Business Strategy (Winter 1987), 60–75.

11. Pradip N. Khandwalla, "Effect of Competition on the Structure of Top Management Control," *Academy of Management Journal* (June 1973), 282–295; Pradip N. Khandwalla, "Properties of Competing Organizations," in *Handbook of Organizational Design*, ed. Paul C. Nystrom and William H. Starbuck (Oxford: Oxford University Press, 1981), I, pp. 79–85.

12. Anil K. Gupta and V. Govindarajan, "Business Unit Strategy, Managerial Characteristics, and Business Unit Effectiveness at Strategy Implementation," *Academic of Management Journal* (March 1984); Danny Miller, Manfred F. R. Kets de Vries, and Jean-Marie Toulouse, "Top Executive Locus of Control and Its Relationship to Strategy-Making, Structure, and Environment," *Academy of Management Journal* (June 1982); Marc Gerstein and Heather Reisman, "Strategic Selection: Matching Executives to Business Conditions," *Sloan Management Review* (Winter 1983).

13. George Steiner, John B. Miner, and Edmund R. Gray, *Management Policy and Strategy*, 3rd ed. (New York: Macmillan, 1986), p. 62.

14. Raymond E. Miles and Charles C. Snow, *Organizational Strategy, Structure, and Process*, (New York: McGraw-Hill), 1978, pp. 37–82.

15. "Leaders of the Most Admired," *Fortune*, January 29, 1990, pp. 40–54.

16. Terrence E. Deal and Allan A. Kennedy, *Corporate Cultures* (Reading, Mass.: Addison-Wesley, 1982), p. 4.

17. Ralph H. Kilmann, Mary J. Saxton, and Roy Serpa, "Issues in Understanding and Changing Culture," *California Management Review* (Winter 1986), 87–93.

18. Jay W. Lorsch, "Managing Culture: The Invisible Barrier to Strategic Change," *California Management Review* (Winter 1986), 95–109.

19. Vijay Sathe, *Culture and Related Corporate Realities*, (Homewood, Ill.: Irwin), 1985.

20. Fay Rice, "Why K mart Has Stalled," *Fortune*, October 9, 1989, p. 79.

21. Tom Peters and Nancy Austin, "A Passion for Excellence," *Fortune*, May 13, 1985, pp. 20–32.

22. T. Peters and R. Waterman, *In Search of Excellence*, (New York: Harper and Row, 1982), chs. 5 through 12.

23. Deal and Kennedy, pp. 14–15.

24. Robert H. Waterman, Jr., "The Seven Elements of Strategic Fit," *Journal of Business Strategy* (Winter 1982), 70.

25. Stephen P. Robbins, *Essentials of Organizational Behavior* (Englewood Cliffs, N.J.: Prentice-Hall, 1984), p. 171.

26. Sathe.

27. Ibid.

28. R. Deshpande and A. Parasuraman, "Linking Corporate Culture to Strategic Planning," *Business Horizons* (May-June 1986), 22–30.

29. Ralph H. Kilmann, Marry J. Saxton, and Roy Serpa, *Gaining Control of the Corporate Culture*, (San Francisco: Jossey-Bass, 1985), pp. 4–5.

Environmental Issue Management

The previous three chapters examined three environmental categories. This chapter describes the systems and methods that a firm should use in monitoring those environments. Whereas Chapters 5 through 7 focused on the areas that should be monitored, Chapter 8 explains how to do the monitoring, and Chapter 9 shows how to analyze the information collected.

The environments must be monitored from two perspectives. The first involves determining the situation as it presently exists, and the second, projecting what the situation is likely to be in the future. Peter F. Drucker summarizes this concept as follows:

> All institutions live and perform in two time periods: today and tomorrow. Tomorrow is being made today—irrevocably in most cases. In turbulent times managers cannot assume that tomorrow will be an extension of today. On the contrary, they must manage for change—as an opportunity and change as a threat.[1]

This quotation highlights the need to manage more than just internal factors and more than just in the present time frame.

Environmental issue management refers broadly to information management issues such as management information systems, decision support systems, environmental scanning and monitoring, and environmental management.

INFORMATION MANAGEMENT APPROACHES

Managers can make better decisions if they have the appropriate information. Effective strategic management requires that different types of information from a wide variety of sources be assembled and organized. These assembling and organizing activities are called *information management*. Information management bridges the gap between the firm's environments and its strategic management activities. Its role is to provide managers with the input needed to formulate effective strategies, and it can play a large part in creating a competitive advantage.[2] Note also that information management is based on effective utilization of information technology, which is one of the most dynamic segments of the environment.[3]

Information management can be somewhat confusing because of terminology such as management information systems, decision support systems, and environmental scanning. Each of these concepts is different and should be melded into an integrated system of information management.

A **management information system (MIS)** is a formal, typically computer-based system, intended to retrieve, extract, and integrate data from various sources in order to provide timely information for managerial decision making.[4] From a slightly different perspective, an MIS is a set of well-defined rules, practices, and procedures by which people, equipment, or both gather and analyze data to generate information needed by decision makers.[5] The best information systems are simple, deliver information to those who need it, and deliver information in a usable form.[6]

An effective MIS can help support and shape an organization's strategy and "lubricate" the overall strategic planning process.[7] MISs have proven successful in storing large quantities of detailed data and in providing information for the decisions that can be anticipated, such as relatively structured and routine decisions. They typically provide management with summary and exception reports. Exception reports contain information only about factors that are abnormal or "out of line." They can be formulated to serve a major environmental scanning role.

A **decision support system (DSS)** is an interactive computer-based system that helps decision makers use data and models to solve both relatively unstructured and complex problems.[8] In many ways, DSSs are more useful than MISs for management because of their interactive nature, timely availability, and flexibility.[9]

Although DSSs are a major step forward for information management, this does not mean that MISs should be discarded. For example, both internal and external data must be gathered for any kind of information management system; an MIS should be designed to provide this data.

Perhaps the ideal structure involves an MIS and a DSS. The MIS should be designed to gather internal and external data both for routine, structured decisions and for environmental scanning purposes. The DSS should provide decision makers with all available data generated by the MIS and with models and software programs appropriate for accessing the data.

THE ENVIRONMENTAL ISSUE MANAGEMENT PROCESS

Regardless of the specific MIS or DSS used, environmental issue management can be viewed as a process comprising four stages:[10]

1. Environmental scanning
2. Identifying key environmental issues
3. Evaluating the impact of environmental issues
4. Formulating strategic responses

The major sections of this chapter focus on each of these steps.

ENVIRONMENTAL SCANNING

Environmental scanning is the process by which a firm seeks information concerning the relevant environments. Effective environmental scanning involves four basic steps:

1. Establishing information needs
2. Identifying general sources of information
3. Identifying specific sources of information
4. Developing the specific scanning system

Establishing Information Needs

The amount and type of information that can be gathered for business decisions is nearly limitless. Not all of it, however, is of equal value in making decisions. Since too much information can be as bad as too little, each firm must determine the right amount and type, given its time and financial constraint. The core problem in information management, then, is gathering the appropriate information—in other words, satisfying specific decision needs.

To pinpoint the information needed, management must first define the problem area (even if in a general way) and analyze it, perhaps with a rough working model. Note that scanning the macro- and task environments may not involve a predetermined problem. At a minimum, however, sufficient data should be gathered to forecast environmental changes and to construct the following profiles:

1. Macroenvironmental profile
2. Task environmental profile
3. Internal situation profile
4. Competitor profiles
5. Customer profiles
6. Supplier profiles

Environmental profiles are discussed and illustrated in Chapter 9.

Establishing information needs is the foundation for acquiring further information. The importance of this process to the total information management process cannot be overemphasized. This step helps reduce the common problems of not having enough information or not having the appropriate information to make a decision.

Identifying General Sources of Information

There are four general sources of information: (1) internal secondary sources, (2) external secondary sources, (3) internal primary sources, and (4) external primary sources. Secondary information has already been gathered for some other purpose, while primary information comes from original research. Each of the four sources can offer information for decision making and should be considered.

Internal secondary sources should be investigated first because they are inexpensive and should be readily available through the management information system. External secondary sources should be consulted next, followed by internal primary sources. External primary sources are pursued last because of the time and expense involved.

Identifying Specific Sources of Information

The four general sources provide a framework for discussing specific sources.

Internal Secondary Sources   Internal secondary data are plentiful and can be manipulated to provide a good information base for decision making. Examples of internal secondary sources include cash register tapes, sales slips, credit records, accounting records, previous research, production reports, and personnel evaluations.

External Secondary Sources   An enormous amount of external secondary data is available, much of it at no cost. Government sources supply a wide range of data in publications such as the *Census of Business, County and City Data Book,* and the *Survey of Current Business.* State and local governments also generate a variety of data. Other external secondary sources include trade association publications, journals, magazines, newspapers, and private organizations (for example, Dun & Bradstreet). Guides or indexes offer an excellent starting point in a search for external secondary data. Guides available in most libraries include the *Business Periodicals Index, Sources of Business Information, Data Sources for Business and Market Analysis,* and *Marketing Information Guide.* C. R. Goeldner and L. M. Disks's article "Business Facts: Where to Find Them" is an excellent place to begin this search.[11]

Internal Primary Sources   Internal primary sources are generally underutilized. The major focus should be on the firm's personnel. Every employee is continually exposed to the firm's internal situation. Many employees, such as buyers and salespeople, also interact with various elements of the macro- and task environments. Salespeople, for example, may be the first to hear of new competitive offerings. Buyers may hear about new, commercialized technology before the scientists do. These sources can contribute valuable information.

External Primary Sources   Data gathered specifically to solve a particular problem or make a current decision can come from a variety of sources, such as consumers, suppliers, competitors, and other groups. External primary sources should be tapped only when the other three sources cannot provide adequate information.

Developing a Scanning System

This fourth step involves assigning responsibility, developing an efficient mechanism for information gathering, and making decisions for disseminating the information within the firm. "The more energy a firm devotes to broad environmental scanning, the greater its capacity to survive."[12]

As Table 8.1 shows, scanning models can be classified as irregular, regular, and continuous.[13] The *irregular scanning model* is the simplest, least effective, and most widely used scanning model. The *regular scanning model* is more effective than the irregular, but the *continuous scanning model* represents the highest level of sophistication and effectiveness. An effective scanning model should focus on the key environmental factors discussed in Chapters 5, 6, and 7 to help management pinpoint relevant changes as they occur.

For example, a firm in a technology-driven industry should have a sophisticated scanning system directed at new technology development. Likewise, a firm which uses retail location as the centerpiece of its strategy should have a scan-

TABLE 8.1 · Scanning Model Framework

	Types of Scanning Models		
	Irregular	Regular	Continuous
MEDIA FOR SCANNING ACTIVITY	Ad hoc studies	Periodically up-dated studies	Structured data collection and process-ing systems
SCOPE OF SCANNING	Specific events	Selected events	Broad range of environ-mental sys-tems
MOTIVATION FOR ACTIVITY	Crisis initiated	Decision- and issue-oriented	Planning process-oriented
TEMPORAL NATURE OF ACTIVITY	Reactive	Proactive	Proactive
TIME FRAME FOR DATA	Retrospective	Primarily current and retro-spective	Prospective
TIME FRAME FOR DECISION IMPACT	Current and near-term future	Near term	Long term
ORGANIZATIONAL MAKEUP	Various staff agencies	Various staff agencies	Environment scanning unit

Source: Liam Fahey and William R. King, "Environmental Scanning for Corporate Planning," *Business Horizons,* August 1977, p. 63. Copyright, 1977, by the Foundation for the School of Business at Indiana University. Reprinted by permission.

ning system that closely scans the available sites, population movements, and competitors' location decisions. The point is that the scanning system should be built around the industry's driving forces and the firm's critical success factors.

The key aspects of designing a data collection system for the chosen scan-ning model involve determining who is best suited to gather the different types of information, assigning responsibility for collecting it, and providing a channel for disseminating the data. Responsibility for collecting data is generally given to the various functional areas of the firm. Exhibit 8.1 depicts the overall flow of information in a firm.

EXHIBIT 8.1 · Information Flow

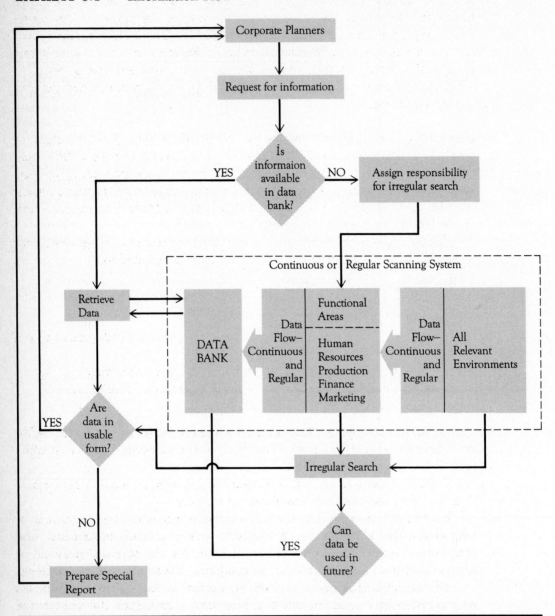

Exhibit 8.1 also highlights the advantage of a well-developed, continuous scanning system. If such a system exists, most requests for information can be filled from the existing data base or bank, with little disruption of other activities. The requests that cannot be filled from the data bank usually require special searches (irregular scanning) of the relevant environment. Firms with poorly developed scanning systems often must make extensive use of special searches, which can be more time-consuming and expensive than a well-planned continuous scanning system.

Competitive Information[14]   Firms can often gain a great deal of insight by monitoring competitors' market signals. A *market signal* is any action by a competitor that provides a direct or indirect indication of its intentions, motives, goals, or internal situation. Some signals sent by competitors represent earnest commitments to action, whereas other signals can be bluffs or warnings. There are several major types of market signals.

First, the competitor may make a *prior announcement* that it will or will not take some action. The prior announcement may be designed to

1. Preempt other competitors
2. Threaten action
3. Test competitors' sentiments
4. Communicate pleasure or displeasure with competitive developments in the industry
5. Minimize the provocation of a forthcoming strategic adjustment
6. Avoid costly simultaneous moves in areas like capacity additions
7. Communicate with the financial community

Second, a competitor may announce results or actions, such as plant additions and sales figures, after the fact. Such announcements ensure that other firms know and take note of the data disclosed.

Third, competitors may publicly discuss or comment on industry conditions, thus revealing their assumptions about the industry.

Fourth, a competitor may discuss its moves in public or in a forum, such as with major customers, where the discussion is likely to reach other firms. This can signal an attempt by the competitor to reduce the potential provocative effects of an action, pre-empt other competitors, or communicate commitment.

Fifth, a competitor's actual tactics—as opposed to tactics it could have used but did not—can be quite revealing. For example, a competitor that chooses the tactics most damaging to other firms is demonstrating direct aggression. Conversely, if its tactics are carefully chosen to minimize damage to other firms, that would signal conciliation.

Sixth, a competitor's sharp divergence from former goals or industry norms may indicate a major readjustment of its goals or assumptions.

Seventh, a competitor may use a cross-parry. A *cross-parry* occurs when a firm initiates a move in one area, and a competitor responds in a different area with a move that affects the initiating firm. The cross-parry can indicate a wish to avoid a destructive set of moves and countermoves, while clearly signaling displeasure. It raises the threat of serious retaliation in the future.

Eighth, a firm may give another kind of warning—a *fighting brand*. It involves the introduction of a product in response to a competitor's threatening move and has the effect of punishing or threatening to punish the source of the threat.

Ninth, the filing of a private antitrust suit against a competitor can be interpreted as a delaying tactic, a signal of displeasure, or in some cases, harassment.

Human Resource Information   A primary responsibility of the human resource function is providing higher-level management with continuous human resource assessment information. Although the components vary from firm to firm and for different jobs within a firm, most assessments contain evaluations of the abilities of the firm's personnel. Examples of other important information and reports include the size and characteristics of the available labor markets, the compensation structure of the firm relative to other industries and competitors, the overall organizational structure, evaluation of the firm's human resource capabilities and cost in light of various strategy alternatives, and the "promotability" of various personnel within the firm.

Another type of human resource report involves analyzing the human resources of competitors or potential acquisition targets. In fact, a major reason for acquiring a particular firm may be to secure some of the skills of its management and key personnel—especially if a company is trying to move into new technology areas.

Production Information   The production function is generally responsible for providing a great deal of information to corporate-level management. Production's primary responsibility for information is normally associated with the cost of production. The information needed by higher-level management often includes projections of costs based on forecasts of relevant environmental conditions, cost forecasts based on proposed internal changes, and interrelated costs due to similar materials, personnel, and equipment being used to produce more than one type of product.

Other possible analyses and reports can involve the following:

1. *Location analysis,* including information such as the cost of labor, the cost of transportation, the total cost of production at a given location, the general attitudes of the population, the political environments, the cultural environments, and any other factors that would make one location better than another

2. *Product quality,* including quality potential, the cost of changing quality, and the quality control procedures utilized

3. *Facility capacity,* including the ideal or potential capacity (the output possible with all equipment and personnel operating at peak efficiency), the real capacity (realistic output in the light of events such as machine breakdowns, machine wearouts, and inventory shortages), any necessary or desirable changes in capacity and the cost of those changes, equipment alternatives, inventory changes, and special skills needed

4. *Materials data,* including information on finished goods, goods-in-process, raw materials inventory, the anticipated availability of key raw materials, and new types of materials

5. *Maintenance and repair,* including regular maintenance and repairs, needed improvements to the plant and equipment, maintenance schedules, repair schedules, maintenance budgets, and repair budgets

6. *Regulatory data,* including compliance with the regulations (for example, those of the Environmental Protection Agency and of the Occupational Safety and Health Agency), actions necessary to attain compliance, the cost of compliance, and likely changes in regulations

7. *Labor-related information,* especially labor relations and problems, unionization, and the adaptability of workers' skills to different tasks

Research and Development Information The R&D area of a business must also provide data to higher-level management. Although the volume of these data may be small when compared with that from other functions, it is no less important. The data provided by R&D typically include new products or production processes relevant to the firm, the practicality of product ideas, and the cost of developing and producing new products. Thus R&D management may be the primary supplier of technology-related data.

Financial Information In many firms, top management requests more information from the financial area than from any other. These requests may come on a regular or irregular basis. Examples of regular requests include items such as the balance sheet, profit and loss statement, statement of retained earnings, and perhaps cash projections and analyses. The timing of these items varies, but annual, quarterly, and monthly patterns are common.

The number of irregular requests tends to be greater in firms that face dynamic environments, in which many environmental opportunities and threats must be evaluated. The specific information supplied irregularly by finance can vary widely but often includes detailed analyses of expenses, budgets, cost of capital, tax forecasts, financial ratios, credit analyses, financial structure, and profitability.

The financial function may initiate the transmittal of several types of information to top management. This information would involve primarily the assessment of financial opportunities (such as a change from one capital source to another that would reduce the cost of capital, favorable new interest rates, or tax changes) and financial threats (such as unfavorable shifts in key financial ratios, disadvantageous new interest rates, or changes in the tax situation).

Marketing Information   As with all the functional areas, marketing can play a vital role in providing information to top management. Note that most marketing textbooks emphasize providing information to the marketing manager rather than the next step—providing information to top management.

Examples of possible regular requests for information by top management are items such as sales volume, advertising expenses, and market share. Irregular requests for information may include analyses of industry attractiveness, market size, market growth rate, competitive intensity, seasonality, relative market share, price competitiveness, sales effectiveness, and perceived product quality. Other examples include requests for average cost per sales call, average number of sales calls per day, profiles of target customers, industry or trade price comparisons, analyses of advertising expenses, and various demographic data.

Sales managers and representatives can be asked for their thoughts regarding competitive strengths, weaknesses, and expected strategic moves. Examples of other data that marketing might prepare include competitive analyses, product comparisons (by consumers), taste tests, market tests, consumer attitude surveys (on almost any marketing-related issue), and evaluations of advertising campaigns.

Marketing can also be assigned specific situations or activities to monitor continuously or periodically as they occur. For example, field salespeople can be instructed to report to the sales manager any changes in competitive strategy encountered in the marketplace, such as price changes and increased trade advertising. Marketing is also responsible for a more general scanning of the various macro- and task environments. This environmental scan is not directed at specific events or activities. Rather, its purpose is to detect (and perhaps evaluate) potential market opportunities and threats. Examples of potential market opportunities discovered by environmental scanning range from the probable departure of a major competitor to the discovery of a major new customer group and new applications of present products. Examples of potential market threats include the entrance of major new competitors, new product breakthroughs, and the departure of major customers.

Organizational Culture Information   Managers can learn much about their firm's culture in a limited amount of time by appointing an insider to examine it using the techniques of outside consultants. The analysis begins with a study of surface indications and proceeds inward to the firm's "unconscious"—that is, typical practices and attitudes of employees that are not normally noticed.

Insider analysts sometimes can probe more deeply into the firm's culture than an outside consultant can, and with much greater precision. However, insiders must beware of their subjectivity; this pitfall often makes it easier to evaluate a competing firm than one's own. The analyst must concentrate on how things are actually done rather than on how they should be done according to official company rules. If lack of objectivity proves an insurmountable problem, an external consultant will be needed.

Clues to a firm's culture are plentiful. Consider, for example, how employees respond to the question, "What do you do for a living?" If they respond "I'm in sales," doubts about the effectiveness of the firm's overall cultural identity might be raised. However, if they respond, "I'm with Ace Industries," a stronger culture is implied. Other diagnostic techniques include the following:[15]

1. *Study the physical setting.* The physical setting makes a statement to the world about the firm. Look also for consistency among locations and internal departments; inconsistency can indicate a fragmented culture.
2. *Evaluate how the firm greets strangers.* Look at the reception/lobby area and the interaction between "greeters" and strangers.
3. *Read what the firm says about itself.* Look at annual reports, advertising copy, press releases, and so on. Firms with strong cultures tend to emphasize the importance of their values and their people. A procedure called content analysis addresses the consistency of written statements over a period of time. Note, too, the accuracy and sincerity of statements.
4. *Analyze the amount of content of internal communications.* People spend their time and effort on what the culture values the most.
5. *Interview employees.* Ask them to discuss the following subjects:
   - The firm's history. This will reveal their understanding of the firm's mythology.
   - Why the firm is successful. They will say what they think is important, thereby reflecting their impressions of the organization's cultural values.
   - The kinds of employees who really get ahead in the firm. They will normally describe their picture of a "hero" of the culture.

- What kind of place the firm is in which to work, the events of an average day, and how things get done. Their answers will disclose the organization's rituals and procedures.

6. *Observe how people spend their time.* What people do is determined by what they value. Find out whether employees habitually arrive late and leave early and whether they frequently complain about other departments and/or management.

7. *Analyze tenure and career path progression.* Short tenure can foster a short-term perspective. Find out what kind of people get promoted; for example, innovators or team players.

8. *Evaluate anecdotes and stories delivered by the cultural network.* People relate experiences they want to share through anecdotes and stories. Pay particular attention to the key point of any given story. Collectively, these points provide strong evidence of what the culture stresses as important.

Employee surveys can supplement these techniques. The Kilmann-Saxton Culture-Gap Survey, for example, is designed to detect the gap between what the culture is and what it should be.[16]

IDENTIFYING KEY ENVIRONMENTAL ISSUES

Step two of the overall environmental issue management process involves identifying key environmental issues through forecasting environmental changes. Management can take a broad-based look at the environment, but although this approach helps pinpoint developments from outside the industry, it also may yield a lot of useless information. Conversely, management can limit the monitoring to areas linked to the firm's activities that are most sensitive to environmental change. This approach focuses effort and resources where they can do the most good, but can miss other events outside the focus.

To develop future strategies for a firm, management must predict the type of environment that the firm will be facing in the short and long term. Consequently, the purpose of **environmental forecasting** is to estimate the timing and the likelihood of the impact of environmental influences. In other words, when will the influences occur and what is the probability of their occurrence? Environmental forecasting provides the basis for making assumptions for the firm's strategic planning efforts.

Management must also choose the specific environmental variables to forecast. Time and money constraints obviously preclude forecasting all possible environmental variables. Certain environmental factors might be monitored with no related forecasting, while published forecasts might be relied upon for others. The environmental factors that should be forecast are those that may strongly influence the firm. The resulting types of forecasts often deal with the economy, political trends, social and cultural trends, technological trends, environmental trends, industry trends, competitors' strategy, customer reactions, and the needs and desires of stakeholder groups.

A number of methods exist for forecasting environmental change. Since they vary in complexity and reliability, each firm should carefully evaluate its needs and capabilities when selecting a forecasting method. Table 8.2 presents short descriptions of the key methods of forecasting.

Many firms find that basic environmental forecasting is beyond their capabilities. For example, few companies have the resources and skills to analyze and accurately predict all changes and trends in the macroenvironment. Consequently, many firms seek basic forecasts from other sources, including governmental agencies, professional research firms, and other analysts. It is critically important that these acquired forecasts be assembled and *evaluated relative to the*

TABLE 8.2 · Summary and Evaluation of Forecasting Techniques

Technique	Description	Cost	Popularity	Complexity	Association with Life Cycle Stage
QUANTITATIVE					
Econometric models	Simultaneous systems of multiple regression equations	High	High	High	Steady state
Single and multiple regression	Variations in dependent variables are explained by variations in the independent one(s)	High	High	Medium	Steady state
Time series	Linear, exponential, S-curve, or other types of projections; forecasts are obtained by smoothing (averaging) past actual values in a linear or exponential manner	Medium	High	Medium	Steady state

(continued)

TABLE 8.2 · (continued)

Technique	Description	Cost	Popularity	Complexity	Association with Life Cycle Stage
QUALITATIVE					
Sales force estimates	A bottom-up approach aggregating salespersons' forecasts	Low	High	Low	All stages
Jury of executive opinion	Marketing, production, and finance executives jointly prepare forecasts	Low	High	Low	Product development
Market research	Learning about intentions of potential customers or plans of businesses	Medium	Medium	Medium	Market testing and early introduction
Scenario	Forecasters imagine the impacts of anticipated conditions	Low	Medium	Low	All stages
Delphi	Experts are guided toward a consensus	Low	Medium	Medium	Product development
Brainstorm	Idea generation in a noncritical group situation	Low	Medium	Medium	Product development

Source: Adapted from J. A. Pearce II and R. B. Robinson, Jr., "Environmental Forecasting: Key To Strategic Management," *Business* (July-September 1983), 6.

firm's specific environment. The ultimate responsibility for this evaluation and interpretation lies with the firm, not with the original forecasters.

To help organize its forecasting activities for macroenvironmental influences, General Electric Co. uses a tool called the **probability/diffusion matrix** (see Exhibit 8.2). The *probability level* is the estimate of the likelihood that an event will occur. The *diffusion base* is the degree of impact the event will have on society. To use the matrix, a number of possible events are organized and assigned a probability ranging from low to high and a diffusion base ranging from low to high. *High diffusion* means widespread impact, whereas *low diffusion* means a narrowly defined impact.

Future mapping offers an alternative approach to forecasting.[17] The basic

---

EXHIBIT 8.2 · Probability/Diffusion Matrix

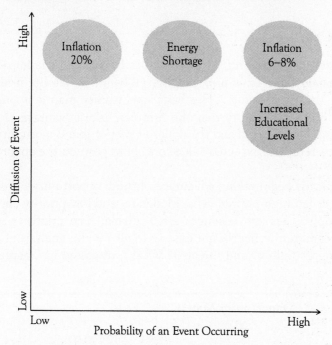

Source: Adapted with permission from Danny R. Arnold, Louis M. Capella, and Garry D. Smith, *Strategic Retail Management*, p. 133. Addison-Wesley Publishing Company, Inc., Reading, Mass., Copyright © 1983.

---

approach involves selecting several potential "end states," or possible outcomes, for an industry (which do not represent forecasts). Managers then work backwards to determine a possible "stream of events" that would most likely lead to the selected end states. Management can then use the streams of events as signals that major changes could be imminent.

EVALUATING THE IMPACT OF ENVIRONMENTAL ISSUES

Management must determine which specific environmental issues are opportunities and which are threats to the firm. Because of limited resources, a firm cannot take advantage of all opportunities nor can it worry about every potential threat. Several available prioritizing models use different approaches for ranking opportunities and threats. Most of these models are based on the expected value concept. The expected value of an event is calculated by multiplying the value of the expected outcome by the probability that the outcome will occur.

Opportunity Matrix

An opportunity matrix prioritizes opportunities by defining the impact that an opportunity could have on a firm and the probability that the firm can take advantage of that opportunity. The basic opportunity matrix is presented in Exhibit 8.3. If the probability that the firm can take advantage of a specific opportunity can be estimated and the dollar impact of that opportunity forecast, the firm can then use the expected value concept to position the opportunity in a matrix cell.

Firms typically begin taking advantage of those opportunities positioned in the three upper-left high-priority cells. Moderate- and low-priority opportunities are pursued only if enough resources are available. The priorities established through the opportunity matrix are used as input for the analysis of strengths, weaknesses, opportunities, and threats (SWOT), discussed in Chapter 9.

EXHIBIT 8.3 · Opportunity Matrix

Impact of Opportunity

		H	M	L
Probability that Firm Can Take Advantage of Opportunity	H	06	03	
	M	01	02	04
	L	05		

Key

High Priority

Moderate Priority

Low Priority

01 Build new plant for Model Z production
02 Expand sales to Latin America
03 Introduce variation of Model A15
04 Consolidate production of Model C and Q at Hartford Plant
05 Open sales office in China
06 Introduce new Model X16

Source: Adapted with permission from a model in a presentation by Ian Wilson, General Electric, at the 1979 Conference on Public Policy and Business Environment at Washington University, St. Louis, Mo.

Threat Matrix

Although some firms use an identical matrix for analyzing threats, we recommend a slightly different version, shown in Exhibit 8.4. The threat matrix looks very similar to the opportunity matrix except that it has an additional impact column. This column is for threats that could destroy the firm, such as bankruptcy. The potential impact of a killer threat with even a moderate chance of occurring must be minimized if the firm expects to remain operational.

Note that a killer threat for one firm may be an irrelevant issue to another firm. Consider the impact of government regulations on the amount of pollution emitted by a plant. A firm with a relatively old, outmoded production facility might see new pollution regulations as killer threats if the cost of meeting these regulations could compromise the firm's ability to stay in business. On the other hand, a company with a new, modern facility that exceeds the required compliance might find the new regulations irrelevant.

The additional column shown in Figure 8.4 for threats with a killing impact also creates a fourth priority category. Besides the low-, medium-, and high-priority categories, an emergency priority is needed for the threats that must be addressed immediately. If the firm considers new pollution control regulations as killer threats, then minimizing their impact becomes an emergency priority. Management must do something at once—for instance, lobby to block or delay

---

EXHIBIT 8.4 · Threat Matrix

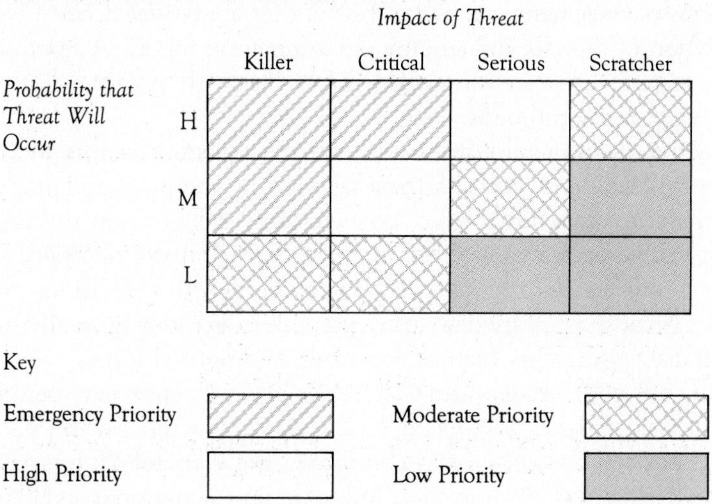

the regulations, appeal for a grace period, seek less expensive ways of complying with the regulations, or perhaps sell or close the plant.

Threats that fall into the emergency priority cells are typically handled by top-level management. Firms seldom have enough time to collect very much additional data on such threats because immediate evasive action is often essential as soon as the threats are identified. Nonemergency threats with a high priority usually allow the firm time to collect additional information. At lower-priority levels, less and less will be done, particularly by high-level management. Lowest-priority threats usually are simply watched. These threats are noted, and someone monitors them through the normal MIS to accumulate information for the time when it might be needed.

The primary reason for differentiating between opportunity and threat prioritizing is the vast difference between potential outcomes of high-priority opportunities and threats. Whereas a missed opportunity results only in opportunity cost, a threat that is not properly identified and avoided can mean actual dollar costs. As already noted, if a firm fails to deflect a killer threat, the firm may cease to exist. In short, companies can afford to overlook a few opportunities but cannot afford to ignore any significant threats.

The priorities established through the threat matrix can also be used as input for the SWOT analysis, which is discussed in the next chapter.

FORMULATING A RESPONSE STRATEGY

A firm's ability to influence and respond to environmental issues affects the types of decisions management can make. Recall that a *proactive decision* is made with the intention of directly influencing environmental forces. A *reactive decision* is made in response to environmental forces but with no intention of directly influencing the environment.

Proactive decisions are most effective for adjusting factors in the internal situation (for example, for changing accounting methods and improving employee morale). Since firms have somewhat less influence on the task environment, proactive decisions are less effective there and the necessity for reactive decisions is greater. In the macroenvironment, reactive decisions are critically important because an individual firm's proactive decisions normally have a more limited impact on factors such as economic and natural forces.

Note, however, that a firm's strategies can influence macroenvironmental factors. Consider these brief examples. Economic factors on the national level can be influenced by decisions at companies like General Motors, AT&T, and IBM. Small firms normally have less influence on the national level but can have a large influence on regional or local economic factors. Both large and small companies can also influence governmental and political factors with various lobbying activities. Some say that Hugh Hefner's *Playboy* magazine was the harbinger of our society's sexual revolution.[18] Almost any firm can damage the nearby natural environment. The technological environment can be changed by any firm's technological breakthrough.

It is also important to recall that reactive decisions regarding the macroenvironment can take two distinct forms. *Passive-reactive decisions* are made after an environmental event occurs and its impact is recognized by management. *Aggressive-reactive decisions* are made in anticipation of an environmental event.

Any decision that can be classified as other than passive-reactive falls into the realm of **environmental management.** Jeffrey Pfeffer contends that "rather than designing the organization to 'fit' the environment, it is more likely that first the organization will attempt to design its environment to fit its present structural arrangements."[19] Pfeffer outlines the methods that can accomplish this task, including managing competition, promoting regulation to reduce competition, managing symbiotic interdependence (that is, working with another firm for mutual benefit), and managing uncertainty, organizational legitimation (enhancing the firm's reputation or image), and political action.

Jay Galbraith partitions environmental management strategies into three categories:[20]

1. *Independent strategies:* the use of internal resources and ingenuity to reduce environmental uncertainty and dependence
2. *Cooperative strategies:* implicit or explicit cooperation with other elements in the environment
3. *Strategic maneuvering:* attempting to change the organization's task environment

Carl P. Zeithaml and Valarie A. Zeithaml drew on Galbraith's typology to develop the specific environmental management strategies shown in Table 8.3. These strategies highlight the need for gathering and understanding environmental information and translating it into useful strategies.[21]

MONITORING THE ENVIRONMENTAL ISSUE MANAGEMENT SYSTEM

The major caution regarding the environmental issue management system is that management too often neglects the system after it is implemented. Firms can quit collecting data for a day or a week or even a month without serious damage; but the longer the firm goes without collecting environmental data, the more likely it

TABLE 8.3 · A Framework of Environmental Management Strategies

Environmental Management Strategy	Definition	Examples
INDEPENDENT STRATEGIES		
Competitive aggression	Focal organization exploits a distinctive competence or pricing, improves internal efficiency of resources for competitive advantage	Product differentiation, aggressive comparative advertising
Competitive pacification	Independent action to improve relations with competitors	Helping competitors find raw materials, advertising campaigns that promote entire industry, price umbrellas
Public relations	Establishing and maintaining favorable images in the minds of those making up the environment	Corporate advertising campaigns
Voluntary action	Voluntary management of and commitment to various interest groups, causes, and social problems	McGraw-Hill's efforts to prevent sexist stereotypes, 3M's energy conservation program
Dependence development	Creating or modifying relationships so that external groups become dependent on the focal organization	Raising switching costs for suppliers, production of critical defense-related commodities, providing vital information to regulators
Legal action	Company engaging in private legal battle with competitor on antitrust, deceptive advertising, or other grounds	Private antitrust suits brought against competitors
Political action	Efforts to influence elected representatives to create a more favorable business environment or limit competition	Corporate constituency programs, issue advertising, direct lobbying

TABLE 8.3 · (*continued*)

Environmental Management Strategy	Definition	Examples
Smoothing	Attempts to resolve irregular demand	Telephone company's lower weekend rates, inexpensive airline fares at off-peak times
Demarketing	Attempts to discourage customers in general or a certain class of customers in particular, on either a temporary or a permanent basis	Shorter hours of operation by gasoline service stations
COOPERATIVE STRATEGIES		
Implicit cooperation	Patterned, predictable, and coordinated behaviors	Price leadership
Contracting	Negotiation of an agreement between the organization and another group to exchange goods, services, information, patents, etc.	Contractual vertical and horizontal marketing systems
Co-optation	Process of absorbing new elements into the leadership or policy-making structure of an organization as a means of averting threats to its stability or existence	Consumer representatives, women, and bankers on boards of directors
Coalition	Two or more groups coalesce and act jointly with respect to some set of issues for some period of time	Industry association, political initiatives of the Business Roundtable and the U.S. Chamber of Commerce
STRATEGIC MANEUVERING		
Domain selection	Entering industries or markets with limited	IBM's entry into the personal computer

(*continued*)

TABLE 8.3 • *(continued)*

Environmental Management Strategy	Definition	Examples
	competition or regulation coupled with ample suppliers and customers; entering high-growth markets	market, Miller Brewing Company's entry into the light beer market
Diversification	Investing in different types of businesses, manufacturing different types of products, vertical iantegration, or geographic expansion to reduce dependence on single product, service, market, or technology	Marriott's investment in different forms of restaurants, General Electric's wide product mix
Merger and acquisition	Combining two or more firms into a single enterprise; gaining possession of an ongoing enterprise	Merger between Pan American and National Airlines, Philip Morris's acquisition of Miller Beer

Source: Carl P. Zeithaml and Valarie A. Zeithaml, "Environmental Management: Revising the Marketing Perspective," *Journal of Marketing* (Spring 1984), 50–51.

is to have serious difficulties because a rapidly changing environment can quickly make sound decisions obsolete.

Disseminating information is a major element in the collection system. Consequently, firms must make sure that the internal channels of communication remain open (see Exhibit 8.1). Serious problems can develop when a communication channel becomes closed for one reason or another. Consider a firm that wants its salespeople to collect information on competitors. This channel can become closed if the salespeople realize that the firm does not utilize their information or if the firm does not acknowledge that it has received the information. As a result, the firm can be more easily damaged by competitors' actions.

Another information problem involves information overload. Getting the *right* information in the right form is critical. Few managers have the time to "glean the wheat from the chaff." Thus the collection and dissemination system must be designed to deliver the right amount of relevant information.

Blockbuster on the Rise

"Wow! What a difference" is the slogan of Blockbuster Entertainment Corporation. Clearly Blockbuster does do something different than other video stores: in only five years it has grown rapidly, becoming the largest video rental chain in the United States. Annual revenues were expected to hit the $1 billion mark in 1990.

In 1986 and 1987, H. Wayne Huizenga and two partners paid a total of $18 million for 35 percent of Blockbuster. In April 1987 Huizenga became chairman of the corporation when its founder left to start another business. At that time, Blockbuster had twenty stores. By the end of 1987: 130. As of mid-1990: 1,200, and counting.

Blockbuster's rental outlets—half of which are franchised—are large (8,000 to 10,000 square feet) and brightly lit. Each store carries nearly 10,000 tapes, roughly twice the average of competitors. Customers can keep the movies for three days, rather than the industry standard one or two. Blockbuster chooses titles—none of them X-rated—with great care, analyzing movie reviews and studying box office takes. At "America's Family Video Store" the target market is similar to that of McDonald's. To better meet the needs of each market, the company is trying to select tapes for each store that will appeal specifically to that neighborhood's viewers.

One key to the financial success of Blockbuster is that it is a rental, not a retail, business. The average cost of a tape is $40. At $3 per rental, the tape is essentially paid for after only thirteen rentals. Also, as long as the share price of Blockbuster stock continues to rise—as of June 1990 the stock was 20 times earn-

ings—the company can use the stock to make acquisitions fairly easily. And, with 50 percent of video rental stores mom-and-pop operations, there are plenty of acquisition targets.

New franchisees pay a one-time franchise fee to Blockbuster; they also pay a fee to "lock in" their rental territory. In addition, Blockbuster sells franchisees their starting inventory. Some analysts feel that this lucrative strategy will keep working only as long as Blockbuster keeps opening new stores—and as long as the video rental market stays hot.

Meanwhile, Blockbuster is trying to attract new customers with a variety of strategies, including a $25 million advertising campaign; joint promotions with Domino's Pizza and McDonald's; and the introduction of Blockbuster cartoon characters in Saturday morning commercials. Blockbuster is also seeking to expand overseas. It already has stores in Britain and hopes to open some in European countries as well as Australia.

Although there are some indications that the video rental market may be cooling, it is expected to grow significantly for the next few years at least. And, with plans for 3,000 outlets, Blockbuster's "difference" will be visible to many home video viewers.

References: Gail De George, "The Video King Who Won't Hit Pause," *Business Week*, January 22, 1990, p. 47–48; Earle Paige and Paul Sweeting, "Industry Ponders Saturation Point: Can Major Chains Continue Expansion?" *Billboard*, January 13, 1990, p. 39; Pete Engardio and Antonio N. Fins, "Will This Video Chain Stay on Fast-Forward?" *Business Week*, June 12, 1989, pp. 72, 75; Erik Calonius, "Meet the King of Video," *Fortune*, June 4, 1990, p. 208.

Several other factors can indicate system deficiencies. First, the forecast and actual environments are different enough to cause incorrect decisions based on forecasts. Although forecasts will seldom be exactly accurate, they should be relatively accurate.

Second, management must often make decisions despite a critical shortage of relevant information. Seldom will a decision maker have all the information desired, but at least the key information must be available.

Third, management may be overwhelmed with too much information, and decision makers may not be able to digest it all. When that happens, quantity often suppresses quality, and can generate false signals.

By and large, whenever needed information is not readily available, there is a problem with the MIS. When this problem occurs, the system must be adjusted. It may require only minor correction (such as changing the form of certain reports) or a complete revamping. Normally, a complete revision is necessary only when major problems exist or keep recurring. However, management should be careful not to just patch up an ineffective system, but rather to make sure that the information generated justifies the cost of the system.

GLOBAL DIMENSIONS

When designing a management information system, companies must take the international arena into account. Even firms with little direct international involvement must maintain some international information. For instance, most firms should at least scan the international environment for new technologies, economic changes, and major political shifts. Information systems for a company with little international involvement can be relatively simple and may simply mean regular reading of the international section of newspapers and periodicals.

Firms with greater international involvement obviously need a more thorough analysis of international issues. The international component of the MIS should be devised much like the domestic component: factors that can greatly influence the firm should be constantly monitored and less significant factors should be monitored less closely.

To help ensure proper interpretation of international developments, many companies employ specialists in international business. These experts, who often concentrate on particular geographical areas, such as Central America, the Middle East, or Western Europe, are recommended for firms with moderate-to-heavy international involvement. They can aid both in interpreting international developments and in setting up international information-gathering systems.

A firm may also need to create and develop environmental profiles for relevant international factors for individual countries or groups of countries.

Resembling the profiles for domestic operations, these profiles should help identify major international threats and opportunities. Such profiles should normally be constructed by experts in international operations.

Notes

1. Peter F. Drucker, "Managing for Tomorrow," *Industry Week*, April 14, 1980, p. 55.

2. Michael E. Porter and Victor E. Millar, "How Information Gives You Competitive Advantage," *Harvard Business Review* (July-August 1985), 149–160.

3. Michael G. Ashmore, "Bringing Information Technology to Life," *Journal of Business Strategy* (May-June 1988), 48–50.

4. Efraim Turban, *Decision Support and Expert Systems*, (New York: Macmillan, 1988), p. 5.

5. Donald F. Heany, *Development of Information Systems* (New York: Ronald Press, 1968), p. 7.

6. Robert E. Cole, "Target Information for Competitive Performance," *Harvard Business Review* (May-June 1985), 100–109.

7. C. Joseph Sass and Teresa A. Kefe, "MIS for Strategic Planning and a Competitive Edge," *Journal of Systems Management*, June 14, 1988, pp. 14–17.

8. Ibid., p. 7.

9. Shelley D. Collier, Lester A. Digman, and Sangjin Yoo, "Decision Support Systems: A New Tool for Strategic Management," *Long Range Planning* (April 1987), 114–124.

10. H. Igor Ansoff, "Strategic Issue Management," *Strategic Management Journal* (January 1980), 131–148.

11. C. R. Goeldner and L. M. Disks, "Business Facts: Where to Find Them," *MSU Business Topics* (Summer 1976), 23–26.

12. Philip Kotler, *Marketing Management*, 4th ed. (Englewood Cliffs, N.J.: Prentice-Hall, 1980), p. 98.

13. Liam Fahey and William R. King, "Environmental Scanning for Corporate Planning," *Business Horizons* (August 1977), 63.

14. This section draws heavily on Michael E. Porter, *Competitive Strategy* (New York: The Free Press, 1980), pp. 75–86.

15. Terrence E. Deal and Allan A. Kennedy, *Corporate Cultures* (Reading, Mass.: Addison-Wesley, 1982), pp. 129–135.

16. R. H. Kilmann and M. J. Saxton, *The Kilmann-Saxton Culture-Gap Survey* (Pittsburgh: Organizational Design Consultants, 1983).

17. David H. Mason and Robert G. Wilson, "Future Mapping: A New Approach to Managing Strategic Uncertainty," *Planning Review* (May-June 1987), 20–29.

18. Hilary Rosenberg, "Playboy: Worn Out at 30?" *Financial World*, June 30, 1983, pp. 40–44.

19. Jeffrey Pfeffer, *Organizational Design* (Arlington Heights, Ill: AHM, 1978), pp. 141–142.

20. Jay Galbraith, *Organizational Design* (Boston: Addison-Wesley, 1977), ch. 14.

21. Carl P. Zeithaml and Valarie A. Zeithaml, "Environmental Management: Revising the Marketing Perspective," *Journal of Marketing* (Spring 1984), 50–51.

CHAPTER 9

Environmental Analysis: Competitive Advantages and Vulnerabilities

Once planners have adequate environmental information, the information must be analyzed to determine the firm's strengths, weaknesses, opportunities, and threats. The purpose of the analysis is to evaluate the firm's present and potential competitive advantages and vulnerabilities. This chapter discusses competitive advantages and vulnerabilities and then turns to more specific analysis techniques.

COMPETITIVE ADVANTAGE

One of the major objectives of environmental analysis is to identify present and potential sources of competitive advantage. A **competitive advantage** involves establishing a distinct, favorable differentiation from rival firms. It also means providing customers with a clear reason to buy from one firm rather than another. Although a firm does not have to "beat the competition" on every conceivable issue, it needs to do so on at least one issue that is important to a sufficiently large group of customers. Competitive advantage can be based on a number of critical success factors, including (1) product differentiation, (2) focusing on specific market segments, (3) focusing on production or distribution channels, and (4) using selective price/cost structures.[1] One study of small businesses found six distinctive competences that commonly lead to competitive advantage: (1) owner and employee ability, (2) a special or unique product, (3) customer service, (4) relative quality of product/service, (5) location, and (6) low cost and price.[2]

Bruce Henderson, former chairman of the Boston Consulting Group, suggests four managerial prerequisites for strengthening a firm's competitive position:[3]

1. *The ability to understand competitive interaction as a complete dynamic system.* How does a firm compete in its core SBUs?
2. *The ability to predict the consequences of a given intervention in the system.* How do the firm and its competitors respond to changing conditions, new opportunities, competitive threats, and so on?
3. *The availability of uncommitted resources.* How does the firm make resource allocation decisions?
4. *The willingness to deliberately act to make the commitment.* How can the firm integrate all of its activities into a committed corporate culture and strategy?

Competitive advantages are achieved by applying the firm's strengths to exploit opportunities and minimize weaknesses and threats. The manner of applying the strengths is a major component of the firm's strategy.

Besides creating a competitive advantage, the firm needs to be able to defend and sustain its advantage. A **sustainable competitive advantage** is one that has a lasting influence on the firm's profitability, which means that the firm must be able to defend the advantage against competitors. Patents and licenses, innovations, organizational flexibility, and superior reputation all help prevent competitive imitation. Pankaj Ghemawat suggests that sustainable competitive advantages result from product innovation, new production processes, and marketing strategies (other than pricing).[4]

Low Cost as a Competitive Advantage

Firms can achieve a competitive advantage through a low-cost or cost-leadership strategy. Porter suggests that a firm's cost position results from cost factors in the firm's overall chain of activities-costs. He configures these cost factors into nine **cost drivers**:[5]

1. *Economies of scale* foster low costs, whereas diseconomies of scale push costs up.
2. Taking advantage of the *learning curve* and *experience curve* can help lower costs. (The learning curve and experience curve are based on the observation that people and firms perform jobs and tasks better and more efficiently the more they do the job or task. These concepts are discussed in more detail in Chapter 10.)

3. A high percentage of *capacity utilization* helps to lower costs, particularly when fixed costs are high.
4. Efficient coordination of the *linkages between activities* can help lower costs when the cost of one activity is influenced by the way other activities are performed.
5. *Sharing activities* with other business units within the organization can provide cost savings.
6. The *extent of vertical integration* can influence costs; more vertical integration, for example, can reduce costs by allowing the business to avoid powerful buyers and suppliers.
7. The *timing of market entry* can influence costs; the first entry can lower costs by establishing a strong brand, and late entries can sometimes achieve lower costs by using the latest and most advanced technology.
8. *Strategic choices and operating decisions* can influence costs—for instance, increasing or reducing customer services, raising or lowering the specifications for purchased materials, and so on.
9. *Location variables* can influence costs through area wage rates, tax rates, energy costs, and so on.

Note that the cost drivers interact and can reinforce each other in a positive manner or counteract another cost driver's potential benefits.

Achieving a low-cost advantage often involves controlling the cost drivers more efficiently than competitors do. Another approach involves doing things differently by modifying activities or relationships among the cost drivers. Examples of potential modifications include changing the production process, automating high-cost activities, using cheaper raw materials, relocating facilities, and vertical integration.[6]

However, overemphasis on lowering cost can become detrimental.[7] Some firms, for example, concentrate all their attention on lowering manufacturing cost while ignoring opportunities to increase purchasing efficiency. Yet the cost of purchased materials may be greater than manufacturing costs. Similarly, some firms tend to ignore costs that represent a fraction of total cost. An automobile manufacturer, for instance, may be able to achieve significant total savings by evaluating each of the thousands of small components that go into a car. If General Motors could save two cents on the air valve for each tire on each car manufactured, the annual savings would be many thousands of dollars. Some firms also seem to misunderstand relationships between costs and the factors that influence cost. For instance, a company may choose a lower-priced component that requires more time to install. This may or may not lower total cost, depending on the cost of labor to install the part. Quite possibly, the greatest error is to make cost reductions that hurt performance, service, or other related factors. For instance, a retailer may decide not to take credit cards in order to reduce cost and, consequently, may lose sales.

Differentiation as a Competitive Advantage

A successful differentiation strategy makes customers value a firm's product or service more highly than competitive offerings.[8] This situation allows the firm to command a price premium, sell more products at a specific price, and achieve greater brand loyalty.

The basis for differentiation can arise anywhere in the activities-costs chain, including these areas:[9]

1. Procurement of raw materials that enhance quality or performance
2. Effective product-related R&D efforts (that is, improved designs, product variety)
3. Effective production-related R&D efforts (that is, improved quality and reliability
4. A high-quality manufacturing process (that is, zero defects)
5. Improve delivery times
6. Marketing activities

It is crucial to remember that differentiation is ultimately defined by the customer; quality is "in the eye of the beholder."

Pursuing a differentiation strategy can cause several problems.[10] All of them revolve around customer desires and perceptions. One problem occurs when the firm's differentiation efforts do not generate a difference that is recognized and valued by customers. For instance, an appliance manufacturer may emphasize its use of an extra coat of paint on all its products. However, if customers are not sure that this helps the quality of a stove, they will not be influenced by the firm's efforts. A price that is too high and better quality than customers desire can also be counterproductive. For instance, suppose a manufacturer of automobile batteries could build a state-of-the-art battery that would cost $200. Would people buy the battery? While some might, most customers would not pay $200 for a battery, regardless of its excellent quality. Such difficulties can be summed up as two overriding problems: (1) not understanding customer desires and perceptions of value and (2) not communicating the differential factors to customers in an effective manner. Essentially, consumers should dictate a firm's differentiating efforts and firms should differentiate only when the factors can be communicated to the target customers in a manner that they can appreciate.

Focus as a Competitive Advantage

The two key factors in pursuing a focus strategy involve selecting the target segments and building a competitive advantage in the chosen segment(s).[11] Target segments must be large enough to be profitable and have growth potential. Furthermore, these segments should not be critically important to major competitors. The firm must have the skills to serve the customers and defend it from competitive inroads.

Building a sustainable competitive advantage within the chosen target segments is based on low-cost leadership or differentiation. Consequently, a focus strategist should use some combination of these approaches.

Sustaining a focus strategy requires the presence of three conditions.[12] First, the focusing firm must be able to defend its position against competitors pursuing broad targets. Second, it needs to erect barriers against potential imitation by competitors. Third, it must not be threatened by conditions that will cause the target segment to shrink or to dissolve into the larger, broader market.

Pitfalls in pursuing a focus strategy include targeting a segment that is not truly different, viewing the targeting decision as permanent, and choosing a segment that cannot be defended or that dries up.[13]

Time as a Competitive Advantage

Rud Istvan, a Boston Consulting Group (BCG) vice president, heads BCG's "Time-Based Competition" effort.[14] He claims that time is the secret weapon of business and offers a "new" management paradigm: *Provide the most value for the lowest cost in the least amount of time.* Istvan also suggests that firms should organize to achieve economies of time rather than economies of scale. Firms that practice time-based competition tend to do the following:[15]

1. Choose time consumption as a critical management and strategic measure
2. Use responsiveness to stay close to the customers, increasing customers' dependence on them
3. Rapidly direct value delivery systems to the most attractive customers, forcing competitors toward the less attractive ones
4. Set the pace of business innovation in their industries
5. Grow faster with higher profits than their competitors

Xerox Corp. used time to its advantage in the 1980s by reducing the time required to bring a product to market from about six years to three years.[16] The shortening of product life cycles has made such strategies even more important.

COMPETITIVE VULNERABILITY

One of the primary dangers of strategic planning is the failure of planners to objectively evaluate a firm's weaknesses and potential threats. Weaknesses and threats make the firm vulnerable to environmental events, particularly those involving competitors.

A **vulnerability analysis** means determining and evaluating the factors that could, by their presence or absence, damage a firm's ability to achieve its objectives. One way to begin a vulnerability analysis is to analyze critical *underpinnings* on which the firm depends for its continued existence. Douglas A. Hurd identifies a number of categories of underpinnings.[17] One involves customer needs and wants filled by the product or service. Certainly, a firm that is satisfying a need has a good chance for success; but if that satisfaction is vulnerable to competitive strategies, the firm is vulnerable. For example, one reason that Federal Express has succeeded so well has been satisfying customer needs for fast, reliable delivery. However, if another firm or the U.S. Postal Service could provide comparable services, Federal Express could be in trouble. Another underpinning involves assets and resources. A firm may have an advantage of having a more modern, efficient plant. Yet the firm may be vulnerable if present or new competitors can build even more efficient plants. Other underpinnings discussed by Hurd include the following:

1. Cost position relative to competition and by major cost components
2. Consumer base, including size, demographics, and trends
3. Technologies
4. Special skills, systems, procedures, organization
5. Corporate identity, including, logo image, products, and corporate culture factors (for example, role models, heroes)
6. Institutional barriers to competition, including regulations, codes, patent laws, and licensing
7. Social values, life styles, common norms, and ideals
8. Sanctions, supports, and incentives to do business, particularly in such fields as medicines, nuclear materials, restaurants, securities, and import and export
9. Customer goodwill, including factors such as customer safety, product quality, and company reputation
10. Complementary products or services in the stakeholder system

The planner must analyze these factors from the perspective of their potential for removal or change. For example, the departure of key managers or unavailability of key raw materials can leave a firm vulnerable. Similarly, changes (particularly

PERSPECTIVE 9.1

Is the Sleeping Giant at UPS Beginning to Awaken?

Profitability and down-to-the-second efficiency have made the United Parcel Service into the giant it is: the largest package delivery company in the world. And it is a wealthy giant, too: 1989 profits were $693 million on $12.4 billion in revenues. For all of its 82 years, the firm has emphasized cost-cutting, saving every penny, even fractions of pennies. Time-and-motion studies are done to shave seconds off each stage of the delivery process. UPS even makes sure its pilots don't use brakes when taxiing before takeoff, in order to save cents on fuel.

In recent years the shipping industry has seen some dramatic changes. Federal Express took the industry by storm when it saw—and filled—a need for overnight service, volume discounts, and efficient tracking of parcels. Other companies joined in, and at the same time the market for international shipping began to burgeon. Although UPS started overnight delivery in 1982, other changes caught the company napping. It began to lose market share.

UPS is now in gear to gain lost ground, however. For one thing, it is expanding its overnight delivery service. It now has its own fleet of 300-plus planes, making it the tenth largest U.S. airline. And it is beginning to offer selective volume discounts, a move it had hesitated to make.

In addition, UPS has budgeted a hefty $1.4 billion for enhanced computerization.

Part of the money is earmarked for an extremely high-tech package-tracking system, due to be operational in 1993. A "dense code" less than an inch square will be packed with twice the information a bar code contains. Scanners and package conveyors will be able to read the code, which will yield information about the sender, destination, contents, value, and so on. There will be no need to rely on a mainframe computer. Two other aspects of the technological push are an automated sorting system that relies on computerized reading of address labels, and electronic clipboards that will digitally record recipients' signatures!

UPS has also invested millions in a bid to get a sizable chunk of the international delivery market. As recently as 1985, UPS's delivery area comprised only the United States, Canada, and a few European countries. It has expanded headlong, now serving 180 countries. The overseas efforts have generated millions of dollars' worth of operating losses, however, partly due to startup costs, vigorous competition, trade barriers, and customs regulation. Chairman Kent Nelson expects the foreign delivery operation to break even by 1993; this, of course, depends on UPS's ability to expand its culture beyond U.S. borders. For example, a European UPS driver may not be readily receptive to such company dictates as always holding the truck keys in the middle finger of the right hand and always fastening the seat belt with the left hand.

Finally, UPS has significantly increased its advertising budget, to $18 million, up from a mere $75,000 in 1981. The company is hoping a successful ad campaign will help increase the share of the international delivery market, which is projected to increase 20 to 30 percent per year through the 1990s.

Such huge investments—coupled with heavy losses in the international market—might spell financial trouble for some companies. But UPS has the wealth to carry it through. (In fact, it even paid cash for 100 planes in its air fleet expansion.) And the firm's history of slow, methodical growth coupled with its efficient management and precise attention to detail make it a force to be reckoned with.

References: Todd Vogel and Chuck Hawkins, "Can UPS Deliver the Goods in a New World?" *Business Week,* June 4, 1990, pp. 80–82; Alicia Orr, "Overseas Carriers Do It All," *Target Marketing,* March 1990, p. 34; Clemens P. Work, "The Flying-Package Trade Takes Off," *U.S. News and World Report,* October 2, 1989, pp. 47, 50; Resa W. King, "UPS Isn't About to Be Left Holding the Parcel," *Business Week,* February 3, 1989, p. 69.

---

if unexpected) in customer preferences or government regulations can also leave the firm vulnerable. The key question for a firm is whether its critical underpinnings are safe from assault by competitors.

A detailed analysis of vulnerabilities involves addressing the following questions:

1. What are the firm's key underpinnings?
2. What would be the impact or consequences of changing or removing each key underpinning?
3. For those changes with major consequences, what is the probability of occurrence?
4. For those major changes likely to occur, how can the firm deal with them?

ANALYZING STRENGTHS, WEAKNESSES, OPPORTUNITIES, AND THREATS

Environmental scanning and analysis should evolve into an analysis of the firm's strengths, weaknesses, opportunities, and threats. This analysis begins with an evaluation of the firm's products and markets, which sets the stage for the development of environmental profiles.

Evaluating Products and Markets

An analysis and evaluation of the firm's products and markets can facilitate the development of the environmental profiles by helping the analyst focus on the most relevant environmental issues. For the firm with multiple products in multiple markets, each individual product/market (P/M) combination may have different competitors and different customers that may respond to a different marketing mix. P/M analysis focuses on the following definitions:

- *Product line:* a family of products from the customer's point of view
- *Market:* a group of customers with needs that respond to a particular marketing mix

The matrix shown in Table 9.1 offers a sound approach to P/M analysis. Each individual P/M cell should be analyzed. The first phase involves establishing market needs, which consists of two basic steps. First, determine the dimensions on which to divide the market, such as benefits (that is, quality, service, economy), end use, type of purchase (that is, straight, modified rebuy, new), volume, psychological dimensions, and evaluative criteria (that is, performance, ease of use, support). Second, determine how the firm can provide the customer groups with satisfaction, which involves effective deployment of the marketing mix elements (product, price, place/distribution, and promotion).

The second major phase involves analyzing the competitors relevant to each P/M cell. The matrix shown in Table 9.2 can facilitate this analysis.

TABLE 9.1 · Product/Market Overview

Product Line Market					Total
Total					

Include the following information in each cell:

1. Total company sales
2. Market share
3. Largest competitor—name and market share

TABLE 9.2 · **Competitor Analysis for Individual P/M Cell**

	Competitor 1	Competitor 2	Competitor 3
Annual sales ($)			
Market share (%)			
Market share trend	up, down, >		
Commitment to P/M	hi, med., low		
% earnings from P/M			
Financial strength			
Investment strategy			
Investment level			
Mfg. skill			
Mfg. cost			
Product charac.			
Price strategy			
Dist. strategy			
Promo. strategy			
OUR SALES			
OUR MARKET SHARE			
TOTAL P/M SALES			

TABLE 9.3 · P/M Approaches

PRODUCT LINE EMPHASIS

Product Line \ Market	I	II	III	IV	Total
A	XX	XX	XX	XX	
B					
C					
D					
Total					

MARKET EMPHASIS

Product Line \ Market	I	II	III	IV	Total
A		XX			
B		XX			
C		XX			
D		XX			
Total					

NICHE EMPHASIS

Product Line \ Market	I	II	III	IV	Total
A			XX		
B		XX			
C			XX		
D	XX			XX	
Total					

In addition to setting the stage for additional analysis, a P/M analysis should also provide cues regarding appropriate business strategy alternatives. For example, four overall approaches to the P/M can be pursued (see Table 9.3):

- **Product line emphasis**
  Product differentiation
  Product development (new products, feature improvements, quality improvements, style improvements)
  Product line development (stretch down, up, or both; line filling; line modernization)
  Cost focus
  Diversification
- **Market emphasis**
  Market penetration (increase rate of purchase, attract competitors' purchases, buy a competitor)
  Market development (find new geographical markets, find new target markets, find new uses)
- **Niche emphasis**
- **Total market**

These approaches are discussed in greater detail in Chapter 12.

Developing Environmental Profiles

Environmental profiles can be useful tools in analyzing the macro- and task environments and the internal situation. An **environmental profile** is a summary of the key environmental factors; each factor is listed and evaluated regarding its influence (positive or negative) on the firm and its significance to (or impact on) the firm.

Table 9.4 presents the basic format for an environmental profile. In the first column, the firm lists the key environmental factors and their components. Marketing factors, for example, would include product quality, pricing, advertising, and so on.

The second column is used to rate each factor according to its overall significance to the firm. A positive rating indicates that the factor is a strength (for the internal profile) or an opportunity (for the macro and task profiles). A negative rating indicates that the factor is a weakness (for the internal profile) or a threat (for the macro and task profiles). For example, a factor of great significance—as increasing interest rates would be to the auto industry—get a rating of -3 (threat). The scale used in this text ranges from $+3$ to -3, but these levels are not magical and can be adjusted according to individual preference.

Obviously, a firm that finds a multitude of factors with high negative scores

TABLE 9.4 · Basic Format for an Environmental Profile

MACROENVIRONMENTAL PROFILE

Environmental Factors	Significance to Firm					
	Opportunity		Neutral		Threat	
Economic factors						
1.	+3 +2 +1		0		−1 −2 −3	

TASK ENVIRONMENT PROFILE

Environmental Factors	Significance to Firm					
	Opportunity		Neutral		Threat	
Customers						
1.	+3 +2 +1		0		−1 −2 −3	

INTERNAL ENVIRONMENT PROFILE

Environmental Factors	Significance to Firm					
	Opportunity		Neutral		Threat	
Human Resources						
1.	+3 +2 +1		0		−1 −2 −3	

should address these items first. The primary benefit of these profiles is that all major environmental factors and their probable impact on the firm are shown in a condensed, manageable format. Opportunities and strengths become more apparent, as do threats and weaknesses. We see that in considering a practical example of the use of environmental profiles and competitor profiles.

The Hayden Company

The Hayden Company (a disguised name) was a bass boat manufacturer in Texas. A consultant was brought in because the firm's problems were pushing it toward bankruptcy. One of the first tasks was to analyze the firm's environmental situation. Tables 9.5, 9.6, and 9.7 present the resulting environmental profiles.

PERSPECTIVE 9.2

Wal-Mart Blinks

Everyone who has ever watched an old-time cowboy movie knows: the Great American Hero does not stumble, does not fall. He (and it should have been she) trods through obstacles (like bullets) with a ghostlike invulnerability because his focus is clear and his heart is pure.

Accordingly, it's hard to think that Sam Walton, a Great American Hero if ever there was one, a man who reportedly through unremitting vision and hard work has become the richest person in the United States, could ever make a mistake. And yet, the founder and motive force of the Wal-Mart discount chain may have done just that.

At least Walton did not err by thinking small. He had the good grace to be not quite right by thinking big—in Texas, and a few other places. And Walton's Hypermart U.S.A. stores *are* big: 225,000-square-foot facilities that sell everything from soft drinks to the refrigerators to cool them in.

Hypermart had the misfortune to come along when the economy was in the midst of what one retail consultant referred to as a "mild recession" in appliance sales in particular and retail sales in general. (Sears had had losing quarters. Cash-starved conglomerates were having trouble finding buyers for famous-name outlets.) Then, too, Walton may not have considered the high costs of operating such huge stores—costs that Wal-Mart, locked into its reputation as a discount retailer, could not entirely pass along to its customers. Also, Wal-Mart's legendary skill at buying cheap may have worked against it. By only buying what it could pick up at a low price, Wal-Mart could not match the variety offered by more specialized retail outlets.

Fear not for Wal-Mart, however. Mighty Sam Walton has not been disarmed. Empowered by its other ventures, Wal-Mart's net income passed $1 billion in 1989, a milestone no other general-merchandise retailer has ever reached. While relentless cost control may have been a contributing factor to the relative lack of success of the Hypermarts, it remains a key to Wal-Mart's position as one of the most successful businesses of its kind of all time.

References: Kevin Kelly and Amy Dunkin, "Wal-Mart Gets Lost in the Vegetable Aisle," *Business Week,* May 28, 1990, p. 48; "Retailer First Wal-Mart: Discounter Nets Over $18," *Discount Store News,* March 12, 1990, p. 7; Steve Weiner, "Retailing," *Forbes,* January 8, 1990, p. 192.

One major advantage of environmental profiles should be apparent from examining the tables; specific problem areas are highlighted by the weighted scores. For instance, few problems existed in the macroenvironment, as indicated by the lack of high negative scores.

The task environment, however, seems to contain several problem areas.

TABLE 9.5 ▪ Macroenvironmental Profile

	Significance to Firm						
Environmental Factors	Opportunity			Neutral	Threat		
ECONOMIC FACTORS							
Increasing fuel prices	+3	+2	+1	0	**(−1)**	−2	−3
Regional economy	+3	+2	**(+1)**	0	−1	−2	−3
National economy	+3	+2	**(+1)**	0	−1	−2	−3
Rising interest rates	+3	+2	+1	0	**(−1)**	−2	−3
GOVERNMENTAL AND POLITICAL							
Possible regulations limiting pleasure boat industry	+3	+2	+1	0	−1	**(−2)**	−3
New lake in area	+3	+2	**(+1)**	0	−1	−2	−3
Decrease in construction of man-made lakes	+3	+2	+1	0	**(−1)**	−2	−3
Safety regulations	+3	+2	+1	0	**(−1)**	−2	−3
SOCIETAL FACTORS							
Increased spending on leisure and recreation	+3	+2	**(+1)**	0	−1	−2	−3
Crowding on lakes	+3	+2	+1	**(0)**	−1	−2	−3
Increasing concern over fuel waste	+3	+2	+1	0	**(−1)**	−2	−3
NATURAL FACTORS							
Increased concern over environmental damage	+3	+2	+1	**(0)**	−1	−2	−3
Many lakes in area	+3	**(+2)**	+1	0	−1	−2	−3
TECHNOLOGICAL FACTORS							
New technology	+3	+2	+1	**(0)**	−1	−2	−3

For instance, there are three −3s related to competitive factors. Intense rivalry existed between firms, and Hayden Company's competition was developing new products and using new marketing strategies. When the changes in demand (indicated under *customers*) are added to the fact that competitors were delivering new products, this problem area is magnified. The factors listed under *substitute products* also add to the same general problem area. The main information gained from the task environment profile is that the character of consumer demand changed and competitors, both direct and indirect, made adjustments whereas the Hayden Company did not.

The internal situation profile indicates even more trouble. For instance, there are problems with human resources related to the owner/manager. (He was not overly fond of this particular profile.) The fact that seven of the nine factors listed under the financial category have −3s indicates tremendous problems. A potential way around some of the difficulties is indicated in the profile, however. Although the firm was on the brink of bankruptcy, a government loan would have given it some breathing space. To obtain the loan, the owner had only to apply for it. There was no other means of avoiding bankruptcy. Without the loan the firm would simply cease to exist; an infusion of money was necessary to implement any other changes.

A competitor profile for one of the Hayden Company's competitors—Bass Boats Unlimited (also a disguised name)—is shown in Table 9.8. Note that the competitor profile differs from the other environmental profiles in several ways. First, the items listed are the key success factors in this particular business and are identical for each competitor. The importance of each factor is also the same for each competitor. The competitor is then rated on its success with each factor. Multiplying the importance times the firm's rating yields a weighted score for each factor. Both the weighted score for each factor and the total weighted score for the competitor can provide useful information. The former indicates the relative importance of each factor or specific strengths and weaknesses of the competitor; the latter allows for the comparison of each competitor's strengths.

Although the financial problems were severe and needed immediate attention, the crucial problem stemmed from marketing. The Hayden Company simply could not sell its boats. There was no sales force and no advertising. The owner/manager thought the fact that his boat was in many ways superior to the competition meant that people would come to him to buy the boat. This did not happen. Most customers could not judge the true structural quality of the boats and, since no written warranty was given, many potential customers believed the product quality to be low. Many boat retailers and buyers thought the boat was also overpriced, off-brand, and outdated. After the financial problems were addressed, the owner needed to seek a great deal of marketing assistance, probably by hiring a good marketing manager.

TABLE 9.6 · Task Environment Profile

Environmental Factors	Significance to Firm						
	Opportunity			Neutral	Threat		
COMPETITORS							
New products	+3	+2	+1	0	−1	−2	(−3)
Pricing structure	+3	+2	+1	(0)	−1	−2	−3
Product life cycle	+3	+2	(+1)	0	−1	−2	−3
New marketing strategies	+3	+2	+1	0	−1	−2	(−3)
Intensity of rivalry	+3	+2	+1	0	−1	−2	(−3)
CUSTOMERS							
Changes in demand	+3	+2	+1	0	−1	−2	(−3)
Wealth changes	+3	+2	+1	(0)	−1	−2	−3
Population changes	+3	+2	+1	(0)	−1	−2	−3
SUPPLIERS							
Raw material availability	+3	+2	+1	(0)	−1	−2	−3
Raw material prices	+3	+2	+1	(0)	−1	−2	−3
Number of suppliers	+3	+2	+1	(0)	−1	−2	−3
New materials	+3	+2	+1	0	(−1)	−2	−3
POTENTIAL ENTRANTS							
Cost of plants	+3	+2	(+1)	0	−1	−2	−3
Ease of entry	+3	+2	+1	0	(−1)	−2	−3
Threat of new entrants	+3	+2	+1	(0)	−1	−2	−3
SUBSTITUTE PRODUCTS							
Different boat models	+3	+2	+1	0	−1	(−2)	−3
Other recreational opportunities	+3	+2	+1	0	−1	(−2)	−3

TABLE 9.7 · Internal Environment Profile

	Significance to Firm						
Environmental Factors	Opportunity			Neutral	Threat		
HUMAN RESOURCES							
Personnel quality	+3	+2	(+1)	0	−1	−2	−3
Management quality	+3	+2	+1	0	−1	(−2)	−3
Organization structure	+3	+2	+1	0	(−1)	−2	−3
Strategic planning	+3	+2	+1	0	−1	−2	(−3)
FINANCIAL							
Cash flow	+3	+2	+1	0	−1	−2	(−3)
Cash position	+3	+2	+1	0	−1	−2	(−3)
Capital structure	+3	+2	+1	0	−1	−2	(−3)
Debt situation	+3	+2	+1	0	−1	−2	(−3)
Bank loan possibility	+3	+2	+1	0	−1	−2	(−3)
Stock sales	+3	+2	+1	0	−1	−2	(−3)
Tax situation	+3	+2	(+1)	0	−1	−2	−3
Government assistance	(+3)	+2	+1	0	−1	−2	−3
Financial planning	+3	+2	+1	0	−1	−2	(−3)
MARKETING							
Product quality	(+3)	+2	+1	0	−1	−2	−3
Pricing	+3	+2	+1	0	(−1)	−2	−3
Sales force	+3	+2	+1	0	−1	−2	(−3)
Advertising	+3	+2	+1	0	−1	−2	(−3)
Warranty	+3	+2	+1	0	−1	−2	(−3)
Image	+3	+2	+1	0	−1	−2	(−3)
PRODUCTION AND R&D							
Facilities	+3	(+2)	+1	0	−1	−2	−3
New product designs	+3	+2	+1	0	−1	−2	(−3)
Scheduling efficiency	+3	+2	(+1)	0	−1	−2	−3
Quality control	(+3)	+2	+1	0	−1	−2	−3

TABLE 9.8 · Competitor Profile for Hayden Company Competitor: Bass Boats Unlimited

Key Success Factors	Importance of Factor to Industry[a]	Firm's Rating[b]	Weighted Score[c]
Product quality	2	2	4
Product mix	2	3	6
Price	3	1	3
Dealer/distribution	2	1	2
Promotion ability	3	1	3
Operations/manufacturing	3	3	9
Overall cost situation	2	2	4
Financial strength	2	2	4
Organization	2	2	4
General managerial ability	3	2	6
Human resource quality	2	3	6
Total weighted score			51[d]

[a]The scale is 3 = high importance, 2 = moderate importance, and 1 = low importance. Note that the rating of each success factor will remain the same for all firms in the industry, and each industry can have its own unique rating scheme.
[b]The scale for the firm's rating is 3 = strong, 2 = moderate, and 1 = weak.
[c]The weighted score is obtained by multiplying the factor's importance by the firm's rating.
[d]The total weighted score is obtained by adding the weighted scores for each success factor. Total weighted scores can be compared for each competitor to get an idea of its relative strength.

One factor in the production and R&D category deserves special attention. The Hayden Company did not really have the capability to develop new hull designs or incorporate new materials into its production process. Since customers wanted different designs and competitors were delivering those boats, the problems were magnified again.

An observation or two about profiles is in order. Many of the factors involved are closely linked. For instance, problems related to funding appear in several sections. Furthermore, several ratings must sometimes be combined to get the true picture. The factors to be combined may even be in different environments (for example, changed customer demands, new boats offered by the competition, and Hayden's inability to develop new products).

Another important point illustrated by the Hayden example is that a good environmental analysis and profile can indicate both the position of the firm and likely solutions to the problems. The owner/manager of the Hayden Company realized that to make the firm profitable he had to obtain a federal loan, start generating cash flow by selling boats, and begin the development of alternate designs. Since this owner did not want to fight the tremendous uphill battle, he simply ceased operations. The profiles were a major reason for his decision.

SWOT Analysis

As we noted in an earlier chapter, SWOT is an acronym for strengths, weaknesses, opportunities, and threats. The purpose of a SWOT analysis is to match strengths and weaknesses with appropriate opportunities and threats. This matching process can be facilitated by using a SWOT matrix. An abbreviated SWOT matrix for the Hayden Company is shown in Exhibit 9.1.

The SWOT matrix is constructed by first listing the strengths, weaknesses, opportunities, and threats—as established through the prioritizing matrices in the appropriate cells.

Next, the strategy analyst methodically compares each relevant pair of lists to uncover logical matches. This process generates four basic categories of matches for which strategy alternatives can be considered.

S/O matches result from matching the firm's major strengths with key opportunities. Essentially, the firm should use its strengths to exploit opportunities.

EXHIBIT 9.1 · Abbreviated SWOT Matrix for Hayden Company

SWOT *Matrix*	*Opportunities* 1. Many lakes in area 2. Increased spending on leisure	*Threats* 1. Strong competition 2. Consumers want different hull designs

Strengths
1. Product quality
2. Government assistance
3. Personnel
	S/O Matches
	1. S – Product quality
	   O – Increased spending on leisure
		S/T Matches
		1. S – Product quality
		   T – Strong competition

Weaknesses
1. No new products
2. Poor marketing skills
3. Weak finances
	W/O Matches
	1. W – No new products
	   O – Increased spending on leisure
		W/T Matches
		1. W – No new products
		   T – Consumers want different hull designs

Thus the Hayden Company might match "product quality" with "increased spending on leisure" and consider focusing on the upper end of the market.

S/T *matches* result from matching the firm's strengths with major threats. The firm should use its strengths to avoid or defuse threats. Hayden Company could match "strong competition" with "product quality" and consider emphasizing the traditional quality characteristics of its boats.

W/O *matches* result from matching the firm's weaknesses with major opportunities. The firm attempts to overcome its weaknesses by taking advantage of opportunities. Hayden Company might match "increased spending on leisure" with "no new products" and consider producing completely new types of leisure products.

W/T *matches* result from matching the firm's weaknesses with threats. Essentially the firm attempts to minimize its weaknesses and avoid threats by undertaking defensive strategies. Hayden Company might match "consumers want different hull designs" with "no new products" and consider hiring a skilled hull designer.

Note that the analyst can modify each SWOT cell to include the ratings assigned to each factor in the environmental profiles. For each match, the absolute value of the relevant ratings for each factor can be multiplied. The resulting sums provide a priority rating for each match. Matches with the largest ratings should naturally be primary targets for analysis.

The following questions can be helpful for each match:

1. Is the match logical? realistic?
2. What is the expected outcome of the match if no action is taken? Note that some matches will not occur if no action is taken, whereas others will occur of their own accord.
3. What action alternatives are possible?
4. What outcomes will the action alternatives generate?
5. What is the cost/benefit of the action alternatives (cost of action versus benefit of outcome)?
6. Can the action alternative/outcome combinations be transformed into objectives/strategies?
7. Do the matches generate competitive advantages? Defendable? Sustainable?

E-SWOT Analysis

E-SWOT is an acronym for *extended*-SWOT analysis.[18] E-SWOT is based on the premise that SWOT analysis ignores several potentially critical matches. For example, a firm might be able to alleviate a weakness by focusing a strength on it. Or three factors may need to be considered as a match, such as S/O *plus* W. E-SWOT includes two additional two-way matches (S/W and O/T), four three-

EXHIBIT 9.2 · E-SWOT Analysis

E-SWOT Matrix	Opportunities 1. 2. 3.	Threats 1. 2. 3.	O/T Matches 1. 2. 3.
Strengths 1. 2. 3.	S/O Matches 1. 2. 3.	S/T Matches 1. 2. 3.	S/O/T Matches 1. 2. 3.
Weaknesses 1. 2. 3.	W/O Matches 1. 2. 3.	W/T Matches 1. 2. 3.	W/O/T Matches 1. 2. 3.
S/W Matches 1. 2. 3.	O/S/W Matches 1. 2. 3.	T/S/W Matches 1. 2. 3.	S/W/O/T Matches 1. 2. 3.

way matches, and the four-way S/W/O/T match (see Exhibit 9.2). Consider, for example, the following four-way match:

- S—government assistance
- W—weak finances
- O—many lakes in area
- T—consumers want different hull designs

This match suggests a strategy of pursuing government loan assistance to enable Hayden Company to acquire the personnel and equipment necessary for producing new hull designs. This strategy is compatible with several of the other factors listed in Figure 9.1 but is countered by a major weakness—lack of marketing skills. The firm probably could not market the new hulls if it had them, which implies that other four-factor matches should be considered.

All cells should be analyzed, including the nonmatching cells, which contain a single variable (that is, strength, opportunity). The questions listed below can help the analyst gain a clearer perspective on the various cells and matches. Note that there is more than one critical question for each single-factor cell and for each of the two-, three-, and four-way matches. Each of these questions provide the analyst with a different perspective.

Single-Factor Cells

- *Strengths*
  a. Which strengths are *not* focused on an opportunity, weakness, or threat? Can the strength be focused?
     > *Note:* A strength does not have to be focused on an opportunity to be beneficial—it can also be beneficial if focused effectively on a weakness or threat. If a strength focuses on nothing, however, consideration should be given to eliminating or disinvesting in the strength.
  b. Which strengths need to be developed more fully? At what cost?
- *Weaknesses*
  a. Which weaknesses are not addressed by a strength?
  b. Can the weakness be eliminated otherwise, such as by a decision? At what cost?
- *Opportunities*
  a. Which significant opportunities are *not* addressed with a strength?
  b. What kind of strength is needed to address untapped opportunities?
- *Threats*
  a. Which significant threats can *not* be addressed with a strength?
  b. Can significant threats be converted into opportunities?

Two-Factor Matches

- For *Strength/Opportunity* matches:
  a. Which significant opportunities can be addressed with each significant strength?

     AND
  b. Which strengths can be focused on a specific opportunity?
- For *Weakness/Opportunity* matches:
  a. Are there significant opportunities that can *not* be pursued because of significant weaknesses?
     > *Note:* Sometimes, an opportunity can be pursued without a significant strength—but certain weaknesses can present barriers.

     AND
  b. Are there weaknesses that could be positioned to benefit from a specific opportunity?
- For *Strength/Threat* matches:
  a. Which significant threats can be addressed with significant strengths?

     AND
  b. Do any threats undermine any of the strengths?

- For *Weakness/Threat* matches:
  a. Are there significant threats that focus directly on specific weaknesses, thereby making the weakness more significant?

  AND

  b. Are there any weaknesses that would make any of the threats more severe?

- For *Strength/Weakness* matches:
  a. Which weaknesses can be reduced or eliminated by applying an existing strength?

  AND

  b. Do any weaknesses undermine any of the strengths?

- For *Opportunity/Threat* matches:
  a. Are there significant threats that could reduce the attractiveness of certain opportunities?

  AND

  b. Are there certain opportunities that could eliminate or reduce the impact of certain threats?

Three-Factor Matches

- For *Strength/Opportunity/Weakness* matches:
  a. Are there weaknesses that reduce the attractiveness of the S/O matches?

  AND

  b. Are there significant strengths that can be applied to various W/O matches to reduce their potential impact?

  AND

  c. Would certain opportunities become more attractive because of successful S/W matches?

- For *Strength/Threat/Weakness* matches:
  a. Are there weaknesses that could reduce the effectiveness of certain S/T matches?

  AND

  b. Are there strengths that could be applied to reduce the potential negative impact of certain W/T matches?

  AND

  c. Could certain threats be defused due to successful S/W matches?

- For *Strength/Opportunity/Threat* matches:
  a. Are there significant threats that could reduce the attractiveness of certain S/O matches?

  AND

  b. Are there certain opportunities that could be made more attractive (or created) if certain S/T matches were pursued effectively?

AND

c. Are there significant strengths that could enhance certain O/T matches by simultaneously reducing the threat and tapping the opportunity?

- For *Weakness/Opportunity/Threat* matches:
  a. Are there significant threats that make certain W/O combinations even more of a problem?

AND

  b. Are significant opportunities made less attractive because of certain W/T matches?

AND

  c. Are there significant weaknesses that could reduce the probability of successfully converting a threat to an opportunity? Or increase the potential impact of a threat?

Four-Factor Matches The simplest way to cope with four-factor matches is to extend the questions for each significant three-factor match by addressing appropriate questions for the fourth factor. For example, after pinpointing significant W/O/T matches, the analyst should seek strengths that could reduce the firm's vulnerabilities or enhance its advantages. Addressing these questions helps to identify precisely the firm's competitive advantages and vulnerabilities.

Opportunities That Become Threats

Although opportunities and threats differ, an ignored opportunity can become a threat. For instance, a firm may have the opportunity to open a branch in a new shopping center. If it decides not to pursue that opportunity and a competitor opens a branch in the center, the opportunity has turned into a threat to the firm.

A firm can also convert a threat into an opportunity. For example, a firm may initially see pollution control regulations as a threat but later use them as an opportunity by refining and selling the chemicals removed from the air or water.

Cautions About Threats

Although certain environmental threats can kill or seriously injure a company, management should not become obsessed with threats. If that happens, management may worry so much about threats that it will not take measures to avoid threats or to exploit opportunities. A firm cannot avoid some threats and must simply cope with them. An example is the threat to the lodging industry of another oil embargo. This threat could be a killer, particularly if it lasted for several months. There is very little that a company such as Holiday Inns can do to avoid this threat, but it can make plans to minimize its negative impact; for instance, it can diversify into other types of businesses. Thus, although management should be concerned about environmental threats, this concern should not overpower other planning that the firm must do or stop the firm from functioning.

GLOBAL DIMENSIONS

Competitive advantages and vulnerabilities are achieved globally in much the same way as they are domestically. The main distinction is that totally different factors may give an advantage or cause vulnerability. For example, a firm may enjoy a strong competitive advantage from its location near major domestic markets. If this location advantage is the only major advantage, the firm may have a major competitive disadvantage in global markets. Similarly, a firm may have products that are viewed as superior at meeting customer demand domestically, but not in other parts of the world. For instance, some countries may not view speed as important enough for Federal Express to be successful there.

Whatever the situation, a company should analyze its advantages and vulnerabilities relative to each country in which it operates. The differences among countries in regard to customer desires, other competitors, and all other environmental elements require this kind of analysis. The analysis done for domestic markets and operations is useless in considering the firm's global situation.

Notes

1. Michael E. Porter, *Competitive Advantage: Creating and Sustaining Superior Performance,* (New York: The Free Press, 1985), pp. 1–3.
2. Charles R. Stoner, "Distinctive Competence and Competitive Advantage," *Journal of Small Business Management* (April 1987), 33–39.
3. Bruce Henderson, "Understanding the Forces of Strategic and Natural Competition," *Journal of Business Strategy* (Winter 1982), 11.
4. Pankaj Ghemawat, "Building Strategy on the Experience Curve," *Harvard Business Review* (March-April 1985), 44.
5. Porter, pp. 70–83.
6. Ibid., pp. 97–115.
7. Summarized from Porter, pp. 115–118.
8. Ibid., ch. 4.
9. Ibid., pp. 135–138.
10. Ibid., pp. 160–162.
11. Ibid., ch. 7.
12. Ibid., pp. 267–269.
13. Ibid., pp. 270–272.
14. Bryan Iwamoto, "It's About Time," *Express Magazine* (Winter 1989), 3–5.
15. Ibid.
16. Gary Reiner, "Cutting Your Competitor to the Quick," *Wall Street Journal,* November 21, 1988, p. A14.
17. Douglas A. Hurd, *Vulnerability Analysis in Business Planning,* SRI International Research Report No. 593 (1977).
18. Danny R. Arnold, Rebecca Porterfield, and Garry D. Smith, "E-SWOT: Extension of a Practical Tool for Small Business," *Proceedings of the SBIDA National Conference* (February 1988), 365–372.

PART THREE

Strategy Selection

If a firm's managers have done what the first nine chapters have suggested, they should understand the environmental situation their firm faces and know where the firm is headed. Thus they should be well prepared to choose strategies that will allow the firm to achieve its goals. Chapters 10 through 12 discuss the strategy selection process.

Chapter 10 examines strategy analysis techniques. It is closely linked to Chapter 9 and its discussion of environmental analysis techniques. Together, Chapters 9 and 10 are transitional, shifting the emphasis from general description to analysis of what a specific firm should do. They also provide the transition to strategy selection, which is explored in Chapters 11 and 12.

Chapter 11 concentrates on the selection of corporate-level strategies and discusses decisions about the scope of operations and the industries or businesses in which a firm will compete. The chapter is built around developing a portfolio of strategic business units that can give a firm strength.

Chapter 12 addresses the selection of business- and functional-level strategies. Decisions considered in this chapter have to do with how the strategic business units intend to compete and how each functional area contributes to helping the entire firm compete and achieve its objectives.

If the management of a firm adheres to the spirit of the material contained in these three chapters, it should be able to develop an appropriate plan and be ready to place that plan into effect.

CHAPTER 10

Strategy Analysis Techniques

Once an organization's environments have been analyzed and appropriate objectives selected, top management is ready to focus on choosing strategies to achieve the objectives. Recall that objectives specify the results the firm intends to achieve and that the environmental analyses provide input concerning what will be needed to accomplish those objectives. Strategic analysis is the analysis of the various strategic alternatives available to a firm that can lead to achieving the firm's objectives in the light of environmental conditions. Strategic analysis, therefore, involves taking the vast amount of environmental data and putting it into a format that leads to the selection of appropriate strategies.

In Chapter 4, you saw that each firm is likely to have various types of objectives. Growth objectives constitute a major type of objectives that each firm should formulate. (Growth objectives are not limited to growth; they can involve maintaining the status quo or planning a decline.) Since firms concentrate a large proportion of their corporate strategies on growth objectives, the strategy selection process discussed in this chapter is geared to achieving such objectives. You need to remember, however, that a firm must also choose strategies focusing on other types of objectives and that similar procedures can be used for selecting these strategies.

Since one of the chief tools for generating strategy alternatives is portfolio analysis, we trace the development of portfolio theory and analysis, discuss several portfolio analysis techniques, and present a sequence of steps for using these techniques. Later in the chapter, we also consider other strategy analysis techniques.

PORTFOLIO ANALYSIS

Portfolio analysis can greatly help strategic planners—provided it is integrated into the strategic management process rather than used as a substitute for it. A firm should be aware that its individual holdings are interdependent and that the sum of its portfolio's contents (that is, the sum of those individual holdings) is different from, and more important than, the individual businesses in that portfolio. Key factors that can be balanced through portfolio analysis include stability of returns, risk, and cash flow.[1] The purpose of portfolio analysis is to provide input to management by helping to eliminate or focus on specific strategies or groups of strategies.

Portfolio analysis has these potential advantages:[2]

1. Provides easily graspable, informative framework
2. Results in differential treatment of businesses (resource allocation, management evaluation and compensation, risk assessment)
3. Gives a chief executive officer support to divest a cash-draining business
4. Enhances the quality of plans
5. Promotes long-run thinking
6. Aids in monitoring competitors
7. Nurtures the entrepreneurial spirit

We discuss problems associated with portfolio analysis and suggestions for optimizing its use later in the chapter.

Firms that compete in one basic industry and offer products that exhibit similar demand characteristics have a one-item business portfolio. Firms in multiple industries face a more involved portfolio analysis task because of multiple-item portfolios. The various portfolio analysis techniques discussed below can be applied to single- or multiple-item portfolios.

Approximately 75 percent of the Fortune 500 firms use some form of portfolio analysis.[3] A variety of portfolio analysis techniques and matrices have been developed, and we discuss several of them in this section. Although we examine them in relation to corporate portfolios, almost all of these techniques can also be modified slightly for use in analyzing business-level portfolios. To set the stage for this discussion, let us first briefly review the development of portfolio theory.

The Development of Portfolio Theory

The increased interest in strategy selection aids was spurred by the Boston Consulting Group (BCG) in the 1960s with their growth/market share matrix. This matrix evolved from the concept of experience curves, popularized by the ongoing Profit Impact of Marketing Strategies (PIMS) study. Both the matrix and the study are discussed later in this chapter.

Experience Curves   The concept of **experience curves** derives from the learning curve concept. **Learning curves** were developed to represent the observation that the number of labor hours it takes to produce one unit of a particular product declines in a predictable manner as the number of units produced increases. Therefore, an accurate estimation of how long it takes to produce the hundredth unit is possible if the production time for the first and tenth is known.

The experience curve includes all costs associated with a product and implies that the per unit costs should fall due to cumulative experience as production volume increases. In a given industry, therefore, the producer with the largest volume and corresponding market share should have the lowest marginal cost.[4] This market share leader should be able to underprice competitors, discourage potential new entrants, and thus achieve a respectable return on investment (ROI). The linkage of experience to cost to price to market share to ROI is illustrated in the graph in Exhibit 10.1.

BCG Growth/Market Share Matrix   BCG's view of the experience curve led to the development of the **growth/market share matrix,** depicted in Exhibit 10.2.

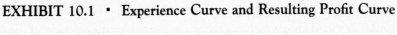

EXHIBIT 10.1 · Experience Curve and Resulting Profit Curve

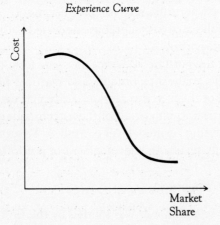

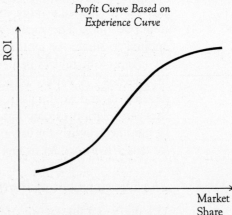

EXHIBIT 10.2 · The BCG Business Portfolio Matrix

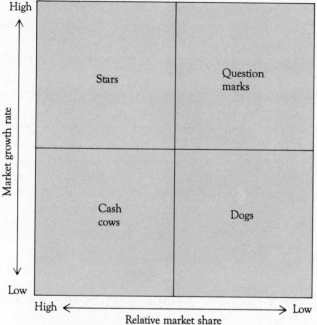

Source: "The BCG Matrix" from *The Product Portfolio Matrix.*
© 1970, The Boston Consulting Group.

The basic idea behind the growth/market share matrix is that the situation of a strategic business unit (SBU) can be summarized in two dimensions—market growth and market share. Market growth results from the combined effect of numerous factors in the macroenvironment and parts of the task environment. Market share stems from the combined effect of numerous factors in the internal environment and parts of the task environment. The better the market growth and the larger the market share, the more likely it is that the firm (SBU) should stay close to its present position. Three key points about the graph should be noted.

First, the horizontal axis represents the market share of each SBU relative to the industry leader. For example, a 0.5 means that the SBU has one-half the market share of the industry leader. The market share axis is drawn in log scale.[5]

Second, the vertical axis concerns the annualized market growth rate for each SBU's particular industry.

PERSPECTIVE 10.1

Dr Pepper/Seven-Up: Courting Heavy Drinkers

If there were no Madison Avenue, would there still be carbonated soft drinks? Probably, but the case of 7UP makes you wonder. The unquestioned leader of the lemon-lime segment of the soft-drink industry in 1985 with a 46 percent market share, 7UP had slipped by 1989, to a 37 percent share. To make matters worse, 7UP lost its leadership position to Coca Cola's Sprite. The probable cause of this change in fortunes was advertising. While cash-rich Coke was pouring money into an aggressive ad campaign for Sprite, Seven-Up, a cash-poor spinoff of Philip Morris, was spending its meager advertising allotment to promote two 7UP spinoffs: 7UP Gold, a cinnamon-flavored beverage that has since evaporated from the market, and Cherry 7UP, whose market share has halved since 1987.

By 1990, the company was again strongly promoting its mainstay products—7UP and Diet 7UP. The promotional device was the red spots which, in the TV commercials, would leap from their place on the label and wreak havoc when no one was looking. With only a small ad budget—the company was able to use more effective computer animation for only one commercial—Seven-Up concentrated its commercials on programs watched by children, who are heavy consumers of soft drinks.

Dr Pepper—which merged with Seven-Up in 1986 to form Dr Pepper/Seven-Up—suffered no decline in the late 1980s. Unlike 7UP the sole occupant of its market niche, Dr Pepper registered growth far in excess of other noncola beverages. Aided by an effective advertising program, Dr Pepper, whose popular base is in the South, had even successfully penetrated new geographic areas. "The Doctor" shared a problem with 7UP, however: lack of promotional money. (A leveraged buyout, Dr Pepper has a huge debt to pay off.) The company decided to concentrate, therefore, on people who already drink Dr Pepper in moderation but are heavy consumers of other soft drinks.

References: Kevin Kelly and Walecia Konrad, "Seven-Up: Where Have All the Bubbles Gone?" Business Week, January 29, 1990, p. 95; Gary A. Hemphill, "Spot to the Rescue: Seven-Up Relaunches Diet, Stars Animated Spot in All Ads," Beverage Industry, November 1989, p. 4; "Pepper Prognosis: No Doctor Needed," Beverage Industry, November 1989, p. 4; Victoria Bushnell, "Image Point's Taylor Animates Leo Burnett's 7-Up Campaign," Back Stage, October 27, 1989, p. 6.

Third, the cash flow situation is different in each quadrant, which leads to the following classifications:

1. *Stars:* High-growth, high-share SBUs that are likely to generate enough cash to be self-sustaining
2. *Cash cows:* Low-growth, high-share SBUs that generate excess cash, which can be used to support other SBUs (especially question marks) and research and development efforts
3. *Question marks:* High-growth, low-share SBUs that normally require a lot of cash to maintain or increase their share. Management must often either invest additional cash to convert these SBUs into stars or phase them out.
4. *Dogs:* Low-growth, low-share SBUs that are often cash traps

The growth/market share matrix can be developed using historical data. Remember, however, that any expected changes should be incorporated into the matrix. Management should pay particular attention to the market growth rate. In many industries, especially developing industries, the expected growth rate may differ substantially from the historical growth rate.

Shared Costs   Experience curve analysis requires that a great deal of attention be devoted to defining the product, the costs to be included, and the market. In the early 1970s, BCG began to doubt the wisdom of focusing cost analyses on one product, and the concept of **shared costs** arose. Consider a firm that manufactures four products, all of which use identical motors that represent 40 percent of the unit cost for each product. What if one product is unprofitable and has a small share of a large, mature market? The logic of the growth/market share matrix would indicate that the company get rid of the unprofitable product. However, spinning off this product would mean cutting back on the total production of motors. This cutback would slow the movement of the other three products down their experience curves because each would have to absorb additional costs. Although developing an accurate shared cost analysis is extremely complicated, some firms, such as B. F. Goodrich, have been able to obtain benefits by using the analysis to add, drop, or retain products.[6]

Criticisms of the Growth/Market Share Matrix   The concept of the growth/market share matrix has come to be widely used. In 1981, for example, approximately half of the one thousand largest U.S. industrial corporations were reported to be using some form of the matrix.[7] However, the matrix has evoked strong criticisms as well from a variety of sources.[8]

1. The matrix does not suggest specific strategies.
2. If new businesses are indicated, the matrix does not tell you where they should come from.
3. The experience curve is useful mostly for products sold on the basis of price alone and there are not many of these businesses.
4. The experience curve is not automatic; costs must be tightly managed.
5. Few companies can implement the concept.
6. Since overall strategy does not need to be changed every year, it begins to be not taken seriously.
7. Cutting price to gain share leads to unprofitable price wars.
8. The experience curve is not relevant for some companies.
9. If growth opportunities do not exist, the matrix is irrelevant.
10. Market share may not deserve the importance the matrix gives it.
11. Balancing cash flow is not as important as profit.

Alternative Portfolio Analysis Techniques

The above criticisms spurred the development of a variety of other **portfolio analysis techniques.** Several of them are described below.

Porter's Model   Critics of the experience curve and the growth/market share matrix have continually found exceptions to the linkage between high market share and profitability, such as Mercedes-Benz of North America, Inc. Exhibit 10.3 highlights the idea that firms with low market share can achieve high ROI.

Firms at the upper left of the curve have small market shares but are profitable producers of highly specialized products or services. Michael Porter (who developed the curve) analyzed the fractional horsepower electrical motor business in the 1970s and positioned Baldor and Gould in this spot. Firms at the upper right end of the curve have large market shares and are also profitable; General Electric and Emerson had that position. Firms stuck in the middle do not have a good market share, a clearly differentiated product, or much profit. Franklin Electric was positioned here.[9]

Based on this analysis, Porter argues that a firm can possess one of two basic types of potentially sustainable competitive advantages: low cost or differentiation.[10] These two alternatives for achieving a competitive advantage, combined with the overall scope of activity sought by the firm, lead to three *generic strategies*: cost leadership, differentiation, and focus. As Exhibit 10.4 illustrates, the focus strategy can be achieved through emphasis on either cost or differentiation.

A *cost leadership strategy* emphasizes producing a highly standardized product, becoming the lowest-cost producer in the industry, and underpricing the competition. A *differentiation strategy* emphasizes producing a product with quality or

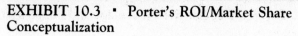

EXHIBIT 10.3 · **Porter's ROI/Market Share Conceptualization**

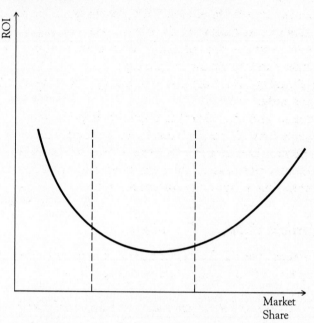

Source: Adapted with permission of The Free Press, a Division of Macmillan, Inc., from *Competitive Strategy: Techniques for Analyzing Industries and Competitors* by Michael E. Porter. Copyright © 1980 by The Free Press.

design features, brand name status, or reputation for service that let it command a higher than average price. A *focus strategy* involves pursuing a narrow competitive scope within an industry by tailoring the product to a small segment (or segments) of the market. Each of these generic strategies is discussed in greater detail in Chapter 12.

A firm lacking a cost or differentiation competitive advantage that it can deploy either in a broad or narrow market is "stuck in the middle" of Figure 10.3. Such firms are at a competitive disadvantage and are lucky to make a reasonable profit. Most industries contain quite a few competitors that are stuck in the middle.

Firms that possess a competitive advantage must strive to maintain it or they will quickly find themselves stuck in the middle. For example, cost leadership can vanish when competitors imitate operations, technology changes, any of the bases by which cost leadership was achieved changes, differentiation parity is

---

EXHIBIT 10.4 · Porter's Competitive Advantage and Scope Matrix

Competitive Advantage

	Lower Cost	Differentiation
Broad Target	1. Cost Leadership	2. Differentiation
Narrow Target	3A. Cost Focus	3B. Differentiation Focus

Competitive Scope

Source: Reprinted with permission of The Free Press, a Division of Macmillan, Inc., from *Competitive Advantage* by Michael E. Porter. Copyright © 1985 by The Free Press.

---

lost, or firms using a cost focus strategy achieve even lower costs. The differentiation advantage can disappear when competitors imitate, the basis or bases of the differentiation become less important to buyers, cost proximity is lost, or competitors using a differentiation focus strategy achieve even greater differentiation in segments. The advantages of a focus strategy can be lost when it is imitated by competitors, the target segment or demand disappears, broad-based competitors overwhelm the segment, or new focusers "sub-segment" the industry.

Porter emphasizes that firms must analyze what is going on in the industry (see the discussion of task environment in Chapter 6) and choose the most promising competitive niche and generic strategy. Management should seek a "defensible competitive position" so that the firm does not have to slug it out with everybody else in the industry.

General Electric's Business Screen General Electric, with the aid of BCG and McKinsey and Co., pioneered the nine-cell **strategic business screen** illustrated in Exhibit 10.5.[11] The vertical axis represents the industry attractiveness. Factors that must be analyzed and weighted to determine an industry's attractiveness

EXHIBIT 10.5 · **General Electric's Nine-Cell Business Screen**

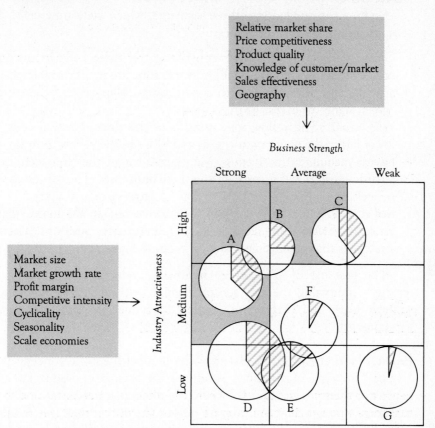

Note: Each lettered circle represents a separate SBU.

Source: Modified by permission from *Strategy Formulation: Analytical Concepts* by Charles W. Hofer and Dan Schendel; Copyright © 1978 West Publishing Company. All rights reserved. p. 32.

include market size, growth rate, profit margins, competitive intensity, cyclicality, seasonality, and scale economies. The horizontal axis represents the firm's strength or ability to compete in the industry. Factors that must be analyzed and weighted include the relative market share, price competitiveness, product quality, knowledge of customer/market, sales effectiveness, and geography. Recall that all of these factors should have been included in the environmental analysis.

Each circle in Figure 10.5 represents an individual SBU. (A firm competing in one industry would have only one circle.) The size of each circle represents the relative size of each industry and the "pie slices" in the circles indicate the SBU's market share.

Each axis is divided into three segments, which yield nine cells. The nine cells are grouped into three zones:

1. *Green zone.* The green zone consists of the three cells in the upper left corner. Firms or individual SBUs in this zone are in a favorable position and are relatively attractive growth opportunities. Management therefore has the "green light" to invest in those areas.
2. *Yellow zone.* The yellow zone consists of the three diagonal cells from the lower left to the upper right. Firms and SBUs in the yellow zone are viewed as having medium attractiveness. Management must therefore exercise caution regarding additional investments in these businesses. The suggested strategy is to seek to maintain share rather than to grow or reduce share.
3. *Red zone.* The red zone consists of the three cells in the lower right corner. Firms and SBUs in the red zone are not in attractive positions. The suggested strategy is that management should begin to make plans to exit the industry.

The best use of GE's screen involves developing current and projected screens. Comparing the two screens should help management identify major strategic issues and alternatives. Table 10.1 summarizes strategies suggested by this approach.

Product/Market Evolution Matrix   The product life cycle concept depicts the "typical" life cycle of a product. Analyzing the balance of products in a portfolio relative to their product life cycles can help direct planners' attention to the need to change strategies and to introduce new products over time (see Exhibit 10.6).

Charles Hofer specifically criticizes the portfolio grids that do not adequately represent new businesses in new industries that are just starting to grow.[12] Hofer's contribution is the **product/market evolution portfolio matrix,** shown in Exhibit 10.7. The horizontal axis categorizes competitive position as strong, average, or weak. The vertical axis divides the stages of product/market evolution into a scale that is equivalent to the more conventional product life cycle (PLC).

Figure 10.7 also illustrates Hofer and Dan Schendel's suggestion that most corporate-level portfolio strategies are variations of one of the three ideal portfolios: (1) growth portfolios (for example, Exxon), (2) profit portfolios (for example, R. J. Reynolds and Philip Morris), and (3) balanced portfolios (for example, General Electric).[13] In the figure, each circle represents the entire market, and each shaded area, the firm's market share.

Peter Patel and Michael Younger developed some diagnostic/decision guidelines, which are closely related to the product/market evolution portfolio matrix.[14] These guidelines are shown in Table 10.2.

TABLE 10.1 · The Position on the Matrix Suggests "Natural" Strategies

Industry strength	Market attractiveness		
	High	Medium	Low
High	Premium: invest for growth • provide maximum investment • diversify worldwide • consolidate position • accept moderate near-term profits	Selective: invest for growth • invest heavily in selected segments • share ceiling • seek attractive new segments to apply strength	Protect/refocus: selectively invest for earnings • defend strengths • refocus to attractive segments • evaluate industry revitalization • monitor for harvest or divestment timing
Medium	Challenge: invest for growth • build selectively on strengths • define implications of leadership challenge • avoid vulnerability —fill weaknesses	Prime: selectively invest for earnings • segment market • make contingency plans for vulnerability	Restructure: harvest or divest • provide no unessential commitment • position for divestment or • shift to more attractive segment
Low	Opportunistic: selectively invest for earnings • ride market • seek niches, specialization • seek opportunity to increase strength (e.g., acquisition)	Opportunistic: preserve for harvest • act to preserve or boost cash flow out • seek opportunistic sale or • seek opportunistic rationalization to increase strengths	Harvest or divest • exit from market or prune product line • determine timing so as to maximize present value

Source: D. D. Monieson, "An Overview of Marketing Planning," in E. B. no. 8, *Effective Marketing Planning: An Overview* (Ottawa: The Conference Board in Canada, 1978), p. 5. Reprinted by permission of the publisher.

Price Sensitivity/Perceived Difference Grid   Developed by The Strategic Planning Associates, the **price sensitivity/perceived difference grid** is a two-dimensional grid that focuses on management's choice between reducing costs or building in more value to the customer (see Figure 10.8).[15] Price sensitivity is plotted on the vertical axis. *High price sensitivity* means that the product costs a great deal

EXHIBIT 10.6 · Product Life Cycle

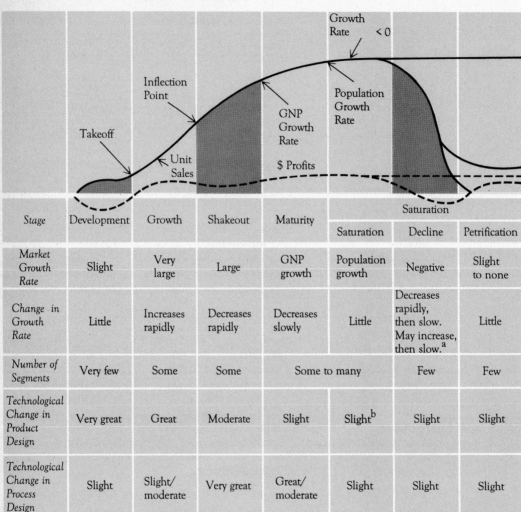

Stage	Development	Growth	Shakeout	Maturity	Saturation	Decline	Petrification
Market Growth Rate	Slight	Very large	Large	GNP growth	Population growth	Negative	Slight to none
Change in Growth Rate	Little	Increases rapidly	Decreases rapidly	Decreases slowly	Little	Decreases rapidly, then slow. May increase, then slow.[a]	Little
Number of Segments	Very few	Some	Some	Some to many		Few	Few
Technological Change in Product Design	Very great	Great	Moderate	Slight	Slight[b]	Slight	Slight
Technological Change in Process Design	Slight	Slight/ moderate	Very great	Great/ moderate	Slight	Slight	Slight
Major Functional Concern	Research and development	Engineering	Production	Marketing, distribution, finance		Finance	Marketing and finance

[*] The rate of change of the market growth rate usually only increases during the decline stage for those products that do not die, i.e., that enter the petrification stage of evolution.

[†] Although the rate of technological change in the basic design of the product is usually low during this stage of market evolution, the probability of a major breakthrough to a different kind of product that performs the same function increases substantially during this period.

Source: C. W. Hofer, "Conceptual Constructs for Formulating Corporate and Business Strategy," Boston: Intercollegiate Case Clearing House, 9-378-754, 1977, p. 7.

EXHIBIT 10.7 · Three Types of Ideal Corporate Portfolios

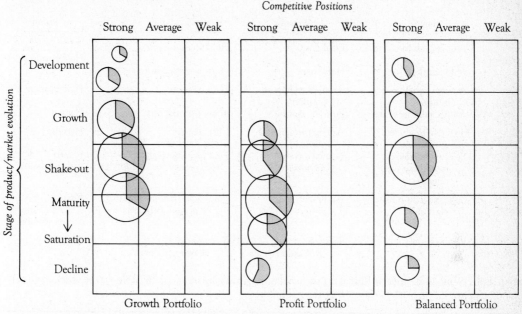

or represents a substantial portion of the customer's budget. *Low price sensitivity* means that the product is inexpensive or a minor item in the budget.

The horizontal axis is a measure of whether the customers perceive a difference between competing products and value these differences enough to pay for them. Each of the four quadrants has different implications in terms of suggested strategy.

First, a *commodity strategy* is recommended for products facing buyers' high price sensitivity and low perceived differences, such as flat steel or gasoline. The commodity strategy is similar to the "increase market share" advice of the experience curve.

Second, a *specialty strategy* is recommended for products facing low price sensitivity and high perceived differences by buyers, such as vintage champagne or narrow-aisle lift trucks. The suggested focus is on continuing efforts to improve the special value that differentiates the product.

Third, a *transitional strategy* is suggested for products facing high price sensitivity and high perceived differences, such as computers. Management should

---

TABLE 10.2 · Strategic Guidelines as a Function of Industry Maturity and Competitive Position

	Embryonic	Growing	Mature	Aging
Dominant	All-out push for share / Hold position	Hold position / Hold share	Hold position / Growth with industry	Hold position
Strong	Attempt to improve position / All-out push for share	Attempt to improve position / Push for share	Hold position / Grow with industry	Hold position or Harvest
Favorable	Selective or all-out push for share / Selectively attempt to improve position	Attempt to improve position / Selective push for share	Custodial or maintenance / Find niche and attempt to protect	Harvest / Phased withdrawal
Tenable	Selectively push for position	Find niche and protect it	Find niche and hang on or phased withdrawal	Phased withdrawal or abandon
Weak	Up or out	Turnaround or abandon	Turnaround or phased withdrawal	Abandon

Source: From William F. Glueck, *Business Policy and Strategic Management,* p. 167 (New York: McGraw-Hill Book Company, 1980), with permission of the publisher.

---

emphasize price and quality but be ready for competitors' product improvements that will attract customers. Environmental analysis and solid financial reserves are critical.

Fourth, a *hybrid strategy* is recommended for products facing low price sensitivity and low perceived differences, such as home insulation or table salt. Management should avoid price wars and talk quality but not spend much on it.

The Number and Size of Advantages Matrix BCG has developed another matrix, which incorporates the number and size of advantages available to the firm. This matrix is based on three premises. First, profitability is the result of a firm's achieving a competitive advantage. Second, the number of ways advantage can be gained and the potential size of the advantage are different in each industry. Third, the magnitude and nature of the advantageous positions alter as the industry evolves.

As shown in Exhibit 10.9, the number of ways advantages can be obtained is plotted on the vertical axis and the size of the advantage is on the horizontal axis. As with other grids, each quadrant can be labeled and has certain strategy implications.

EXHIBIT 10.8 · The Price Sensitivity/Perceived Difference Grid

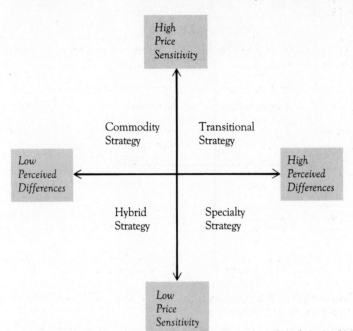

Source: Drawn from verbal description in Walter Kiechel III, "Three (or Four, or More) Ways to Win," *Fortune*, October 19, 1981, p. 183.

First, firms in *stalemate industries*, such as the paper and steel industries, possess small advantages and have few ways to achieve them. The suggested strategy is to push for rigid cost control, squeeze cash, look for new opportunities, and look for the opportunity to exit the industry with minimum injury.

Second, firms in *volume industries*, such as the denim and aluminum industries, have large advantages but few ways to achieve them. The suggested strategy is to cut costs by increasing volume. Firms with large advantages should "attack" the have-nots, firms without competitive advantages should withdraw or seek competitive advantages other than price.

Third, firms in *specialization industries*, such as the automobile industry, have large advantages and many ways to achieve them. The suggested strategy is to manage to maintain position and spend to prevent competitors from building the same advantages.

EXHIBIT 10.9 · Number and Size of Advantages Grid

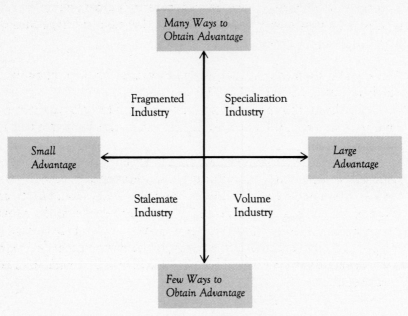

Source: Drawn from verbal description in Walter Kiechel III, "Three (or Four, or More) Ways to Win," *Fortune,* October 19, 1981, p. 184.

Fourth, firms in *fragmented industries,* such as the restaurant industry, possess small advantages and many ways to achieve them. The suggested strategies are to minimize investment, try to improve profitability, maintain position, and be cautious about expanding.

This avenue of analysis emphasizes the importance of a good analysis of the task environment. Innovative ideas and technology can change the nature of an industry (remember the technology life cycle). For example, a determined competitor, such as McDonald's, moved out of a fragmented industry by creating a unique competitive advantage.[16]

Corporate Development Matrix The **corporate development matrix** is designed to help assess the potential of existing and proposed businesses and products.[17] It is based on two questions:

1. Can this business or product be made more valuable to the customer through *value leveraging?* (Value leveraging or leveraging customer value refers to increasing a business's or product's value to the customer.)
2. Can this business or product maintain or increase its competitive cost advantage through *system innovation?*

A business is assigned a high or low priority based on its position in the matrix, which is illustrated in Exhibit 10.10.

Losers have little potential and should be sold or closed. *Winners* have the potential for continued value leveraging and system innovation and should be nourished.

Watch and wait businesses have high potential for value leveraging, but low potential for achieving a competitive cost advantage. Essentially, the firm can carve out a profitable niche through specialization. Retaining its competitive advantage involves staying ahead of competitors relative to the relevant CSFs.

Businesses classified as *unstable cash bonanzas* typically have high achievable competitive cost advantage, but little potential for further leveraging of customer value. They may be stable temporarily but are vulnerable to competitive maneuvers.

EXHIBIT 10.10 · Corporate Development Matrix

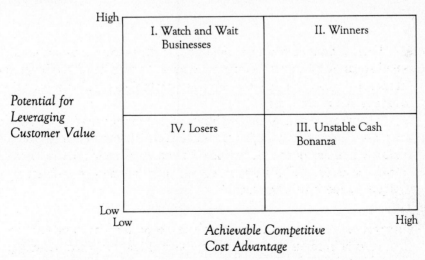

Portfolio Summary Matrix One technique that has been intentionally saved until last can be referred to as the **portfolio summary matrix.** It is presented now because it is derived from and may provide the best general summary of portfolio analysis techniques.

As shown in Exhibit 10.11, the horizontal axis represents the firm's competitive strength and the vertical axis represents the industry's market growth potential. The matrix looks much like the BCG market growth/share matrix but is

---

EXHIBIT 10.11 · Portfolio Summary Matrix

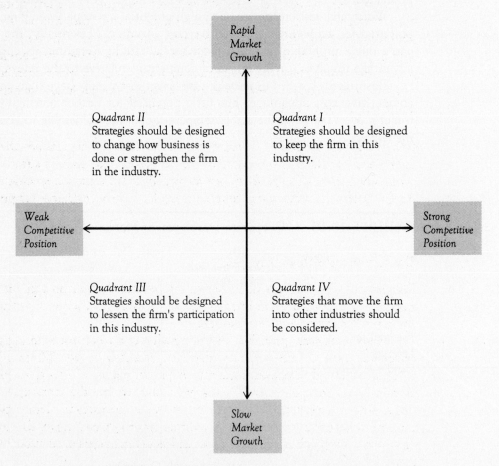

Rapid Market Growth

Quadrant II
Strategies should be designed to change how business is done or strengthen the firm in the industry.

Quadrant I
Strategies should be designed to keep the firm in this industry.

Weak Competitive Position

Strong Competitive Position

Quadrant III
Strategies should be designed to lessen the firm's participation in this industry.

Quadrant IV
Strategies that move the firm into other industries should be considered.

Slow Market Growth

Source: Adapted from Arthur A. Thompson, Jr., and A. J. Strickland III, *Strategic Management: Concepts and Cases,* 3rd ed. (Plano, Tex.: Business Publications, 1984), p. 97. Copyright 1984 Business Publications, Inc.

designed to overcome some of the problems associated with the BCG matrix and incorporate other conceptual advances. The substitution of competitive position for market share, for example, allows much more flexibility. Incorporating concepts such as those proposed by Porter allows more appropriate analysis and positioning (on the matrix) for firms with low market shares but strong competitive position. Hewlett-Packard, for example, would be positioned in the question mark quadrant of the BCG matrix. It would be a star, however, in the portfolio summary matrix because it is in a strong competitive position even with its low market share.

The key to using the portfolio summary matrix (or any of the other strategy selection aids) is good environmental analyses. Essentially, the firm's position on the competitive position axis is drawn primarily from the internal situational analysis and partially from the task environmental analysis. The position on the market growth axis is drawn primarily from the analysis of the macroenvironment and partially from the task environment analysis. Thus the matrix can be viewed as a synthesis of the total environmental analysis. The portfolio summary matrix can be extremely helpful in selecting a strategy.

Other Portfolio Models   There are a variety of other approaches that a firm might find beneficial. Among them are the directional policy matrix, business profile matrix, product performance matrix, risk-return model, stochastic dominance approach, stock price/return on equity matrix, and the margin return model.[18]

Conducting Portfolio Analysis

The portfolio analysis process can be pursued as the second step of strategy selection. Do not lose sight of the idea that portfolio analysis is only one step of the overall strategy selection process.

Many readers are probably wondering what to do with the seemingly diverse conceptualizations and portfolio matrices presented above. While all of the techniques described can be criticized on various points, all can yield benefits in certain situations. In general, managers should choose the technique that appears most appropriate. If the technique yields inadequate, inappropriate, or unclear indications, they should try another technique and might also consider a customized approach.[19] Whatever the technique, managers need to take these six steps:

1. Choose the levels of organization for analysis
2. Specify the units of analysis
3. Choose the dimensions of a portfolio matrix

4. Gather and analyze data
5. Construct and analyze the portfolio matrices
6. Specify the desired portfolio

Choosing Levels of Organization for Analysis   Management must determine for which levels of the organization it will perform a portfolio analysis. Analysis only at the top level in multiple business firms can lead to an average portfolio position for all products, which can often lead to inappropriate strategies. For example, should a firm that produces shampoo, shaving cream, bath soap, toothpaste, and other personal care items position all of these products in one SBU? If market growth rate, market share, and other key factors differ for these products, averaging the factors would be misleading.

Ideally, firms should develop a hierarchical structure of portfolios and corresponding strategies; the hierarchy should begin at the individual product level and culminate at the corporate level (which would include all lower-level portfolios). As a general rule, the portfolio should be constructed to include all major options management has for using its resources. Although traditional portfolio analysis has concentrated on products or entire industries, market segments can also provide a useful level of analysis.[20] In fact, a study found that 72 percent of the Fortune 1000 considered each SBU as a portfolio consisting of product/ market segments.[21] General Electric, for example, uses a five-level portfolio approach: product, product line, market segment, SBU, and business sector.

Specifying Units of Analysis   After determining the levels of analysis, management must select the units of analysis, or strategic business units (SBU). However, the selection of these components for further analysis and positioning on the portfolio matrix can be clouded by planners' preconceptions from dealing with existing operating units and industry classification schemes.[22] Philippe Haspeslagh noted in 1982 that more than half of the firms introducing portfolio analysis found that they had to establish SBUs different from existing operating units.[23]

Choosing the Dimensions of a Portfolio Matrix   The dimensions or matrix axes must be selected and defined. The specific dimensions selected provide the foundation and direction for the data gathering and analysis in the next step. Selecting the axis involves choosing the number of variables to include in each dimension. BCG's growth/market share matrix is an example of single-variable dimensions and GE's business screen is an example of composite- (or multiple-) variable dimensions.

Defining the dimensions involves choosing the specific variables to measure. GE now uses six variables to define industry attractiveness: market size, growth,

---

PERSPECTIVE 10.2

Amax: Sometimes More Is More, and Sometimes More Is Less

Everyone knows that "buy low and sell high" applies to stock-market investors. It might not occur to the man in the street, however, that the maxim also applies to top executives of natural-resources companies deciding how deeply they wish to go into different natural resources. Will demand for copper increase in the next few years? Consider increasing the company's involvement in copper. Will the natural gas balloon go flat? You may want to sell your holdings. The idea is simple. All you have to do is divine the future before the other players drive up the price of what you want to buy, or drive down the price of what you want to sell. It takes a nimble prophet to prosper in the cyclical world of natural resources. Nimble and resilient. It is not enough to have been right yesterday. You have to be right tomorrow, too.

Witness the case of Allen Born, who took over the presidency of nearly bankrupt Amax Inc. in 1985 and immediately saw the light reflecting off aluminum. Accordingly, Born concentrated Amax's efforts on that metal and got rid of less profitable natural-resource investments. The results were inspiring. Two years later Amax showed a profit of nearly three-quarters of a billion dollars.

Then aluminum, as is the way of natural resources, began to slump. Born prescribed di-versification as a remedy for Amax. In 1988, he sold a 25 percent stake in two aluminum smelters to Japanese interests; Amax's profits from the sale of aluminum ingots correspondingly fell. This was bad short-term news, considering that aluminum accounted for four-fifths of Amax's profits. It would become good long-term news, however, if the receipts from the sale were invested in the resources of the near future. Unfortunately, Amax had a problem investing these receipts in any resources at all. Born was outbid in efforts to acquire a coal producer and a nickel, zinc, and copper producer.

Meanwhile, takeover-minded stockholders raised their holdings in Amax's undervalued stock. Increasingly profitable as a company or not, Amax owned valuable natural resources that could be sold off separately at a profit.

References: Monica Roman and Lisa Driscoll, " 'We're Like a Honey Pot With the Bees Swarming,' " *Business Week,* June 11, 1990, p. 82; Gene G. Marcial, "Mining Amax for a Takeover? Pay Dirt May Be Near," *Business Week,* January 22, 1990, p. 66; Bob Regan, "Amax Earnings Down in 4th Quarter, Fiscal Year," *American Metal Market,* February 8, 1990, p. 2.

profitability, cyclicality, ability to recover from inflation, and world scope. Business strength is defined by nine variables that are divided into two categories: market position (domestic market share, world share, share growth, and share compared with the leading competitor), and competitive strength (leadership in quality, technology, cost, marketing, and relative profitability).

Defining the key dimensions also involves choosing the measurement units (such as dollar sales or unit sales), necessary adjustments (such as per capita sales), time (such as quarterly or annual data), and data sources used (such as company shipments, wholesale and retail audits, or consumer diaries and reports). Choosing the appropriate measurement units can be especially complex since different yardsticks can produce different results.

Management must exercise extreme care in selecting and constructing a portfolio matrix. Yoram Wind and others compared the portfolio position of fifteen firms according to four standardized portfolio models.[24] They found only one firm classified consistently by all four models tested. The classification of the other fourteen firms were highly sensitive to (1) definition of dimensions (or axis), (2) the specific rule used to divide a dimension into low and high categories, (3) the weights assigned to the variables constituting the composite dimensions, and (4) the specific portfolio model used.

Gathering and Analyzing Data   A variety of data must be gathered and analyzed at this point. Four areas are critically important.

1. *Industry attractiveness.* The overall purpose of this assessment is to determine the positive and negative attributes and risk inherent in each industry. Hofer and Schendel suggest that a weighted evaluation (for each relevant factor) should be used.[25]
2. *Competitive position.* Competitive position must be analyzed to determine the firm's potential in a particular industry. The overall competitive position can be determined by analyzing and rating the firm on selected key competitive factors and comparing this rating with competitors' ratings.[26]
3. *Opportunities and threats.* Management might benefit from an explicit analysis of opportunities and threats separate from the assessment of industry attractiveness.[27]
4. *Resource/skills.* Management should realistically appraise whether the firm has resources and skills that could materially alter the firm's competitive standing in each industry.[28]

Constructing and Analyzing Portfolio Matrices   Management is now ready to construct portfolio matrices based on one or more of the portfolio analysis approaches discussed earlier. The first efforts should focus on locating the present matrix position of each of the firm's businesses. This combination represents the firm's present portfolio of businesses. Management should then forecast expected positions on the matrix, which would essentially represent the firm's anticipated portfolio. Although most portfolio matrices rely on historical data, management should consider forecasting data for at least four different scenarios: (1) current trends continue, (2) all environmental conditions are favorable, (3) disaster strikes, and (4) the situation most likely to occur.

Management can now analyze the gap between the present portfolio position and the forecast position. The purpose of this *gap analysis* is to determine whether the aggregate performance of the forecast portfolio can be expected to achieve the firm's objectives. Three basic steps must be undertaken. First, management should compare and rate the relative short-run and long-run attractiveness of each individual business.

Second, management should evaluate the overall balance of the forecast portfolio. Questions such as the following must be addressed:[29]

1. Does the portfolio contain enough businesses in attractive industries?
2. Does the portfolio contain too many losers or question marks?
3. Does the proportion of businesses in mature or declining industries indicate slow corporate growth?
4. Are there enough cash cows to finance stars and question marks?
5. Will the portfolio generate both adequate profits and cash flow?
6. Is the portfolio overly vulnerable to unfavorable economic trends?
7. Are there too many businesses with weak competitive positions?

Third, as a result of analyzing the portfolio balance, management can compare the projected performance of the entire portfolio with corporate objectives. Depending on the outcome of this comparison, management may want to seek to develop a new portfolio that has the desired performance characteristics.

Specifying the Desired Portfolio   A desired portfolio that is expected to generate the desired performance by achieving corporate objectives should be selected. Top management must realize, however, that portfolio matrices are not designed as substitutes for decision making. For example, BCG's matrix indicates that "dogs" are not desirable, but a multinational may cherish its foreign dogs as hedges against currency fluctuations. Management must be involved in this decision and be prepared to select corporate strategy that can deliver the desired portfolio.

The Role of Portfolio Analysis

As we have noted, portfolio analysis can aid in strategy selection if it exploits management's creativity and imagination rather than becoming an exercise in paper shuffling. It should be obvious by now, however, that portfolio analysis hniques are not quite the equivalent of a crystal ball. They are not intended to the final word or give definitive answers; they are intended to provide input for nagers as part of the strategy selection process. Strategic planning and management involves much more than just portfolio analysis and is far too complex to be capsuled into a simple four- or nine-quadrant matrix.

One specific problem that portfolio analysis does not address involves the generation of new growth opportunities. Haspeslagh, for example, found that, although portfolio analysis should be concerned with all resource allocations, many companies focus solely on allocating capital resources. They ignore allocation of human resources and strategic expenses, such as R&D and marketing research, necessary to generate new business.[30]

Despite this qualification, when portfolio analysis is integrated into the strategic management process, the combination can be extremely helpful. Three specific benefits to be derived are the generation of good strategies, the promotion of more selective resource allocation tradeoffs, and the improvement and intensification of management's review process of business plans.[31]

ADDITIONAL STRATEGY-GENERATING TECHNIQUES

Other viable strategy-generating approaches and techniques include Michael Porter's competitive advantage approach and the PIMS (profit impact of market strategies) approach.

Porter's Competitive Advantage Approach

Porter contends that portfolio analysis is too restricted and proposes three different approaches for generating strategy alternatives.[32] The *restructuring* approach focuses on adding value by shifting strategy, replacing management, or redeploying assets, thereby changing the business and perhaps the industry. Firms pursuing this approach would tend to seek industries on the brink of change or underdeveloped companies.

The *transferring-skills* approach focuses on sharing expertise that can yield a competitive advantage through lower cost or differentiation. The *sharing-activities* approach focuses on exploiting relationships and related processes and systems among business to lower costs or increase differentiation for the units.

These three approaches differ from portfolio analysis in several ways. First, they emphasize the relationships between the various SBUs and between the corporate and business levels, whereas portfolio analysis stresses independent SBUs. Second, the relationships emphasized are difficult to measure, whereas portfolio analysis emphasizes more objective criteria. Third, Porter's approaches do not lend themselves to graphic representation.[33]

Porter suggests a seven-step approach for generating strategy alternatives:

1. Identify interrelationships among present SBUs
2. Select the core businesses that will serve as the foundation of the corporate strategy
3. Create horizontal organizational mechanisms to facilitate the interrelationships among core businesses, including laying the groundwork for future, related diversification
4. Pursue diversification opportunities that take advantage of shared activities
5. If opportunities for shared activities are exhausted, pursue diversification through skills transfer
6. If skills transfer is not promising, pursue restructuring, if it fits the skills of management
7. Pay dividends so that the shareholders can be the portfolio managers

The PIMS Approach

PIMS (profit impact of market strategies) is conducted by the Strategic Planning Institute. The PIMS project is an ongoing empirical study of 250 firms with more than 2,000 individual business units. Its major focus is on determining which environmental and internal company variables influence the firm's return on investment (ROI) and cash flow. More than thirty factors have been correlated with profitability, with seven variables appearing to have the greatest influence on the ROI: (1) competitive position, (2) industry/market environment, (3) budget allocation, (4) capital structure, (5) production processes, (6) company characteristics, and (7) "change action" factors.[34]

Factors correlated with a high ROI include the following:[35]

- High market share (particularly for vertically integrated firms), but low market share does not damage ROI for customized products
- High relative market share (firm's market share divided by the combined market share of the three largest competitors
- High product quality, particularly in low-growth markets
- Market growth rate
- High degree of vertical integration, but only late in the product life cycle
- High new product activity, but only in the late stages of the product life cycle
- Above-average R&D ratios, but only in the late stages of the product life cycle

- High marketing expenditures, but only in the late stages of the product life cycle; can damage ROI during introductions
- Low investment-to-sales ratio (investment intensity)
- Low inventory levels
- High capacity utilization
- High productivity, particularly in high-growth markets

The PIMS data do have several limitations, which the planner must be aware of:[36]

1. ROI may not be the only, or even the major, investment criterion.
2. The value for market share is based directly on the manager's definition of the relevant market.
3. The value of other variables, such as product quality, is based on subjective judgment.
4. PIMS definition of product/service category may be very different (broader or narrower) from the way a given firm defines it.
5. PIMS data is historical and does not forecast the future.
6. The high correlation between market share and ROI is probably not conclusive; firms with high market share do not always have high ROI, and firms with low market share sometimes do have high ROI.[37]

The PIMS project provides detailed reports to subscribers, which show the ROI that a specific SBU should expect (given factors such as those identified above). Based on answers to questions, for example, such as market share level and level of investment, PIMS will provide the average ROI from its database for all similar firms. Such a report helps planners understand what to expect if conditions continue as they are now. Furthermore, planners can obtain additional input regarding which variables can be altered to generate the greatest positive change in ROI. This input generates strategy alternatives.

GLOBAL DIMENSIONS

As with many other aspects of strategic management, the basics of strategy analysis remain much the same for both domestic and global operations. The most important point to remember is that the analysis must be done for each and every relevant country. For instance, a soft drink manufacturer might determine that there is little likelihood for market growth in the United States but substantial growth potential in Central or South America. Likewise, the firm's competitive strength or market share may differ significantly from one country to another.

Notes

1. See Richard N. Cardozo and David K. Smith, Jr., "Applying Financial Portfolio Theory to Product Portfolio Decisions: An Empirical Study," *Journal of Marketing* (Spring 1983), 110–119; and Harper W. Boyd, Jr., and Jean-Claude Larreche, "The Foundations of Marketing," in *Review of Marketing,* ed. Gerald Zaltman and Tom Bonoma (Chicago: American Marketing Association, 1978), pp. 41–72.

2. K. Giddens-Emig, "Portfolio Planning: A Concept in Controversy," *Managerial Planning* (November-December 1983), 4–14.

3. R. G. Hamermesh, "Making Planning Strategic," *Harvard Business Review* (July-August 1986), 115–120.

4. Pankaj Ghemawat, "Building Strategy on the Experience Curve," *Harvard Business Review* (March-April 1985), 143–149.

5. For additional reading, see D. C. Hambrick, I. C. MacMillan, and D. L. Day, "Strategic Attributes and Performance in the BCG Matrix—A PIMS-Based Analysis of Industrial Product Businesses," *Academy of Management Journal,* 25, No. 3 (1982), 510–531; and George S. Day, "Diagnosing the Product Portfolio," *Journal of Marketing* (April 1977), 29–38.

6. Walter Kiechel III, "The Decline of the Experience Curve," *Fortune,* October 5, 1981, pp. 139–145.

7. Philippe Haspeslagh, "Portfolio Planning: Uses and Limits," *Harvard Business Review* (January-February 1982), 58–73.

8. For points 1 through 6, see Walter Kiechel III, "Corporate Strategists Under Fire," *Fortune,* December 27, 1982, pp. 24–29; for 7 and 8, Kiechel, "The Decline of the Experience Curve," pp. 144–145; and for 9 through 11, Walter Kiechel III, "Oh Where, Oh Where Has My Little Dog Gone? Or My Cash Cow? Or My Star?" *Fortune,* November 2, 1981, pp. 148–154.

9. Michael E. Porter, *Competitive Strategy* (New York: The Free Press, 1980), pp. 34–46.

10. This section draws heavily on Michael E. Porter, *Competitive Advantage: Creating and Sustaining Superior Performance* (New York: The Free Press, 1985), pp. 11–21.

11. For additional reading, see Boyd and Larreche; and George A. Steiner, John B. Miner, and Edmund R. Gray, *Management Policy and Strategy* (New York: Macmillan, 1982), pp. 213–217.

12. C. W. Hofer, "Conceptual Constructs for Formulating Corporate and Business Strategies" (Boston: Intercollegiate Case Clearing House, 9–378–754, 1977), p. 3.

13. C. W. Hofer and Dan Schendel, *Strategy Formulation: Analytical Concepts* (St. Paul, Minn.: West, 1978), p. 183.

14. Peter Patel and Michael Younger, "A Frame of Reference for Strategy Development," *Long Range Planning* (April 1978), 6–12.

15. Walter Kiechel III, "Three (or Four, or More) Ways to Win," *Fortune,* October 19, 1981, p. 184.

16. Ibid., p. 188.

17. Alan J. Rowe, Richard O Mason, Karl E. Dickel, and Neil H. Snyder, *Strategic Management: A Methodological Approach,* (Reading, Mass.: Addison-Wesley, 1989), p. 59.

18. Each approach is discussed, respectively, in the following sources: S. J. Q. Robinson, R. E. Hichens, and D. P. Wade, "The Directional Policy Matrix—Tool for Strategic Planning," *Long Range Planning* (June 1978), 8–15, and D. E. Hussey, "Portfolio Analysis: Practical Experience with the Directional Policy Matrix," *Long Range Planning* (August 1978), 2–8; Robert V. L. Wright, "A System for Managing Diversity," in *Marketing Management and Administrative Action,* ed. Stuart Henderson Britt and Harper W. Boyd, Jr.

(New York: McGraw-Hill, 1978); Yoram Wind and Henry Claycamp, "Planning Product Line Strategy: A Matrix Approach," *Journal of Marketing* (January 1976), 20; Yoram Wind, "Product Portfolio: A New Approach to the Product Mix Decision," in *Proceedings of the August 1974 American Marketing Association Conference*, ed. Ronald C. Curhan (1974), p. 460; Vijay Mahajan, Yoram Wind, and John Bradford, "Stochastic Dominance Rules for Product Portfolio Analysis," *Management Science*, Special Issue of PIMS Studies on Marketing Planning Models, ed. Andy Zoltners (1981); Kiechel, "The Decline of the Experience Curve," p. 154; and Jagdish N. Sheth and Gary L. Frazier, "A Margin-Return Model for Strategic Market Planning," *Journal of Marketing* (Spring 1983), 100–109.

19. Yoram Wind and Vijay Mahajan, "Designing Product and Business Portfolios," *Harvard Business Review* (January-February 1981), 155–165.

20. Day, p. 29.

21. Haspeslagh, p. 65.

22. Gary L. Frazier and Roy D. Howell, "Business Definition and Performance," *Journal of Marketing* (Spring 1983), 59–67.

23. Haspeslagh, p. 65.

24. Yoram Wind, Vijay Mahajan, and Donald J. Swire, "An Empirical Comparison of Standardized Portfolio Models," *Journal of Marketing* (Spring 1983), 89–99.

25. Hofer and Schendel, pp. 72–75; see also W. R. King, "Using Strategic Issue Analysis," *Long Range Planning*, 15, No. 4 (1982), 45–49.

26. Hofer and Schendel, p. 78.

27. For additional reading, see H. Weihrich, "The TOWS Matrix-A Tool for Situational Analysis," *Long Range Planning*, 15, No. 2 (1982), 54–66; and D. A. Hurd, *Vulnerability Analysis in Business Planning*, SRI International Research Report, No. 593 (1977).

28. Hofer and Schendel, p. 80 and R. T. Lenz, "Strategic Capability: A Concept and Framework for Analysis," *Academy of Management Review*, 5, No. 2 (1980), 225–234.

29. Arthur A. Thompson, Jr., and A. J. Strickland III, *Strategic Management*, 3rd ed. (Plano, Tex: Business Publications, 1984), p. 142.

30. Haspeslagh, p. 67.

31. Ibid., p. 72.

32. This section is drawn from Michael Porter, "From Competitive Advantage to Corporate Strategy," *Harvard Business Review* (May-June 1987), 50–60.

33. Leslie W. Rue and Phyllis G. Holland, *Strategic Management; Concepts and Experiences*, 2nd ed. (New York: McGraw-Hill, 1989), p. 158.

34. See George S. Day and David B. Montgomery, "Diagnosing the Experience Curve," *Journal of Marketing* (Spring 1983), 44–58.

35. George S. Day, *Analysis for Strategic Market Decisions* (St. Paul, Minn.: West Publishing Company), pp. 115–165; Robert D. Buzzell and Frederik D. Wiersema, "Modeling Changes in Market Share: A Cross-Sectional Analysis," *Strategic Management Journal* (January-March 1981), 27–42; Mark J. Chussil, "Responses to PIMS: Fact or Folklore?" *Journal of Business Strategy* (Spring 1984), 93–96; Don Collier, "Strategic Planning Systems Design and Operation," *Journal of Business Strategy* (Fall 1989), 76–77; George Day and David B. Montgomery, "Diagnosing the Experience Curve," *Journal of Marketing* (Spring 1983), 44–58; Bradley T. Gale, "Can More Capital Buy Higher Productivity?" *Harvard Business Review* (July-August 1980), 78–86; Sidney Schoeffler, "Capital-Intensive Technology vs. ROI: A Strategic Assessment," *Management Review* (September 1978), 8–14.

36. Carl R. Anderson and Frank T. Paine, "PIMS: A Reexamination," *Academy of Management Review* (July 1978), 603.

37. John E. Prescott, Ajay K. Kohli, and N. Venkatrama, "Is the Relationship Between Market Share and Business Profitability Spurious? An Empirical Assessment," *Proceedings of the Academy of Management* (1984), 36; Vasudevan Ramanujam and N. Venkatraman, "An Inventory and Critique of Strategy Research Using the PIMS Database," *Academy of Management Review* (January 1984), 147.

CHAPTER 11

Selecting Corporate Strategies

Every business entity has a game plan. Although some business game plans are implicit, the probability of success is much greater if the game plan is explicit. The overall explicit game plan is referred to as the **corporate strategy,** and it focuses on achieving corporate objectives. This chapter considers the selection of corporate strategies. Business- and functional-level strategy alternatives, which are more specific, are discussed in Chapter 12.

Corporate strategy is most relevant to diversified firms with several lines of business. Management of this type of firm faces three fundamental questions:

1. Which businesses should we stay in?
2. Which businesses should we get out of?
3. Which new businesses should we get into?

Corporate-level planners should concentrate on forming a workable whole from a diverse set of businesses, and corporate strategy should provide direction to the total set of activities. Corporate strategies thus deal with (1) shaping what an organization does and does not do and (2) adjusting the make-up and emphasis among the organization's chosen business activities.[1]

Corporate strategy is also relevant for firms currently involved in a single business. Single-business firms must address the same basic questions as the multiple-business firms, but the scope of the questions is obviously more limited. Depending on the characteristics of the single-business firm, many of the strategy alternatives that we discuss in this chapter may be impractical because of inadequate resources.

Often called **grand strategies** or **master strategies,** the strategies for achieving a firm's growth objectives can be classified in a variety of ways. We focus on four categories: growth strategies, stability strategies, decline or defensive strategies, and closure strategies. As we discuss specific strategy alternatives for each of these four categories, keep in mind that different firms may choose different objectives and strategies to achieve basically the same ends.

Each of the corporate strategy alternatives that we consider can be pursued through an internal or an external approach. Growth through internal avenues involves using the existing corporate resources and competencies to develop the strategies. Some observers believe that management should exhaust internal options for growth before pursuing external options.[2] Growth through external avenues means acquisitions of, mergers with, or joint ventures with other companies. Each of these external options is discussed later in the chapter. To facilitate understanding, we also present examples of both internal and external business strategies appropriate for carrying out corporate strategies. Once we have examined the various strategies, we explore the strategy selection process. The outcome of this process should be an acceptable strategy and relevant contingency strategies.

The simple grid shown in Exhibit 11.1 can help distinguish among the various corporate strategy alternatives. Essentially, each of the generic corporate strategies discussed in this chapter is derived from changing one or more of five basic elements: product, market, industry, industry level, and technology. Note the close relationship between these elements and the components of a mission statement given in Chapter 4.

To help illustrate the various types of corporate strategies, let us consider a hypothetical company—Cannon Consolidated Industries, Inc. (CCI). Here is a brief description of CCI:

> CCI owns and operates three separate businesses, with a total of five major SBUs. The three businesses are
>
> > **Cannon Furniture Company,** which manufactures and distributes high-quality, high-priced living room and bedroom furniture.
> >
> > **Cannon Clock Company,** which manufactures and distributes top-line grandfather clocks and mantel clocks.
> >
> > **Cannon Apparel Company,** which produces knit sport shirts, mass-marketed under other firms' names.
>
> CCI's chairman is Charlotte Cannon, and each of her three sons serves as president of a company. Although no longer active in the day-to-day business operations, Cannon makes all major strategic decisions for CCI. She typically leaves business-level strategy up to each company's president.

To help focus the discussion, we will refer to CCI throughout the chapter.

EXHIBIT 11.1 · Strategy Change Grid

Product	Market	Industry	Industry Level	Technology
Current or New	Current or New	Current or New	Current or New	Current or New

GROWTH STRATEGIES

Most U.S. firms have growth as one of their objectives and therefore employ some type of growth strategy. The popularity of growth strategies has several possible sources:[3]

1. Growth and progress are ingrained in the value system of many Americans and many view them as the quickest way to get rich.
2. Managers often gain financial rewards and continued employment when they achieve growth in sales and profits.
3. Many managers want to be known for making a contribution to their firm and expanding the company is often viewed as the major contribution.
4. Investors and others with a financial interest in the firm frequently pressure managers to stress high growth.
5. Many people believe that a firm must grow in order to survive.

A researcher who studied fifty-three high-growth companies concluded that companies with the highest growth rates

1. Choose industries that were growing more rapidly than the economy
2. Concentrated on the market segments within fast growing industries
3. Entered the market earlier than competing firms
4. Operated in multinational markets[4]

Other researchers have noted that firms should strive to become large in fast-growing markets, get out of small nongrowth markets, select specific market segments, and not try to compete against larger firms.[5]

Growth strategies fall into three categories: concentration strategies, integration strategies, and diversification strategies. Each category contains several specific types of strategies.

Concentration Strategies

Concentration strategies are master strategies that center on improving current products and/or markets without changing any other factor. In pursuing such a strategy, a firm essentially attempts to exploit available opportunities with current products or in current markets by doing what it is already doing, only better. Exhibit 11.2 shows the general strategy change grid for concentrated growth strategies.

A concentration strategy indicates that corporate-level strategists intend to stay in the same basic business. Sometimes, the corporate strategists will simply inform business-level planners that they are to pursue a concentrated growth strategy without specifying which one, thereby forcing the decision and implementation burden on the business level. This is the approach taken by Charlotte Cannon of CCI.

In other situations, however, a specific concentrated growth strategy will be specified at the corporate level. It can then be carried out at the business level or, particularly if an external acquisition is called for, at the corporate level.

We look briefly at three concentrated growth strategies here and discuss them in greater detail in the next chapter.

Market Penetration   Market penetration involves seeking growth for current products in current markets, normally through more aggressive marketing efforts.[6] The strategy change grid for a market penetration strategy appears in Exhibit 11.3.

Charlotte Cannon of CCI could specify a market penetration strategy for each of CCI's businesses or she could specify it for one of the businesses while choosing other strategies for the remaining two businesses. The president of each

---

EXHIBIT 11.2 · Strategy Change Grid for Concentrated Growth

Product	Market	Industry	Industry Level	Technology
Current or New	Current or New	Current	Current	Current

EXHIBIT 11.3 · **Strategy Change Grid for Market Penetration**

Product	Market	Industry	Industry Level	Technology
Current	Current	Current	Current	Current

---

business would typically be responsible for selecting the more detailed business-level strategies needed for implementing the market penetration strategy.

Although these examples of market penetration are internally focused, an external focus is also possible. The firm might consider acquiring or seeking greater control of one or more of its director competitors, which is often called horizontal integration. The widespread acquisition of small breweries in recent years by the larger breweries, such as G. Heileman, illustrates horizontal integration. Firms choosing this strategy must be careful not to run afoul of government antitrust regulations and laws.

If Cannon chose to pursue the external approach to market penetration for one or more of her businesses, it might involve acquiring another furniture manufacturing business that specialized in a different style of living room or bedroom furniture. Implementing such a plan would normally occur at the corporate level. Essentially, Cannon would acquire the other firm and either leave it as a separate business entity or charge the president of Cannon Furniture Company with assimilating it into the existing furniture business.

Market Development Market development involves seeking growth by entering new markets with current products. Exhibit 11.4 presents the strategy change grid for market development strategies.

CCI could employ a market development strategy for any or all of its three businesses. Again, Cannon could specify this strategy and leave the details to each business unit.

Product Development Product development involves seeking growth by developing new products for current markets. These new products can be developed internally, acquired through licensing agreements, or acquired through merger with or acquisition of another firm. The strategy change grid for product development appears in Exhibit 11.5.

EXHIBIT 11.4 · Strategy Change Grid for Market Development

Product	Market	Industry	Industry Level	Technology
Current	New	Current	Current	Current

Once again, CCI could deploy a product development strategy for any or all of the three business units. On the other hand, Cannon could conceivably specify a different concentrated growth strategy for each business: Cannon Furniture Company, for example, could pursue market penetration; Cannon Clock Company, market development; and Cannon Apparel Company, product development.

Integration Strategies

Integration strategies are appropriate for firms that are in strong industries but hesitate to or cannot initiate one of the concentrated growth strategies (perhaps because of saturated markets). An integrative growth strategy is appropriate when available opportunities are compatible with the firm's objectives and existing long-term strategies, strengthen the organization's position in its primary business, and permit fuller exploitation of the firm's technical talent. The two corporate strategies for integrative growth can be implemented on the corporate

---

EXHIBIT 11.5 · Strategy Change Grid for Product Development

Product	Market	Industry	Industry Level	Technology
New	Current	Current	Current	Current

EXHIBIT 11.6 · Strategy Change Grid for Integration

Product	Market	Industry	Industry Level	Technology
New	New	New	New	Current

---

level through acquisitions or on the business level through internal development.[a] Since each strategy involves moving to a different industry level, the strategy change grid for each is modified for industry level (see Exhibit 11.6). However, even though moving to a different level of the same industry could mean dealing with different products and technology, the core or basic products, markets, industry, and technology remain the same.

Backward Vertical Integration   In backward vertical integration, a company seeks growth by acquiring ownership or increased control of supply sources. In internal backward integration, the firm creates its own source of supply, perhaps by establishing a subsidiary company. The external approach entails the purchase or acquisition of an existing supplier.

Backward integration is attractive when suppliers are experiencing fast growth or have great profit potential. It is also attractive if there is uncertainty regarding availability, cost, or reliability of deliveries of future supplies. Its additional benefit is converting a current cost center into a potential profit center.

Furthermore, backward integration can be an excellent way to ensure a workable degree of commitment from suppliers. The overall merchandising strategy of Sears, Roebuck, for example, requires dependable supplies of goods at the right price and quality. Consequently, a large portion of Sears merchandise has historically been supplied by firms in which Sears has an ownership interest.[7]

Along with the benefits, backward integration can bring problems. They range from the often large capital requirements and increased complexity in the management process to organizational inflexibility and imbalances in capacity at each production stage.[8]

---

[a]The term *horizontal integration* is sometimes used to refer to a strategy that involves acquiring competing firms in order to obtain new products, services, and/or markets—which is actually one of the concentration strategies.

Backward vertical integration for CCI could mean acquiring or establishing a lumberyard to supply the furniture business, a machining company to make internal clock mechanisms, or a knitted-goods firm to supply the apparel business.

Forward Vertical Integration   When pursuing forward vertical integration, a firm seeks growth by acquiring ownership or increased control of channel functions closer to the ultimate market, such as sales and distribution systems.

A firm can accomplish forward integration internally by establishing its own production facility (if it is a supplier of raw material), sales force, wholesale system, or retail outlets. It can achieve external forward integration by acquiring firms that already perform the desired function.

Forward integration is attractive when intermediaries closer to the customer are experiencing fast growth or a firm is receiving unsatisfactory service—for instance, because of costly inventory pileups or frequent production shutdowns. Raw materials producers sometimes find forward integration attractive as a way of increasing the opportunity for product differentiation, thereby avoiding the intensity of price competition associated with commodities. Many firms have sought the benefits offered by forward integration, including Sherwin-Williams and Xerox. Forward integration poses the same potential problems as backward integration.[9]

Forward vertical integration for CCI could involve acquiring or establishing retail stores that sold furniture, clocks, or clothing.

Diversification Growth Strategies

Diversification growth strategies may be appropriate for firms that cannot achieve their growth objectives in their current industry with their current products and markets. Other reasons for a firm to diversify include the following:[10]

1. Markets of current business(es) are approaching the point of saturation or decline of the product life cycle.
2. A current business or businesses are generating excess cash that can be invested elsewhere more profitably.
3. Synergy is possible from new business (for example, because of common component part, costs can be spread among more units).
4. Antitrust regulations prohibit expansion in present industry.
5. A tax loss can be acquired.
6. The international sector can be entered quickly.
7. Technical expertise can be gained quickly.
8. New, experienced executives can be attracted or current executives can be held (for example, if they are productive but bored).

Pursuing a diversification strategy essentially means changing the characteristics of the business, which requires extreme care in formulating and implementing specific strategies. The risk inherent in a diversification strategy can be reduced somewhat by following five general guidelines.[11] First, make sure that management understands the significance of a diversification strategy and selects it because of distinctive skills. Second, ensure that the firm's skills match those needed for success in the new situation. Third, test the decision before taking action, for instance, by evaluating the market size, market access, reactions of potential customers, and production problems. Fourth, identify the point of no return before too many resources are allocated. Fifth, evaluate potential human problems and the possible influence of the strategy on corporate identity.

Three corporate strategies for diversification growth follow.

Concentric Diversification Concentric diversification involves seeking growth by appealing to new markets with new products that have a meaningful technological or marketing fit or synergy with existing products. Generally, a firm that is concentrically diversified will have a recognized base; for instance, Sears is known for its retail base, although it is in numerous other businesses related to retailing (such as credit). The key to concentric diversification is to take advantage of at least one of the firm's major internal strengths. A manufacturer of cassette tapes (for example, Memorex) diversifying into the production of flexible discs for personal computers illustrates internal concentric diversification based on technology. Procter & Gamble's extensive product line illustrates internal concentric diversification based on expertise in marketing household products through supermarket channels. External concentric diversification for Memorex, for example, would have involved the aquisition of another company that already manufactured flexible computer discs. Exhibit 11.7 illustrates the change grid for a concentric diversification strategy.

EXHIBIT 11.7 · Strategy Change Grid for Concentric Diversification

Product	Market	Industry	Industry Level	Technology
New	New	Current or New	Current	Current or New

CCI could pursue a concentric diversification strategy at the corporate level by acquiring (1) a firm that manufactures relatively inexpensive office furniture, (2) a manufacturer of radio/clock combinations, or (3) a firm that produces dress shirts.

Horizontal Diversification   Horizontal diversification involves seeking growth by appealing to current markets with new products that are technologically unrelated to present products. The strategy change grid for a horizontal diversification strategy is shown in Exhibit 11.8.

Even though a technological fit is not sought, some aspect of the new product must provide a meaningful strategic fit. For example, new but technologically unrelated products might fit a firm's objectives relative to present channels of distribution or target customer demands. A firm that emphasizes records and tapes for the teenage market, for example, might publish a magazine oriented toward teenagers or manufacture products (perhaps tape recorders) that music outlets might also carry. Before pursuing horizontal diversification, management must make certain that the firm possesses or can obtain the competencies needed for success, such as technological, production, and marketing skills.

CCI could pursue a horizontal diversification strategy at the corporate level by acquiring (1) a firm that manufactures lamps or carpet (for the furniture business), (2) a firm that manufactures antique-looking, expensive, stained-glass decorative pieces (for the clock business), or (3) a firm that produces socks or caps.

Conglomerate Diversification   Conglomerate diversification involves seeking growth by appealing to new markets with new products that have no technological relationship to current products. The strategy change grid for a conglomerate diversification strategy appears in Exhibit 11.9.

EXHIBIT 11.8 · Strategy Change Grid for Horizontal Diversification

Product	Market	Industry	Industry Level	Technology
New	Current	Current or New	Current	New

EXHIBIT 11.9 · **Strategy Change Grid for Conglomerate Diversification**

Product	Market	Industry	Industry Level	Technology
New	New	New	Current or New	New

Note that other factors must still provide a meaningful strategic fit. Conglomerate diversification may be pursued to offset certain deficiencies, such as seasonality, lack of cash or earnings power, lack of certain skills, or a lack of attractive environmental opportunities. Firms sometimes pursue conglomerate diversification because they have available financial resources and believe that another firm's stock is undervalued.

Although conglomerate diversification can be an internal strategy, it is most often focused externally. Firms such as Litton, Textron, and Gulf & Western use this external approach; their primary criterion for such a move is whether the opportunity meets minimum standards for long-run profit potential. Diversification by other firms is sometimes conglomerate in nature because their current markets and businesses are so narrow as to preclude any other form of diversification.

CCI could pursue a conglomerate diversification strategy by acquiring virtually any company that fits the above criteria. For example, CCI could purchase a grocery store, a farm, or an electronics firm.

Conglomerate diversification is not without its pitfalls. The primary caution has to do with the firm's competencies, including managerial competencies. For example, can management bail the new business out of any potential trouble? Second, if too high a premium is paid to get into a growth industry, stockholder earnings may be impaired. Third, synergies are not guaranteed.[12] Fourth, conglomerate diversification intended to offset seasonal and cyclical downturns has often been unsuccessful.[13]

STABILITY STRATEGIES

A **stability strategy** (or *neutral strategy*) dictates that the company keep doing what it has been doing to maintain competitive position; no major changes are made in products, markets, or production methods. This strategy does not necessarily imply inaction. Growth is possible, but will be slow and nonaggressive. Firms can consciously pursue a stability strategy when management is satisfied with the status quo; sometimes, however, a stability strategy is pursued without a conscious decision being made. Firms most likely to pursue a stability strategy are (1) small, privately owned firms, (2) large, dominant firms, and (3) heavily regulated firms. This strategy is also common after periods of rapid growth.

A stability strategy can be pursued through any of the specific strategies discussed in the growth strategy section; the firm just uses the strategy unaggressively. For example, large, dominant firms in mature industries can use market penetration to maintain a competitive position. Similarly, they can pursue product development by the slow introduction of new products.

DECLINE STRATEGIES

Decline strategies (sometimes referred to as *defensive strategies*) are generally short-run reactions to poor management or to unexpected environmental events, such as competitors' actions. They are appropriate when a firm needs to regroup to improve efficiency after a period of fast growth, when long-run growth and profit opportunities are unavailable in an industry, during periods of economic uncertainty, or when other opportunities are simply more attractive than those being pursued. Three corporate strategies for a planned decline follow.

Retrenchment

Retrenchment simply means falling back and regrouping. The term *retrenchment* is sometimes defined rather broadly, similarly to our conception of decline strategies. We define retrenchment more narrowly as a temporary or short-run strategy that focuses on a *turnaround*, or the alleviation of organizational inefficiencies or temporary environmental problems. Management often directs attention to such issues as reducing operating expenses and improving productivity. Specific activities vary according to the situation and include reduced hiring, laying off personnel, dropping marginal products, and closing marginal facilities. Charlotte Cannon of CCI could, for example, order each business to reduce manufacturing costs by 10 percent and allow each president to choose the specific retrenchment strategy for his business.

Retrenchment is closely linked to the other decline strategies, particularly divestiture. In fact, the primary difference between retrenchment and divestiture is often a matter of degree or scale of the decline. The more permanent the decline objective, the more likely is the strategy to be a divestiture strategy, particularly when major assets or divisions are sold.

Divestiture

Divestiture occurs when a firm sells or closes one of its businesses to achieve a permanent change in the scope of operations. This might happen when the management of a diversified firm recognizes that one of its businesses has turned sour or does not have the expected strategic fit with other businesses. Often it offers the least costly way of rectifying a mistake.[14]

Divestiture results in a reallocation of resources to surviving businesses and/or new business opportunities. CCI, for example, could immediately sell one of its three businesses or simply close it down (which would be liquidation for that business). Note that a retrenchment strategy can become a permanent divestiture strategy if new opportunities do not become available. Note also that a divestiture strategy is sometimes pursued because of technological changes or antitrust requirements.

Harvest

Harvest involves seeking to maximize cash flow in the short run, regardless of the long-term effect. Harvesting is generally pursued for businesses that have a dim future and little likelihood of being sold for a profit but are capable of yielding cash during the harvesting. Expenditures are generally slashed to increase the cash yield, which typically accelerates the demise of the business. CCI could pursue a harvest strategy for its clock business by laying off employees, purchasing no new raw materials, cutting prices, and taking other necessary actions to slowly squeeze the last profits out of the business. Any of these strategies—harvest, retrenchment, or divestiture—can evolve into a more permanent closure strategy.

CLOSURE STRATEGIES

When all else fails, management can simply close down the firm. The two basic closure strategies are liquidation and declaring bankruptcy.

Liquidation

Liquidation occurs when the entire firm ceases to exist, either through sale or dissolution. Although liquidation can occur because of court-ordered bankruptcy proceedings, planned liquidations can occur in an orderly manner. For example, a firm might decide that it cannot compete successfully in the current industry and recognizes that it does not have the resources necessary to pursue other promising strategies. To minimize losses, the firm might attempt to liquidate immediately by selling out or taking other measures (for example, conserving cash) to make its asset base more attractive to potential suitors. Cannon of CCI, for example, could recognize that none of her sons was capable of managing the combined businesses and decide that the total wealth of all four parties would be maximized if she sold CCI and retired, thereby leaving her sons with a large capital base and the opportunity to seek other employment.

Bankruptcy

A strategy that deserves special attention is **bankruptcy**. Bankruptcy basically means that a firm is unable to pay its debts. However, U.S. bankruptcy law allows for two distinct types of bankruptcy and each is named for the section (or chapter) of the law. *Chapter 7* involves bankruptcy in which the assets of the firm are liquidated. The court-ordered procedure for closure mentioned in the preceding section is called Chapter 7 bankruptcy. *Chapter 11* bankruptcy is very different, for the firm is protected from creditors and other contract holders until it can rehabilitate itself. The assets of the firm are controlled by the courts during the time the firm is in Chapter 11, and management can make few asset-related decisions without the courts' concurrence. The idea behind Chapter 11 is that if the company has time, it can work its way out of its difficulties. Thus Chapter 11 is a defensive strategy, and most firms that seek Chapter 11 protection do, in fact, eventually resume normal operations.

COMBINATION STRATEGIES

Firms can implement multiple corporate strategies simultaneously for both short- and long-term benefits.[15] For example, any large retail chain could conceivably use all of the following corporate strategies at the same time:

- Market penetration, by focusing more efforts on improving its fashion image
- Product development, by introducing new products, such as video games
- Backward integration, by acquiring or developing production capabilities for various existing products, such as paints or knit shirts
- Horizontal diversification, by introducing personal computers, real estate sales services, or banking services
- Divestiture, by selling or closing less profitable businesses that supply various products

When a firm seeks growth through external acquisitions of other multiple-business firms or through mergers with them, a combination strategy almost always results.

In a different context, a firm may, over a period of time, pursue a sequential combination strategy. That means pursuing one particular corporate strategy in order to later pursue another. A firm that intends to diversify, for example, may first seek divestiture of several businesses as a means of securing adequate capital for the diversification strategy. Similarly, a firm wishing to concentrate in present businesses because of high industry attractiveness may first pursue a vertical integration strategy to gain greater control of distribution channels or sources of supply. The chief executive officer of Philips, a large Dutch electronics firm, used a combination strategy when he pared down the firm to four core businesses by divesting and closing dozens of marginal firms, laying off twenty-four thousand workers, modernizing designs and styling, improving marketing, and speeding up new product development.[16]

EXTERNAL CORPORATE STRATEGY OPTIONS

As mentioned earlier, a firm can pursue growth strategies through external focus. The two major options are mergers and acquisitions and joint ventures.

Mergers and Acquisitions

The terms *acquisition* and *merger* are closely related and sometimes used interchangeably; the resulting company structure is somewhat different. A **merger** occurs when two or more firms combine to form a single, new company. Mergers are often the result of firms mutually agreeing to combine and create a new name and identity, issue new stock, implement a new organizational structure, and make other changes.

An **acquisition** occurs when one firm purchases another and absorbs or adds it to existing operations, often as an operating subsidiary or division. The absorbed firm may retain its individual identity, however, if the identity is an important strategic element. Both Allied Department Stores and Federated Department Stores have used this approach successfully, as have many financial holding companies. In other situations, especially vertical integrations, the acquired firm often loses its individual identity when the parent becomes the only customer or supplier.

Merger and Acquisition Versus Internal Development   An acquisition or merger can be more desirable than internal development for several reasons. First, a firm may want to implement its strategy, such as entering a new market or developing a new product, in the relatively near future. The time element can be crucially important when the opportunity is expected to exist for only a short time. While internal development could take years, acquisition or merger might allow practically instant implementation of the desired strategy.

Second, the cost of upgrading internal competencies can be greater than the cost of acquiring a firm that already has the necessary distinctive competencies. This high cost can result from the high barriers to entry in the sought industry. Conversely, if the new business opportunity is closely related to existing businesses, the barriers to entry may be low and favor internal development.

Third, internal development generally results in the firm becoming a new competitor in the relevant market. This can create a situation of oversupply that may reduce the attractiveness of the market; external acquisition or merger is a way to avoid this situation.

Fourth, internal development tends to be uncertain and risky. Acquiring an established firm may provide more of a known quantity.

Problems with Mergers and Acquisitions   There are three basic problems associated with mergers and acquisitions.[17] First, can the right firm to pursue be found? For example, should the firm seek a presently weak company at a low price or a strong firm at a high price? Second, what is a fair price?[18] Third, does the target firm want to be acquired or merged? Some firms fight takeover bids, which means that a careful "unfriendly" takeover strategy must be developed.[19] Other problems include the following:[20]

- Straying too far afield from present businesses
- Merging disparate corporate cultures
- Counting on key managers staying
- Assuming that a market growth will continue
- Leaping before looking or inadequate planning
- Swallowing too large a company

Merger Guidelines   A former CEO of Rockwell International Corporation suggests ten guidelines for successful mergers and acquisitions:[21]

1. Specify the objectives.
2. Specify the benefits for the stockholders of both firms.
3. Ensure that the managers of the acquired firm are competent or can be made competent.
4. Ensure that the resources of the two firms are compatible and offer synergistic possibilities.
5. Involve both CEOs in the entire merger process.
6. Clearly define the business or purpose of the acquiring firm.
7. Examine the strengths, weaknesses, and other performance factors of both firms.

8. Create a climate of trust between the organizations by anticipating a merger and dealing with it early and openly.
9. Make the right advances, and make them smoothly and tactfully.
10. Exercise a minimum of control over the new firm and maintain or improve the status of the newly acquired managers.

Lionel L. Fray, David H. Gaylin, and James W. Down offer guidelines from a slightly different perspective:[22]

1. Develop a comprehensive acquisition plan as part of the overall corporate development strategy.
2. Acquire a firm that meets sound financial and strategic criteria.
3. Understand the industry's and the firm's driving forces and critical success factors.
4. Understand the opportunities, devote the resources to pursuing the opportunities, and develop management commitment to take advantage of it.
5. Evaluate management of the target firm relative to competence and fit with existing management.
6. Purchase at a price that allows an attractive return, and determine this price early.

The Acquisition Process   The acquisition process consists of three broad phases: (1) identifying, evaluating, and screening prospects, (2) bidding and negotiation, and (3) integration.

The *identifying, evaluating, and screening* of prospective acquisition targets occurs after the firm has performed a thorough internal analysis, including specification of the strategic rationale for pursuing an acquisition strategy and the criterion for acquisitions. Potential targets can be identified through a research approach or an opportunistic approach (or a combination of the two).[23]

- A *research approach* involves analyzing broad sectors of the economy, with successive narrowing of choices.[24] Once a broad group of acceptable sectors has been identified, the competitive character of each sector should be evaluated. After the number of sectors is pared to a few, promising candidates can be identified.
- An *opportunistic approach* does not consist of a strategic analysis process. Rather, it involves learning about potential acquisition targets from personal contacts as well as from financial entrepreneurs who serve as brokers. The key characteristic of this approach is that potential targets are not compared; each opportunity must be evaluated individually.

Regardless of the approach, it is critical that the right company be acquired.[25]

The *bidding and negotiation* phase actually begins with negotiation. The beginning point involves seeking broad agreement between the parties relative to how the two companies will mesh, how the stockholders will benefit, and how the transaction will be handled. If this phase is successful, the bidding and details of the transition can be worked out.

The price bid for a firm should naturally be as low as possible. The overall financial evaluation should determine the maximum price to pay, primary areas of financial risk, potential for earnings and cash flow, and the best way to finance the acquisition.

The *integration phase* should be based on a sound transition plan, which should address the following issues:[26]

1. Merging of function and systems to avoid duplication
2. The degree of autonomy given to the acquired unit
3. Defining the reporting relationships and requirements needed
4. Defining how to handle compensation, benefits, and company perquisites

Defenses Against Raiders   An investor who buys a large block of a firm's stock with the intention of a takeover is termed a **corporate raider**. Often, the target firm's management does not favor the takeover and the attempt is called a **hostile takeover**. There is considerable debate about the ethics of both hostile takeovers and defenses against them. As discussed earlier, there are many good and bad reasons for takeovers. There are also many good and bad reasons for management to resist a takeover. One good reason, for example, is that there is not a good fit between the two firms. Generally, all of the good reasons center on protecting stockholders and employees. Bad reasons, on the other hand, typically pertain to protecting managers and their jobs. Regardless of the reason, the target firm wishing to avoid a takeover has several possible defenses:[27]

- *Pac-Man defense:* The target firm becomes the aggressor by buying the attacker's stock.
- *Self-tender:* The target firm offers to buy its own stock.
- *White knight:* The target firm finds a more compatible third party to purchase it.
- *Poison pill:* The target firm issues more securities or takes on more debt.
- *Greenmail:* The target firm purchases its own shares from a suitor for more than the current market price.
- *Shark repellents:* The target firm changes its bylaws to stagger the terms of directors so that it takes several years to get a majority of board members or requires a supermajority to approve a tender offer (75 to 80 percent).

In addition to these defenses, the target firm can maintain a relationship with legal or financial advisers who have special knowledge of mergers or dilute the voting power of stockholders by issuing more common stock.

Joint Ventures

Joint ventures occur when two or more firms join forces to accomplish something that a single organization is not suited for. The ownership of both firms remains unchanged.

The Rationale for Joint Ventures   Joint ventures typically arise for one of four reasons. First, international joint ventures are sometimes necessary to surmount political or cultural barriers. In fact, occasionally, joint ventures with foreign firms are the only legal avenue for competing in that foreign country.

Second, joint ventures sometimes develop because a specific mutually beneficial strategy is beyond the financial means of any individual firm. The Alaskan pipeline illustrates this situation.

Third, certain projects have tremendous risk associated with them. A joint venture can spread this risk.

Fourth, joint ventures may be used when two (or more) firms possess different competencies (such as technical expertise) needed for a single endeavor. For example, there have been several joint ventures between firms possessing private branch exchange (PBX) technology and those with advanced office automation products and technology. Examples of these pairings include Honeywell and L. M. Ericsson, AT&T and Phillips, and IBM and Rolm Corporation.[28]

Joint Venture Strategies   Staffan Gullander proposes three basic joint venture strategies: the spider's web, go together–split, and successive integration strategies.[29]

The **spider's web strategy** is typically employed by smaller firms in industries dominated by a few large firms. Essentially, the small firm enters a joint venture with one large organization and, as quickly as possible, enters another joint venture with a different organization. These multiple linkages form counterbalancing forces in the industry.

The **go together–split strategy** entails a long-term joint venture between two or more firms, which then separate. It is appropriate for projects of a definite life span, such as construction projects.

The **successive integration strategy** involves a series of joint ventures, beginning with a weak relationship and progressing toward stronger relationships. It can ultimately end in a merger, either friendly or hostile.

It seems to be relatively easy to make mistakes about joint ventures, particularly with foreign firms. Apparently, these mistakes usually stem from poor managerial judgment and do not necessarily lead to termination of the joint venture. Examples of problem areas include rapidly changing environments, uncertainty of environmental conditions, increases in a partner's skill level, cultural differences, frequent management transfers, and technological incompatibility.[30]

Strategic Alliances: A Special Case   Joint ventures based on the participating firms' distinctive competencies are a special form of joint ventures, which can be referred to as **symbiotic marketing** or **strategic alliances.** Although most business relationships are symbiotic in nature, Lee Adler uses the term *symbiotic marketing* to refer to relationships other than the traditional marketer–marketing intermediary relationship. He defines the term as "an alliance of resources or programs between two or more independent organizations designed to increase the market potential of each." In reality, symbiotic marketing is essentially a strategic alliance from a marketing perspective.[31]

Specific strategic alliance modes include the following:[32]

- Equity position
- Licensing
- Technology exchange
- Consortium
- Joint product development
- Joint technology development
- Marketing agreements
- Manufacturing agreements
- Joint product/service marketing
- Shared distribution facilities
- Joint sales organization
- Joint service
- Tie-in advertising and/or sales promotion
- Franchising

Strategic alliances offer an alternative method of developing the various master growth strategies. These examples illustrate the point:[33]

1. *Market penetration:* a firm's credit card holders given a discount when using another firm's product or service
2. *Market development:* a bank or savings and loan automatic teller machines located in a grocery store
3. *Product development:* a soft drink company and distiller producing and marketing a line of soft drink mixers
4. *Backward vertical integration:* a firm helping its suppliers develop appropriate quality control programs, cut costs, and improve product quality and reliability
5. *Forward vertical integration:* franchising
6. *Horizontal integration:* one firm turning a rival into a partner, as when a U.S. automobile firm has certain models manufactured by a rival
7. *Horizontal diversification:* a legal services firm and tax preparation firm residing together

8. *Concentric diversification:* the efforts of IBM, CBS, and Sears to develop videotex
9. *Conglomerate diversification:* the entry of a financial services firm and a movie producer into cable television programming

CORPORATE STRATEGIES AND FIRMS PERFORMING BELOW POTENTIAL

A special situation is faced by companies performing below their potential relative to internal strengths and external opportunities. This type of firm is often in a weak competitive position and can generally improve this position by making the right kind of adjustments. Such firms must consider formulating a **turnaround strategy.**

There are two general types of turnaround strategies. First, management can consider an *operations turnaround.* This type of turnaround is based on the assumption that the firm's basic corporate objectives and strategies are sound and appropriate. Specific alternatives include:

1. Increasing revenue, for instance, by increasing advertising, raising or lowering price, and improving customer service
2. Reducing costs, perhaps by job reductions and productivity improvement
3. Improving cash flow, for example, by selling assets and dropping marginal products

An operations turnaround strategy is—the managers hope—a short-run expedient to return the firm to a break-even profit or cash flow situation.

Second, a *strategic turnaround* can be pursued when the firm's objectives or corporate strategy is not yielding the desired performance. One of the more unusual aspects of a strategic turnaround is that it is often selected by the board of directors rather than by top management. This happens because the top management may have to be removed entirely; Schendel and his colleagues reported that thirty-nine of the fifty-four firms studied had significant managerial (including CEO) changes during turnarounds.[34] Whoever makes the decision must determine whether the industry potential is sufficient to make the turnaround effort worthwhile and whether the firm has the basic competencies to accomplish the turnaround. If a turnaround strategy is not pursued, the alternatives normally involve divestiture or liquidation.

SELECTING CORPORATE STRATEGY

Management should now be in an excellent position to select an overall corporate strategy, or a combination of strategies, that:

1. Adds new business units to the portfolio
2. Deletes business unit(s) from the portfolio
3. Modifies business strategies of one or more business units
4. Modifies corporate performance objectives
5. Focuses on altering those conditions (for example, through political action) responsible for forecast subpar performance
6. Maintains the status quo[35]

Before selecting the corporate strategy, several factors must be considered. Some of these factors are objective, but others are somewhat subjective. The key influencers of corporate strategy are industry strength and corporate strength, objectives, CEO's attitudes, internal politics, financial resources, the firm's skills, familiarity with and commitment to previous strategy, degree of external dependence, competitors' reactions, stakeholders' reactions, and timing.

Industry Strength and Corporate Strength

A firm's strength of position relative to competing firms can have a major impact on the strategy selection process. Weak and dominant firms are likely to select different types of strategies (see Exhibit 11.10).

Weak firms should normally select strategies that will increase their strength or else they must exit the industry. Weak firms in fast-growth industries may use a concentration strategy (but will often have to use the turnaround approach). If these attempts to become stronger are unsuccessful, the firm is likely to use divestiture or liquidation. In mature industries, strategies focusing on becoming stronger are less viable, especially if the total market size is small. Shifting resources out of the industry with one of the diversification or decline strategies is the typical solution. Weak firms in declining industries are even more likely to use decline or diversification strategies.

Typically, firms with strong competitive positions can select growth strategies different from those chosen by weak firms. A dominant firm should generally try to consolidate and exploit its position and, if possible, seek opportunities in other industries with greater growth potential. In fast-growth industries, dominant firms are more likely to choose one of the concentration or integrated growth strategies and/or concentric diversification. Dominant firms in mature industries are more likely to use diversification strategies. In declining industries, diversification strategies, especially conglomerate diversification, are the most likely choices.

Objectives

The specific set of objectives chosen by management has a strong, direct influence on the choice of strategies, regardless of the analysis process just discussed.

EXHIBIT 11.10 · Portfolio Summary Matrix

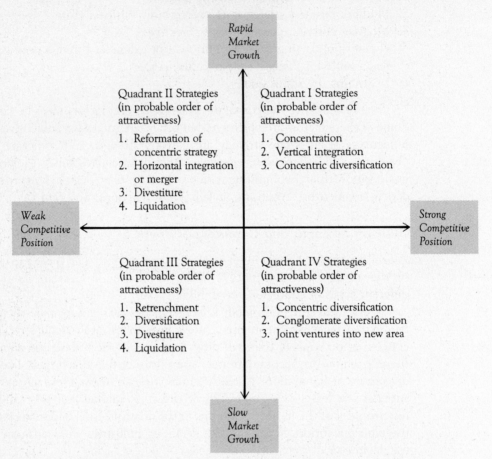

Rapid
Market
Growth

Quadrant II Strategies
(in probable order of
attractiveness)

1. Reformation of
   concentric strategy
2. Horizontal integration
   or merger
3. Divestiture
4. Liquidation

Quadrant I Strategies
(in probable order of
attractiveness)

1. Concentration
2. Vertical integration
3. Concentric diversification

Weak
Competitive
Position

Strong
Competitive
Position

Quadrant III Strategies
(in probable order of
attractiveness)

1. Retrenchment
2. Diversification
3. Divestiture
4. Liquidation

Quadrant IV Strategies
(in probable order of
attractiveness)

1. Concentric diversification
2. Conglomerate diversification
3. Joint ventures into new area

Slow
Market
Growth

Source: From Arthur A. Thompson, Jr., and A. J. Strickland III, *Strategic Management:
Concepts and Cases,* 3rd ed. (Plano, Tex.: Business Publications, 1984), p. 97. Copyright ©
1984 Business Publications, Inc.

Management, for instance, may choose simply not to grow fast or even to
contract despite a strong competitive position in a rapid growth market. There
are many ways to justify such a decision. In a firm with one owner or a closely
held firm, the owner/managers may not want to work as hard as they have in the
past. The key point is that all objectives have to be analyzed to determine
whether a specific strategy fits in with the entire set of objectives rather than with
only the growth objectives.

PERSPECTIVE 11.1

If Cleanliness Is Next to Godliness, Is Toothpaste a Moral Cleanser?

The promotion of toothpaste has been linked to health, happiness, and social approval, but never, before Bifluor 1450, to the triumph of good over evil. The new product with the name that sounds more like a radioactive isotope than a dentifrice is being aggressively—and creatively—promoted by Colgate-Palmolive, the number-two firm in U.S. toothpaste sales. The Bifluor campaign features a television commercial in which a man in white competes against a man in black in a modernistic, chess-like game. The man in white, of course, represents Bifluor 1450, and his victory is celebrated with the pulsing of the product name on a series of cathode ray tubes. "When Colgate advances," we are then told, "harm retreats."

However more inventive Colgate may be in trying to increase its percentage of the toothpaste market, it is not the only manufacturer so engaged. At the lower end of the market-share continuum, Chesebrough-Pond—to give just one example—is reintroducing Close-Up toothpaste with a more traditional appeal to that brand's effectiveness as a breath freshener.

Meanwhile, Warner-Lambert, manufacturer of Efferdent, is trumpeting its Fresh 'n Brite toothpaste as just the suds to remove stains from dentures. As the name suggests, Fresh 'n Brite will not only whiten dentures but also enhance the quality of the denture-wearer's breath.

In the same market segment Block Drug Co.'s Dentu-Creme, the number-one seller, is refusing to face its competition with a smile. Dentu-Creme is now starring in an I-clean-better-than-you TV commercial against Efferdent. The confrontation may be less dramatic than Bifluor's struggle against evil, but it is the sort of thing that is proven to have worked.

References: Debbie Seaman, "Colgate Chess Ads Sell Toothpaste," *ADWEEK Western Advertising News,* January 22, 1990, p. 31; Laurie Freeman, "Close-up Goes Back to Its Roots," *Advertising Age,* January 22, 1990, p. 40.

Attitudes of the CEO

The opinions of the firm's chief executive officer may strongly influence the strategy selection. For example, the CEO may not want his or her decisions questioned or changed, regardless of supporting evidence. For example, many observers thought that ITT Corporation held certain assets for many years past their useful life, but the CEO would not make the decision to let go of them.[36]

The CEO's attitude toward risk also strongly affects the firm's strategy, especially regarding new markets or industries. Risk-averse CEOs attempt to minimize the firm's exposure to risk and therefore are willing to accept less than optimal profitability. At the opposite extreme, a "risk lover" views risk as necessary for success and rewards and tends to focus on high-risk projects and opportunities for profit. Between these two extremes are managers who view risk as a fact of life and find some risk acceptable; these managers tend to seek a balance of high- and low-risk projects.

Being risk prone or risk averse is not inherently good or bad; the appropriateness may depend on the circumstances. A recent research study found that managers of higher-performing SBUs with "build" objectives showed a greater willingness to take risks. Conversely, managers of higher-performing SBUs with harvest strategies had little inclination to take risks.[37]

Internal Politics

A firm's internal political situation can sway strategy selection. Although power typically resides with the CEO, *dominant coalitions* can exert considerable influence in the strategic management process.[38] A coalition forms when mutual interest draws individuals and subunits together to enhance their position on major strategy issues.

Financial Resources

A firm's financial resource base also influences (and can sometimes dictate) strategy selection. Firms with large or easily transformed resources are in a position to pursue a variety of growth opportunities. Conversely, firms with limited to illiquid resources are in a more difficult position. Some firms can tap the capital markets for additional funding, but others cannot. These latter firms are likely to be forced to forgo identified profit opportunities because they cannot afford the "entry fee."

Skills

Another large influence on strategy selection is the quality and variety of a firm's skills. Walker Lewis of the Strategic Planning Associates has developed the *field theory approach*, which focuses management's attention on developing skills that are useful across several different product lines. To develop these skills, management needs to analyze the products made, the firm's customers for these products, the places where the products are sold, and the value-adding skills.[39] The results of this analysis help guide skill development, as well as the search for acquisition and new product strategies that will exploit the existing set of skills.

Familiarity with and Commitment to Previous Strategy

Although top management's familiarity with and commitment to previous strategy can enhance the strategy selection process, it can also cause problems. If executives remain committed to a given strategy and pursue it for several planning periods, inertia can ensue, and inertia reduces the impact of subsequent strategic planning. In addition, managers tend to increase their commitment to previous strategies when the strategies begin to falter.[40] This fact strengthens the view that key executives should be replaced after extended periods of poor performance by the firm.

Degree of External Dependence

Some firms depend to an extreme degree on one or more external coalitions, such as suppliers or customers. To maintain the necessary relations with the key coalition, these firms may have to choose a strategy that would not normally be selected. Consider, for example, a firm that relies heavily on one customer, such as General Motors. This firm may have to produce certain products that would otherwise not be produced in order to carry the full line of products demanded by General Motors. Essentially, the greater a firm's dependence, the lesser are its decision-making range and flexibility.

Competitors' Reactions

Competitive reactions to strategy alternatives require careful evaluation. Any strategy that is likely to elicit an immediate and strong response from a powerful competitor must take such a response into account. The likelihood of a strong reaction may reduce the attractiveness of the strategy and suggest a more indirect approach.

Stakeholders' Reactions

Reactions expected from the firm's stakeholders will also effect the choice of strategies. Consider the following examples:

1. Firm A wants to pursue a strategy that involves deleting several products from its product line. If many customers demand a complete product line, firm A may need to consider other strategies.

2. Firm B wants to pursue a strategy that involves immediate and drastic reduction of inventories and purchases, but numerous small suppliers for which firm B is the only customer would be out of business. If firm B expects to purchase the same products in the future, other, less damaging, strategies might be needed.

3. Firm C has the largest market share in the industry and wants to pursue a strategy of concentration involving a merger with the firm that has the next largest market share. If the antitrust division indicates that this merger would significantly lessen competition in the industry, firm C should look for another corporate strategy.

Timing

Proper timing can be critical to the success of a firm's strategies. For example, a firm wishing to divest one business in order to vertically integrate by acquiring a different business might need to time each transaction carefully because of financial demands.

Another aspect of timing involves the *strategic window* concept.[41] The basic idea is that opportunities exist for a finite time period because customers, technology, competitors, channels, and laws evolve and change over time. This limited period when there is a strategic fit between the opportunity and the firm's competencies is referred to as the strategic window. While the strategic window is open, the firm should be investing in the opportunity. Because of evolutionary changes in subsequent periods (for example, competitors seizing the opportunity), the strategic window will close and the firm will be forced to seek other opportunities.

EVALUATING THE SELECTED STRATEGY

To evaluate the strategies selected, management should ask and answer several penetrating questions about them. The most important question is: *Will the strategies achieve the objectives?* The seven supporting questions listed below can be viewed as selection criteria. Each criterion suggests a multitude of additional questions; a few of these additional questions are provided as examples.[42]

1. Is the strategy consistent with the environment?
   a. Is the strategy acceptable to the firm's major stakeholders?
   b. Does the strategy provide a differential competitive advantage?
2. Is the strategy consistent with internal policies, styles of management, philosophy, and operating procedures?

    a. Does the strategy conflict with other strategies?

    b. Is the existing organizational structure compatible with the strategy?

3. Is the strategy appropriate in the light of financial, physical, and human resources?

    a. What are the financial consequences of allocating capital to this strategy?

    b. Are there identifiable and committed managers to implement the strategy?

4. Are risks in pursuing the strategy acceptable?

    a. Do the potential benefits justify the risks?

    b. What are the consequences of failure?

5. Does the strategy fit the product life cycle and market potential?

    a. Is the strategy appropriate for the present and future?

    b. Is the strategy compatible with the product life cycle?

6. Can the strategy be implemented efficiently and effectively?

    a. Does the strategy fit managerial and employee capabilities?

    b. Is the timing appropriate?

7. Are there other important considerations?

    a. Have the major factors influencing success been evaluated accurately?

    b. Are all key assumptions realistic?

As already noted, these seven criteria can be used to compile a formidable list of questions. These additional questions should be formulated and answered; some can be answered quickly while others require a more rigorous analysis.

CONTINGENCY PLANS

A strategic plan is based on assumptions and forecasts of macro-, task, and internal environmental factors. Since forecasting is an inexact science, strategists should develop alternative strategies, or *contingency plans,* to be followed in the event that key assumptions and forecasts are in error. Developing contingency plans involves three key steps:[43]

1. *Identify key variables.* These variables should be the factors that are most important to the success of a strategy and can indicate that a strategy is not working as planned.

2. *Establish trigger points.* Each key variable should have a trigger point, which is the amount of variation from the forecast that triggers a change in the strategy or activates the contingency plans.

3. *Select alternative strategies.* Alternative strategies, or contingency plans, can vary in the amount of detail. The most important consideration is that they provide direction for strategists.

The major advantages of developing contingency plans are to shorten reaction time and alert management as to when changes are needed. Charles Schwab & Co., the discount brokerage firm, developed contingency plans to cope with the possibility of a major San Francisco earthquake. When an earthquake did occur in 1989 (interrupting baseball's World Series), Schwab was prepared. The major plans had already been thought through.[44]

GLOBAL DIMENSIONS OF CORPORATE STRATEGY

One of the most fundamental international corporate strategy decisions involves the scope on which a firm intends to compete. A firm has these basic alternatives:[45]

1. *Full global scope:* compete worldwide in the full product line of the industry
2. *Limited global scope:* compete worldwide, but only in selected portions of the industry offering
3. *National scope:* compete only in selected countries
4. *Protected national scope:* compete only in selected countries that have erected governmental barriers (for example, high tariffs, requiring a high proportion of local content in product) by concentrating on effective dealings with that market and government

Although firms entering the international arena have similar corporate strategy options, the execution of each strategy alternative may be somewhat different. In the remainder of the chapter, we briefly consider the strategy options related to entering foreign markets.

Market Development

Entry into foreign markets is a special form of market development. The key to this strategy is whether the firm's current products can be successful in the foreign country. One firm, for example, tried to sell its gelatin dessert in a country in which only 3 percent of the population owned refrigerators.[46]

Backward Vertical Integration

A backward vertical integration strategy is available to the firms that are currently supplied by a foreign company. Internal vertical integration would obviously involve establishing a new production facility in a foreign country. For either strategy, political and legal barriers must be analyzed and surmounted.

Forward Vertical Integration

Forward vertical integration generally involves the development (either internally or externally) of sales or distribution outlets in foreign countries. One interesting pattern of development involves foreign students attending U.S. universities. There are many instances of successful students returning to their country as the first employee and sales manager (or entrepreneur with an exclusive national distributorship) for a U.S. firm in that country.

Diversification

Neither concentric nor conglomerate diversification strategies are particularly popular international strategies because of the problems inherent in entering new markets (especially those with unfamiliar cultures) with new products. (See Chapter 2.) A firm might still consider a diversification strategy, however, if potential opportunities were sufficiently attractive.

Joint Ventures

D. F. Channon and M. Jalland suggest that joint ventures and licensing agreements are sound strategies for entering foreign business.[47] Although not without problems, joint ventures can often surmount financial hurdles and legal and political barriers in foreign lands.[48]

Notes

1. Arthur A. Thompson, Jr., and A. J. Strickland III, *Strategic Management: Concepts and Cases,* 3rd ed. (Plano, Tex.: Business Publications, 1984), pp. 79–81.
2. James A. Belohlav and Karen Giddens-Emig, "Selecting a Master Strategy," *Journal of Business Strategy* (Winter 1987), 76–82.
3. Leslie W. Rue and Phyllis G. Holland, *Strategic Management* (New York: McGraw-Hill, 1989), p. 41.
4. Peter Gutmann, "Strategies for Growth," *California Management Review* (Summer 1964), 31–36.
5. Michel Chevalier and Bernary Catry, "Don't Misuse Your Market Share Goal," *European Business* (Winter-Spring 1974), 43–50.
6. Philip Kotler, *Marketing Management,* 5th ed. (Englewood Cliffs, N.J.: Prentice-Hall, 1984), pp. 58–59.
7. Peter F. Drucker, *Management: Tasks, Responsibilities, Practices* (New York: Harper & Row, 1974), p. 686.
8. Arthur A. Thompson, *Economics of the Firm: Theory and Practice* (Englewood Cliffs, N.J.: Prentice-Hall, 1977), ch. 2.
9. Kathryn Rudie Harrigan, "Quick Change Strategies for Vertical Integration," *Planning Review* (September 1986), 32–37.

10. William F. Glueck, *Business Policy and Strategic Management* (New York: McGraw-Hill, 1980), p. 211.

11. Bernard Ramanantson and Jean-Pierre Petrie, "Diversification—The Key Factors to Success," *Long Range Planning,* February 1986, pp. 31–37.

12. Thompson and Strickland, p. 86.

13. Drucker, p. 767.

14. Clark E. Chastain, "Divestiture: Antidote to the Merger Mania," *Business Horizons* (November-December 1987), 43–49.

15. Claudia Bird Schoonboven, "Combining Strategies Pays Off Fast, Even in Turbulent Markets," *Planning Review* (July-August 1987), 38–41.

16. Jonathan Kapstein, Thane Peterson, and Lois Therrien, "Look out, World, Philips Is on a War Footing," *Business Week,* January 15, 1990, pp. 44–45.

17. See Alfred Rappaport, "Strategic Analysis for More Profitable Acquisitions," *Harvard Business Review* (July-August 1979), 99–110 for methods of evaluating how much to pay for an acquisition.

18. Thompson and Strickland, pp. 90–93.

19. David B. Jemison and Sim B. Sitkin, "Acquisitions: The Process Can Be a Problem," *Harvard Business Review* (March-April 1986) pp. 107–116.

20. Steven E. Prokesch and Wiliam J. Powell, Jr., "Do Mergers Really Work? *Business Week,* June 3, 1985, p. 90.

21. Willard F. Rockwell, Jr., "How to Acquire a Company," *Harvard Business Review* (September-October 1968), 121–132.

22. Lionel L. Fray, David H. Gaylin, and James W. Down, "Successful Acquisition Planning," *Journal of Business Strategy* (Summer 1984), 46.

23. J. L. Frier, "Acquisitions Search Program," *Mergers and Acquisitions* (Summer 1981), 35–39.

24. H. W. Ebeling, Jr., and T. L. Doorley III, "A Strategic Approach to Acquisitions," *Journal of Business Strategy* (Winter 1983), 44–54.

25. Zane Markowitz, "Acquiring the Right Company," *Journal of Business Strategy* (September-October 1988), 43–46.

26. Fray, Gaylin, and Down.

27. Charley Blaine, "Terms of Business," *USA Today,* January 27, 1986, p. 3E.

28. "Honeywell Finds a Swedish Partner," *Business Week,* August 22, 1983, p. 42.

29. Staffan Gullander, "Joint Ventures and Corporate Strategy," *Columbia Journal of World Business* (Spring 1976), 106–108.

30. Marjorie A. Lyles, "Common Mistakes of Joint Venture Experienced Firms," *Columbia Journal of World Business* (Summer 1987), 79–83.

31. Lee Adler, "Symbiotic Marketing," *Harvard Business Review* (November-December), 59–71.

32. P. Rajan Varadarajan and Daniel Rajaratnam, "Symbiotic Marketing Revisited," *Journal of Marketing* (January 1986), 7–17.

33. Ibid.

34. Dan Schendel, G. R. Patton, and James Riggs, "Corporate Turnaround Strategies," *Journal of General Management* (Spring 1976), 3–11.

35. Thompson and Strickland, p. 120.

36. Geoffrey Colvin, "The De-Geneening of ITT," *Fortune,* January 11, 1982, pp. 34–39.

37. Anil K. Gupa and V. Govindarajan, "Build, Hold, Harvest: Converting Strategic Intentions into Reality," *Journal of Business Strategy* (March 1984), 34–47.

38. Richard M. Cyert and James G. March, *A Behavioral Theory of the Firm* (Englewood Cliffs, N.J.: Prentice-Hall, 1963).

39. Walter Kiechel III, "Corporate Strategists Under Fire," *Fortune,* December 27, 1982, p. 39.

40. Barry M. Staw, "Knee-Deep in the Big Muddy: A Study of Escalating Commitment to a Chosen Course of Action," *Organizational Behavior and Human Performance* (June 1976), 27–44.

41. Derek F. Abell, "Strategic Windows," *Journal of Marketing* (July 1978), 21–26.

42. George A. Steiner, John B. Miner, and Edmund R. Gray, *Management Policy and Strategy* (New York: Macmillan, 1982), pp. 240–244; George S. Day, "Tough Questions for Developing Strategies," *Journal of Business Strategy* (Winter 1986), 60–68.

43. J. L. Cooley, Jr., *Corporate and Divisional Planning*, (Reston, Va.: Reston Publishing, 1984), p. 436.

44. "Charles Schwab's Little Red Book," *Fortune*, November 1989, p. 104.

45. Adapted/reprinted with permission of The Free Press, a division of Macmillan, Inc. from *Competitive Strategy: Techniques for Analyzing Industries and Competitors* by Michael E. Porter. Copyright © 1980 by The Free Press.

46. For an excellent documentation of incidents illustrating such blunders, see David Ricks, Marilyn Y. C. Fu, and Jeffrey S. Arpan, *International Business Blunders* (Columbus, Ohio: Grid, 1974).

47. D. F. Channon and M. Jalland, *Multinational Strategic Planning* (New York: AMACOM, 1978), ch. 7.

48. William R. Fanning and Carol B. Gilmore, "Developing a Strategy for International Business," *Long Range Planning* (June 1986), 82–84.

CHAPTER 12

Selecting Business- and Functional-Level Strategies

Just as every firm must have corporate-level strategies, it must also have business-level and functional-level strategies. Business-level strategies outline how a business will compete within its industry. If a firm operates only one business, its corporate- and business-level strategies are basically the same. In multiple-business firms, though, the business-level strategy (also called divisional, or SBU, strategy) of each component business is distinct.

Each business (or corporate strategic business unit—SBU) must formulate strategies designed to achieve and support the corporate objectives and strategies. Although the strategic planning process at the business level consists of the same basic steps as those used at the corporate level, the specific details are naturally different. Business-level environmental analysis, for example, focuses more directly on factors that can have an impact on the business than does corporate-level analysis. Consequently, analysis of the task and internal environment tends to be more important. Also, business-level objectives tend to be more narrowly defined, emphasizing shorter-term goals. Strategies at the business level focus more strongly on product and market variables.

Within a business, each functional area must formulate functional strategies that support and contribute to achieving the business-level objectives and help to carry out business-level strategies. Again, the basic steps of the strategic planning process are the same, but the specific details are different. For example, environmental analysis focuses on how to achieve various functional objectives.

This chapter is organized around perspectives of business-level strategies. The discussion focuses on generic strategies, concentration strategies, market entry strategies, product life cycle strategies, and competitive strategies.

GENERIC STRATEGIES

As discussed in Chapter 10, strategists at the business level of the organization should consider the three **generic strategies:** cost leadership, differentiation, and focus.[1]

Cost Leadership

A **cost leadership strategy** emphasizes producing a highly standardized product, becoming the lowest-cost producer in the industry, and underpricing the competition. Sources of a firm's cost advantage, which vary according to the industry and the industry structure, include economies of scale, proprietary technology, preferential access to raw materials, product configuration, level of service provided, process technology, and so on.

As Michael Porter points out, cost leadership can be attractive because it can

- give the firm above-average returns.
- defend the firm against competitive rivalry because it is not very vulnerable to competitive pricing strategies.
- defend the firm against powerful buyers because buyers can exert pressure only to drive prices down to the level of the next most efficient competitor.
- defend the firm against powerful suppliers by providing flexibility to deal with input cost increases.
- provide substantial barriers to entry because of the potential high cost of those factors which contribute to the low cost position.
- put the firm in a favorable position to defend against substitute products.[2]

Note that pursuit of a cost leadership strategy does not eliminate the need to address differentiation. Customers must still see the producer's product as comparable with competing products. Therefore, low cost will provide a competitive advantage only if the producer achieves competitive parity or proximity relative to the key bases of differentiation.

Differentiation Strategy

A **differentiation strategy** emphasizes producing a product with such quality or design features, brand name status, or reputation for service that it commands a higher than average price. The product's unique aspect must match some characteristic valued by many consumers—for instance, brand image, design image, technology quality, features, customer service, dealer network, or some combination of these.

Differentiation has several potential advantages:[3]

1. It can provide protection against competition due to brand loyalty, which supports higher prices.
2. It can increase margins because of the ability to charge higher prices.
3. The higher margins provide flexibility for dealing with supplier power, such as raising prices.
4. It can mitigate buyer power because there are no comparable alternatives.
5. It can provide entry barriers because of customer loyalty and the necessity for competitors to overcome the product's uniqueness.
6. It can fend off competitive substitutes because of customer loyalty.

Pursuit of a differentiation strategy does not allow the firm to ignore costs. The price differential charged must more than offset the cost of differentiating the product. Otherwise, the firm does not achieve a competitive advantage. Furthermore, the company seeking differentiation should aim at cost parity or proximity relative to competitors. Cost should therefore be reduced in areas that do not affect differentiation.

Focus Strategy

A **focus strategy** involves pursuing a narrow competitive scope within an industry by tailoring the product to a small segment (or segments) of the market. There are two variants of the focus strategy. First, a *cost focus strategy* exploits differences in the cost situation in some segments. The production and delivery systems that best serve the target customers normally differ from those used for other segments. Second, a *differentiation focus strategy* emphasizes the special needs of buyers in certain segments.

Either focus strategy must exploit the differences in the chosen segment if the strategy is to succeed. Furthermore, competitors must not be meeting the needs of these segments.

A firm that does not possess a cost or differentiation competitive advantage that it can deploy either in a broad or narrow market is "stuck in the middle." Such firms are at a competitive disadvantage and are lucky to make a reasonable profit. Most industries contain quite a few competitors that are stuck in the middle.

Firms that possess a competitive advantage must strive to maintain it or they will quickly find themselves stuck in the middle. Cost leadership, for example, can be lost when competitors imitate operations, when technology changes, when any of the bases by which cost leadership was achieved changes, when differentiation parity is lost, or when firms using a cost focus strategy achieve even lower costs. The differentiation advantage can be lost when competitors imitate, when the basis or bases of the differentiation become less important to buyers, when cost proximity is lost, or when competitors using a differentiation focus strategy achieve even greater differentiation in segments. The advantages of a focus strategy can be lost when it is imitated by competitors, when the target segment or demand disappears, when broad-based competitors overwhelm the segment, or when new focusers "subsegment" the industry.

Porter emphasizes that firms must analyze what is going on in the industry (see the discussion of task environment in Chapter 6) and choose the most promising competitive niche and generic strategy. Management should seek a "defensible competitive position" so that the firm does not have to slug it out with everybody else in the industry.

CONCENTRATED GROWTH STRATEGIES

Concentrated growth strategies at the business level focus on product and/or market elements. Although integration and diversification strategies can also be pursued at the business level (and are discussed below), the major focus of business-level strategy is typically one of the three concentrated growth strategies: market penetration, market development, or product development.[4] Each is discussed in detail in this section.

The main difference between the corporate and the business view of the concentration strategies is that the scope or scale of the relevant SBU is different. Whereas corporate-level planning addresses each business or major market type (for example, home appliances) as an SBU, at the business level SBUs are generally defined more narrowly. The home appliance corporate-level SBU, for example, could be divided into four product line SBUs, such as stoves, refrigerators, air conditioners, and washer/dryers, at the business level.

As part of the discussion of each business-level strategy alternative, examples of corresponding functional-level analyses, decisions, and strategies are presented and examined. Table 12.1 shows the major areas of analysis and decision making for each functional unit. The strategies designed by each functional unit must, of course, complement the business-level strategies.

Before going further, we need to resolve a potential semantic confusion about the terms *objective* and *strategy*. Thus far we have defined an *objective* as a desired result or outcome, and a *strategy* as the game plan for achieving one or more objectives. These definitions still hold for each individual level of analysis, but not between the levels. Assume, for example, that a business has chosen

---

TABLE 12.1 · Key Analysis and Decision Areas at the Functional Level

MARKETING	1. Consumer analysis
	2. Product line and brand strategy
	3. Pricing
	4. Distribution/location
	5. Promotion
PRODUCTION	1. Quality control
	2. Plant site location
	3. Purchasing
	4. Facility and equipment maintenance
	5. Scheduling
HUMAN RESOURCES	1. Employee promotion procedures
	2. Training
	3. Compensation
	4. Hiring
FINANCE	1. Capital structure
	2. Dividend policy
	3. Working capital
	4. Financial markets
RESEARCH AND DEVELOPMENT	1. Technical innovation
	2. Technical development
	3. Product imitation

---

market penetration as its chief business-level strategy. This strategy, once it is transmitted to the funcitonal level, changes and becomes an *objective*.

Market Penetration Strategy

A **market penetration** strategy, which involves seeking growth in current markets with current products, may be pursued along two basic avenues.[5] First, a firm can increase its market share if it can accomplish one of the following:

1. *Increase the rate of purchase of the product.* Customers' rate of purchase is a function of purchase frequency and purchase amount. A firm might, therefore, attempt to persuade customers either to use the product more often or to use more of the product on each occasion. The primary selling point of Johnson & Johnson's Baby Shampoo, for example, is that it is mild enough to use every day. Other firms encourage customers to use two applications of

PERSPECTIVE 12.1

Gillette's $300 Million Razor

Gillette's single most expensive project ever saw the light of day in January of 1990. This was a cartridge razor that took over ten years and $200 million to research, develop, and tool. An extra $110 million was budgeted for media advertising in 1990, including ultra-expensive Super Bowl ads.

Gillette was willing to spend so much money because its cartridge razors had been losing market share to disposable razors marketed by Bic and other companies—including Gillette. Gillette found it worthwhile to fight the trend toward disposable razors. The company made almost three times as much per cartridge for its Atra and Trac II razors as it did for the throw-away models.

The extremely high cost of the razor was partly the result of the technical difficulties of building a razor with floating parts in it. The new razor has springs that follow facial contours to give a closer shave; it's called the Sensor because—according to the Super Bowl ads—"it can sense the individual needs of your face." At the outset, however, there were no springs that would do this effectively, so Gillette had to develop them. And the spring design would not allow for the use of the styrene plastic that Gillette had been using for its handles, so the company developed a new plastic, called Noryl.

Early indications pointed to success: after an early 1990 promotional blitz, including the Super Bowl spots, the razors were in such demand that Gillette cut down on advertising and increased production. If the razor continues to meet with such success, Gillette will increase its already commanding two-thirds share of the North American and European market. The company should also improve its profit margin significantly by moving people away from the disposable razors.

References: Keith H. Hammonds, "How a $4 Razor Ends Up Costing $300 Million," *Business Week,* January 29, 1990, pp. 62–63; Allison Fahey and Wayne Walley, "Sensor Sensation: Gillette Cuts Ads to Satisfy Demand," *Advertising Age,* February 5, 1990, p. 4; Bob Garfield, "Somehow, Gillette's 'Best' Idea Seems Better This Time Around," *Advertising Age,* January 29, 1990, p. 60.

their shampoo each time. In addition, finding or simply emphasizing a new use for a product can sometimes increase the rate of purchase by present customers.

2. *Attract competitors' customers.* Taking customers away from competitors often involves emphasizing one of the elements of the marketing mix (product,

price, place, and promotion). For example, a firm could launch an advertising campaign that features a famous personality extolling the quality of the firm's products.

3. *Buy a competitor.* If other opportunities for increasing market share are not attractive, a firm can consider purchasing one of its direct competitors (which is sometimes referred to as horizontal integration). To be classified as a market penetration strategy, the purchase must involve a firm that carries the same basic product lines and competes in the same markets. Otherwise, it would actually be an example of horizontal diversification (discussed in Chapter 11 and later in this chapter).

Second, market penetration can also involve *increasing the total size of the market* by converting nonusers of the firm's product in the current target markets into users. For example, since all women currently do not use hair-styling mousse, female nonusers could become new users. Note that if the new users come from outside the present target markets (for example, if they are men), the strategy employed has probably been market development.

Functional-Level Plans   At the functional level, the primary burden for supporting a business-level market penetration strategy is typically shouldered by the marketing function. Almost all of the approaches discussed above require an extensive analysis of present or potential customers. Questions like the following must be addressed and answered by the marketing research staff:

- Why do customers buy our product?
- Why do other consumers not buy our product?
- Why do other consumers buy our competitor's product?
- How do customers use our product?
- What do customers like about our product?
- What do customers not like about our product?
- What additional features would customers like?

After the questions have been answered, the marketing staff is in a position to fine-tune the marketing mix to achieve greater penetration. Since no change can be made in the product, marketing's major options include adjusting the price, finding new or better outlets, selecting new advertising media or different promotional techniques, changing the major theme of promotion, or hiring more salespeople.

The research and development and human resource functions usually play little or no part in a market penetration strategy. The production function needs to be ready to increase output if the strategy succeeds. Similarly, the financial function should be prepared to provide the funds necessary for increased demand for raw materials, inventories, and perhaps credit.

Market Development Strategy

Market development at the business level involves seeking new markets for current products, that is, finding new users from markets not presently penetrated. There are three ways to accomplish this:[6]

1. *Find new geographical markets.* Large firms that have completely blanketed the United States might have to look overseas for new markets. However, many large firms with nationwide operations have not necessarily exhausted all geographical possibilities. McDonald's Corp., for example, has outlets seemingly everywhere, but many opportunities for new locations are still available. Smaller firms might consider simply expanding into the next town or even across town.

   When internally focused, this effort commonly involves finding new distributors, expanding the sales force, or opening new outlets. Hanes Companies, Inc., for example, was one of the first firms to successfully market pantyhose (L'eggs) outside of the traditional channels (department stores and women's clothing outlets). External avenues for market development would involve horizontal integration with a company that appeals to different target markets.

2. *Find new target markets.* This approach involves finding an entirely new group of target customers within the present geographical markets. Hair-styling mousse, for example, could be positioned as a men's product, as was done with hair spray several years ago. Personal computer firms, too, are constantly seeking new software that will open up new target markets for their products. Other specific efforts might involve developing new channels of distribution or simply using different advertising media.

3. *Find new uses.* Many products have multiple uses that the firm can exploit. Each new use can represent an entirely new target market. In most situations, the product will have to be transformed to tap the new use. In this situation, the market development strategy actually generates a new product life cycle, thereby joining with a product development strategy. The uses of nylon, for example, have been expanded over time from parachutes to women's stockings, blouses and shirts, automobile tires, upholstery, and carpeting.[7]

Functional-Level Plans   The functional-level plans and activities needed to pursue a market development strategy are basically quite similar to those discussed for a market penetration strategy. Marketing still bears the primary burden but focuses its efforts in slightly different directions, such as toward customers in other geographical areas. R&D would have more responsibilities if this strategy involved finding new uses for the product that required converting it into a different form.

Product Development Strategy

A **product development** strategy consists of developing new products for current markets or customers. This strategy can focus either on individual products or on the firm's overall product line.

Individual Product Development   Four specific approaches are available for pursuing the development of individual products.[8]

1. *Feature improvements.* New products can arise from modifying, adding to, or rearranging present features or content. These changes generally aim at improving the product by expanding its versatility, safety, or convenience. Adding a self-propelling feature to a lawn mower, for example, increases the mower's convenience. Annual introduction of a "new model" can also result from this strategy. The major benefits of this approach are that it can usually be done quickly, and it tends to generate enthusiasm for salespeople, dealers, and customers.
2. *Quality improvements.* This approach aims at improving the product's reliability, speed, durability, taste, or other characteristics. Different versions of the product can also be developed that vary in quality. For example, a single company may sell various grades of oil, grease, and gasoline.
3. *Style improvements.* The aesthetic appeal of a product can be enhanced by changing its color, package design, texture, and so on.
4. *Model additions.* Different models or sizes can be developed. Most hand tools and power tools, for example, are available in a variety of models and sizes.

Any of these approaches can result in a "new" product. New products can also arise from consideration of the firm's overall product line.

Product Line Development   Among the major alternatives available for improving a firm's product line, some involve adding new products, and one involves upgrading existing products.[9]

First, management should consider *line stretching,* that is, lengthening the product line beyond its present dimensions. It can use one of these three approaches:

- *Downward stretch.* When its product line is positioned on the high end of the market, a firm can consider adding individual products to plug gaps in the lower end. Both IBM and Caterpillar have chosen this approach and launched smaller, less expensive units of their basic products. Failure to cover the lower end of the market leaves opportunities for encroachment by competitors. This strategy, however, is not without potential problems. The new products can lure customers away from the current products, and they can force competitors to seek the upper end of the market.

- *Upward stretch.* An upward stretch involves adding products to serve the upper end of the market. In the personal computer market, for example, Tandy Corp. has sought to stretch upward by bringing out more sophisticated units. The major pitfalls of this approach are that the new product is likely to face stiff, entrenched competition, and that it is difficult to convince customers of the added quality in the new product.
- *Two-way stretch.* When a firm occupies the middle range of the market, it might consider a two-way stretch by bringing out new products at both the high and low ends of the market. Texas Instruments followed this approach in the hand-held calculator market.

Second, a *line-filling* decision involves adding more items within the range of the present product line. The major consideration for this decision involves ensuring that consumers will actually see the new products as different and that they will buy them not in place of, but in addition to, the present products.

Third, a *line-modernization* decision might be made when the product line length is acceptable, but the line needs adjustments to update style or incorporate technological advances. Firms in areas that are experiencing rapid technological change, such as the computer/information processing area, are forced to continually modernize. They must decide whether to upgrade the entire product line (probably a heavy cash drain) or take a piecemeal approach (allowing competitors to keep up).

A product development strategy also calls for considering several other major issues. Specifically, a structure for developing new products and extensions of current products must be developed, and strategy alternatives over a product's life cycle should be considered.

The New Product Development Process   The overall process for innovation and the product development strategy are basically the same and generally referred to as the **new product development process.** Various new product development systems have been proposed, and we summarize the steps involved.[10]

1. *Idea generation.* Estimates of the number of new product ideas needed to generate one successful product range from forty to sixty.[11] The major sources of ideas for new products and services include customers, R&D scientists and engineers, salespeople, members of channels of distribution (such as dealers), competitors, and top management. Management must design and coordinate a system to solicit ideas. The purpose of this idea generation step is to provide a number of good ideas, whereas the purpose of the remaining steps is to reduce the number of ideas.

2. *Idea screening.* The first major "go/no go" decision is made during this idea-screening stage. In making this decision, managers must avoid two types of errors. An error of omission involves reaching a "no go" decision on a product or

service that would have actually been profitable for the firm. This type of error can be especially embarrassing when a competitor makes a successful and profitable "go" decision on the same idea. An error of commission brings about a "go" decision that results in product failure or generates less than the firm's targeted rate of return.

3. *Concept and product development.* This step entails translating a general idea for a product (for example, a throwaway cigarette lighter) into a specific product concept (for example, a small, thin, adjustable butane lighter with "lifetime" fuel and flint for 99 cents) and then testing the product concept. The testing requires obtaining consumer reactions to either the concept (if possible) or the product. The purpose is to evaluate whether the product's appeal warrants further consideration.

4. *Concept evaluation.* Concepts that have survived until this point must still pass several additional evaluations. The first major evaluation is often called the business analysis: it comprises forecasting sales, costs, and profits. Note that firms will need to develop tentative marketing strategies as a basis for the sales forecast, R&D must design the product, and production managers must design the production facility to form the basis for the cost forecasts. Normally, the financial managers are then responsible for the profitability analysis.

If the concept passes the business analysis, R&D should develop and produce a prototype and test it for physical and functional characteristics. Production must make sure that the product can be made in sufficient quantity. Marketing personnel may also extend this test to include various forms of consumer testing, such as in-home placement tests.

5. *Final product evaluation and development of marketing strategy.* This step often begins with market testing, that is, introducing the product to the market in an authentic, but limited, setting. The purpose of test marketing is to evaluate the product's performance (as well as the marketing strategy) and to identify potential problems before committing to a full-scale introduction of the product. The results of the test marketing should permit final forecasts of profitability and approval of marketing strategies. Production personnel must concurrently determine the specific plant and equipment necessary to produce the forecast sales.

6. *Monitoring system.* A system for continuous monitoring and evaluation of new product performance must be developed and integrated with the firm's normal control procedures.

7. *Product introduction.* This is the commercialization stage, in which full-scale introduction of the product begins. A successful "roll-out" involves making decisions regarding timing, the geographical strategy (for example, local, regional, or national introduction), target prospects, the marketing mix, and the amount of money to be spent.

Functional-Level Plans   Although the specific plans and activities undertaken by the various functional areas vary according to the approach taken for product development, several generalizations can be made. All the plans and activities focus on change—whether changing an existing product or changing the product line by adding a new product.

Marketing's burden again consists of gathering and analyzing information about consumers and their attitudes toward the firm's product(s), competing products, and potential new products. If changes are indicated, marketing personnel typically collaborate with R&D to launch the new product development process. R&D will also often generate ideas for new products. Before spending a great deal of money on the ideas, however, marketing should be included in the process. Regardless of the source of an idea, R&D typically is responsible for developing the technical concept and marketing is responsible for addressing the commercial feasibility.

Production personnel should also be involved early in new product deliberations. They must consider the production implications of the new product, including more refined cost estimates.

The financial function can assist by consolidating the financial projections. In addition, it is responsible for analyzing the capital investment required and, eventually, securing the needed capital.

The human resources function will be especially important if the proposed product changes call for hiring additional employees or employees with specialized skills. If such employees are not readily available, a developmental human resources strategy must be formulated. For example, special arrangements with a local trade school could be made to train a certain number of potential employees for electronics or welding positions.

MARKET ENTRY STRATEGIES

Before considering strategy alternatives available during the life of the product, strategists must evaluate and select a market entry strategy. The three basic alternatives are (1) being first, (2) being early, and (3) being late.[12]

Enter-First Strategy

Being first in the market is inherently attractive to many individuals because it connotes leadership, innovation, and being number one.[13] Being first does have a number of potential advantages. First, the firm can be the first to benefit from its learning and experience curve, which may provide a cost advantage relative to competitors that enter the market later. Second, the firm can often benefit from customer inertia, thereby making it more difficult for competitors to take customers away. Third, the first firm in the market begins with initiative and momentum, which provides the opportunity to continually stay one step ahead of competitors. Fourth, perhaps the greatest attraction of being first is the opportunity to dominate the market (which does not always happen).

Porter adds the following advantages:[14]

1. The reputation gained
2. The pre-emptive position gained
3. The buyers' cost of switching from the first firm to competing firms, once the initial purchasing has occurred
4. Greater choice of channels of distribution
5. Favorable access to facilities, imports, and other scarce resources
6. Opportunity to define standards, which later competitors may be forced to adopt
7. Creation of barriers, such as patents and special status or agreements with customers or regulatory agencies
8. High early profits due to the unavailability of the product from other sources

Along with the potential advantages, being first in the market brings several distinct problems.[15] It demands extreme concentration of effort, such as on one clear, major vision and objective. Maintaining a leadership position also requires continual striving to avoid the loss of all that has been invested. Furthermore, too much success may attract competitors, which may force the first firm to cut prices. On the other hand, a firm that introduces a product too early may find its reputation permanently damaged.

Being first in the market allows a company to use a **pre-emptive strategy,** which involves moving first to secure an advantageous position that competitors' are discouraged or barred from duplicating. Pre-emption can be achieved through actions such as these:[16]

1. Expanding production capacity before demand increases, in an attempt to discourage competitors' expansion
2. Using long-term contracts to tie up key raw material sources and/or suppliers
3. Locking in the best geographical locations
4. Securing the largest and/or most prestigious customers
5. Establishing strong consumer image
6. Locking in the best distributors

Note that certain pre-emptive strategies—such as expanding production ahead of market demand—can also be used long after entering the market.

Enter-Early Strategy

An early entry into the market, but not the first entry, can occur in two very different contexts. On the down side, a firm can lose the race to be first, thereby forcing it into the "early" category. This second-place finisher is likely to put up a strong fight for share, primarily because of previous commitment to a strategy and commitment of resources. Although this firm has all the disadvantages of being first and none of the advantages, it can wage a successful battle if it possesses and is willing to commit adequate resources to the fight. A weak effort, however, is destined to defeat.[17]

Being second in the market has some potentially significant advantages. The greatest potential advantage may be the opportunity to gain insight as to what works and what does not work. The early entry can keenly observe what occurs in the market, develop different strategies for overcoming obstacles, and develop strategies that focus on the first entry's actions (for example, based on customer reactions, eliminate product "bugs").

The early entry may face reduced risk. Many things can go wrong when entering the market first because of risk in demand, risk in technological obsolescence, and so on. Consequently, many firms are more comfortable with an early-entry strategy, which they can pursue perhaps by developing a superior imitative product.

Along with the lower risk, the early entry may find that most of the opportunity is still available in the marketplace. Demand should already be established, but the lack of other competitors leaves the market largely untapped.

The early entry faces two potential handicaps. A strong competitor entering the market first can erect some formidable barriers, which the early entry must overcome. Furthermore, at least slightly less market potential exists at the time the second competitor enters the market.

Enter-Late Strategy

Although on the surface a late market entry may not appear to be an attractive strategy, it carries some significant advantages. Late entrants

1. Can include the latest technological improvement in their product and production processes (for example, consider IBM's late entry into the personal computer market)
2. May be able to achieve greater economies of scale because demand can be established more accurately, thereby facilitating the design of optimal size plants
3. May be able to obtain better terms from suppliers or customers since earlier

entrants may be tied to less favorable agreements, made initially to help establish the market

4. May be able to offer lower prices, if they can avoid wasting resources and take advantage of opportunities for lowering the cost of R&D and marketing

5. Can attack existing competitors' specific weak spots[18]

The late entry confronts the same two hurdles as the early entries: barriers to early entry and less market potential. These problems become more severe as the product enters the maturity and decline stages of its product life cycle.

PRODUCT LIFE CYCLE STRATEGIES

It is appropriate to look at strategy alternatives after market entry and as they arise over the life of the product. The general idea underlying the **product life cycle** (PLC) concept is that products and services have a limited life span: introduction to growth to maturity to decline.[19] At some point in the decline stage, a product modification or deletion decision essentially terminates the PLC. We discuss strategies for the PLC stages in the next four sections.

Introduction Stage Strategies

The key strategy decisions in the **introduction stage** involve the four basic elements of the marketing mix. Although all four elements can be adjusted, the price and promotion elements are more easily adjusted. Let us, therefore, work with combining price and promotion into four strategy alternatives.[20]

First, a *rapid skimming strategy* involves combining high prices and high levels of promotion. The high prices are designed to skim a lot of profit from the market while the high promotion is designed to help accelerate the rate of market penetration. Rapid skimming can be effective when most consumers are unaware of the product but potentially highly interested in it, and the firm wants to build brand preference to defend against expected competition.

Second, a *slow skimming strategy* results from high prices and low promotion levels. The key difference between this strategy and rapid skimming is that the firm prefers low promotion, which helps keep marketing expenses down, over improving brand preference. Slow skimming is more desirable when the market size is relatively small, consumers are aware of the product and are not price sensitive, and competition presents little threat.

Third, a *rapid penetration strategy* combines low prices with heavy promotion in an attempt to obtain and maintain a large market share. This strategy is appropriate when the market potential is large, consumers are unaware of the product but are price sensitive, strong potential competitors exist, and favorable economies of scale are possible.

Fourth, a *slow penetration strategy* involves low prices to foster market penetration and low levels of promotion to keep expenses down. Two key assumptions underlie this strategy: that consumers are price sensitive but not promotion sensitive. In addition, the market should be large and highly aware of the product.

Growth Stage Strategies

Rapidly increasing sales characterize the **growth stage** of the PLC. In this stage, one of the dominant business issues involves securing the resources to grow along with the market. Marketing activities tend to be a major application of these resources. The following guidelines can help direct these marketing activities:[21]

1. Concentrate on improving quality, adding new features, and developing new models
2. Focus on tapping new market segments
3. Search for new distribution channels
4. Shift the focus of advertising themes from creating awareness to generating product acceptance and trial
5. Concentrate on the proper timing for price reductions to tap the next "layer" of consumers

Although the five guidelines focus on growing as rapidly as possible, management must not lose sight of the forthcoming maturity stage. The firm must also devote attention to developing the distinctive competencies and stamina to withstand the more intense competitive rivalry characteristic of the maturity stage.[22] The firm should consider pruning the product line, increasing sales to present customers, and giving more emphasis to process innovation, cost reductions, purchase of rival firms at bargain prices, and international expansion.[23]

Maturity Stage Strategies

The **maturity stage**, marked by a stable (or stagnant) industry sales curve, usually lasts much longer than the other stages of the PLC. Rather than simply defending current market share, management should seek strategies that fit market opportunities. A firm can choose among three sound alternatives:[24]

1. Focusing on finding previously untapped market segments
2. Relaunching the product with improved quality, new features, or style improvements

3. Improving efficiency wherever possible—for instance, in production, distribution channels, or other marketing mix elements

Decline Stage Strategies

Falling sales and low or nonexistent profits characterize the **decline stage**. If sales are expected to continue declining, management should consider modifying or deleting the product. Although decisions to modify or delete a current product may focus on capitalizing on opportunities, this section is oriented toward overcoming present or anticipated problems.[25]

Carrying a weak product can be very costly for a company now and in the future, especially if it precludes the development of new product opportunities. To ensure effective handling of aging products, firms should establish a system to identify, analyze, and recommend courses of action for products in the decline stage. A five-step process is outlined below:

1. Establish a product review team (include representatives from at least the marketing, finance, and production functions).
2. Determine necessary inputs or key performance measures (such as profitability, market share, gross profit margins, and ROI).
3. Routinely monitor all products and assign to categories, such as (a) acceptable current and projected performance—no changes needed; (b) acceptable current and projected performance—could benefit from changes; and (c) unacceptable current or projected performance—changes needed. A product could be assigned to category b or c above because of (1) declining sales, market share, or profitability; (2) changes in consumer attitudes toward the product; (3) new competitive products or activity; (4) changes in governmental regulations regarding the product (for example, red dye No. 2 and saccharin); (5) changes in resource availability; or (6) technological advances.
4. Evaluate in detail each product in categories 3b and 3c and generate and evaluate alternative strategies, such as (a) leave the product alone; (b) modify the marketing strategy (for example, change product features, position, pricing, and distribution channels); (c) concentrate on the strongest markets or products and phase out other efforts; (d) harvest; (e) sell entire product line; or (f) drop completely.
5. Select an alternative. Explicit attention should be given to the product modification/deletion decision for products in their decline stage. These decisions can have a greater and more immediate impact on profit than new product development decisions.

COMPETITIVE STRATEGIES

The most appropriate competitive strategies depend on a variety of factors, including the firm's objectives, strategies, resources, target customers, stage of the product life cycle, competitors' marketing strategies, and the character of the economy.

The primary objective of a competitive strategy is to be strong at the critical *decisive point*.[26] The overall environmental situation and specific competitive strategies will cause the decisive point to change, thereby mandating modified or new strategies.[27]

The similarities between competitive strategy and military strategy have been noted in business literature.[28] In both competitive strategy and military strategy, critical decisions must be made with limited resources, under conditions of risk and uncertainty, while facing severe competition. William A. Cohen translated military strategy and the "principles of war" into his twelve "principles of marketing strategy." These twelve principles are modified slightly to form twelve "principles of competitive strategy":[29]

1. *Objective:* Every strategy must have an objective that focuses on attaining a specified and decisive goal, which implies minimizing costs in resources and time.
2. *Initiative:* Initiative implies action rather than reaction, which supports the maintaining of an offensive attitude to control the time and place of action.
3. *Concentration (principle of mass):* Perhaps the most fundamental concept, it involves allocating resources to achieve a competitive advantage at a decisive point.
4. *Economy of force:* Resources should be concentrated on the decisive objective, and only a minimum of them allocated to secondary efforts.
5. *Maneuver:* Management must position resources to assist in accomplishing the objective and should consider, economic, psychological, and timing factors.
6. *Unity of command:* For every assigned mission, there should be one responsible manager, to ensure unity of effort and efficient utilization of resources.
7. *Coordination:* Organizational units must cooperate, tasks must be integrated, and the overall strategy must by planned and implemented.
8. *Security:* Accurate intelligence is required to prevent competitors from gaining an unanticipated advantage, and information about the firm's capabilities and intentions must be protected.
9. *Surprise:* The firm should accomplish its purpose before competitors can react effectively; it can do so with the aid of secrecy and deception, as well as through variation of methods, innovation, audacity, or speed of action.

10. *Simplicity:* Even simple strategies can be quite difficult to execute; complex strategies can be an exercise in futility.
11. *Flexibility:* Managers should remember Murphy's Law, "Everything that can go wrong will go wrong." The strategic plan should contain contingency plans to facilitate coping with problems and taking advantage of opportunities.
12. *Exploitation:* The firm needs to maintain pressure when winning until it achieves maximum success.

Diversion and Dissuasion Strategies

Achieving a competitive advantage by concentrating resources at the decisive point involves a variety of considerations. Bruce Henderson succinctly states one perspective: "Induce your competitors not to invest in those products, markets, and services where you expect to invest the most."[30] He also suggests six **diversion and dissuasion strategies:**[31]

1. *Appear to be unworthy of attention*—such as by "staking out" a small niche or portion of the market; once you accomplish this successfully, repeat the pattern for another small niche.
2. *Appear to be unbeatable;* for instance, convince competitors that if they follow your firm's lead, they will not succeed because the firm will equal or better any actions that they take or resources that they commit.
3. *Avoid attention* by following the principle of security and not forewarning competitors about new products, strategies, capabilities, or policies until it is too late for them to respond.
4. *Redirect attention (feint),* perhaps by focusing competitors' attention on major volume areas (current activity) rather than high-potential areas (future intentions).
5. *Practice self-discreditment*—for example, by overstating and overpublicizing the potential impact of actions.
6. *Appear to be irrational* by taking actions that seem illogical because they are impulsive or emotional.

These strategies are particularly appropriate for a weaker competitor facing a strong competitor, as in the situation discussed in the next section.

Competitive Position Strategies[32]

The primary focus of this section is on another key issue, the firm's size and competitive position in the market. To simplify the discussion, we have divided firms into four competitive categories: market leaders, market challengers, market followers, and market nichers. Alternative competitive strategies are discussed for each category under the assumptions of fast-growth or stable-growth objectives and concentration growth strategies. Thus each of the marketing objectives and strategies derives from one of the concentration strategies discussed earlier.

Strategies for Market Leaders Many markets contain a firm that is the acknowledged market leader. If the market leader selects a fast-growth objective and a concentration strategy, the marketing planners can choose from two basic marketing growth objectives. First, the firm can seek to *expand the size of the total market* by attracting new users, finding new uses, or increasing usage of the product per use occasion.

Second, the market leader can choose to *increase market share* to achieve fast-growth objectives. The marketing strategy can involve one of the strategies discussed for increasing the size of the market or adjusting one of the elements of the marketing mix.

Market leaders that choose a stable-growth objective and a concentration strategy generally must also select a marketing objective that can protect the present market share. Protecting market share does not necessarily indicate a passive approach to marketing strategy. Market leaders such as Procter & Gamble and General Motors cannot afford to be passive but must be constantly on the alert for attacks by able challengers.

Four broad strategies for protecting market share are available. An **innovation strategy** assumes that "someone will come up with something better, so it might as well be us." Consequently, the market leader tries to lead the industry in such areas as developing new products, services, and means of distribution.[33] Another positive approach to preserving market strength, a **fortification strategy** focuses on maintaining reasonable prices and on introducing new product sizes, forms, and brands.[34] A **confrontation strategy** often involves a quick and direct response to a challenger. This strategy can take the form of promotional wars, price wars, and dealer "pirating." A rather negative approach, a **harassment strategy,** can end up in the court system. A firm practicing this strategy attempts to influence major suppliers or distributors, have salespeople criticize the challenger, or even hire away key personnel.

Market leaders must always be on the lookout for trouble. Stanley F. Stasch and John L. Ward identified three categories of factors that point to the likelihood of attacks by competitors:[35]

1. *External forces:* (a) government or environmental challenge, (b) a random catastrophe for the leader, (c) a change in the status of industry technology, such as the emergence of a substitute technology and the expiration of pat-

ents, and (d) a new personality entering the industry, such as a new corporate parent or a competitor from a related industry.

2. *Market structure and characteristics of the leader:* (a) there is no strong number two competitor, (b) the leader charges high prices because of skimming strategy, to maintain a high-quality image, or the leader has high costs, (c) a new positioning opportunity emerges, (d) the leader is relatively small, and (e) the number two competitor can expand geographically.

3. *Leader's behavior:* (a) lethargic leadership because of conservatism, financial goals, relatively inconsequential market, fear of cannibalizing, or preoccupation, (b) significant strategic weaknesses, and (c) alienation of key distributors.

Strategies for Market Challengers   Market challengers may be quite large but are not number one in the market. Fast-growth corporate objectives and a concentration growth strategy strongly imply a marketing growth objective of gaining additional market share. Before considering how to accomplish this market share objective, strategists must carefully evaluate its appropriateness.

A high share strategy tends to work best when financial resources are adequate, when the firm's position will be viable even if the fight for market share is stopped, and when government regulations do not interfere.[36] Pankaj Ghemawat recommends addressing the following questions before launching a strategy to increase market share:[37]

1. Does my industry exhibit a significant experience curve?
2. Have we defined the industry broadly enough to take into account interrelated experience?
3. What is the precise source of cost reduction?
4. Can my firm keep cost reductions proprietary?
5. Is demand sufficiently stable to justify using the experience curve?
6. Is accumulated output doubling fast enough for the experience curve to provide much strategic leverage?
7. Do the returns from the experience curve strategy warrant the risks of technological obsolescence?
8. Is demand price sensitive?
9. Are there well-financed competitors that are already following an experience curve strategy or are likely to adopt one if my company does?
10. Is there a significant antitrust risk?

A high market share strategy does not always generate a high return on investment. One research study found that market share leaders with low profitability were more often located in regional and fragmented markets, faced unstable environments and deteriorating market conditions, had low value added factors, had a poor reputation for quality, charged higher prices, faced higher costs, did not focus resources effectively, and had a poor strategic fit with environments.[38]

The strategists must determine from which firm to take the share. One approach is a head-on or direct attack on the market leader. This approach can be effective, but the challenger must have a strong, sustainable competitive advantage or the market leader must have an exploitable weakness.

A second approach involves *guppy strategy,* or *taking share away from other smaller and weaker competitors.* Many of the larger beer brewers, for example, have grown through acquisition of smaller brewers.

A third approach is much more indirect. The challenger tries to *bypass* or take an *end run* around the market leader, thus avoiding a direct confrontation. For example, the firm could expand into new geographical areas or concentrate on the next generation of technology. Peter Drucker refers to this sidestepping of a leader's strength as *entrepreneurial judo* and contends that it is made possible by five bad habits of entrenched firms:[39]

1. The *NIH (not invented here) syndrome,* or managers' conviction that nothing can be good unless they themselves thought of it
2. The tendency to focus only on high-profit market segments and ignore smaller niches
3. Ignoring customers' definition of quality and relying on technical definition of quality
4. Maintaining a premium price to achieve a high profit margin and ignoring other measures such as return on investment (ROI) and return on assets (ROA)
5. Trying to use a single product to satisfy everyone in the market

A fourth approach involves *guerrilla strategies.* A smaller challenger can use a guerilla attack to choose the time, place, and conditions that best suit it rather than the market leader. Typical guerrilla strategies include (1) focusing on a narrow niche that is weakly defended by competitors, (2) focusing on fronts where competitors are overextended (for example, faster delivery times), and (3) launching small scattered raids, perhaps through intense bursts of promotional activity and selective price cutting.

Any combination of marketing mix factors can be used to gain market share. C. Davis Fogg found five strategies to be most important.[40]

1. Maintaining lower prices than competitors
2. Introducing product innovations (or modifications) or stimulating new needs
3. Improving service, especially faster delivery to service-conscious customers

4. Fielding a larger and better sales force or building a better distribution system
5. Increasing and improving advertising and promotion

Fogg also points out five key pitfalls in implementing a strategy to gain market share: moving too slowly, not doing enough, not following through, underestimating competition, and not knowing when to quit.[41]

Strategies for Market Followers   Market followers do not choose to challenge the market leaders. Although their market share is usually smaller than the leader's, their overall profitability can be as good or better. The followers' marketing objective is generally to protect their existing market share, which does not necessarily mean a passive approach without strategies. Followers must continually strive to maintain their present customers and get their share of new customers. The key to success for market followers is deploying the elements of the marketing mix in a profitable way that does not provoke intense competitive retaliation.

Strategies for Market Nichers   Market nichers attempt to find and occupy small niches in the market that the major firms are likely to overlook or ignore. Successful market nichers tend to segment their markets carefully, use research funds efficiently, grow at a carefully chosen rate, and have strong CEOs who have pervasive influence.[42] Serving these niches effectively normally involves some form of specialization—for instance, by customer characteristics, geography, product line, product feature, service, or quality. Drucker proposes three separate niching strategies (which are similar to Porter's generic strategies):[43]

1. The *tollgate strategy* involves creating a situation in which customers feel that they cannot do without the product. It requires that the product be essential, the risk of not using it be greater than the cost of the product, and the market be so limited that whoever occupies it controls it and prevents others from entering.
2. The *specialty skill strategy* involves possession of a skill not possessed by competitors. The skill must generally apply to something new, be truly different, and be continually upgraded. (Opportunities for this strategy usually exist in rapidly evolving market/industry situations.)
3. The *specialty market strategy* involves tapping a market that is unique and different and not being served by competitors.

GLOBAL DIMENSIONS OF BUSINESS STRATEGY[44]

Multinational firms are normally composed of subsidiaries that operate on a virtually autonomous basis. With the exception of limited shared product development, competition in the international arena is on a country-by-country basis. Key differences between countries that must be addressed include (1) cost structures, (2) market structures, (3) roles of foreign governments, and (4) the ability to monitor foreign competitors and their goals and resources.

Firms engaged in global competition may encounter a variety of impediments, especially in an emerging global industry. Transportation and storage costs may offset any available economies of scale, particularly for bulk products such as fertilizer and prestressed concrete. National markets may demand different product varieties. When customers are numerous and individual purchase amounts are small, the firm may have to try to penetrate entrenched channels of distribution. Furthermore, larger products may entail the acquisition and training of local sales forces, and local repair may also be required. Another hurdle may come from factors such as short fashion cycles and rapidly advancing technology, which may prevent the firm from responding appropriately. Still other drawbacks stem from the fact that the marketing tasks can vary substantially in each country and that the firm may face a variety of governmental obstacles, such as tariffs and duties, preferential procurement from local firms by government, preferential taxes for local firms, and insistence on local R&D or locally produced components for the product.

Besides these relatively specific handicaps, global firms also face some unique strategic issues. First, the firm's global competitors may have home governments that influence their position in global competition. The home government, for example, might provide R&D funds, help the firm negotiate in world markets, help finance sales through central banks, or partially or completely own the firm. Second, host governments in major global markets can obstruct global firms in ways described in the preceding paragraph. Third, global competitors are likely to have coordinated worldwide strategies for markets, facilities, and investments. Fourth, competitor analysis in global industries is extremely difficult.

Addressing these impediments and strategic issues requires the firm to have or develop distinctive competencies that offer international competitive advantages in its industry.[45] The key sources of global competitive advantages include: (1) product cost lower than in other countries; (2) product quality significantly greater than in other countries; (3) production, purchasing, logistical, and marketing economies of scale; (4) proprietary product technology; (5) mobility of production; and (6) global experience.

A firm seeking a global scope has a number of strategic alternatives. The four basic ones are as follows:

1. *Broad-line global competition:* The firm competes worldwide with the full industry product line. This requires substantial resources and a long time horizon; the firm must strive to reduce impediments.

2. *Global focus:* The firm competes worldwide in a particular segment of the industry; it seeks a segment with low impediments.

3. *National focus:* The firm competes in selected countries; it focuses on particular needs to outcompete global firms.

4. *Protected niche:* The firm competes in selected countries, where governmental restraints (such as a required high proportion of local content in the product) virtually exclude global competitors.

The point here is that a firm must be careful when competing globally and should select an alternative that provides a defensible position. For instance, only a very large, powerful firm is likely to select broad-line competition because it exposes the firm to virtually all other firms in the industry, some of which place major resources in a segment or country. The other three alternatives are generally more defensible, especially for smaller firms. For example, a firm that selects a national focus can become very competitive in the selected countries.

Notes

1. Adapted/reprinted with permission of The Free Press, a division of Macmillan, Inc. from *Competitive Strategy: Techniques for Analyzing Industries and Competitors* by Michael E. Porter. Copyright © 1980 by The Free Press.

2. Ibid., pp. 35–36.

3. Ibid., pp. 37–38.

4. Philip Kotler, *Marketing Management: Analysis, Planning, and Control,* 5th ed. (Englewood Cliffs, N.J.: Prentice-Hall, 1984), pp. 58–59.

5. Ibid.

6. Ibid.

7. Theodore Levitt, "Exploit the Product Life Cycle," *Harvard Business Review* (November-December 1965), 81–94.

8. Kotler, p. 58.

9. Ibid., pp. 475–479.

10. See Yoram J. Wind, *Product Policy: Concepts, Methods, and Strategy* (Reading, Mass.: Addison-Wesley, 1982), p. 228; and Alfred Oxenfeldt, *Executive Action in Marketing* (Belmont, Calif.: Wadsworth, 1966), pp. 364–367.

11. See C. Davis Fogg, "Planning Gains in Market Share," *Journal of Marketing* (July 1974), 39; "The Rebuilding Job at General Foods," *Business Week,* August 25, 1973, p. 50; and *Management of New Products,* 4th ed. (New York: Booz, Allen & Hamilton, 1968), p. 9.

12. Peter Drucker, *Innovation and Entrepreneurship,* (New York: Harper & Row, 1985), pp. 208–218.

13. William A. Cohen, *The Practice of Marketing Management* (New York: Macmillan, 1988), p. 369.

14. Michael E. Porter, *Competitive Advantage,* (New York: The Free Press, 1985), pp. 186–188.

15. Drucker, p. 210.

16. Ian MacMillan, "Preemptive Strategies," *Journal of Business Strategy* (Fall 1983), 18–26.

17. Subhash C. Jain, *Marketing Planning and Strategy,* 2nd ed. (Cincinnati: Southwestern, 1985), pp. 607–611.

18. George S. Yip, "Gateways to Entry," *Harvard Business Review* (September-October 1982), 89.

19. Wind, pp. 46–49.

20. Kotler, pp. 362–366.
21. Charles W. Hofer and Dan Schendel, *Strategy Formulation: Analytical Concepts* (St. Paul, Minn.: West, 1978), pp. 164–165.
22. Hofer and Schendel, pp. 164–165.
23. Porter, *Competitive Strategy*, pp. 241–246.
24. R. G. Hamermesh and S. B. Silk, "How to Compete in Stagnant Industries," *Harvard Business Review* (September-October 1979), 163–165.
25. Wind, pp. 528–543; and Kotler, pp. 371–372.
26. William A. Cohen, "The Application of Historical Military Strategy Concepts to Marketing Strategy," in *Development in Marketing Science*, ed. John C. Rogers III et al., (Logan, Utah: Academy of Marketing Science, 1983), VI, 263–265.
27. Derek F. Abell, "Strategic Windows," *Journal of Marketing* (July 1978), 26.
28. For example, see Harry L. Hansen, "Creative Marketing Strategy," *Boston Conference on Distribution* (Boston: International Marketing Institute, 1959); Philip Kotler and Ravi Singh, "Marketing Warfare in the 1980s," *Journal of Business* (Fall 1980), 67–81; William A. Cohen, "War in the Marketplace," *Business Horizons* (March-April 1986).
29. William A. Cohen, "Historical Military Strategy Principles Advocated for Winning Marketing Wars," *Marketing News*, April 12, 1985, p. 23.
30. Bruce D. Henderson, *Henderson on Corporate Strategy* (New York: Abt Books, 1979), p. 11.
31. Ibid, pp. 14–15.
32. This section draws heavily on Kotler, pp. 383–413.
33. Roland W. Schmitt, "Successful Corporate R & D," *Harvard Business Review* (May-June 1985), 124–128; James Brian Quinn, "Managing Innovation: Controlled Chaos," *Harvard Business Review* (May-June 1985), 73–84.
34. Steven C. Wheelwright and Robert H. Hayes, "Competing Through Manufacturing," *Harvard Business Review* (January-February 1985), 99–109.
35. Stanley F. Stasch and John L. Ward, "When Are Dominant Market Leaders Likely to Be Attacked?" in *1984 AMA Educators Proceedings*, ed. Russell W. Belk et al. (Chicago: American Marketing Association, 1984), p. 225.
36. William E. Fruhan, Jr., "Pyrrhic Victories in Fights for Market Share," in *Strategic Management*, ed. Richard G. Hamermesh (New York: Wiley, 1983), pp. 124–125.
37. Pankaj Ghemawat, "Building Strategy on the Experience Curve," *Harvard Business Review* (March-April 1985), 149.
38. Carolyn Y. Woo, "Market-Share Leadership—Not Always So Good," *Harvard Business Review* (January-February 1984), 50.
39. Drucker, p. 220.
40. Fogg, p. 30.
41. Ibid., p. 38.
42. R. G. Hamermesh, M. J. Anderson, Jr., and J. E. Harris, "Strategies for Low Market Share Businesses," *Harvard Business Review* (May-June 1978), 98.
43. Drucker, pp. 233–242.
44. This section draws heavily on Porter, *Competitive Strategy*, pp. 275–299.
45. John Alie and Robert R. Miller, "Manufacturing Strategies in an Era of International Competition," *Industrial Management* (May-June 1986), 6–7.

PART FOUR

Taking Action

The previous chapters have dealt with ways of determining what a firm wants to accomplish and how. Part Four focuses on putting the plans into action.

Many companies spend a great deal of time determining objectives, analyzing environments, and selecting strategies. Such analysis and planning are very well and good, but they serve only to get a company started. Chapter 13 discusses the importance of careful planning of implementation, and gives some specific guidelines.

Chapter 14 covers the final step in the strategic management process: evaluating and controlling performance. This step is vital because it ensures that the selected strategies are indeed helping the firm achieve its objectives. In addition, information gleaned from the evaluation and control process can be used as the basis of strategic plans for the next planning period.

CHAPTER 13

Implementing the Strategies

Far too often companies seemingly assume that implementation of strategic plans will occur automatically. It does not occur automatically, however; it requires the same careful analysis and planning as the other aspects of the strategic management process. Firms that do not plan adequately for implementation are no better off than those that do not plan at all.

In the case of poor implementation, management often views the strategic planning phase as an exercise in futility: large chunks of time are spent on developing strategic plans, but these plans fail to bring satisfactory results. This situation does not necessarily indicate a problem with the strategic planning components. What it does signal is that strategic planning has not been extended to strategic management by properly incorporating the implementation and/or control elements. Until effective implementation occurs, the strategic plans are literally paperwork exercises. The implementation phase transforms the plans into action.

Implementing strategic plans is not always an easy task. A study of implementation found that these ten problems cropped up most frequently:[1]

1. Implementation took more time than originally allocated.
2. Major problems that surfaced had not been anticipated.
3. Implementation activities were poorly coordinated.
4. Competing activities and crises distracted attention from implementing decisions.
5. The employees involved lacked sufficient capabilities.
6. Lower-level employees were inadequately trained and instructed.
7. Uncontrollable factors in the external environment had an adverse impact.
8. Departmental managers did not provide adequate leadership and direction.
9. Key implementation tasks and activities were not defined in sufficient detail.
10. Information systems used to monitor implementation were inadequate.

This investigation also identified five rules that firms with successful implementation track records tended to follow:[2]

1. The plan must be communicated to all the employees whom it will affect.
2. The idea or concept represented by the strategic decision must have a sound purpose and be well formulated.
3. Management must obtain commitment and involvement from employees.
4. Management must provide sufficient resources for the project, including money, manpower, technical expertise, and time.
5. Management must develop an implementation plan by setting goals and keeping a record of accomplishment.

In this chapter, we examine what corporate-level management should do to ensure proper implementation of strategies. We emphasize five major steps:

1. Review objectives, environments, and strategies
2. Evaluate, adjust, and commit resources
3. Develop organizational structure
4. Introduce the changes or strategies
5. Re-evaluate the strategic plan

The steps are designed to make successful implementation more likely; that, in turn, would enhance the probability of achieving the firm's objectives.

Timing is as crucial as the planning itself. Management must not get so mired in the planning that it fails to act. Thus the major steps discussed in this chapter should be considered thoroughly but also as quickly as possible so that strategies can be put into operation within a reasonable time frame.

REVIEWING OBJECTIVES, ENVIRONMENTS, AND STRATEGIES

The first major step in implementing strategic plans is to review previous analyses and decisions regarding objectives, environments, and strategies. The aim is to ensure that those responsible for implementation have a firm grasp of the strategies, the reasons for pursuing them, and the relevant objectives. The review also serves as the final assessment of the objectives and strategies. For example, the objectives should be evaluated to make sure that they are still viable and that all major factors have been taken into account.

From a philosophical perspective, analyzing the firm's external environments (as described in Chapters 5 and 6) helps strategists determine *what strategies are possible and desirable*. One of the primary purposes of analyzing the internal environment is to determine *how the strategies can be implemented*. Consequently, much of the material discussed in Chapter 7 is also relevant to implementation issues and should be reviewed in conjunction with this chapter.

The review of earlier analyses gives management the opportunity for detecting and assimilating the environmental changes that have occurred since the major environmental analysis was conducted. Managers must also carefully pinpoint any factors that might have a major impact on the implementation phase.

As mentioned above, the primary reason for this review is to ensure that those responsible for implementation have a thorough understanding of the objectives and strategies. All analysis, objectives, and strategies should have been compiled into a written document or strategic plan. If the strategic plan has been written and no major environmental changes have occurred, this review can be relatively quick and painless. However, if need be, management can, and should, adjust the plan. The understanding gained from the review should greatly facilitate the adjustment and fine-tuning process.

EVALUATING, ADJUSTING, AND COMMITTING THE RESOURCES

Once it has thoroughly reviewed and understood the strategies and plans, management must evaluate, adjust, and commit the firm's resources. In this context, *resources* is broadly interpreted to mean all resources, including personnel and their activities, equipment, and financial resources.

The chief purpose of this step is to develop appropriate programs, budgets, and procedures. A *program* is a detailed statement of activities or steps needed to accomplish something. For example, a corporate subunit might develop programs for training, recruiting, advertising, plant modernization, and new product development. *Budgets* lay out the costs of the activities specified by the programs. *Procedures* are systems of sequential steps or techniques specified to perform a particular task or job. Procedures serve as guides to employees in areas such as grievance handling, raises, promotion, purchasing, and credit. Although it might seem obvious that programs, budgets, and procedures guiding the firm's day-to-day activities should be linked directly to the strategic plan, this situation does not always exist.[3]

Evaluating

An overall evaluation of resources should have been conducted as part of the firm's internal situation analysis and also as part of the strategy selection process.

PERSPECTIVE 13.1

NeXT Computing

After Steve Jobs, the *wunderkind* cofounder of Apple Computer, left that company in 1985, everyone wondered what he would do next. What he did next was NeXT: with $7 million of his own money, he founded NeXT Inc. and soon raised over $100 million from investors to support the development of a new computer.

NeXT's personal computer was introduced in late 1988 and began shipping in September 1989. A sleek black box with a huge screen, it has a nearly three-dimensional interface, soft-touch buttons, sound quality to match a compact disc, and other new features that met with accolades at the computer's unveiling. But customers seem to have balked at both the computer's high price tag and some technical problems—specifically, technology that does not conform to industry standards. For example, NeXT relies on an optical disk for storage rather than on floppy or hard disks, and the optical disk drive it uses is not compatible with other optical disk drives. In addition, it uses a UNIX operating system, but not the version of UNIX that is expected to become the industry standard.

The NeXT personal computer does seem to be popular for desktop publishing, because it excels at displaying how a page of print will really look. The company has not released precise figures, but analysts think sales have been disappointing. But, as one industry observer notes, even if NeXT doesn't corner the personal computer market, it can still generate sizable revenues: a mere 1 percent of that market could translate into $400 million to $500 million in worldwide revenues.

Jobs is making some moves to bolster NeXT in the market. He is making some concessions to the clamor for standardization, such as ordering a chip that will facilitate the use of accessories, such as floppy-disk drives, that NeXT doesn't sell. He is also turning attention to marketing. And, significantly, he is selling some of NeXT's technology to industry giant (and Apple rival) IBM.

So what will happen with NeXT? The jury's still out. Just remember that people were initially skeptical about Jobs's Macintosh, which is now wildly popular. And, for one, Dan'l Lewin, NeXT's vice-president of sales, discounts the importance of matching industry standards, saying that improvement depends on changing the common denominator.

References: Richard Brandt, "So Far, So-So, for Steve Jobs's New Machine," *Business Week,* January 29, 1990, pp. 76–77; Gordon Graham, "Waiting for the NeXT Wave," *Canadian Business,* January 1990, pp. 75–77; John Daly, "A Computer War Game: Internal Problems and an Old Ally Confront Apple," *MacLean's,* March 12, 1990, p. 50ff.

A re-evaluation may be necessary at this point to ensure that the company has or can obtain the quantity and quality of resources required to implement each selected strategy. This re-evaluation may also force management to re-analyze the cost of implementation. For example, one firm analyzed by the authors found that the cost of implementing an operations turnaround strategy for one of its plants would exceed $400,000, which would be more than the expected benefits of the strategy.

The essential question to be answered is, Do we have the resources to effectively pursue the strategies that have been selected? If any resource deficiencies are discovered, those resources must be adjusted. Three broad issues relevant to resource quality merit discussion here.

Management Characteristics and Strategy   Having the right kind of manager responsible for implementing various types of strategic thrusts and specific strategies may be critical to the success of a business. Marc Gerstein and Heather Reisman describe the characteristics needed by general management for seven different strategic postures, ranging from startup, to new acquisition.[4]

- **Startup**

  Description: high financial risk, limited management cohesiveness, no experience, organization, systems, or procedures

  Management thrust: creating an organizational vision, core business and technical expertise, and management team

  Management characteristics needed: a hands-on approach; knowledge in key technical and functional areas; organizing, staffing, and team-building skills; high levels of energy, stamina, and charisma

- **Dynamic growth in existing business**

  Description: new markets, products, technology; moderate-to-high financial risk; rapid and unequal growth in organization sectors; multiple demands, conflicting priorities, and changing power bases; inadequate resources to meet all demands; constant dilemma between doing current work and building support systems for future

  Management thrust: managing rapid change, increasing market share in key markets, building toward achieving vision and mission

  Management characteristics needed: clear company vision; sound strategic planning, financial planning, team building, crisis management, and staffing skills; ability to take risks and balance priorities; high energy level

- **Extracting profit/rationalizing existing business**

  Description: need to invest selectively in short run, but unattractive industry in long run; internal stability, moderate-to-high managerial and technical competence, most systems and relationships adequate

Management thrust: efficiency, stability, management succession, sensing signs of change

Management characteristics needed: good technical knowledge and administrative skills; orientation toward relationships, management development, management succession, efficiency (rather than growth); sensitivity to changes and ability to anticipate problems

- **Redeployment of efforts in existing business**

Description: low-to-moderate short-term risk, but high long-term risk; bureaucratic resistance to change; mismatches between organizational skills, resources, and strategies; operations-oriented management—little or no strategic planning

Management thrust: managing change and establishing effectiveness in limited business sphere

Management characteristics needed: skills in change management, persuasion, sensitivity to people, systems, organizing, and staffing; moderate risk taking

- **Turnaround of existing business**

Description: business worth saving, but characterized by poor results, weak competitive position, low morale, inadequate systems, inadequate relationships with external stakeholders, lack of leadership, and limited resources and skills

Management thrust: rapid and accurate problem diagnosis, fixing short-term problems and setting up long-term solutions

Management characteristics needed: orientation toward taking charge and risks; analytical and diagnostic skills regarding finances, business strategy, crisis management, and negotiations; high energy level and ability to handle pressure

- **Liquidation/divestiture of poorly performing business**

Description: need to cut losses and make tough decisions because of little opportunity for turnaround; weak competitive position, unattractive industry, or both

Management thrust: cutting losses and making tough decisions and the best deals

Management characteristics needed: a risk taker who is tough-minded, willing to do the "dirty work" and to be the "bad guy," and prefers respect to popularity; highly analytical approach to cost versus benefits

- **New acquisitions**

Description: acquisitions resulting from any of the above situations or from the need to integrate acquired company with parent at some levels and pressure on new management to "prove themselves"

Management thrust: integration and establishing sources of information and control

Management characteristics needed: skills in analysis, relationship building, interpersonal influence, communications, and establishing instant credibility relative to the new organization

C. W. Hofer and M. J. Davoust propose that management characteristics be matched with strategies suggested by levels of industry attractiveness (IA) and competitive position (CP):[5]

1. **Strategy:** *invest/grow strongly* (strong CP/high IA)
   Managerial type: *mature entrepreneur*—takes calculated risks to further the goals of the organization and should balance focus in the present and future
2. **Strategy:** *invest/grow selectively* (average CP/high IA)
   Managerial type: *planner entrepreneur*—places emphasis on future planning
3. **Strategy:** *Dominate/delay/divest* (weak CP/high IA)
   Managerial type: *turnaround entrepreneur*—strives to improve the competitive position of the firm before it is pushed out of the industry; often comes from outside the firm and has reputation for success in failing firms
4. **Strategy:** *invest/grow selectively* (strong CP/medium IA)
   Managerial type: *sophisticated planner*—focuses on the external environment and on carefully pinpointing opportunities for growth—typically has experience in the contingency management approach.
5. **Strategy:** *Earn/protect* (average CP/medium IA)
   Managerial type: *profit planner*—focuses on strategic planning, quantitative decision-making tools, and information systems to optimize use of the organization's resources and talents
6. **Strategy:** *Harvest/divest* (weak CP/medium IA)
   Managerial type: *turnaround specialist*—focuses on the present in order to improve the position of the firm immediately or milk the firm if turnaround is unsuccessful; often comes from outside the firm
7. **Strategy:** *earn/protect* (strong CP/low IA)
   Managerial type: *professional manager*—focuses on conserving competitive strengths and typically is a stable, experienced leader
8. **Strategy:** *harvest/divest* (average CP/low IA)
   Managerial type: *experienced cost cutter*—takes maximum advantage of every opportunity to succeed in the present, with less concern about future
9. **Strategy:** *harvest/divest* (weak CP/low IA)
   Managerial type: *professional liquidator*—concentrates on the present in order to divest the business as quickly and painlessly as possible; may possess only minimal skills in strategic, long-term planning; often comes from outside the firm

Commitment of Personnel   Successful implementation of strategies is dependent heavily on the commitment of personnel throughout the organization, from the executive suite to the lowest levels. Firms that enjoy this commitment possess a high-quality resource that can often overcome other minor deficiencies. This commitment does not come automatically, nor is it easy to obtain. Management's major task is to convince all personnel that the best way to achieve their personal objectives is by helping the organization accomplish its objectives. To attain this goal, management may need to use a variety of conceptual approaches and tools, such as change management, leadership, and motivation. The commitment of personnel implies that a spirit of performance permeates the company.

Spirit of Performance   The *spirit of performance* is an attitude that fosters a willingness to support and strive toward organizational objectives and to accept and even initiate appropriate changes. A pervasive spirit of performance is valuable because it implies a sense of moving ahead. Ideally, this attitude motivates both individual and organizational performance.

Quality circles, which are very popular in Japan and are becoming more popular in the United States, illustrate formal attempts to create a spirit of performance. The quality circle concept is a formalized version of participative management, in which workers are encouraged to evaluate their responsibilities and activities and suggest improvements. The purpose is to obtain better performance from the workers (and, therefore, the firm) because the workers want to perform better, rather than because superiors demand it.[6]

Allocating and Committing the Resources

Implementing strategies often calls for resource adjustments, which are performed by top-level management and by functional area managers and personnel. These adjustments can relate to resource quality or quantity. Human resource skills (including those in the executive suite) may need upgrading for effective pursuit of a particular strategy or reduction of an existing deficiency. In the case of a temporary cash deficiency, adjusting the quantity of cash resources by financial means or by converting other assets may solve the problem.

Top management also has the duty to ensure that the functional areas make necessary adjustments. Sometimes one or more of the functional areas may not want to move in new directions and top management has to convince those people to make the changes or to implement the changes that have been selected.

The primary issue here is to provide adequate resources for executing the firm's strategies. A frequent mistake is to skimp on the resources, but halfhearted attempts at implementation will usually fail, even if the strategy is correct and all the planning properly done.

The strategic window concept, discussed in Chapter 11, also applies to resource commitment. Since some opportunities last only a short time, a firm unprepared or hesitant to commit the necessary resources may find that the window has closed—that is, the opportunity has passed—before it can act. Although several firms often identify the same opportunity, only those that act quickly will be able to take advantage of it.

Decisions on reallocating resources vary according to whether the firm is growing or declining.[7] During periods of **growth,** new resources can be directed toward "needy" areas without decreasing allocations to other areas. In other situations, some firms will establish priorities centrally and dictate resource allocation. At the opposite extreme, some firms encourage internal competitive bidding for resources and use strategy-related criteria for allocating. This approach can be set up as an *investment bank.* In between these two extremes, *constrained bidding* has various internal units bidding for additional resources but within defined constraints.

The main issue in resource allocation for firms experiencing **decline** involves reducing some area's resources in absolute terms to maintain other areas and/or to support promising new developments. Centrally imposed, constrained bidding, and competitive bidding can also be employed to reduce resources.

A major part of committing resources entails allocating capital and preparing budgets. Each of these points is discussed below.

Capital Allocation   Although management must consider the availability of capital while developing corporate strategies, the allocation of capital to various competing uses generally occurs after corporate strategies are selected. The key problems relate to getting capital in the form of cash and allocating the cash to the most efficient uses. It is critical to note that generating profits does not necessarily guarantee the availability of cash. Profits resulting from increased sales volume, for example, may be used to increase other assets, such as inventory or accounts receivable. Although profits should eventually generate cash, financial management has the burden of determining when the cash will be available and whether the cash flow will be large enough to meet cash requirements.

Capital allocation involves the following steps:

1. Establish (or review) the general guidelines.
2. Analyze demands for capital.
3. Analyze the financial structure.
4. Analyze sources of capital.
5. Select sources of capital.

The competing internal demands for capital are often varied and sometimes enormous. Naturally, executives responsible for a particular operation or project favor equipment and other expenditures that would let them to do their job better or lower their operating costs. Top management can try to regulate these competing demands by translating corporate objectives and strategy into guidelines that state general areas where investment will or will not be made. For example, a firm with which the authors are familiar faced declining demand for the type of products manufactured at one particular plant. Therefore, it adopted a policy of making no major investment in fixed assets for this plant.

In analyzing the demands for capital from the company's various functions, management may find that current assets, especially inventories and accounts receivable, are absorbing a large proportion of the firm's available capital. It also needs to consider earnings distribution, and, in particular, determine the balance between stockholder dividends and the amount reinvested in the firm.

Capital budgeting is a method of determining which competing demands for capital to endorse and which to reject. Its key components are (1) describing all proposals in detail (including dollar amounts of investment and returns expected), (2) screening out all proposals that are inconsistent with corporate or functional objectives and strategy; (3) analyzing incremental costs and incremental revenues (or reduced costs); (4) ranking each proposal, perhaps through the net present value (NPV) or internal rate of return (IRR) approaches (note that the payback method is still often used); and (5) choosing alternatives, beginning with proposals with the highest rates of return. This last step will continue until the capital available is exhausted or until the next project's rate of return is below acceptable standards. The efficiency of the capital budgeting process can be enhanced by requiring additional analyses when appropriate—as in the case of lease versus purchase decisions.

Once it has decided among the competing demands for capital, management must analyze the firm's financial structure. A firm's financial structure consists of the various types and amounts of capital (all debt and equity) that the company uses. Analyzing it is important because the existing financial structure affects the attractiveness (either positively or negatively) of specific sources of capital. The cost of the firm's various capital sources, in turn, determines the firm's cost of capital, which influences the firm's profit. The financial structure can also be used to alter the firm's financial leverage, which affects the level and timing of cash needs and the firm's profit picture by influencing the break-even point.[8]

A company's overall objectives and strategy also have a bearing on its financial structure. Indeed, objectives and strategy should dictate the allocation of capital.

The financial structure must be compatible with the nature of the capital needs. For example, capital needed to finance a temporary expansion of inventory or accounts receivable would not normally be obtained from issuing new common stock. Furthermore, firms needing large amounts of capital for long periods of time (such as utilities) normally do not seek this capital from their local bank.

Analyzing the financial structure has two specific purposes. First, management needs to examine the desirability of the present structure periodically, especially when the relative attractiveness of any source of capital changes (whether or not currently used by the firm). Second, it must ascertain that the company has the desired financial structure when new capital is needed.

The next step is analyzing the various sources of capital. A variety of factors influence the sources of capital chosen by a firm: the size of the company, the existing financial structure, the nature of its assets, the amount and stability of earnings, and the conditions existing in the financial markets at the time when the capital is raised. Maintaining the firm's attractiveness to the various financial markets is important, for if the firm cannot obtain sufficient capital, it may not be able to execute its preferred strategy. Capital can be obtained from owners or stockholders, long-term and short-term creditors, and internal sources.

Finally, management needs to select one or more of these sources of capital. In making this decision, it should weigh three key factors: (1) the specific use for the capital, (2) the cost of capital, and (3) the rights and restrictions granted with new securities.

Budgets   Budgets are important tools for implementation and managerial control. In a sense, budgets are the firm's projected operating plans. Unlike financial statements, which deal with historical data, budgets are concerned with the future. The basic types of budgets include the cash budget, capital budget, sales budget, merchandise or inventory budget, and various expense budgets.

DEVELOPING ORGANIZATIONAL STRUCTURE

For a new business, one of the most important considerations in implementing a strategy is developing an **organizational structure.** For an ongoing business, the structure used in the past should be analyzed to ensure that it remains appropriate for executing the strategies. This section discusses types of structures, the key factors that can influence organizational structure, and the key steps in selecting a structure.

Types of Organizational Structures

Management must select a relevant basis for organizing the firm. A wide variety of organizational types are available, and we examine several major ones next.

EXHIBIT 13.1 · Functional Organization

Functional Organization   Firms with **functional structures** are divided into units or departments devoted to the various functional areas, such as marketing, production, and finance (see Exhibit 13.1). A functional structure is fairly easy to understand and is used by most firms at some point in their development. Its specific advantages can include (1) enhanced operating efficiency if tasks are routine and repetitive, (2) fuller exploitation of benefits of specialization, (3) simplified training of management specialists, and (4) heavy emphasis on professional standards and affiliation.

The major problem with the functional structure is that very frequently it leads to conflict among the separate functional units about the goals and strategies that should be established. Too often functional specialists attach more importance to their functional area than to the whole firm. Other potential problems include (1) a lack of coordination between functions, (2) overspecialization and narrow managerial perspectives, (3) limited development of general managers, and (4) forcing of profit responsibility to the top.

Product Organization   As Exhibit 13.2 shows, personnel and activities can be separated according to products or product categories. The resulting **product structure** is relatively easy to understand and is used by many firms. Procter & Gamble, for example, has used this form effectively for many years. Key advan-

EXHIBIT 13.2 · Product Organization

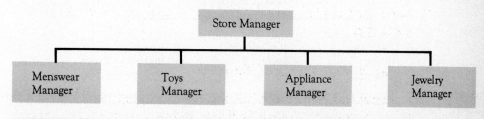

tages of the product structure include (1) relatively easy assignment of profit responsibility, (2) more effective coordination of efforts between the functional areas, (3) better development of general managers, (4) better understanding of the offerings of a business, and (5) greater likelihood that the consumer will be considered in decisions.

As for possible disadvantages, (1) battles between the product managers for resources may become highly political and counterproductive, (2) few specialized managers are developed, and (3) certain corporate-level strategies or tasks may be slighted, depending on the product manager's expertise or interests (for example, a product manager whose background is in production might slight marketing issues, and vice versa).

Geographical Organization   Firms with **geographical organizational structures** are organized on the basis of geographical divisions (see Exhibit 13.3). This structure seems to work very well in organizations with extensive distribution systems. It has these specific advantages: (1) strategies and programs can be tailored to needs of specific markets, (2) functional activities can be coordinated and focused on specific markets, (3) development of general managers is fostered, and (4) economies of local operations can be exploited.

Some of the potential disadvantages are that (1) consistent firmwide practices are difficult to maintain, (2) more managers are required, (3) duplication of staff services is likely, and (4) centralized decision making and control are difficult to maintain.

Customer Organization   A business can be organized around customers or customer types (see Exhibit 13.4). For example, a firm might have an industrial division and a consumer sales division while another firm might have a domestic sales division and an international sales division. Although the **customer organizational structure** is seldom used as the only, or even the primary, organizational type, it is often used at some level in the overall structure—for instance, to

---

EXHIBIT 13.3 · Geographical Organization

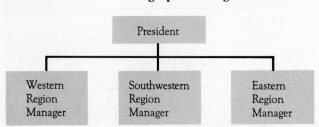

EXHIBIT 13.4 · Customer Organization

divide marketing personnel and activities. The major potential advantages of this form include (1) greater understanding of customers, (2) greater likelihood that the customers will be prominently considered in all decisions, and (3) greater efficiency in directing sales efforts.

Key drawbacks might include (1) counterproductive battles for resources, (2) lack of specialization, and (3) occasional inappropriateness for activities other than marketing and sales. These disadvantages often diminish significantly when the customer structure is used to augment other organizational types (for example, the functional type) rather than as the primary structure.

SBU Organization   The **strategic business unit (SBU) structure** is a relatively new organizational type, dividing the firm according to product/market segments (see Exhibit 13.5). This form is essentially a variation of the product structure or the customer structure. The SBU structure is generally needed only by large firms with somewhat diverse activities. Its advantages closely resemble those of the product organizational structures. The greatest disadvantages are its complexity and potential duplication of effort.

The SBU structure is being used by firms such as General Electric Co., General Foods Corporation, and Armco Inc. Some think this will be a primary

EXHIBIT 13.5 · SBU Organization

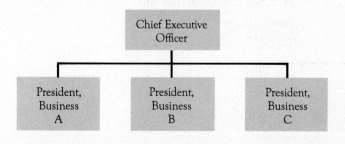

structural type for the future.[9] As more firms (including smaller firms) diversify, the use of this form will become more important.

Hybrid Organization   Most businesses need a structure that combines two or more of the "pure" forms just discussed. A firm will often use one type as its main structure and then incorporate other structures as needed (see Exhibit 13.6). The major potential advantage of the **hybrid structure** is that the combinations may allow the firm to gain the advantages offered by the primary structure while at least diminishing the impact of the disadvantages. Its other advantages are that (1) it can handle very complex situations, (2) it can be effective for very large firms, and (3) it allows for specialization of organizational types (for example, marketing-oriented structure can be used for marketing while another type can be devised for other activities).

In one sense, the disadvantages of the hybrid structure mirror the advantages. The structure may (1) be a complex structure, (2) result in overorganizing a smaller business, and (3) emphasize the weaknesses of each type rather than the advantages. Correct usage, however, should minimize these drawbacks.

EXHIBIT 13.6 · Hybrid Organization

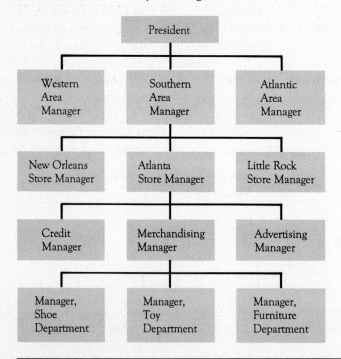

Matrix Organization Like a hybrid organization, a **matrix organization** also combines two or more other structural types.[10] The functional form, for example, is often combined with one of the other pure types of structures (see Exhibit 13.7). The managers of each pure type (functional and product in Exhibit 13.7) are on the same level within the firm in that they report to the same authority level and each has the same general degree of authority. Each manager has the authority to make decisions relating to his or her area of responsibility. Each functional manager listed in Exhibit 13.7 has authority over his or her function and each product (or project) manager has authority over a product (or project).

As Exhibit 13.7 illustrates, there is a significant problem with the matrix structure: each subordinate has two superiors. This arrangement violates one of the principles of management—the unity of command principle. Despite this problem, however, the matrix structure can work quite well if management and employees are committed to the organization's objectives.

The key to making the matrix structure work is that everyone completely understands the specific authority of each manager. Top management must foster this understanding and also ensure that neither of the bosses tries to usurp the authority of the other. If this understanding develops and the managers react

EXHIBIT 13.7 · Matrix Organization

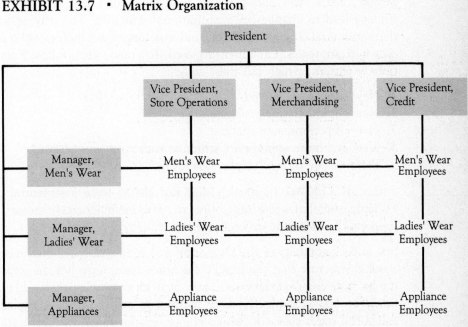

appropriately, the matrix structure could offer great promise for many businesses. Its principal benefit stems from combining the expertise of multiple managers.

Factors That Influence Organizational Structure

No single factor determines an organization's structure. Rather, structure is influenced by multiple factors, and these factors vary from situation to situation. There are seven key factors:

1. Strategy
2. Size and complexity of organization
3. Technology
4. Environmental turbulence
5. Top management's attitudes
6. Attitudes of personnel
7. Geographic considerations

Let us look at each of them more closely.

Strategy   It is now generally accepted that strategy and structure are inseparable in the management of modern organizations.[11] Nearly thirty years ago, A. D. Chandler studied a variety of large U.S. corporations, such as DuPont, General Motors, Sears, and Standard Oil, and concluded that changes in corporate strategy lead to changes in organizational structure. The driving force behind these structural changes is that the old structure causes inefficiencies in achieving corporate strategies. Chandler proposed that many firms follow a similar evolutionary pattern, which has these stages:[12]

1. New strategy is created.
2. New administrative problems arise.
3. Overall performance declines.
4. New and more appropriate structure is devised and adopted.
5. Performance returns to previous levels.

Although a change in strategy may not always force a structural change (for example, some firms may raise prices to cover inefficiencies),[13] research generally supports the idea that structure follows strategy.[14]

Size and Complexity of the Organization   Management should seek an organizational structure that can handle the firm's operations, but the structure should not be more complex than necessary. Structural complexity should match operations (or task) complexity. One method of analyzing the complexity issue is called the *stages approach*, which comprises four stages of organization (see Exhibit 13.8).[15]

EXHIBIT 13.8 · **Organization Stages**

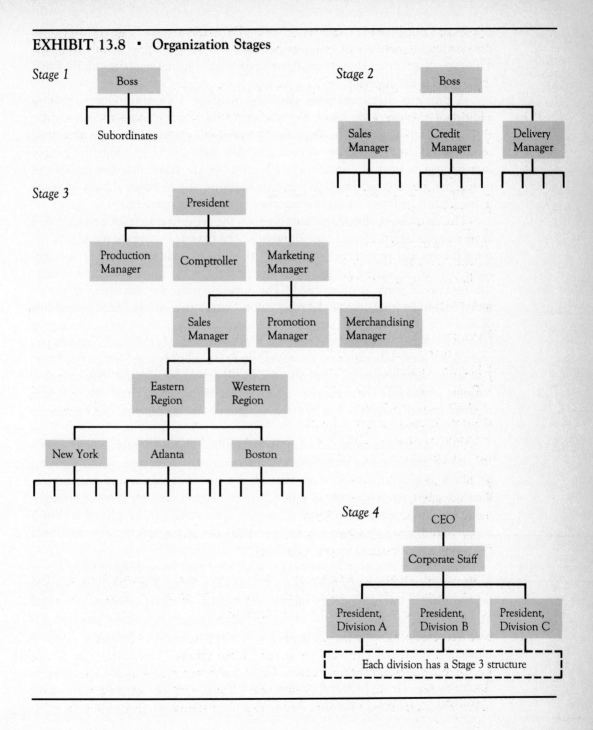

Stage 1 organizations represent the simplest organizations. The typical managerial structure consists of one superior and a limited number of subordinates. This type of structure is most appropriate for small businesses, particularly when the owner is the superior.

A problem that sometimes develops in Stage 1 organizations is that as additional employees are hired, the manager/owner finds it more and more difficult to adequately handle the business. In management terms, the span of control becomes too large for the owner/manager. Although the ideal number of people in a manager's span of control is not known, we do know that the number of people can become too large. When this happens, the manager should be ready to adjust the structure by adding another layer of management.

This extra layer of management changes the organization from a Stage 1 to a *Stage 2* organization. Thus Stage 2 organizations have two layers of management, the top layer and an intervening layer. Although the additional layer of management may be organized according to any of the specific forms discussed earlier, the functional form is often used. The superior may, for example, name an individual to be in charge of the production, marketing, or the credit operations of the firm. The Stage 2 structure, although not very complex, can handle relatively large businesses by simply expanding the number of middle managers and adding more subordinates. However, there is a point beyond which the Stage 2 structure simply does not provide the flexibility to handle the very complex business situations. For example, when a firm becomes so large that it needs regional sales managers or has multiple production facilities, it should consider a Stage 3 structure.

Organizations at *Stage 3* tend to be centralized and have relatively complex structures, with three or more layers of management. The Stage 3 structure can be much broader in scope than that of the first two stages and can handle virtually any type of business. If a firm becomes larger, another layer of management can be added or additional managerial personnel can be placed within a layer. The Stage 3 structure can be used with any of the specific organizational types discussed above.

The *Stage 4* structure is needed by large firms that have designated SBUs or divisions complex enough themselves to warrant a Stage 3 structure. A Stage 4 organization is therefore decentralized and consists of a combination of several Stage 3 organizations. Stage 4 structures often require corporate headquarters and have large managerial staffs at the various divisions or strategic business units.

Technology The nature and complexity of a firm's technology can affect organizational structure. Firms that focus on high technology, for example, often have narrow spans of control. The structure must be arranged to enhance the firm's ability to incorporate or otherwise react to rapid technological change. Unfortunately, structure often lags behind the needs of technology, which generally creates a time lag before technology can be fully exploited.[16] Firms that exploit technology tend to have (1) top managers who have a technical education and technical experience, (2) managers who allocate capital to projects oriented toward supporting and maintaining the firm's technological leadership, and (3) organizational systems and structure congruent with the technological system and ensuring close coordination between business and technological decision making.[17]

Environmental Turbulence   The level of environmental turbulence appears to influence structure. Stable environments can be handled well by firms with mechanistic structures that emphasize centralization of decision making along with fairly rigid directives, rules, and procedures. Conversely, firms that have experienced success in turbulent environments tend to have organic structures with decentralized decision making, flexible procedures, integrative departments, and cross-functional teams.[18]

Top Management's Attitudes   The attitudes of top management may also affect the structure of an organization. Traditional managers are likely to prefer traditional structures, such as the functional type, and are much less likely to embrace structures such as the matrix form. Generally, traditional managers prefer centralized control; they are not likely to favor decentralized structures with a great deal of employee input.

Attitudes of Personnel   The personnel should also be considered in selecting organizational structures. Highly educated and/or trained employees are likely to prefer more open management structures. Highly regimented structures, such as the functional, are often preferred by lower-level and highly technical personnel, probably because these structures are less ambiguous. Besides, in a functional structure, there may be more opportunity for affiliation with similar technical workers.

Geographic Considerations   Geographic expansion or decentralization forces new divisions of labor, which in turn create a new organizational structure. Note that firms that have geographic decentralization may attempt to retain centralized decision making. Over time, however, decentralized decision making tends to become more and more important as a firm increases in size.

Future Organization Trends   Changing environmental conditions will probably force corresponding changes in organizational structures. Such structural changes could be brought about, for example, by changes in the role of government, new technology, international competition, and alterations in the attitudes of employees and managers. Some analysts feel that new structures must be developed, giving lower-level employees and managers a much larger voice in the organization and reducing the number of middle-level managers. This change would involve much more delegation of authority to lower-level managers and employees than is done at present.[19]

One writer feels that organizations of the future will have flatter structures, more employee networking to get the job done, and be more oriented toward people.[20] One publication described four philosophies that may be increasingly important in the future and suggested how each might affect the structure of companies.[21]

1. *Meritocracy:* Large companies structured like small, entrepreneurial companies that maximize profits and reward those employees who work hardest
2. *Egalitarianism:* Companies characterized by bureaucracy, increased regulation, and powerful unions
3. *Corporatism:* Large companies that place a high value on efficiency, which requires close cooperation between labor, management, and business
4. *Humanism:* Small, decentralized, worker-owned, worker-managed corporations that focus on improving the quality of life

In practice, of course, a corporation would be more likely to adopt elements of several of these philosophies rather any one of them entirely.

Perhaps the *dynamic network* organizational form will also become popular. This structure is a broad, loose network on independent organizations that work together to accomplish tasks currently accomplished by a single organization. This loose structure has four characteristics:[22]

1. *Vertical disaggregation.* Business functions now generally performed within a single organization are performed by independent organizations within the network.
2. *Brokers.* As a result of vertical disaggregation, there will be a need for middlemen or brokers to negotiate between each organization and the other independent organizations needed for proper functioning of the network.
3. *Market mechanisms.* Market mechanisms such as contracts and payment are used to hold together major functions. They replace traditional control devices such as progress reports and personal supervision.
4. *Full-disclosure information systems.* Computerized information systems are used as substitutes for lengthy, trust-building processes based on experience.

Organizing for Performance

The purpose of analyzing the organizational types and factors that influence structure is to arrive at a structure that enhances the firm's performance. The structure should be efficient and effective in achieving the firm's objectives. The most advanced structure, which utilizes the latest in organizational theory, is absolutely useless unless it is can achieve the firm's objectives. Because of certain prejudices and biases, such as the desire for more power, management sometimes installs structures that are not focused on implementing the firm's strategies. For instance, it is very easy for top management to adopt the matrix organizational structure without defining the authority of the people involved. When this occurs, the higher-level managers become more powerful.

The following five steps are useful for designing an organization's structure:[23]

1. Identify strategy-related critical tasks and key functions. Although much of a firm's total work effort can be routine (for example, payroll systems) and not likely to change along with strategy changes, certain crucial tasks and functions often have to be done exceedingly well for a strategy to succeed. These crucial tasks and functions vary for each firm. For example, firms seeking cost leadership in a price-sensitive industry must concentrate on tight cost controls. Conversely, firms focusing on high-quality luxury items generally must focus on distinctive styling, manufacturing craftsmanship, and sophisticated promotional appeals. Generally, management must identify those activities that need to be done exceptionally well.

2. Study the relationships among routine activities and those that are strategically significant. These relationships are important because they usually form the basis for grouping into organizational units. Gaining proper understanding involves pinpointing how activities are linked: by type of customer served, distribution channels used, technical skills used, production processes, flow of material, geographic territories, and so forth. The key is to find those relationships that connect one part of the strategy to another. Note that diversified firms with unrelated businesses may need to create separate and independent structures for each.

3. Group activities into organizational units. Management should use the critical tasks and key functions as the primary building blocks of the organization's structure. Thus activities crucial to strategic success occupy a central position in the structure and get the visibility and attention they deserve.

4. Determine the degree of authority and independence for each organizational unit. The key issues here are to decide at what level major decisions should be made relative to business units and what is the most workable means of aligning the overall corporate strategy and individual business strategies. Although there are no specific, universal rules for choosing between centralization

decentralization, a general guideline is that a unit's role in contributing to strategic success should determine its rank and placement in the hierarchy of authority.

5. Provide for coordination among the units. Coordination among structural units can involve a variety of activities. Positioning units in the authority hierarchy is a primary method of coordination. Coordination can also be enhanced through information meetings, project teams, special task forces, and standing committees. Furthermore, the strategic management process can foster coordination through formal strategy reviews and the overall interaction and negotiation necessary during annual strategic planning and budgeting.

Management should refrain from changing the organizational structure drastically unless it is absolutely essential. When that necessity does arise, changes in the structure should be made as quickly and as efficiently as possible. The problems associated with this and other changes and the ways to overcome some of them are discussed next.

INTRODUCING CHANGES

Strategies, especially new ones, often require various changes for or during the implementation phase. Top management must plan and introduce such changes carefully; the goal should be managed change. All too often firms spend much time, effort, and many resources selecting strategies and then doom the strategies to failure by not properly introducing them. For instance, after spending many hours with relatively high-priced consultants, management may decide that it needs a new organizational structure. Then it introduces the new structure without much thought to potential resistance from employees who must operate within the structure. The manner of introducing the change can sometimes be more important than the absolute quality of the change. Xerox Corp. spent two years developing a plan for changing its technology-oriented style.[24] The plan involved "unfreezing" the old style, introducing the change (new management techniques), and "refreezing" the new style with appropriate rewards and sanctions. Proper introduction of a change generally involves four steps:[25]

1. Forecast potential resistance.
2. Reduce potential resistance.
3. Reduce actual resistance.
4. Refreeze the status quo.

Each of these steps is discussed below.

J. P. Morgan & Co.: Take Caution or Take Risk?

J. P. Morgan & Co. is one of the best-known banking institutions in the world. Historically, it has been a well-run but somewhat conservative bank: an image persists of white-gloved treatment of blue-blooded clients. There is no doubt that Morgan has done well in banking: Morgan Guaranty Trust, its main banking unit, is the only bank in the country with a AAA bond rating.

In the early 1980s, Morgan decided to get into investment banking. One reason was that commercial lending had begun to erode throughout the industry, so the bank had to look elsewhere for revenue sources. And investment banking offers great potential for profit.

However, the world of money is fluid: just as J. P. Morgan was warming up to the idea of investment banking, the mergers and acquisitions market, to give just one example, was cooling down. Suddenly there was less business to go around. After having made a profit of $1 billion in 1988, Morgan posted a loss of $1.3 billion in 1989. Much of the loss can be explained by the reserves Morgan set aside to take care of loans made to Third World countries.

Many analysts believe that Morgan's relative lack of success in the investment banking business is the result of its conservatism, which leads to success in banking but not necessarily in investment banking. But this is not to say that Morgan has been less than inventive in its new line of work. It was in the forefront in petitioning the Federal Reserve Bank of New York to permit it to underwrite corporate stocks. It helped create ADRs, the American depository receipts that make it easier for Americans to invest in foreign companies. And it was one of the first banks to introduce techniques allowing corporations increased flexibility in repricing dividends of variable-term preferred stocks.

Could, would, and should J. P. Morgan become less cautious and more of a risk taker? On the one hand, conservative investment banking might be the key to success in the conservative 1990s (particularly given some of the problems at other investment banking houses). On the other hand, the bank might have to approach its new venture with more flexibility if it is to reap the profits needed to justify its multimillion-dollar outlay. There are in fact some signs that things are already changing: for example, in the summer of 1989 Morgan offered to underwrite a large issue of junk bonds in a takeover attempt.

References: John Meehan and Richard A. Melcher, "It's a Jungle Out There for J. P. Morgan," *Business Week,* January 29, 1990, pp. 84–85; Rosalyn Retkwa, "Auction or Sabres? Hybrid Issues Offer Maximum Flexibility," *Corporate Cashflow Magazine,* February 1990, p. 20; Robert M. Garsson, "Underwriting Ruling Shifts to Final Step," *American Banker,* February 16, 1990, p. 2; Michael Weinstein, "J. P. Morgan's Preston: Getting Ready to Pass the Puck," *American Banker,* October 5, 1989, p. 21.

Forecasting Potential Resistance to Change

It is vital for management to gain an understanding of the potential resistance to a proposed change before the change is introduced. Resistance to change stems from self-interest (threat to job, status, or power), disagreement with the assessment that change is needed, anticipated unpleasant consequences, or simple unwillingness to upset the status quo.

Three distinct reactions to change are possible: *acceptance* and two forms of rejection. One form is *active rejection* by employees; they dislike the change and openly fight it. The more difficult rejection for management to detect and cope with is *passive rejection:* employees behave as though they are accepting change but take various subtle actions to try to prevent or sabotage it.

Although the exact reaction to a change is hard to predict, management should try to get a sense of what to expect. Since large changes normally involve a major shift from the status quo, they commonly incur more resistance. Furthermore, the longer a firm has been doing something in a certain way, the greater is the likelihood of resistance. A variety of data-gathering and diagnostic techniques—such as questionnaires, interviews, and observation—can help management estimate the degree of resistance to change.[26] A good feel for the amount of resistance that will occur can often be obtained by simply talking and, especially, listening to employees. To forestall or lessen this resistance, management can take several actions.

Reducing Potential Resistance to Change

Perhaps the best way to reduce resistance to change is for management to demonstrate (before the change is made) both the necessity of change and its benefits. Lewin's **force field theory** is a good starting point for understanding resistance reduction.[27] Kurt Lewin contends that the status quo is maintained by forces that operate around the current situation. Some of these forces push toward change while others act to restrain change, which creates a state of equilibrium, or status quo. Movement toward change is possible only if one of the forces is adjusted. If management can reduce the forces restraining change, the probability of acceptance will rise.

Management can also decrease potential resistance to change by soliciting more input from employees regarding the specific change.[28] This is often called *shared power or shared change.* Conversely, *unilateral change* decisions generally encounter the greatest resistance. Other, more specific, techniques for reducing potential resistance to change include team building, intergroup meetings, and quality circles.[29] Most of these techniques are geared to convincing workers that change is needed and allowing them to share in the introduction so that resistance is minimized.

Reducing Actual Resistance

If management has properly identified the level, nature, and sources of potential resistance and has done everything possible to reduce it, the introduction of change can be relatively painless. Nevertheless, some resistance is likely to remain, and management must be able to handle it to ensure eventual acceptance of the change.

A major step forward in managing change is a realization by management that resistance is natural and generally unavoidable. One way of managing this resistance is simply to allow it to run its course; it may disappear after a short period of time. If the resistance is minor and expected to be temporary, it would be a serious mistake for management to adjust the change simply because some people were initially opposed to it.

Introducing the change with great confidence helps prevent resistance from overpowering it. Management should present the change as the sole—and highly effective—answer to a problem situation. Such confidence on the part of management may spread to the employees as well.

Once the change is in place, management may lessen any residual resistance by sharing or entering into a type of problem-solving situation with employees. The purpose is to ask for the employees' assistance and thus make them feel that they are helping to implement the change.[30]

Leadership Styles[31]   Management's leadership style in introducing a change can have a strong impact on the level of actual resistance. Leadership styles can range from very active to very passive. Active resistance reduction makes use of management's power—for example, management forcefully tells employees to accept the change (an autocratic style). Although this is generally the least preferred style, it can be appropriate when the change is large and significant. Consider, for example, a turnaround strategy (discussed in Chapter 11) that calls for significant changes, such as changes in the organizational structure, top management, and general personnel areas. Turnaround strategies often provoke heavy resistance and need the guiding hand of managers who specialize in turnarounds. These managers tend to be extremely autocratic and capable of using the necessary power.

Normally, however, a more participative style of leadership is recommended for introducing change. By and large, securing the employees' voluntary cooperation is more fruitful than obtaining their unwilling obedience.

Conflict Management   Actual resistance to change can erupt into outright conflicts. Conflict refers to the deliberate, overt behavior of active resistance. It arises because of perceived incompatibility between an individual's goals and those of the organization or another individual.[32]

Allaying these conflicts requires the use of an appropriate conflict management style. Five such styles can be identified by combining a manager's degree of cooperativeness and degree of assertiveness: competitor, avoider, accommodator, compromiser, and collaborator.[33]

Competitors are high on assertiveness and low on cooperativeness. Power oriented, they approach conflict with a win/lose attitude and strive to eliminate it through suppression, intimidation, and coercion. However, such efforts tend to aggravate the struggle without uncovering constructive acceptable solutions.

Low on both assertiveness and cooperativeness, *avoiders* may conform out of indifference or refuse to take a position of any kind. This style is most appropriate when the conflict situation has relatively minor implications or when there is a need to reduce tension, regain perspective, or obtain additional information.

Competitors' opposites, *accommodators* are low in assertiveness and high on cooperativeness. They take a smoothing approach, which sometimes shows too little concern for personal goals. Accommodating, however, can fit various situations, for example, when maintaining harmony is important.

Compromisers are moderate on both assertiveness and cooperativeness and allow each participant to share in some degree of winning and losing. Although this style can lead to less than ideal solutions, it can also be the only practical approach capable of yielding results in the time allotted.

High in both assertiveness and cooperativeness, *collaborators* take a problem-solving approach and view conflict as an opportunity for constructive contribution. As they strive to depersonalize the conflict, they also make an effort to legitimize the goals, opinions, attitudes, and feelings of others.

Any of these styles can be appropriate for managing conflict. Management must try to match the right style with the specific situation.

Intraorganizational conflict may be destructive, constructive, or both. If not handled properly, it may have noxious consequences, such as inefficient operations and employee turnover. The positive effects of conflict can be summarized as follows:[34]

1. Conflict energizes people. Even if not all of the resulting activity is constructive, at least it wakes up people and gets them moving.
2. Conflict usually involves a search for a resolution. This search may lead to the discovery and implementation of needed organizational changes.
3. Since conflict is a form of communication, the resolution of conflict may open up new and lasting communication channels.
4. Conflict often provides an outlet for pent-up tensions and allows individuals to concentrate on the primary responsibilities.
5. Conflict may prove to be an educational experience, for the participants may become more aware and more understanding of their opponents' functions and problems.

Refreezing the Status Quo

Regardless of the specific techniques used to manage resistance, management must eventually create a harmonious situation—in other words, refreeze the status quo.[35] The old status quo is altered by the change, and management has to establish the new situation as an acceptable status quo. If management has had to coerce workers to accept the change, some fence mending will likely be needed. For example, managers hired to implement turnaround strategies often move on to other organizations (at their own or the firm's discretion) after the changes have been made. New managers then have a better opportunity to create a harmonious status quo. Even when changes encounter little resistance, management still needs to restate and re-establish an acceptable status quo.

The following tips can prove helpful in changing an organization's culture:[36]

- Understand your old culture first—you must know where you are before you can chart a new course.
- Encourage those employees who are bucking the old culture to offer their ideas for a better one.
- Find the best subculture in the organization and make sure it is highly visible to others.
- Do not attack the culture head-on; rather, help employees find their own new ways to accomplish their tasks, and a better culture will follow.
- Do not count on a vision to work miracles—it can act only as a guiding principle for change.
- Figure on five to ten years for significant organizationwide improvement.
- Live the culture you want—actions are more powerful than words.

Effective conflict management can facilitate the introduction and implementation of future changes. However, management will not always succeed in introducing change and managing conflicts. If the upheaval and resistance is severe enough to compromise the firm's ability to thrive, management may have to consider changing the strategy.

RE-EVALUATING THE STRATEGIC PLAN

Strategic planning is a dynamic process that should foster the evolution of effective strategies. Even after the strategic plan is developed, management must recognize that the plan may require periodic adjustments. Although massive adjustments should occur infrequently, they should be considered if the situation warrants. The implementation phase provides an excellent opportunity to thoroughly re-evaluate the strategic plan. Strategic plans sometimes appear quite logical and appropriate, yet cannot be implemented effectively for any of several reasons, such as inadequate or unsuitable resources, inadequate decoupling from previous plans and commitments,[37] employee resistance, or poor communication systems. When the time, effort, and cost of implementing begin to approach the expected return, management should carefully reassess the strategic plans. Specific issues to examine include the continued relevance of the stated objectives, changes in the environmental situation, and the strategies themselves.

However, strategies should not be adjusted every time some minor problem arises. Adjustments should be made only after careful evaluation and only if the new strategy can generate more benefits than can be gained from implementing the original strategy.

GLOBAL DIMENSIONS OF IMPLEMENTATION

Although the basics of implementation for multinational firms are the same as for other firms, specific issues and their resolutions are often different because of a different set of influencing environmental factors. In the rest of the chapter, we first review some of the key conflicts and problem areas and then address the evolution of multinational firms.[38]

Problem Areas of International Implementation

Many of the issues presented here are more aptly described as areas of conflict that lead to implementation problems. The cause of most problems encountered by international managers can often be traced to a conflict between the basic values held by two or more groups of people. Some issues relate to cultural conflicts, others are more individual in nature, and still others pertain to structural problems.

Individualism   A society's attitudes toward individualism or independence can affect the implementation of certain strategies. Whereas personal accomplishment and self-expression are considered virtues in American culture, similar individualism is not deemed particularly important in other cultures. In the Chinese culture, for example, conformity and cooperation have a much higher value.

Informality   In many cultures, Americans are viewed as too informal and casual. Latin Americans, for example, tend to prefer formal public receptions and processions and expect outsiders to carefully observe all amenities of personal etiquette and hospitality. In a related matter, the American tendency to get straight to the issue rather than participate in informal small talk makes people from many countries, such as Saudi Arabians and Latin Americans, uncomfortable.

Materialism   The tendency in Western culture to attach status to certain physical objects is not shared by all cultures. Many other cultures place more emphasis on finding and enjoying aesthetic and spiritual values.

Time Orientation   Americans tend to view time as a scarce resource and, therefore, emphasize efficient use of time. Other cultures view time as an unlimited and unending resource.

Authority   Many cultures view managerial authority and the concept of employee participation in management quite differently from Americans. Managers in some cultures, including those of much of Russia, South America, and the Middle East, have virtual absolute authority. Conversely, participative management is practiced in some countries, such as Japan, more than in the United States.

Other differential cultural issues can also influence a multinational firm's ability to implement strategy successfully. Examples include rank and social status, the impact of social institutions, the role of women, language, and nonverbal communication. Other environmental issues include political instability, currency instability, competition from state-owned enterprises, pressures from national governments, nationalism, and patent and trademark protection.

To help alleviate these problems, an international expert or, even better, a specialist on a specific country is often needed. The same types of country- or region-specific experts that have been discussed in previous chapters can and usually are used. They can often pinpoint likely implementation problems and advise on how to reduce these problems. The international specialists can also help U.S. executives gain a better understanding of foreign cultures and how to treat members of a particular culture.

A special problem with implementation is the level of international engagement. Typically, a firm evolves into multinational statures. This process may require many structural changes over time.

The Evolution of a Multinational Firm

As firms evolve into multinational enterprises, they often go through several distinct, but overlapping, stages. Note that same firms may skip certain stages and that the rate of evolution can vary substantially.[39]

Stage 1 begins with the firm receiving an inquiry about one of its products from a potential distributor, such as a foreign businessperson or independent importer/exporter. If profitable sales result, other foreign channels may be sought, such as an export merchant, an export commission house, resident buyer, broker, or international manufacturers' agents.

Stage 2 features an export manager. The initial reactive posture changes into a proactive posture as management decides to take more direct control of exports. An export manager (with a small staff) is appointed to actively seek foreign markets.

Stage 3 features an export department and direct sales. Eventually, the company may need to establish a full-fledged export department or division on the same level as the domestic sales department. As the firm increases sales made directly to importers located in foreign countries, it drops the domestic export middlemen.

Stage 4 involves sales branches and subsidiaries. Additional growth of international sales can force the establishment of foreign sales branch offices to handle sales and promotion work. These sales branches can evolve into more autonomous subsidiaries, which are incorporated and domiciled in foreign countries.

Stage 5 begins when the firm initiates assembly operations in one or more foreign countries. For a variety of reasons, including lower tariffs on unassembled goods, export of unassembled goods to be assembled in a foreign country can sometimes prove more profitable.

Stage 6 involves production abroad. Because of high tariffs, quotas, or absolute bans on certain products, a firm sometimes finds it impossible to expand into other foreign markets without local production facilities. Three common production alternatives are contract manufacturing, licensing, and direct investment in manufacturing facilities.

Stage 7 entails integration of foreign affiliates. At some point, management may decide to integrate all foreign sales and production affiliates into one multinational enterprise. The direction of this new enterprise takes on a global perspective as strategic plans are more often made at the company headquarters.

The various stages may call for different organizational structures and may evolve quickly. Like any other changes, these structural changes may be resisted, making implementation more difficult. Again, an international specialist may be able to help reduce or control the resistance to change as the organization evolves.

Notes

1. Larry D. Alexander, "Successfully Implementing Strategic Decisions," *Long Range Planning*, 18, No. 3 (1985), 91–97.

2. Ibid.

3. J. M. Hobbs and D. F. Heany, "Coupling Strategy to Operating Plans," *Harvard*

Business Review (May-June 1977), 119–126.

4. Marc Gerstein and Heather Reisman, "Strategic Selection: Matching Executives to Business Conditions," *Sloan Management Review* (Winter 1983).

5. C. W. Hofer and M. J. Davoust, *Successful Strategic Management* (Chicago: Kearney, 1977), pp. 44–53.

6. See William Ouchi, *Theory Z* (Reading, Mass.: Addison-Wesley, 1981).

7. Gerry Johnson, Kevan Scholes, and Robert W. Sexty, *Exploring Strategic Management* (Scarborough, Ont.: Prentice-Hall Canada, 1989), p. 270.

8. See Anthony F. Herbst, *Capital Budgeting* (New York: Harper & Row, 1982), pp. 160–169.

9. William K. Hall, "SBU's: Hot New Topic in the Management of Diversification," *Business Horizons* (February 1978), 25.

10. See Jay R. Galbraith, "Matrix Organizational Designs," *Business Horizons* (February 1971), 29–40; and Stanley M. Davis and Paul R. Lawrence, "Problems of Matrix Organizations," *Harvard Business Review* (May-June 1978), 131–142.

11. R. E. Miles and C. C. Snow, *Organizational Strategy, Structure and Process* (New York: McGraw-Hill, 1977), p. 7.

12. A. D. Chandler, *Strategy and Structure* (Cambridge, Mass.: MIT Press, 1962), p. 14.

13. J. R. Galbraith and D. A. Nathanson, *Strategy Implementation: The Role of Structure and Process* (St. Paul, Minn.: West, 1978), p. 139.

14. Galbraith and Nathanson, p. 47; P. H. Grinyer and M. Yasai-Ardekani, "Strategy, Structure, Size, and Bureaucracy," *Academy of Management Journal* (September 1981), 471–486; and P. Lorange, *Implementation of Strategic Planning* (Englewood Cliffs, N.J.: Prentice-Hall, 1982), p. 109.

15. See Malcolm S. Salter, "Stages of Corporate Development," *Journal of Business Policy* (Spring 1970), 23–27; J. Thomas Cannon, *Business Strategy and Policy* (New York: Harcourt Brace Jovanovich, 1968), pp. 525–528; Donald H. Thain, "Stages of Corporate Development," *The Business Quarterly* (Winter 1969), 32–45; and Chandler, ch. 1.

16. P. G. W. Keen, "Communications in the 21st Century: Telecommunications and Business Policy," *Organizational Dynamics* (Autumn 1981), 54–67.

17. A. I. Frohman, "Technology as a Competitive Weapon," *Harvard Business Review* (January-February 1982), 97.

18. See P. R. Lawrence and J. W. Lorsch, *Organization and Environment* (Homewood, Ill.: Irwin, 1967), p. 138.

19. Robert H. Guest, "Management Imperatives for the Year 2000," *California Management Review* (Summer 1986), 62–69.

20. Burke Sashkin, "Organizational Development in the 1990's," *Journal of Management*, 13, No. 2 (1987), 393–413.

21. "Evolving Corporate Management," *The Futurist* (September-October 1986), 49.

22. Raymond E. Miles and Charles C. Snow, "Organizations: New Concepts for New Forms," *California Management Review* (Spring 1986), 62–73.

23. See Arthur A. Thompson, Jr., and A. J. Strickland III, *Strategy Formulation and Implementation*, rev. ed. (Plano, Tex.: Business Publications, 1983), p. 313; LaRue T. Hosmer, *Strategic Management: Text and Cases on Business Policy* (Englewood Cliffs, N.J.: Prentice-Hall, 1982), ch. 10; and Cannon, p. 316.

24. Norman Deets and Richard Morano, "Xerox's Strategy for Changing Management Styles," *Management Review* (March 1986), 31–35.

25. See Michael Beer, *Organization Change and Development* (Santa Monica, Calif.: Goodyear, 1980); and Edgar F. Huse, *Organization Development and Change* (St. Paul, Minn.: West, 1980).

26. Huse, p. 92–97.

27. Kurt Lewin, *Field Theory in Social Science* (New York: Harper & Row, 1951).

28. Lester Coch and John R. P. French, Jr., "Overcoming Resistance to Change," *Human Relations*, 1, No. 4 (1948), 512–532.

29. Edward E. Lawler III and Susan A. Mohrman, "Quality Circles After the Fad," *Harvard Business Review* (January-February 1985), 65–71.

30. R. T. Lentz and Marjorie A. Lyles, "Managing Human Problems in Strategic Planning Systems," *The Journal of Business Strategy* (Spring 1986), 57–64.

31. See Arthur G. Bedeian and William F. Glueck, *Management*, 3rd ed. (Chicago: The Dryden Press, 1983), pp. 494–517.

32. See, for example, Robert Albanese, *Managing: Toward Accountability for Performance* (Homewood, Ill.: Irwin, 1978), p. 424.

33. Based on Kenneth W. Thomas, "Conflict and Conflict Management," in *The Handbook of Industrial and Organizational Psychology*, ed. Marion D. Dunnette (Chicago: Rand McNally, 1976), p. 900.

34. Leslie W. Rue and Lloyd L. Byars, *Management* (Homewood, Ill.: Irwin, 1977), pp. 249–250.

35. Lewin.

36. Brian Dumaine, "Creating New Company Culture," *Fortune*, January 15, 1990, p. 128.

37. Hobbs and Heany, pp. 119–126.

38. This section draws heavily on Arvind Phatak, *International Dimensions of Management* (Boston: Kent, 1983).

39. Ibid.

CHAPTER 14

Evaluating and Controlling Performance

The last major step in the strategic management process is to evaluate and control the firm's performance. Management must ensure that the strategies are generating the performance necessary to achieve the stated objectives. Effective evaluation and control benefit the firm by helping to accomplish objectives, providing clear guidelines on expected performance from personnel, and directing energy through employee performance/reward expectations.[1]

Although the control phase is the "concluding" step of strategic management, it provides information that becomes part of the basis of strategic planning for the next planning period. Essentially, the output of control becomes input for subsequent internal situation analyses. A significant portion of the feedback to management derives from control procedures. Control, therefore, closes the loop of planning, as shown in Exhibit 14.1.

Exhibit 14.2 illustrates a control process, consisting of these six steps:

1. Determine what to control.
2. Set control standards.
3. Measure performance.
4. Compare performance with standards.
5. Determine the reason for deviations.
6. Take corrective action.

We discuss each of these steps and then, briefly, the controlling of the overall control system itself.

DETERMINING WHAT TO CONTROL

Before considering specific factors to control, management must understand that there are three primary types of control.[2] **Strategic control** focuses on evaluating strategy and is practiced both after the strategy is formulated and after it is implemented. **Management control** concentrates on the progress of major subsystems toward accomplishing strategic objectives. (For example, are quality control objectives being met?). **Operational control** applies to the performance of individuals and work groups. For example, are individual sales quotas being met? (Some authors group management control and operational control together and refer to them as tactical control.) Each of these types of control is not a separate and distinct entity and, in fact, may be indistinguishable from the others. Furthermore, similar measurement techniques, such as return on investment (ROI), may be used for each type of control. This chapter, therefore, explores the process of control and examines specific control factors.

Sometimes managers may find it quite difficult to determine what specific factors to monitor and control. Essentially, control procedures should be devel-

EXHIBIT 14.1 · Planning Loop

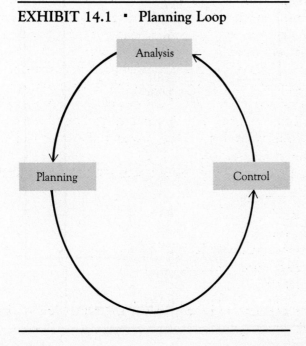

EXHIBIT 14.2 · Control Process

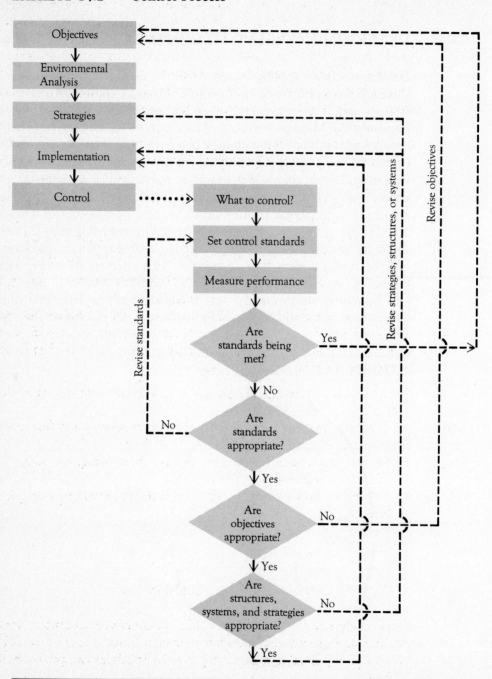

oped for any performance factor or result viewed as important. Performance factors can be grouped into two broad categories: people and things (such as money, materials, computers, supplies, information, and equipment).

Four aspects of the performance factors can be managed and controlled: quantity, quality, time, and cost. Controlling people, for instance, involves making an effort to regulate the quantity, quality, timing, and cost of their performance. Controlling equipment means regulating the quantity, quality, and costs of the output and attempting to efficiently use available equipment or machine time.[3]

Each aspect of control may need additional categorizing. When planning cost control, for example, a manager should consider four categories:[4]

1. *Productive costs:* contribute directly to the value of the product or service
2. *Support costs:* provide no direct value to the customer but are necessary to support production
3. *Policing costs:* incurred to prevent something from going wrong
4. *Waste costs:* for efforts that yield no productive, support, or policing benefits

Managers can broaden this approach to include the quantity, quality, and time for any activity in their area of responsibility.

Part of the decision regarding what to control involves the concept of **responsibility centers.** A responsibility center is a smaller, identifiable corporate unit that is accountable for certain aspects of the business. The basic types of responsibility centers include these four:[5]

1. *Revenue center:* exerts control over income (for example, the sales department)
2. *Cost center:* exerts control over different types of costs (for example, the production department or R&D)
3. *Profit center:* exerts control over profits (for example, a product division or subsidiary company)
4. *Investment center:* exerts control over return on capital (for example, a subsidiary company)

SETTING CONTROL STANDARDS

Once management has determined what performances to control, it should establish **control standards** for each performance factor. Effective control is impossible without standards. Conversely, concise standards can greatly facilitate the control process.

Conciseness of Standards

Standards must be concise. If specific goals have been formulated for a performance factor, setting the standards is relatively simple. For example, consider a sales goal of $1 million for the next year. This sales goal meets all the criteria for sound objectives (for example, measurability and specificity) discussed in Chapter 4. Such a sales goal dictates the standard: $1 million in sales for next year. Additional standards can be developed for various territories, salespeople, or months, much like the hierarchy of objectives was developed in Chapter 4. If specific goals have not been set, more specificity must be added at this point.

Surrogate Standards

Setting standards, however, is sometimes much more difficult because the objectives are ill defined or because surrogate standards are necessary. **Surrogate standards** are needed when performance cannot be measured directly. Standards for social responsiveness, for example, may have to be stated in terms of the number of dollars given to charity or the number of handicapped workers hired.

Surrogate standards may also be needed when performance is difficult or impossible to measure. Consider the issue of measuring the effectiveness of advertising performance. Good advertising should have a positive impact on sales volume, but what proportion of sales increases should be attributed to advertising? Other factors (such as price and competition) also affect sales. Surrogate standards—consumer attitudes, consumer intentions to purchase, and audience size or recall—can be helpful and more meaningful in this situation.

Tolerance Limits

Most standards should also include **tolerance limits.** Since actual performance seldom conforms perfectly to plans, deviations from plans should be expected as part of the normal state of affairs. Tolerance limits establish the boundaries within which these deviations can occur and still be considered in conformance with the original plan. As Exhibit 14.3 demonstrates, the boundaries are generally referred to as upper control limits and lower control limits. We discuss the actual use of tolerance limits later.

MEASURING PERFORMANCE

Obtaining appropriate and timely information is a crucial issue in **performance measurement.** This section presents several information guidelines, discusses a variety of measurement techniques, and describes selected performance measurement problems.

EXHIBIT 14.3 · Tolerance Limits

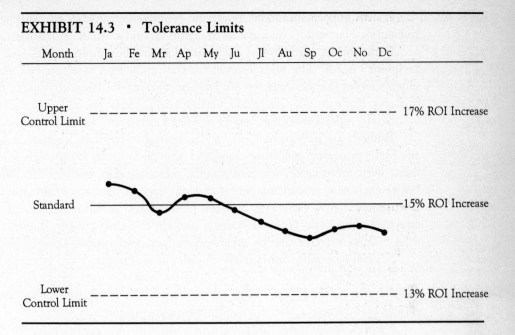

Information for Performance Measurement

Information useful for performance measurement can come from many sources. The management information system (MIS) discussed in Chapter 8 should deliver a wealth of such information. Although not always trustworthy, informal information, such as conversations with subordinates or feedback from customers, can also be useful. Management must specify what information is really needed to measure and evaluate performance. The following guidelines can be helpful.[6]

First, reporting systems should generate only enough information to provide a reliable picture of performance. Any additional information causes unnecessary costs and unnecessary management efforts to assimilate it.

Second, necessary information includes information on all strategically meaningful variables (for example, sales volume and unit costs) and on symptoms of potentially significant trends (for example, increasing absenteeism or employee turnover).

Third, reports should be structured to portray performance or symptoms in a way that can lead to action. Thus issues that call for immediate action should be highlighted. Issues that are merely "interesting" should be omitted or minimized so as not to obscure actionable information.

Fourth, reports should be timely and generated often enough to allow corrective action, but not so frequent as to create an undue drain on managerial time.

Fifth, the type and flow of information should be simple and tailored to each recipient's needs. The sales analysis for the production manager can usually be much simpler (for example, by products only) than the sales analysis for the sales manager (for example, by product, salesperson, territory, and customer type).

Sixth, reports should generally be aimed at flagging exceptions to standards.

Budgets are important tools for managerial control. In a sense, budgets are the firm's projected operating plans and serve as vehicles for providing management with information for performance measurement. Budgets are formulated before each new accounting period and can then be used to continually monitor performance. Any variations between planned and actual achievements can be analyzed. The basic types of budgets include the cash budget, capital budget, sales budget, merchandise or inventory budget, and various expense budgets.

Several general comments are in order at this point. First, efficient budgeting and control practices do not necessarily imply cost minimization. Effective control can entail either increased or decreased expenditure. The firm's goal should be optimum rather than minimum expenditure.

Second, budgets should provide for variability. Variability refers to the concept that many expenses are related to the level of activity or sales volume.

Third, budgets should permit flexibility. Flexibility refers to the concept of giving managerial discretion to override budgeted figures. Remember that amounts budgeted before a planning period were set with less information than a manager will have during the planning period. As conditions change, budgeted amounts may also have to change.

Fourth, a crucial part of budgetary control involves analyzing the variations between expected and actual performance, explaining why the variation occurred, and evaluating the desirability of the variation. An unexpected increase in utility rates is unavoidable; an increase in insurance expense may be desirable because of improved coverage. Variations are not necessarily mistakes.

Fifth, systematic budgeting and related cost control activities are extremely important, but management must guard against budgeting and cost control systems that are too expensive or cumbersome. The benefits must justify the cost and effort.

Measurement Techniques

The choice of the appropriate measurement technique obviously depends on the performance factor to be measured. If stated properly, the performance standard should dictate the measurement technique. We examine several measurement techniques in this section.

Marketing Measures   Five major categories of marketing performance measures and analysis can be distinguished.[7]

First, *sales analysis* involves analyzing and comparing actual sales with sales goals. This analysis can focus on variances due to price or volume changes or on specific categories such as products and territories.

Second, *market share analysis* concentrates on calculating and analyzing the relationship of a firm's sales volume to that of its competitors. The basic idea is to remove the influence of the environment on the firm's performance. An increase in sales volume, for example, does not necessarily indicate good performance if competitors are improving even more. Four basic market share measures are (1) overall market share, (2) share of target market, (3) share as percentage of combined sales of top three competitors, and (4) share as percentage of leading competitor. Market share analysis also involves analysis for changes in overall market share and perhaps for breakdowns such as product line and region. One useful way to analyze these changes is to track the changes in the key variables that influence market share.

Third, analysis of *marketing expense-to-sales ratios* helps to ensure that the firm is not overspending to achieve its sales goals. The component ratios for the overall ratio might include sales force/sales, advertising/sales, sales promotion/sales, marketing research/sales, and sales administration/sales.

Fourth, *customer attitude tracking* (of customers, dealers, and other marketing system participants) can provide important qualitative indications of marketplace developments. The key assumption is that attitudes change first and are followed by changes in purchasing behavior, which are then shown in sales reports. Thus attitude tracking can help management judge the effectiveness of various efforts (such as promotion) and initiate earlier strategic adaptations. The major techniques for attitude tracking include the use of complaint and suggestion systems, customer panels, and customer surveys.

Fifth, *efficiency analysis* focuses primarily on controlling the efficiency of the sales force, advertising, sales promotion, and distribution activities. Indicators of sales force efficiency include the average number of sales calls per day, average time per sales call, average revenue per sales call, and average cost per sales call. Indicators of advertising efficiency include the average cost per thousand customers reached, before/after measures of consumer attitudes, and the number of inquiries per ad. Indicators of sales promotion efficiency include the percentage of coupons redeemed and display costs per sales dollar. Indicators of distribution efficiency include cost per delivery and average number of deliveries per day.

Financial Measures   There are many financial measures used for control. In fact, financial measures are probably the most widely used measures of performance. Often these involve ratio or related analysis. Some common ratios are presented below (a more extensive list appears in the Appendix, along with definitions and relevant formulas).

Profitability ratios may be the most important financial measures. They include return on investment (ROI), return on assets (ROA), and return on equity (ROE), profit margin, and so on.

Liquidity ratios are also important. They include the current ratio and quick ratio. The purpose of these ratios is to help determine if the firm can pay its debt.

Activity ratios are used to help determine if a firm is using its assets wisely. The ratios include inventory turnover, asset turnover, and the like.

Leverage ratios include debt-to-equity, debt-to-assets, and other variations of these. They are used to help determine if a firm has too much or too little debt.

Beyond the ratios mentioned here, there are literally hundreds of possible analyses based on the income statement and balance sheet and other financial statements.

Human Resource Measures   Several types of human resource measurement techniques are also available. *Production measures* focus on quantity and/or quality of output or results (for example, the number of telephones produced or sold). *Personal measures* include absences, tardiness, accident frequency, and rate of wage or salary advancement. *Judgmental measures* pertain to certain types of employees, such as managerial, technical, and professional employees. This judgment may take the form of rating scales, comparisons, checklists, or critical incidents.[8]

Human resource management is also very likely to be involved with performance appraisals of individual workers. Although *performance appraisals* are typically conducted by an employee's immediate supervisor, human resource management often plays a large part in developing appraisal measures and procedures and in evaluating the appraisals. For instance, the sales manager will generally evaluate the performance of his or her salespeople, but human resource personnel are likely to provide both the rating instruments and the specific methods for determining performance.

Performance appraisals can be used to accomplish two broad purposes: company purposes, when the results serve as the basis for salary, promotion, and transfer decisions, and developmental purposes, when the appraisal is designed to improve the employee's performance and career development through self-learning and personal growth. These two types of appraisals should not normally be combined. Among the more specific aims of appraisals are improved motivation, improved managerial understanding, better basis for planning, training, and development, and reduced favoritism.[9]

Production Measures   The production function requires a wide variety of control standards and measures. Three categories of control standards and measures are precontrol (of inputs), concurrent control (of processing or transformation), and postcontrol (of outputs).

Precontrol concentrates on predetermining standards and measures for the quantity and quality of resource inputs. Since capital and labor resources are discussed in Chapter 12, only materials are discussed here. Precontrol of the quality of incoming material involves selecting appropriate inspection procedures, such as counting, measuring, and checking for damage. In recent years, inspection based on statistical sampling has gained popularity.[10]

Precontrol of material quantity focuses on maintaining efficient inventory levels, which involves balancing ordering costs and inventory carrying costs. Consequently, production managers must determine how many of each item to order and how often to order each item. The details of this type of analysis can be found in literature on the economic order quantity (EOQ).[11]

Concurrent control relates to how much and when outputs will be produced and is often called production scheduling. Some firms employ staff who specialize in preparing production schedules. Popular tools for production scheduling include various network models, such as the Program Evaluation and Review Technique (PERT)[12] and linear programming models.[13]

Whereas precontrol and concurrent control procedures increase the likelihood of high-quality, efficiently produced output, *postcontrol* focuses on analyzing the output. Two techniques are widely used for postcontrol. *Standard cost analysis* involves estimating and combining the direct labor, direct materials, and overhead costs to find actual per unit costs. Actual unit costs are then compared to standard unit costs to find the cost variance, which must be analyzed.[14] *Statistical quality control* procedures aim at detecting low quality or defective output. Statistical sampling theory is used to help reduce the amount of time and cost devoted to maintaining desired quality.[15]

Audits   Control can also involve periodic evaluations or functional-level audits. An audit is a systematic examination of the components of a functional area. The task is to pinpoint present weaknesses, potential problems, and potential opportunities.

Besides the better-known accounting audits, there are other management audits, human resource audits, social audits, SBU audits, and marketing audits.[16] Relatively formal audit procedures can be found for some functional areas and can be used as is or tailored to fit the firm's needs. If formal procedures are unavailable or inappropriate, customized procedures can be developed.

The scope of an audit of one of the functional areas can range from very broad to very narrow. The broad-based audit is a horizontal audit that entails an evaluation of the entire operations of the function. The focus is often on problem definition. A vertical audit is narrower in scope but entails a more in-depth

PERSPECTIVE 14.1

General Motors and the "Quality Perception Gap"

You are in business to sell a product and for years you do it successfully. Then, over a five-year period, you lose over 20 percent of your business. A two-step corrective policy seems reasonable enough: First, ask former and prospective customers what they think the problem is. Two, try to solve that problem.

Such was the situation in which General Motors found itself in 1990. From 1984 to 1989 the company's market share had plummeted, from 44 percent to 35 percent. Such was one of the solutions GM considered: it surveyed customers and came to the conclusion that people thought the quality of GM products wasn't what it had been. GM had, in the parlance of its vice president for consumer market development, a "quality perception gap." Her suggestion for bridging that gap: a corporate ad campaign to tell the country that quality mattered at GM.

In GM's divisions—Cadillac, Buick, Pontiac, Oldsmobile, and Chevrolet—some felt this sort of corporate-image campaign was an intrusion. Historically, the divisions had operated with a great deal of autonomy, although for some years now engineering and design had become more centralized. (The 1985 acquisition of Hughes Aircraft was intended to accelerate that trend. Hughes's sophisticated technological capacity would be used to develop engineering innovations for all GM cars.) A campaign to promote GM quality would cut into the marketing budgets of the various divisions.

There were also reservations from those at GM who felt that promoting GM quality would do more to raise questions than to quiet suspicions. Does such a campaign amount to an admission that quality had slipped? Nevertheless, one marketing consultant found that GM had improved the quality of its vehicles considerably in the last few years—in fact, more so than other domestic automakers.

References: "Shirley Young: Pushing GM's Humble-Pie Strategy," *Business Week*, June 11, 1990, pp. 52–53; David Woodruff, "GM and Hughes: Is the Marriage Fizzling?" *Business Week*, February 12, 1990, p. 54; Raymond Serafin and Cleveland Horton, "GM Splits on Quality Pitch," *Advertising Age*, March 26, 1990, p. 1.

analysis of one specific component, such as the firm's university campus recruiting component of human resources.

The periodic audits should be viewed as an integral part of the overall control process. As with the other components of control, however, they should not become an end in themselves and the benefits must justify the costs.

Problems with Performance Measurement

Intervening variables may greatly influence performance, making it quite difficult to isolate the actual performance levels. Consider, for example, measuring the performance of an assembly line worker. The work on many assembly lines occurs in a sequential fashion, which means that the performance of one worker is influenced by the quantity and quality of work performed by those earlier in the sequence. Thus simply counting the output may not give a true picture of performance in some situations.

Performance measurement can also consume much time and money. For example, accurate measurements of advertising effectiveness may be very desirable but have an unfavorable cost/benefit ratio.

The subjective nature of some performance measures can also create problems, especially in the case of personnel measures. A key issue involves the relative quality of the evaluator. An evaluator with considerable experience in the job or activity being evaluated can often deal much better with the subjective nature of some jobs. For instance, teaching is an activity that is difficult to measure objectively; however, someone with teaching experience can often judge quality reasonably well. For this reason, peer evaluation is sometimes used.

COMPARING PERFORMANCE WITH STANDARDS

Some managers set standards and measure performance, but do not compare the two. However, without such comparisons, control becomes overly subjective and random.

Comparing performance and standards also emphasizes the necessity for measuring performance in the same terms used for setting the standards. For example, standards for advertising media might be stated in terms of number of households reached and average frequency of exposure to the advertisement. Measurements of reach and frequency should, therefore, be used for the comparison. Measures of sales volume should not be used in this situation.

The concept of tolerance limits can facilitate this comparison. A control chart similar to that in Exhibit 14.3 can be constructed and used to structure the comparison. As long as actual performance is within the upper and lower control limits and negative trends are not apparent, management will take no action. If performance exceeds the limits or negative trends arise within the limits, management should take further action.

DETERMINING THE REASON FOR DEVIATIONS

In finding out why actual performance has deviated from the standards, both positive and negative deviations should be investigated. Note that deviations from standards do not necessarily indicate performance problems. Many standards, such as those represented by the financial ratios (see Appendix), are interrelated and seemingly inadequate performance on one standard may be acceptable. Consequently, management should examine other related standards to make sure that a problem actually exists. If the deviation does represent a problem, management should initiate a quick review of its possible causes. A general checklist such as the following can be helpful:

1. Are the standards appropriate for the stated objectives and strategies?
2. Are the objectives and corresponding standards still appropriate in the light of the current environmental situation?
3. Are the strategies for achieving the objectives still appropriate in the light of the current environmental situation?
4. Are the firm's organizational structure, systems (for example, information), and resource support adequate for successfully implementing the strategies and therefore achieving the objectives?
5. Are the activities being executed appropriate for achieving the standard?

If the cause of the deviation is not found quickly, management should continue the investigation in more depth; for instance, it can expand the general checklist by adding more specific questions for each major area.

TAKING CORRECTIVE ACTION

The five steps of the control process that we have now discussed all focus on enabling management to take the sixth step—corrective action. The checklist we have just presented suggests the following five general areas for corrective action.

Revising the Standards

Although this situation is uncommon, it is possible that the standards are not in line with the objectives and strategies selected. For instance, a firm may have an objective related to reduction of inventory costs but may set the standard in terms of reducing average inventory by a specific amount. Reducing average inventory may or may not reduce total inventory costs because ordering costs may increase. Being out of line with the standard may actually help achieve the objective.

Revising the Objectives

If the standards are appropriate for the stated objectives, management might find that the objectives themselves are no longer appropriate in the light of current environmental conditions. Sudden changes, such as in interest rates, can make even the most carefully planned objectives obsolete for many companies. In these circumstances, adjusting the objectives can be much more logical and sensible than adjusting the performance.

Revising the Strategies

If the objectives and standards appear appropriate, the performance deviation may be caused by inappropriate strategies. For example, management might find that an original strategy involving market development is not working because the specific market chosen is much smaller than expected.

A strategy that was originally appropriate can become inappropriate during a period because of environmental shifts. One retailer, for example, was pursuing a market development strategy in the early 1980s that involved building new outlets. Several of these new construction projects were abandoned in midstream when the prime interest rate rose above 20 percent.

Revising the Structure, Systems, or Support

Inadequate performance can sometimes be traced to an inadequate organizational structure, systems, or resource support. Successful implementation of strategies is severely compromised without these factors. Since each of them is discussed elsewhere in this text, only brief examples are provided here. Management may want to revise the organizational structure by adding regional or district sales managers when geographical expansion is not yielding the expected sales volume. Flurries of new product introductions by competitors can decrease the impact of a firm's own new products. Management may therefore need to expand its management information system to facilitate the flow of competitive information. Increased resource support (for example, more money) may be needed to successfully implement any strategy, such as backward or forward integration.

Revising Activities

The most common adjustment, especially if the strategic planning process has been relatively successful, involves activities. Many times this adjustment involves fine-tuning one or more of the implementation procedures. Examples of such adjustments range from additional coaching by management and additional employee training to more positive incentives, more negative incentives, and improved scheduling. Most of these adjustments are designed and executed by functional managers.

Remembering the Interrelationships

Management must remember that adjustments in any of the above areas may require adjustments in one or more of the other factors. Adjusting the objectives, for example, is likely to require different strategies, standards, resources, activities, and perhaps organizational structure and systems. New strategies are not likely to warrant new objectives and standards, but may need adjustments in the other factors. At the other extreme, fine-tuning activities does not normally call for additional major adjustments.

CONTROLLING THE STRATEGIC PLANNING PROCESS

One of the most critical aspects of control involves monitoring the strategic planning process to ensure that it is functioning properly and contributing to the firm's overall performance.[17] As discussed in Chapter 1, strategic planning holds much promise for those firms that can use it efficiently and effectively. However, the process cannot be ignored once it is launched. As more and more firms implement a strategic planning system, more and more difficulties arise. One troublesome area, for example, involves barriers that inhibit strategic thinking, including the following deadly assumptions:[18]

1. My top team is a closely knit group.
2. Our team controls our organization.
3. If it's long-term, it's strategic.
4. Established corporate strategy means clear divisional or overall strategy.
5. Stable organizations do not need strategy.
6. Our long-range plans tell us where we're going.
7. Our top team is bright, talented, experienced; therefore, they've got what it takes to set strategy.

Three of the most critical barriers to strategic planning are lack of management time to devote to planning, conflict between short- and long-term planning, and middle management's lack of understanding and skill in strategic planning.[19] Other common shortcomings in strategic planning and corresponding solutions appear in Table 14.1.

TABLE 14.1 · Strategic Planning Shortcomings and Solutions

1. *Shortcoming:* Inadequate line management involvement (the top-down approach does not work well when used alone).[a,g]

   Solution: Require line managers rather than staff managers to do the planning. Staff managers should provide assistance to the line managers as needed.[c,d]

   Solution: Hire consultants *only* to help set up the strategic planning framework, not to do any planning.[c]

   Solution: Adopt an entrepreneurial style of strategic management.[h]

2. *Shortcoming:* Poor preparation of line managers for the job.[b]

   Solution: Line managers usually need training in strategic analysis and participative skills.[b]

3. *Shortcoming:* Inadequate top management involvement (the bottom-up approach does not work well when used alone).[a,g]

   Solution: Make sure that everyone in the organization (including the CEO) understands that the CEO is the chief planner and that full management participation is the norm.[c,h]

   Solution: Participative strategy development often requires cultural change at the upper levels of corporations and their business units.[d]

4. *Shortcoming:* Ritualized, routinized, procedure-driven approaches that lead to a lack of flexibility.[a]

   Solution: Separate strategic planning from resource allocation, budgeting, and profit planning; match all factors after the strategic plans are finalized.[c,d,f]

   Solution: Develop a formal, systematic, uniform approach and use objective thinking and planning to encourage risk taking and innovation. Flexible, winning plans are the aim, not thick planning books. Turbulent environmental conditions can make the planning more important than the plan.[c,d,h]

5. *Shortcoming:* Inadequate information bases for action planning.[b,h]

   Solution: Make sure that MIS is properly designed relative to continuous input and output that is appropriate for strategic planning at all levels. Furthermore, impress upon all employees the importance of providing input.[h]

6. *Shortcoming:* Overdependence on long-term forecasts.[e,h]

   Solution: Maintain a skeptical (but not cynical) attitude toward all forecasts, particularly when experience is limited.[c]

7. *Shortcoming:* Extrapolating from the past.[a]

   Solution: Planners must obviously evaluate historical conditions and results, but must be forward looking and plan for the future. This perspective is particularly important in complex and turbulent environments.[a]

8. *Shortcoming:* Overreliance on quantitative goals.[e]

   Solution: Use judgment as filter. Goals for some areas simply cannot be adequately quantified.

9. *Shortcoming:* Vaguely formulated goals[b]

   Solution: Define specific action plans.[b]

(continued)

TABLE 14.1 · (continued)

10. *Shortcoming:* Failure to recognize differences in businesses, markets, industries, and people.[a]
    Solution: Planning and plans must be adapted to the situation at hand.[d]

11. *Shortcoming:* Failure to define business and segments appropriately.[b]
    Solution: Define strategic business units so that one executive can control the key variables essential to the execution of the strategic business plan.[b]

12. *Shortcoming:* Badly handled reviews of business unit plans.[b]
    Solution: Pay close attention to business-level strategies: force units to plan well; and plan for healthy conflict and reconciliation during review phase.[b,d]

13. *Shortcoming:* Short-term perspective and overemphasis on short-term goals.[a,e]
    Solution: Avoid a "home-run" mentality (expect payoff to come slowly), and relate short-term goals to long-term goals.[d,f]
    Solution: Shift the compensation system away from rewarding only short-term successes.[h]

14. *Shortcoming:* Too much emphasis and time wasted on developing vague, long-term plans.
    Solution: Plan only up to the time horizon dictated by the nature of the firm and industry. Uncertainty makes planning for longer time horizons an exercise in futility.[c]

15. *Shortcoming:* Overestimating strengths and underestimating weaknesses.[c]
    Solution: Evaluate the firm's strengths and weaknesses continually and objectively.[c]

16. *Shortcoming:* Overlooking key competitive issues, such as potential competitors and technological developments in other fields.[a]
    Solution: The concept of the business in which a unit is engaged must be formulated from the outside in so that the unit can effectively interact with the environment.[b]

17. *Shortcoming:* Overemphasis on the *plan.*
    Solution: Equal emphasis must be placed on both strategy formulation and strategy implementation.[c]

18. *Shortcoming:* Inadequate linkage of strategic planning with other control systems.[b]
    Solution: Completely integrate the strategic planning system into the organization's culture, structure, and control system to make it a "living, breathing document."[b,c]

19. *Shortcoming:* Too few or too many planning resources.[a]
    Solution: Marshal all resources for the first big planning task. Make the first group of resources self-liquidating, leaving only a modest group to orchestrate updates and adjustments.[a]

20. *Shortcoming:* Resistance by corporate culture.[h]
    Solution: Encourage full participation in the strategic planning process at all levels of the organization.[h]

Sources:

[a] Alex R. Oliver and Joseph R. Garber, "Implementing Strategic Planning: Ten Sure-Fire Ways to Do It Wrong," *Business Horizons* (March-April 1983), 49–51.

[b] Daniel H. Gray, "Uses and Misuses of Strategic Planning," *Harvard Business Review* (January-February 1986), 89–97.

[c] William A. Dimma, "Competitive Strategic Planning," *Business Quarterly* (Spring 1985), 22–26.

TABLE 14.1 · (*continued*)

[d] Richard G. Hamermesh, "Making Planning Strategic," *Harvard Business Review* (July-August 1986), 115–120.

[e] Robert H. Hayes, "Strategic Planning—Forward in Reverse?" *Harvard Business Review* (November-December 1985), 111–119.

[f] Lawrence G. Hrebiniak and William F. Joyce, "The Strategic Importance of Managing Myopia," *Sloan Management Review* (Fall 1986), 5–14.

[g] Milton C. Lauenstein, "The Failure of Strategic Planning," *The Journal of Business Strategy* (Spring 1986), 75–80.

[h] Larry J. Rosenberg and Charles D. Schewe, "Strategic Planning: Fulfilling the Promise," *Business Horizons* (July-August 1985), 54–62.

Management must also recognize that the strategic planning process evolves over time. R. T. Lenz views this evolution as consisting of three phases, which must be managed and shaped: introduction of the process, consolidation, and a "fork in the road."[20] The introduction phase focuses primarily on designing and introducing the process. The consolidation phase finds management confident about the strategic planning process and its usefulness in guiding and coordinating strategy. The "fork in the road" phase occurs when various attitudes and actions begin to undermine the process. They include the following:[21]

- Treating strategic planning as a science
- Too much emphasis on numbers
- Leaving line managers out of the process
- Too much standardization of inputs and analyses
- Misapplication of analytical techniques

CONTROLLING THE CONTROL SYSTEM

Control systems operating out of control can do more damage than good. Without proper care, a variety of problems can develop.

Behavior Focused on the Control System

The overall purpose of a control system is to foster performance that moves the organization toward achieving its goals. Consequently, the system should encourage goal-oriented behavior. However, a strong control system sometimes causes employees to focus their behavior directly on the control system, rather than on the firm's goals. In essence, the system may generate behavior that makes employees look good on the control system's measures.[22] For example, a faculty member whose salary is partially based on teaching skills as measured by student evaluations may give higher grades in order to get higher scores rather than work to be a better instructor.

A related problem involves confusion between means and ends. The control system should provide a means for accomplishing goals and not be an end in itself. Results are more important than standards. Behavior that achieves desired results should be rewarded, even if standards are circumvented.

Invalid Data

Control systems can also produce invalid data about what can be and has been done. The budgetary component of a control system provides a good case in point. The problem of invalid data arises when managers underestimate revenues and overestimate costs in an attempt to build some slack into the measures used to judge their performance. Control systems that provide rewards based on the accuracy of budget estimates can partially alleviate this problem (but they may foster undesirable budget-oriented behavior).[23]

Overcontrol

An otherwise well-conceived control system can lead to managerial overcontrol. The overcontrol problem can manifest itself in several ways. For instance, the absolute volume of control information can overwhelm those responsible for control. To illustrate, the authors encountered one manager who insisted on having a computer printout on his desk each morning when he arrived at work. The printout contained daily performance information for every conceivable standard. However, it would have taken this manager six to seven hours each day to read the report. Rectifying the situation meant having the manager analyze the frequency of receiving control information. Obviously, some performance factors needed comparing with standards every day, but many other comparisons gained significance only with varying degrees of lapsed time. The timing of these comparisons was, therefore, changed to a periodic (rather than continuous) basis—once a week, month, quarter, or year.

Overcontrol can also mean overdirecting and overregulating employees' behavior. Employees can be so overwhelmed with rules, policies, and regulations that they lose all initiative.

Cost Versus Benefits

Management should carefully analyze the cost of controlling each performance factor and compare the costs with the expected benefits. The relevant costs include both direct financial costs and indirect costs, such as lost time, negative attitudes, lowered job expectations, dysfunctional job behavior, and adverse customer relations. Potential benefits can include time savings, improved morale, improvements in quality, and conservation of resources.

Although some costs and benefits are difficult to compute, management must attempt to estimate the cost. For instance, stringent controls on work breaks might cause a work stoppage or promote union-organizing attempts. Management must consider the costs of these actions and the probability of their occurrence. If management does not want a union and had barely won in past attempts to organize workers, then disliked controls may trigger a win by the union. In such situations, management must be sure that the performance being controlled is enough out of line to run the risk of unionization. For instance, if only a few workers are abusing work breaks, a solution (corrective action) involving only those workers is likely to be better than new work rules.

GLOBAL DIMENSIONS OF CONTROL

The control process is virtually identical for both multinational and domestic firms. The scope and execution of control activities, however, is likely to be different. As a firm achieves multinational scale, obviously the scope of control activities must increase. The multinational firm must also exercise control in additional areas, such as foreign exchange. Currency fluctuation and economic instability may make control activities, such as setting standards and measuring performance, much more complicated.

The execution of control might also need adjustments. For instance, in some cultures, changing a standard even when it is wrong may be viewed as an admission that management is ineffective. Management must also allow workers to save face in some cultures—for instance, when employees are reprimanded for failure to perform adequately. As with other strategic management activities, a good adviser on specific cultures can be invaluable in reducing these problems.

Notes

1. Robert Albanese, *Managing: Toward Accountability for Performance* (Homewood, Ill.: Irwin, 1978), p. 136.

2. James M. Higgins, *Organizational Policy and Strategic Management: Text and Cases.* 2nd ed. (Chicago: The Dryden Press, 1983), p. 207.

3. Albanese, p. 136.

4. Peter F. Drucker, *Managing for Results* (New York: Harper & Row, 1964), pp. 78–84.

5. L. G. Hrebiniak and W. F. Joyce, *Implementing Strategy* (New York: Collier Macmillan, 1984), ch. 7.

6. Arthur A. Thompson, Jr., and A. J. Strickland III, *Strategy Formulation and*

Implementation (Plano, Tex.: Business Publications, 1983), pp. 380–381.

7. Philip Kotler, *Marketing Management,* 5th ed. (Englewood Cliffs, N.J.: Prentice-Hall, 1984), pp. 746–760.

8. John M. Ivancevich, James H. Donnelly, Jr., and James L. Gibson, *Managing for Performance* (Plano, Tex.: Business Publications, 1983), pp. 485–487.

9. Ibid., pp. 480–483.

10. Michiel R. Leenders, Harold E. Fearon, and Wilbur B. England, *Purchasing and Materials Management,* 7th ed. (Homewood, Ill.: Irwin, 1980), pp. 132–143.

11. Ibid., pp. 162–195.

12. Richard J. Hopeman, *Production and Operations Management* (Columbus, Ohio: Merrill, 1980), pp. 91–104.

13. Ibid., pp. 303–323.

14. Charles T. Horngren, *Cost Accounting* (Englewood Cliffs, N.J.: Prentice-Hall, 1982), pp. 200–216.

15. Hopeman, pp. 465–491.

16. For each one see, respectively, J. Martindell, *The Appraisal of Management* (New York: Harper & Bros., 1962); P. H. Mirvis and B. A. Macy, "Human Resources Accounting: A Measurement Perspective," *Academy of Management Review* (April 1976), 74–83; P. Ogan and S. Ma-tulich, "Human Resource Accounting: Dead or Alive," *Atlanta Economic Review* (July-August 1976), 13–16; D. R. Melville, "Top Management's Role in Strategic Planning," *The Journal of Business Strategy* (Spring 1981), 57–65; and Kotler, pp. 767–770, and Philip Kotler, William Gregor, and William Rogers, "The Marketing Audit Comes of Age," *Sloan Management Review* (Winter 1977), 25–43.

17. Steven R. Baldwin and Michael McConnell, "Strategic Planning: Process and Plan Go Hand in Hand," *Management Solutions* (June 1988), 29–36.

18. Benjamin Tregoe, "Seven Assumptions That Kill Strategic Thinking," *Chief Executive* (Autumn-Winter 1981).

19. Erik G. Rule, "Making Strategic Management Work," *Business Quarterly* (Winter 1987), 33–36.

20. R. T. Lenz, "Managing the Evolution of the Strategic Planning Process," *Business Horizons* (January-February 1987), 34–39.

21. Ibid.

22. Edward E. Lawler III and John Grand Rhode, *Information and Control in Organizations* (Menlo Park, Calif.: Goodyear, 1976), 83–94.

23. Ibid.

HOW TO ANALYZE A CASE

To gain an understanding of how to analyze a case, it is necessary first to understand why cases are used. The basic reason for using cases is to allow you to apply the various techniques you have studied in this and other courses to real-world situations. The process of analysis or overall approach may be more important than generating specific, accurate answers. It is the process of analysis with which this chapter deals.

This experience will allow you to sit vicariously in the place of an individual with responsibility for decisions. The case study offers a level of involvement that should give you a true feel for the managerial decision-making process. The argument is often made that not enough information is available to make a decision, but remember that in many "real-world" cases complete information is not available. Also, managers often don't have time to come up with "perfect" solutions. If a manager asks, "Is the decision needed Thursday, or is it needed correctly?" in many cases the answer is "Thursday."

A six-step process for case analysis is recommended. The six steps are:

1. Analyze the firm's present and likely future position.
2. Analyze the firm's objectives and the likelihood of achieving them.
3. Evaluate the alternatives that may help achieve the firm's objectives.
4. Select the solution(s) from the alternatives.
5. Develop plans to implement the solution(s).
6. Consider back-up solution(s).

Using these six steps does not guarantee a proper analysis, but it does offer a logical sequence that, when diligently and vigorously pursued, can be of significant benefit in analyzing classroom cases and in real-world situations.

ANALYZE THE FIRM'S PRESENT AND LIKELY FUTURE POSITIONS

This first step is extremely critical to the remainder of the case analysis process. If a manager, consultant, or student can develop a thorough understanding of a firm's present and likely future position, he or she has an excellent chance of generating appropriate problem solutions. Note that this analysis follows closely with the environmental analysis discussed in Part Two (Chapters 5–9). You may wish to review this material before proceeding further.

The primary focus of both the macro- and task environmental analyses should be on identifying factors that can have a significant impact on the firm. You should also consider the probability of these environmental events and trends occurring and whether the impact will be positive or negative. Case writers often indicate some of these factors, but you must identify others from outside sources such as newspapers, journals, government publications, and trade publications.

Although the macro- and task environments are important, this chapter focuses primarily on the analysis of the internal situation. Two broad categories of analysis are discussed: financial analysis and marketing/behavioral analysis.

Financial Analysis

Analysis of financial performance and position is an important part of a firm's internal situation analysis and helps form the basis for further planning. Financial performance and position are reported by the firm's balance sheet and income statement. Examples of each of these statements are shown in Tables A.1 and A.2.[1]

Ratio analysis is frequently used to help evaluate a firm's financial performance and position. Ratio analysis involves evaluating the relationship(s) between two or more financial variables.

Types of Ratios

Ratios can be divided into four categories.[2] First, **profitability ratios** measure the firm's ability to turn each dollar of revenue into profit (operating efficiency) and to produce profits from each invested dollar (financial efficiency). Second, **liquidity ratios** measure the firm's ability to pay current liabilities (also called short-term solvency). Third, **leverage ratios** measure the firm's use of debt and ability to meet scheduled repayments. Fourth, **activity ratios** measure the firm's ability to generate sales and profits from assets. Specific key ratios for each of these ratio types are summarized in Table A.3.

---

[1]Detailed discussion of each of the financial statements can be found in almost any basic accounting or corporate finance textbook.

[2]Smith/Arnold/Bizzell/Arnet, *Policy Expert* (Boston: Houghton Mifflin Company, 1991).

TABLE A.1 · Nike, Inc.

Nike, Inc. Consolidated Balance Sheet (in thousands)

	1989[1]	1988[2]	1987[2]	Industry (1989)[3]
ASSETS				
Current assets:				
Cash & equivalents............	$ 85,749	75,357	126,867	33,482.00
Accounts receivable	$296,350	258,393	184,459	59,318.00
Inventories...................	$222,924	198,470	120,663	89,636.00
Deferred income tax	$ 18,504	8,569	10,576	
Prepaid expenses	$ 14,854	12,793	6,717	
Total current assets	$638,381	553,582	449,282	195,617.00
Property, plants and equip......	$154,314	112,022	96,988	41,127.00
Less accum. depreciation	$ 64,332	54,319	48,508	
Net; property; plants & equipt...	$ 89,982	57,703	48,480	—
Goodwill	$ 81,899	84,747		
Other assets.................	$ 15,148	13,063	14,081	26,891.00
Total assets...................	$825,410	709,095	511,843	263,635.00
LIABILITIES AND SHAREHOLDERS' EQUITY				
Current Liab:				
Current portion of long term debt....................	$ 1,884	1,573	4,800	13,182.00
Notes payable to bank	$ 39,170	135,215	43,145	2,109.00
Accounts payable	$ 71,105	50,288	28,036	35,591.00
Accrued taxes payable	$ 76,543	59,073	8,309	—
Income tax payable............	$ 27,201	8,617	39,792	
Total current liabilities	$215,903	254,766	124,082	83,836.00
Long-term debt..................	$ 34,051	30,306	35,202	19,509.00
Non-current deferred income taxes and purchased tax benefits	$ 13,352	11,949	14,242	
Redeemable preferred stock........	$ 300	300	300	
Shareholder's equity				
Common stock a stated value Class A — convertible 14,295 & 14,453 shares outstanding	$ 171	173	174	
Class B — 23,004 & 22,650 shares outstanding......	$ 2,700	2,696	2,705	

(continued)

TABLE A.1 (continued)

	1989[1]	1988[2]	1987[2]	Industry (1989)[3]
Capital in excess of stated values	$ 74,227	69,737	83,542	
Foreign currency translation adjustment	$ −2,156	−1,157	−1,938	
Retained earnings	$486,862	340,325	253,534	
Net equity.	$561,804	411,774	338,017	160,290.00
Liabilities & equity	$825,410	709,095	511,843	263,635.00

Sources:

[1]1989 Nike Annual Report. Reprinted by permission of Nike, Inc.
[2]1989 Nike Annual Report. Reprinted by permission of Nike, Inc.
[3]Industrial Norms and Key Business Ratios; Dun & Bradstreet Publications, 1989.

TABLE A.2 · Nike, Inc.

Nike, Inc. Income Statement (in thousands, except per share data)

	Ending May 31			
	1989[1]	1988[1]	1978[1]	Industry[2]
Revenue	1,710,803	1,203,440	877,357	600,000.00
Cost & expenses:				
Cost of sales	1,074,831	803,380	596,662	
Selling and administrative	354,825	246,583	204,742	
Interest	13,949	8,004	8,475	
Other expenses. . . .	−3,449	−20,722	−6,201	
Income before income taxes	270,647	166,195	73,679	222,000.00
Income taxes , ...	103,600	64,500	37,800	
Net income	167,047	101,695	35,879	27,600.00
Net income per common share	4.45	2.70	0.93	
Average number of common and common equivalent shares	37,572	37,639	38,393	

Sources: 1989 Nike Annual Report

[1]1989 Nike Annual Report. Reprinted by permission of Nike, Inc.
[2]Industrial Norms and Key Business Ratios; Dun & Bradstreet Publications, 1989.

TABLE A.3 · Summary of Key Financial Ratios

Ratio	How calculated	What it shows
PROFITABILITY RATIOS		
1. Gross profit margin	$\dfrac{\text{Sales} - \text{Cost of goods sold}}{\text{Sales}}$	An indication of the total margin available to cover operating expenses and yield a profit.
2. Operating profit margin	$\dfrac{\text{Profits before taxes and before interest}}{\text{Sales}}$	An indication of the firm's profitability from current operations without regard to the interest charges accruing from the capital structure.
3. Net profit margin (or return on sales)	$\dfrac{\text{Profits after taxes}}{\text{Sales}}$	Shows after-tax profits per dollar of sales. Subpar-profit margins indicate that the firm's sales prices are relatively low or that its costs are relatively high or both.
4. Return on total assets	$\dfrac{\text{Profits after taxes}}{\text{Total assets}}$ or $\dfrac{\text{Profits after taxes} + \text{Interest}}{\text{Total assets}}$	A measure of the return on total investment in the enterprise. It is sometimes desirable to add interest to after-tax profits to form the numerator of the ratio since total assets are financed by creditors as well as by stockholders; hence it is accurate to measure the productivity of assets by the returns provided to both classes of investors.
5. Return on stockholders' equity (or return on net worth)	$\dfrac{\text{Profits after taxes}}{\text{Total stockholders' equity}}$	A measure of the rate of return on stockholders' investment in the enterprise.
6. Return on common equity	$\dfrac{\text{Profits after taxes} - \text{Preferred stock dividends}}{\text{Total stockholders' equity} - \text{Par value of preferred stock}}$	A measure of the rate of return on the investment which the owners of common stock have made in the enterprise.
7. Earnings per share	$\dfrac{\text{Profits after taxes} - \text{Preferred stock dividends}}{\text{Number of shares of common stock outstanding}}$	Shows the earnings available to the owners of common stock.

(continued)

TABLE A.3 · **Summary of Key Financial Ratios**

Ratio	How calculated	What it shows
LIQUIDITY RATIOS		
1. Current ratio	$$\frac{\text{Current assets}}{\text{Current liabilities}}$$	Indicates the extent to which the claims of short-term creditors are covered by assets that are expected to be converted to cash in a period roughly corresponding to the maturity of the liabilities.
2. Quick ratio (or acid-test ratio)	$$\frac{\text{Current assets} - \text{Inventory}}{\text{Current liabilities}}$$	A measure of the firm's ability to pay off short-term obligations without relying upon the sale of its inventories.
3. Inventory to net working capital	$$\frac{\text{Inventory}}{\text{Current assets} - \text{Current liabilities}}$$	Indicates the extent to which the firm's working capital is tied up in inventory.
LEVERAGE RATIOS		
1. Debt to assets ratio	$$\frac{\text{Total debts}}{\text{Total assets}}$$	Measures the extent to which borrowed funds have been used to finance the firm's operations.
2. Debt to equity ratio	$$\frac{\text{Total debt}}{\text{Total stockholders' equity}}$$	Provides another measure of the funds provided the creditors versus the funds provided by owners.
3. Long-term debt to equity ratio	$$\frac{\text{Long-term debt}}{\text{Total stockholders' equity}}$$	A widely used measure of the balance between debt and equity in the firm's overall capital structure.
4. Times-interest-earned (or coverage ratios)	$$\frac{\text{Profits before interest and taxes}}{\text{Total interest charges}}$$	Measures the extent to which earnings can decline without the firm's becoming unable to meet its annual interest costs.
5. Fixed charge coverage	$$\frac{\text{Profits before taxes and interest} + \text{Lease obligations}}{\text{Total interest charges} + \text{Lease obligations}}$$	A more inclusive indication of the firm's ability to meet all of its fixed-charge obligations.

Ratio	How calculated	What it shows
ACTIVITY RATIOS		
1. Inventory turnover	$\dfrac{\text{Sales}}{\text{Inventory}}$	When compared to industry averages, it provides an indication of whether a company has excessive inventory or perhaps inadequate inventory.
2. Fixed assets turnover	$\dfrac{\text{Sales}}{\text{Fixed assets}}$	A measure of the sales productivity and utilization of plant and equipment.
3. Total assets turnover	$\dfrac{\text{Sales}}{\text{Total assets}}$	A measure of the use of all the firm's assets; a ratio below the industry average indicates the company is not generating a sufficient volume of business given the size of the asset investment.
4. Accounts receivable turnover	$\dfrac{\text{Annual credit sales}}{\text{Accounts receivable}}$	A measure of the average length of time it takes the firm to collect the sales made on credit.
5. Average collection period	$\dfrac{\text{Accounts receivable}}{\text{Total sales} \div 365}$ or $\dfrac{\text{Accounts receivable}}{\text{Average daily sales}}$	Indicates the average length of time the firm must wait after making a sale before it receives payment.
OTHER RATIOS		
1. Dividend yield on common stock	$\dfrac{\text{Annual dividends per share}}{\text{Current market price per share}}$	A measure of the return to owners received in the form of dividends.
2. Price-earnings ratio	$\dfrac{\text{Current market price per share}}{\text{After-tax earnings per share}}$	Faster growing or less risky firms *tend* to have higher price-earnings ratios than slower growing or more risky firms.
3. Dividend payout ratio	$\dfrac{\text{Annual dividends per share}}{\text{After-tax earnings per share}}$	Indicates the percentage of profits paid as dividends.
4. Cash flow per share	$\dfrac{\text{After-tax profits} + \text{depreciation}}{\begin{array}{c}\text{Number of common shares}\\\text{outstanding}\end{array}}$	The discretionary funds over and above expenses available for use by the firm.

Source: From *Strategic Management: Concept and Cases,* Fifth Edition by A. A. Thompson, Jr. and A. J. Strickland III, pp. 289–290. © 1990 by Richard D. Irwin, Inc. Reprinted with permission.

Using Ratios

Standard or ideal figures for the various ratios cannot be determined. However, a reasonable analysis using these financial ratios is still possible. Two types of comparisons are useful: (1) a firm's present ratio values with those of similar firms and (2) a firm's present ratio values with its own previous ratio values.

Secondary sources of industry and trade ratios are readily available in references such as Dun & Bradstreet, Standard and Poor, *Annual Statement Studies* published by Robert Morris Associates, the Federal Trade Commission's *Quarterly Financial Report,* and the *Almanac of Business and Industrial Financial Ratios.* Other secondary sources of ratios include trade associations, banks, brokerage houses, and other financial institutions. It is important to understand that these sources usually provide averages and ranges of ratio values for a particular classification of firm. These ratio values should not be viewed as ideal, but simply as indications of other firms' performance. Table A.4 presents key ratios for the Nike Company along with industry averages.

TABLE A.4 · Nike, Inc

Ratios

Liquidity Ratios	1989	1988	1987	Ind. Avg.[1]
Current ratio	2.96	2.17	3.62	2.33
Quick ratio	1.92	1.39	2.65	1.26
Gross profit margin	15.82%	13.81%	8.40%	37.00%
Operating profit margin	16.64%	14.48%	9.36%	37.00%
Debt to assets ratio	31.94%	41.93%	33.96%	39.20%
Debt to equity ratio	38.43%	61.87%	36.71%	52.30%
Return on total assets	20.24%	14.34%	7.01%	10.47%
Return on stockholders' equity	29.68%	24.62%	10.53%	17.22%
Net sales to net working capital	267.99%	217.39%	195.28%	306.72%
Net sales to net worth	3.05	2.92	2.60	3.74
Net income to net worth	29.73%	24.70%	10.61%	17.22%
Retained earnings to net income	291.45%	334.65%	706.64%	0.00%

[1]Industrial Norms and Key Business Ratios; Dun & Bradstreet Publications, 1989.

Trend Analysis

Analysis of trends can be very helpful when comparing present ratio values with previous ratios. A change in the value of a ratio normally indicates that a change has occurred or is occurring in the firm's financial position or performance. This trend analysis can help alert management to potential problems before they get out of hand. Note that ratio comparison only indicates a change; in-depth analysis is required to determine the cause of the change and its implications.

Consider the three years of ratios for the Nike Company in Table A.4. Let us compare Nike's ratios with those for the athletic shoe industry, with specific attention to any major divergences first. The current ratio of 2.96 compares to the industry average of 2.33. This difference could mean that Nike's current assets are too high or that its current liabilities are too low. A similar situation applies to the quick ratio. The firm has some combination of high assets or low liabilities compared to other companies within the same industry.

Comparison of the gross profit margin at 15.82 to that of the industry at 37 indicates that the company's gross profit is lower than that of other comparable firms in the industry. This level should be a signal to management that the company is operating at a profit margin lower than comparable firms. This action may be a part of the firm's overall desire to be more competitive in pricing its products, or it may reflect inordinate costs that comparable firms do not have. A similar situation exists with operating profit margins.

Third, Nike's ratio of net sales to net working capital, 268, is lower than the industry average, 306. Because the company's current quick ratios are higher than those of the industry, this ratio indicates that Nike may make inefficient use of their working capital. It may also indicate that working capital is higher than it needs to be for current business conditions.

The company's return on total assets is 20, compared to the industry average of slightly over 10. Thus, the firm has a very high return on its total assets. This is probably predictable, since the quick and current ratios are higher than the industry average while the debt-to-assets ratio is lower than the industry average. It may also indicate that the firm is in a position to use this strength in its return on assets for future growth.

To be meaningful, all of the above ratios must be considered simultaneously and interpreted. Try to relate the following interpretation to the above ratio. Nike appears to be experiencing solid increases in sales. Further, the firm is seeking these sales increases by retaining profits in the firm, increased borrowing, maintaining low working capital and current assets, and expanding current liabilities.

The du Pont System of Financial Analysis

The **du Pont system** of financial analysis has received widespread recognition in American industry. The system combines activity ratios and profitability ratios to show how they interact to determine the firm's return on investment (ROI). As shown in Figure A.1, the profit margin on sales and the asset turnover ratio are multiplied to yield return on asset investment according to the following formulas:

Net profit margin $\times$ asset turnover = ROI

Therefore,

$$\frac{\text{Profit}}{\text{Sales}} \times \frac{\text{Sales}}{\text{Assets}} = \text{ROI}$$

Nike's net profit margin after taxes was 9.7 percent and asset turnover was 2.1 times. These ratios combine to yield an ROI of 20.4 percent.

The usefulness of the du Pont system is in showing how various changes will eventually impact the ROI. Assume that Nike's management finds an opportunity to reduce cost of goods sold. How much would cost of goods sold have to be for the ROI to become 25 percent? Earnings as a percent of sales would have to increase to 11.9 percent ($2.2 \times 11.9 = 25$). To do so, net income must increase to $203,585 ($203,585 / 1,710,803 = 0.119%). Therefore, total costs (specifically, cost of goods sold) must decrease by $36,538 ($203,585 − $167,047). Hence, cost of goods sold would have to be $1,038,293 ($1,074,831 − $36,538) or decrease by 3.4 percent. Other changes can also be traced through the du Pont system to gauge their impact on ROI.

Cautions for Using Ratios

Ratios are only signs that a deviation is apparent. As in all control cases such deviation indicates an event, not a cause. Management must determine what has caused the event and what action, if any, to take.

All such deviations must be taken in context. Refer to *Policy Expert* by Smith, Arnold, Bizzell, and Arnet (Boston: Houghton Mifflin, 1991) for potential courses of action and examine the array of decisions. Remember, ratios indicate events that have already occurred and may or may not indicate a problem. An isolated deviation may not forecast future events. Management must always determine both why the event happened and what the event means. Care must also be taken in measuring the organization against the industry. It may be that the organization being examined is much better (or perhaps worse) than the industry. Such positions must be examined to determine why.

All factors, both internal and external, must be examined to assure the best possible course of action.

FIGURE A.1 · Modified Du Pont System Applied to Nike, Inc.

Note: **All figures in thousands.**

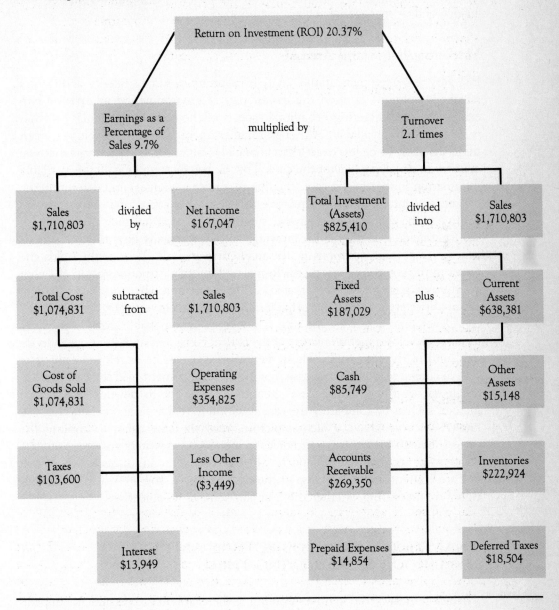

Other types of financial-related analysis such as breakeven and expected value may also be useful. Rather than attempt to put these and the many other valuable techniques in this chapter, we suggest that you make use of your old finance and/or managerial accounting textbooks.

Marketing/Behavioral Analysis

In a very real sense quantitative analysis (contrary to some students' and faculty members' opinion) is often the easiest part of environmental analysis. When examining the marketing/behavioral aspects of the firm, few formulas or other precise tools are available. Although number forecasts may be developed, even these are likely to be less exact than financial analysis. The key point is that you must try to develop a feel for the case. That is, you must analyze all the available information (either in the case, the library, or other sources) and determine the present and future conditions relative to the firm's markets and marketing and relative to the people and personalities in the case. Questions such as how large is the total market, is the market growing, and who actually buys the firm's products are important questions in the marketing analysis. Who really holds the power in the company, how do the formal and informal structures compare, what are the real goals of the owners and/or managers, and what are the individual personalities are a few of the behavioral questions to investigate.

Developing a feel for the firm is not easy. One possible method involves trying to develop a mental picture of the typical customer, of the various individuals, and of the firm itself. These mental images can be developed only after several careful readings of the case. For instance, you might read the case once to obtain an overview of the case situation. Then, try to develop the mental picture, such as by comparing the case situation to real firms and people that you know. Once you have a mental picture, read the case again to confirm the images. Search for any inconsistencies (remember case writers may intentionally create some inconsistencies) and revise your mental picture if necessary. When you are content with your grasp of the case situation, you are ready to concentrate on pinpointing whether the firm can achieve its objectives.

ANALYZE THE FIRM'S OBJECTIVES AND THE LIKELIHOOD OF ACHIEVING THEM

The second major step involves examining the firm's objectives and any impediments to achieving the objectives. Although case writers sometimes specifically state the firm's objectives, you may be forced to extrapolate the true objectives from the case material. Analyzing the firm's position and likely future position is extremely important for doing this. The behavioral analysis often holds the key to determining the firm's true goals. Even with careful reading and analysis, the firm's goals may be difficult to discern in some cases. In these cases, it is usually safe to assume that the firm's major objective is "to do better," especially relative to profit.

After you are reasonably satisfied with your understanding of what the firm wants to accomplish, you must determine if there are likely to be any difficulties in achieving those objectives. This is sometimes called problem identification, although problem and/or strategic issue identification is a more accurate term. It is difficult to overemphasize the importance of correct problem or issue identification. If correct, a good solution is much easier to achieve; if incorrect, the probability of developing a good solution is rather remote.

A good approach to adequately defining the overall problem or issue begins by listing any specific problems or symptoms discovered in the quantitative and qualitative analysis discussed above. It may be helpful to underline all problems and symptoms mentioned in the case and then list all aspects of the financial analysis that are out of line. (The underlining should be done on the second or third reading of the case.) You should also list relevant environmental elements not specifically mentioned in the case that could affect the firm.

The list of problems and symptoms must be organized into a format that can help point to a concise problem or issue definition. The environmental profiles discussed in Part Two can be useful for this purpose. Once the environmental profiles are developed, one or possibly two areas will stand out as possessing the most problems and symptoms. The category with the most significant problems and symptoms is likely to be the major problem or issue.

Symptoms must be distinguished from problems. Symptoms are the outward signs or results of a problem. Although treating symptoms may provide temporary relief, it seldom solves the basic problem. Note that the information gained from financial analysis is likely to indicate symptoms rather than problems. A cash flow "problem," for example, is often a symptom of a more basic problem in areas such as sales and/or expense control. The key point is that you should analyze each symptom and problem by asking why did it occur or why is it a problem.

The analysis of problems and symptoms should result in pinpointing the major problem or issue in the case. Other problems that can affect the ability of the firm to survive may also be indicated. A major problem or issue (related more to the long-run success of the firm) and a critical subproblem or symptom (usually financial in nature) may be discovered. The critical subproblem must often be solved first.

EVALUATE THE ALTERNATIVES THAT MAY HELP ACHIEVE THE FIRM'S OBJECTIVES

Once the major problem(s) or issue(s) have been identified, you are ready to begin generating and evaluating alternative solutions. Virtually all problems have numerous potential answers. Each potential solution must be examined carefully to determine whether it should be selected as the solution to the case at hand. Remember that the process of evaluating alternatives has a large impact on the alternatives selected. Note that the importance of well-conceived and well-presented evaluations may be even greater in a case course than in the real world, because your solutions cannot undergo a final judgment.

One important aspect of evaluating alternatives involves considering both the positive and negative points of each alternative. Essentially, you should ask the question, "If I were to select this alternative, what would happen?" Both positive and negative consequences should be considered. Remember to consider several different environmental forecasts. Allow yourself to think broadly, both in listing alternatives and evaluating the consequences.

Another important aspect of evaluating an alternative involves considering how the alternative will be implemented. Implementation need not be fully developed at this point, but it must be considered. An alternative that is impossible to implement is not likely to be a good solution. For instance, if an alternative requires the spending of $500,000 and the firm already has a liquidity problem, it may be difficult to raise the funds needed to implement the solution.

SELECT THE SOLUTION(S)

Selecting an appropriate solution should be relatively easy if the preceding steps have been adequately performed. Although there may not be a clear-cut answer, the evaluation of alternatives and their consequences should provide ample information for the selection decision. It is important to discuss why a particular solution was selected. The major reasons can be drawn from the preceding step.

There may be many reasons why one alternative is selected as the recommended solution. The reasons may range from an alternative being the best of a group of good alternatives to its being the least onerous of several bad alternatives. Whatever the reason for selecting an alternative, you should select one or a combination of alternatives as your solution and justify your selection.

The selection of a solution is not the end of a good case. The solution chosen must be developed more completely, including the plans for implementation and control.

DEVELOP PLANS TO IMPLEMENT THE SOLUTION(S)

The plans for implementing the recommended solution are an important element of a good case solution. The major problem or issue, the key alternatives, and the most likely solution are sometimes stated in the case. For these cases, an implementation plan is both the largest and most important element of your analysis. For other cases, your solution can dictate implementation, which would make the implementation section of your analysis shorter and less significant.

There are several keys to developing a good plan for implementation. One is to carefully review the firm's present and anticipated future position, especially the financial position. This review helps to ensure that the firm can implement the selected solution, which is especially helpful when the solution requires extensive capital resources. The review should also pinpoint any special competencies that can be exploited and any shortcomings that must be minimized.

Implementation issues should be considered throughout the case analysis, particularly while evaluating the alternatives. Plans for implementation should be completely developed in this section. If you have been evaluating alternatives and selecting a solution with implementation in mind, this section should be relatively easy to develop.

When this step is completed, the firm's problem(s) or issue(s) should be corrected. One last step is recommended.

CONSIDER BACK-UP SOLUTIONS

Regardless of the quality of the decision maker, the solution chosen will not always work. There are many reasons why a solution might not be effective, including environmental changes, incorrect forecasts, incorrect analysis of alternatives, a poorly conceived solution, and implementation difficulties. You should consider the possibility that your solution may be wrong and develop a back-up solution. This solution should be implemented when it becomes evident that the selected solution is not working.

Part of the recommendation for the back-up solution should deal with when it will be implemented. An event in any of the environments could trigger a change in solutions. For example, if your solution was selected based on a forecast that travel will increase in the United States, you may want to make adjustments for the possibility of gasoline prices going up or for availability becoming a problem. In other cases, the back-up solution might be triggered by the failure of the primary solution rather than by an environmental event. You should determine how long the primary solution should be given to work and what are the desired early effects of the primary solution. If this date passes with little change in the early indicators, the back-up solution should be triggered.

SUMMARY

A six-step process is recommended for case analysis. The six steps are as follows:

1. Analyze the firm's present and likely future positions.
2. Analyze the firm's objectives and the likelihood of achieving them.
3. Evaluate the alternatives that may help achieve the firm's objectives.
4. Select this solution(s) from these alternatives.
5. Develop plans to implement this solution(s).
6. Consider back-up solution(s).

The use of this process should aid significantly in performing a case analysis.

You should not consider these six steps as an absolutely sequential process. Although these steps are listed in the order they would most likely be addressed, they represent a process or system where each step is related to both the preceding and subsequent steps. For instance, the evaluation of alternatives should include consideration of implementation and back-up solutions.

Another important consideration is the fact that the case will seldom provide all the information you would like to have. This situation is representative of the real world. There are almost always a few pieces of additional information that would facilitate decision making. However, we must select strategies and make decisions without all the desirable information.

One other problem you may encounter is bad information. Sometimes there is conflicting information given in the cases. This conflicting information is often provided by the case characters. You may want to ask yourself why that individual would make certain statements. This is also representative of the real world. You must learn to evaluate conflicting data and determine the real situation.

The most important element of good case analysis involves thinking. Case analysis may be one of few times in your education when you really need to think. Many courses involve memorizing lists and facts, but case courses are different. There are no canned answers or procedures that will always work. It is also one of your few peeks at what you might be doing in real managerial positions.

INDEX

Page numbers followed by f refer to figures. Those followed by t refer to tables.